MEMOIRS

Translated by Richard and Clara Winston

Documents translated by Jan van Heurck

MEMOIRS

József Cardinal Mindszenty

MACMILLAN PUBLISHING CO., INC.
NEW YORK

The translation from Hungarian to English of Documents, 2, 4, 32, 33, 64, 69, and 71 have been taken from *Cardinal Mindszenty Speaks* (New York, London, Toronto: Longmans, Green, Inc., 1949).

© 1974 by Verlag Ullstein GmbH, Frankfurt/M. · Berlin · Wien Propyläen Verlag

English translation copyright © 1974 by Macmillan Publishing Co., Inc.

Macmillan Publishing Co., Inc.
866 Third Avenue, New York, N.Y. 10022
Collier-Macmillan Canada Ltd.

Library of Congress Cataloging in Publication Data

Mindszenty, József Cardinal, 1892–
    Memoirs.

    Translation of Erinnerungen.
    I. Mindszenty, József Cardinal, 1892–
BX4705.M5565A2813   262'.135'0924[B]   74-19494

ISBN 0-02-585050-4

FIRST AMERICAN EDITION 1974

Memoirs was originally published in German under the title *Erinnerungen*.

Printed in the United States of America

Contents

Illustrations

(*following page 96*)

The cardinal's birthplace in Mindszent.
Portrait of the cardinal's family.
The cardinal's mother and two sisters.
Veszprém.
Esztergom.
Baron Vilmos Apor, bishop of Győr.
Lajos Shvoy, bishop of Székesfehérvár.
Chrysostom Kelemen, chief abbot of the monastery at Pannonhalma.
Jusztinian Cardinal Serédi.
Count János Mikes, bishop of Szombathely.
Mindszenty in 1924.
Mindszenty in 1946.
German soldiers, 1945.
Russian soldiers advancing, 1945
Wartime Budapest.
Hungarian refugees.
Matyas Rákosi addressing crowds at a demonstration.
The May 1 demonstration, 1945.
Mass meeting in Budapest, 1948.

Chronology of Events 1944-1956

1944

March 3, 1944
Jószef Mindszenty becomes bishop of Veszprém.

March 19, 1944
Military occupation of Hungary by the Germans. The German aim is to prevent Hungary from concluding a separate peace with the Allies.

March 25, 1944
Primate Jusztinián Serédi consecrates József Mindszenty a bishop.

June
The Sztójay government confines the Jews to ghettos; the Hungarian bishops issue a pastoral letter vigorously protesting this action.

July
Regent Horthy forms a military government.

August–October
After the eastern part of Hungary has been lost to the advancing Russians, Regent Miklós Horthy appeals to the Soviet High Command for an armistice. On October 16 he issues a radio call to the Hungarian troops to cease hostilities. The chief commander of the first Hungarian army, Béla Dalnoki Miklós, went over to the

Russian side. The Germans seize Horthy and force him to relinquish his power to Ferenc Szálasi, the leader of the Arrow Cross men.

October 31
Memorandum of protest from the bishops of western Hungary to the Arrow Cross premier.

November 27
Bishop Mindszenty is arrested.

December 21
A provisional National Assembly is convened in Debrecen. It appoints a provisional government. The ministries are assigned to representatives of a coalition called the Independence Front, in which the following parties are united: The Smallholders party, the National Peasant party, the Communist party, the Social Democratic party, and the Civil Democratic party. An effort to found a new Christian-Socialist party is frustrated.

December 24
Soviet troops begin the siege of Budapest. Bishop Mindszenty is taken to Kőhida prison near the Austrian border.

1945

January 18
Soviet troops occupy the left bank of the Danube and take Pest, the eastern part of the capital.

January 20
A Hungarian government commission signs the armistice in Moscow; on the Russian side General Voroshilov signs in behalf of the Allies.

January 30
Mátyás Rákosi, first secretary of the Communist party, arrives in Hungary.

February 13
Soviet troops occupy Buda, the western part of the capital.

March 15
The provisional government passes the agrarian reform bill. Of a total of 25,000 acres of agricultural land, fully one third are affected by this reform. As a result smallholdings of from 3 to 14 acres become the rule in Hungary.

March 29
Primate Jusztinián Serédi dies in Esztergom. The apostolic nuncio, Angelo Rotta, is expelled from Hungary.

April 4
The last German troops leave the country, which remains henceforth under Soviet occupation.

April
The government moves to Budapest, where life begins to resume its normal course. Economic difficulties lead to inflation.

May 24

The Hungarian bishops issue their first postwar pastoral letter.

July 17

Beginning of the Potsdam Conference.

September

A uniform elementary school, consisting of eight classes in which children are educated until the age of fourteen, replaces the several existing types of schools.

September 16

Pope Pius XII appoints József Mindszenty as archbishop of Esztergom and primate of Hungary.

October 7

The new primate is enthroned in Esztergom.

October 17

The college of bishops publishes a pastoral letter pleading the cause of the deported, the interned, and the prisoners of war and protesting against measures of collective retaliation being applied to the civilians of German extraction in Hungary.

November 1

The bishops' pastoral letter is read throughout the country during the election campaign.

November 4

In the elections the Smallholders party wins 57.7 percent of the votes, the Social Democratic party 17.4 percent, the Communist party 17 percent, and the National Peasant party approximately 8 percent. These parties form a coalition government which has virtually no opposition (only 3 percent). Zoltán Tildy, chairman of the Smallholders party, becomes premier. There are 16 ministers: 7 Smallholders, 4 Social Democrats, 4 Communists, and one representative of the National Peasant party. Mátyás Rákosi and Árpád Szakasits hold the posts of deputy premiers. Ernő Gerő becomes minister of transportation, Imre Nagy minister of the interior.

November 30

Primate Mindszenty leaves for Rome.

1946

January 1

The coal mines, 485 of the power plants, and the associated chemical plants are placed under government control.

February 1

Parliament proclaims Hungary a republic and elects Zoltán Tildy president.

February 21

In St. Peter's, Primate Mindszenty receives his cardinal's hat from Pope Pius XII.

March 12

The law for the "protection of the democratic system and the Republic" (the "hangman's law") is promulgated. The Communists, Social Democrats, and National Peasant parties form a "left bloc" inside the government coalition and organize a demonstration against the deputies from the right wing of the Smallholders party. Under pressure of this demonstration the Smallholders party expels twenty-three deputies from its ranks. The expelled members form a new opposition party under the chairmanship of Dezső Sulyok, the Hungarian Freedom party.

March 23

The Communist party charges Imre Nagy with "lack of vigor" and relieves him of his post as minister of the interior. It appoints László Rajk as his successor. Rajk begins a campaign against the Catholic schools.

August 1

By introducing a new unit of currency, the forint, accompanied by drastic reductions in wages and energetic rounding up of the stocks of gold in private hands, the government succeeds in halting the most severe inflation in the country's history, which since 1945 had constituted Hungary's greatest economic problem.

Autumn

The State Security Service uncovers a "conspiracy" allegedly aimed at overthrowing the Republic. It turns out that some of the members of the conspiracy come from the ranks of the Smallholders. The "unmasking of the plotters" is aimed at weakening the Smallholders party, which is now forced to expel additional members.

November 16

Beginning of the deportation of Hungarians from Slovakia to the Sudetenland.

November 28

Nationalization of a number of segments of heavy industry.

1947

February 10

In Paris the Hungarian delegation, headed by Ernő Gerő, signs the peace treaty.

February

In order to force further nationalizations, the Communist party launches fresh attacks on the Smallholders party. It involves Béla Kovács, secretary general of the Smallholders party, in the recently discovered conspiracy. Parliament, however, refuses to lift Béla Kovács' immunity.

February 21

The Soviet Control Commission arrests Béla Kovács, charging him with anti-Soviet machinations.

March

The trial of the "conspirators" is held. The leaders are condemned to death, the others receive long prison terms.

May 28

Nationalization of the three largest banks in the country.

May 30

Alleging confessions extracted by coercion from Béla Kovács, the Soviet Control Commission declares that the conspiracy was instigated by Premier Ferenc Nagy personally. Nagy, who is on vacation in Switzerland at this time, resigns. Lajos Dinnyés becomes the new premier.

June 13–July 11
Cardinal Mindszenty goes to Ottawa for the world Marian congress.

July 22
Shortly before the elections the minister of the interior dissolves the Hungarian Freedom party.

July 29
Several deputies of the Freedom party and of the Smallholders party found a new opposition, the Hungarian Independence party, under the chairmanship of Zoltán Pfeifer.

August 15
Opening of the Marian Year in Esztergom.

August 31
General elections in which 60.2 percent of the votes are won by the government coalition, the Communist party taking 21.5 percent, the Social Democratic party 14.8 percent, the Smallholders party 15.2 percent, and the National Peasant party 8.7 percent. Of the opposition parties, the Democratic People's party (with a Christian-centrist tendency) under István Barankovics receives 16.1 percent of the votes, and Zoltán Pfeifer's party 14.4 percent.

September 15
The Allied Control Commission ceases its functions. On the pretext of guarding the link with the Soviet occupation forces in Austria, the Soviet troops remain in Hungary.

October 24
In a letter to Premier Dinnyés, Cardinal Mindszenty protests against the restrictions on freedom of conscience.

December 8
Tito visits Hungary. Yugoslavia and Hungary sign a treaty of friendship.

1948

February 18
Signing of the Hungarian-Soviet friendship treaty in Moscow. On this occasion Stalin proposes a toast to the equal rights of small nations.

March 2
Under pressure from the Communist party, which is seeking a fusion with the two working-class parties, the Social Democratic party expels some of its leading members (Szélig, Bám) who are opposed to such a union.

March 25
Nationalization of businesses with more than one hundred employees.

June 12–14
At separate congresses the Social Democratic and the Communist parties decide to fuse. A joint congress confirms the new program and new statutes, which virtually mean that the Social Democratic party is absorbed by the Communist party.

June 16

Parliament votes secularization of the schools, the new law to take effect on July 1.

June 28

The Cominform issues a statement denouncing Tito.

July 30

Zoltán Tildy resigns; he will remain in a villa under house arrest until 1956. On August 3 he is replaced by Árpád Szakasits.

August 5

Minister of the Interior László Rajk becomes foreign minister. His successor as minister of the interior is János Kádár.

August 20

Rákosi in his Kecskemét speech announces government support for the formation of production cooperatives; in practice this means collectivization.

September

Intensified reorganization of the technical high schools and universities. A Communist party resolution criticizes both the organization of the people's colleges and the "nationalism" of the peasant youth, whom it accuses of petty-bourgeois ideology.

September 1948–March 1949

Large-scale purge in conjunction with a checkup on all members of the Communist party. The consequence is expulsion of some 100,000 members—"former Social Democrats or unreliable elements."

December 26

Arrest in Esztergom of József Cardinal Mindszenty, who is charged with treason. He is sent to the Andrássy Street jail in Budapest.

1949

February 3–5

Trial of Cardinal Mindszenty.

February 8

Hungary's primate is sentenced to life imprisonment.

March 15

Congress of the Independence Front; its name is changed to People's Front. László Rajk becomes its general secretary. A barbed-wire fence (the "Iron Curtain") is built along the western frontier.

April

Arrest of the American correspondent Noel Field. It later develops that the purpose of the arrest is to obtain confessions implicating László Rajk.

April 9

In *Szabad Nép* Mátyás Rákosi publishes an article on the true nature of people's democracies. In theory and practice this article constitutes an announcement of the dictatorship of the proletariat.

May 15

General elections are held under the aegis of the People's Front. The single list receives almost 100 percent of the vote.

May 30

Arrest of László Rajk.

July 6

The court of appeals approves the verdict against Cardinal Mindszenty.

August 20

Ratification of a new Constitution which is faithfully modeled on the Soviet Constitution.

September 5

Obligatory religious instruction in the schools is abolished.

September 15–20

Trial of Rajk, which serves to justify the attacks on Yugoslavia and in domestic policy makes possible consolidation of Rákosi's absolute rule.

October 22

Election of district councils from a single list of Popular Front candidates. As in all following elections, nearly 100 percent of the votes go to the single list.

Production competition to celebrate Stalin's impending seventieth birthday. In the course of this competition the Stakhanovite system is developed in Hungary. At the beginning of the following years this results in a raising of quotas, which in turn means acceleration of the tempo of work and a corresponding reduction in wages.

December 21

Pompous ceremonies for Stalin's seventieth birthday.

December 28

Nationalization of businesses with more than ten employees. Industry is now completely in the hands of the Communist government.

1950

January 1

The first Five Year Plan takes effect. It concentrates on the development of heavy industry; it aims for exceeding the capacities and resources of the country. The new plan is associated with the slighting of agricultural techniques and intensified collectivization.

April 24

Árpád Szakasits, former leader of the Social Democrats and president of the Republic, is arrested and forced to resign.

May–August

A wave of arrests of former Social Democrats. On June 9 the mass removal of monks and nuns also begins.

August 30

The Catholic college of bishops arrives at an agreement with the government; it draws subsidies and obtains the return of several schools.

September 7

Dissolution of the monastic orders.

1951

February 25–March 2

Second congress of the Hungarian Communist party. Increase of the planned quotas far beyond the capacities of the country. Imminent institution of complete collectivization is announced.

April 15

Introduction of bread rationing. Serious economic difficulties loom.

May 19

The bill is passed creating the notorious government bureau for church affairs.

May 22–26

At the meeting of the Communist party's central committee violent new attacks on the enemy within the party are launched. Since March, János Kádár, Géza Losonczy, Cyula Kállai, Sándor Zöld, and many other prominent Communists have vanished from the political scene. Most of them were tried in secret trials and many condemned to death.

June 15

Forcible deportation begins of "class enemies" from Budapest and western Hungary to the eastern parts of the country.

June 22

Trial of József Grősz, archbishop of Kalocsa and chairman of the college of bishops since Mindszenty's arrest. Grősz is sentenced to fifteen years in the penitentiary for espionage and conspiracy.

July 21

The Catholic college of bishops takes the oath of allegiance to the Constitution. The seminaries for the training of priests are abolished.

November 20–30

By drastic price increases, which are far out of line with wages, the central committee shifts the burden of the country's economic predicament to the consumer. Simultaneously the rationing system is abolished; despite the nuisance of ration cards that system had at least permitted people to obtain essential consumer goods at moderate prices.

1952

March 9

Rákosi's sixtieth birthday is celebrated with pompous ceremonies in honor of the "Hungarian Stalin," the "father of his people."

June 27–28

The Communist party central committee feels forced to concede the existence of economic difficulties; but it shifts responsibility to the people by appealing to the spirit of sacrifice, and to scapegoats in the form of "saboteurs."

August 15

Rákosi reaches the peak of his power. He has himself elected premier.

October 5–14

Nineteenth congress of the Communist party of the Soviet Union. Stalin calls Hungary the vanguard of socialism.

December

Bishop József Pétery of Vác is arrested.

1953

February

Secret arrest of Péter Gábor, chief of the AVO, the secret police.

March 3

Death of Stalin.

May 15

Elections. Total victory for the single list.

June 16–20

World congress of the peace movement in Budapest, with great display of Picasso's dove of peace. Elaborate ceremonies.

June 17

Uprising in East Germany.

June 27–28

Meeting of the central committee at which new directives are adopted. These show a degree of liberalization and indicate a weakening of Rákosi's power.

July 2–6

Rákosi offers to resign as premier. He is succeeded by Imre Nagy, whose inaugural speech makes a great sensation. In addition to a reorganization of the economy, Imre Nagy announces measures of political liberalization. He condemns the terror, the arrests, and deportations, and promises to put an end to all that. Henceforth, he pledges, the peasants will be allowed to withdraw from the cooperatives.

July 26

The peasants are promised tax relief.

July 30

Agricultural credit is eased.

August 20

General amnesty. End of the deportations and further easing of agricultural credit.

August 28

First agreement with Yugoslavia, concerning border incidents.

December 13

Easing of payments in kind to be made by farms; debts can be paid off by long term installments.

1954

Spring

Cardinal Mindszenty, seriously ill, is released from the prison on Conti Street and transferred to the prison hospital at the Budapest reception prison.

March 13

Conviction of Péter Gábor and his accomplices—though their names are not mentioned—for "offenses against socialist legality" is announced.

May 24–29

Third congress of the Hungarian Communist party. After Rákosi's report, in which there is mention of democratization but not of any readiness to make concessions. Imre Nagy announces the reconstitution of the government apparatus and the formation of new People's Front. He pledges that it will be organized on democratic principles.

June

Release of János Kádár, Géza Losonczy, László Rajk's wife, Gyula Kállai, and other communist leaders. The penal camps for political prisoners are closed.

August 12

A new Patriotic People's Front is formed.

September

Rationalization campaign: Attempt to reduce the number of employees in government and in some factories. This takes the form of surprise firings which engender general panic. In addition, the considerable unemployment gradually becomes a burden.

October 23–24

Congress of the Patriotic People's Front.

October 26–27

At the meeting of the central committee of the Communist party, Imre Nagy wins a temporary new victory over the advocates of the previous economic policy.

October 28

In an article in *Szabad Nép* Imre Nagy announces intensified democratization and the release of additional innocent persons who are still in prison. He condemns the methods of rationalization and the time chosen to put them into effect.

December 21

On the tenth anniversary of the provisional government Rákosi fiercely attacks "the June line."

1955

January 2

At a meeting of the presidium of the People's Front, Rákosi declares that the right deviationists represent the greatest danger to the country.

February 6

Resignation of Malenkov.

February

The Communist party's theoretical magazine, *Társadalmi Szemle*, publishes an editorial criticizing Imre Nagy's political line.

March 2–4

The central committee condemns Imre Nagy's course. Suslov takes part in the meeting as a representative of the Communist party of the Soviet Union.

April 18

Imre Nagy is expelled from the central committee and relieved of all his offices. His successor as premier is András Hegedüs.

May 14

Signing of the Warsaw Pact. Hungary is represented by András Hegedüs. The pact provides that Soviet troops may remain in Hungary even after the evacuation of Austria, but must not intervene in the internal affairs of Hungary.

July

Cardinal Mindszenty is taken to Püspökszentlászló.

July 17

Commutation of Mindszenty's sentence. (In reality he continues to be held under guard in a rural manor house.) Beginning of the Geneva Conference.

October 14

Archbishop Grősz is taken to Püspökszentlászló.

November 2

Primate Mindszenty and Archbishop Grősz are transferred to Felsőpetény.

December 6

The central committee issues a decree against writers, condemning their attitude as right deviationism.

1956

February 14–25

Twentieth congress of the Communist party of the Soviet Union.

February 21

Rehabilitation of Béla Kun, the leader of the first communist government of 1919 in Hungary, who had been executed in the period of the great purges in the USSR.

March 12

Rákosi reports to the central committee about the twentieth congress. The resolution of the Hungarian central committee evokes widespread dissatisfaction because it does not take into account the decisions of the twentieth congress.

March 27

At a meeting of the section of the Communist party for the Thirteenth District of Budapest (Angyalföld, an important working-class district), Rákosi publicly acknowledges Rajk's innocence. György Litván, a young teacher, openly calls upon him to withdraw from the political arena.

May 1

Failure of the demonstration for the "workers' holiday." Only half of the usual crowd attends.

April–May

Lively discussion in the Petőfi literary circle, which had been established the previous year. The first important debate deals with economic problems.

May

Release of Zoltán Tildy, Béla Kovács, and a number of Social Democratic leaders.

May 11

Amnesty for József Grősz, the archbishop of Kalocsa, who now becomes head of the Catholic Church of Hungary.

May 18

Rákosi practices public self-criticism but does not succeed in satisfying public opinion.

May 20

The lowest category of wages are raised.

June 16

Philosophical debates in the Petőfi circle. György Lukács condemns Stalinist dogmatism.

June 28–29

The events in Posen.

June 30

Central committee resolution against the Petőfi circle.

July 27–28

Meeting of the central committee in the presence of Mikoyan. Rákosi resigns. Ernő Gerő succeeds him as secretary general of the Communist party. Partial reshuffling of the politburo and the central committee; several rehabilitated politicians are taken into the latter. Reduction in the size of the army. Mihály Farkas is expelled from the party—a first indication that Imre Nagy may be readmitted.

October 6

State funeral for László Rajk and his three executed comrades.

October 13

Debate on agriculture in the Petőfi circle. Forced collectivization of the peasants is rejected. Cooperatives based on voluntary membership are declared a necessity. The demand is raised for the return to power of Imre Nagy.

October 14

Imre Nagy is readmitted to the Communist party.

October 16

The university students of Szeged once more organize in the autonomous student association known as MEFESZ, which had been absorbed by DISZ, the communist youth organization.

October 15–23

A delegation headed by Ernő Gerő visits Yugoslavia. Among the members are János Kádár, István Kovács, and Antal Apro.

October 19–21

The events in Poland.

Tuesday, October 23

Szabad Nép, the central organ of the Communist party, in its morning edition gives vigorous support to the Polish people's aspirations. *Szabad Ifjuság*, the communist youth newspaper comes out as a leaflet and likewise backs the demands of the Poles. MEFESZ, the student association, also issues a newspaper which contains most of the sixteen points adopted the night before (the demand for the withdrawal of the Soviet troops is omitted).

An announced demonstration is first forbidden, then approved by the ministry of the interior. The demonstrators assemble before the monuments to the two great revolutionaries of 1848, the poet Petőfi and General Bem, the rebel of Polish descent. Huge crowds fill the main streets and assemble in front of Parliament. Gerő addresses them. Nagy appears briefly on the balcony of the Parliament building. At 10 P.M. the AVO fires the first shots at the demonstrators in front of the radio station. At the same time there are demonstrations in the major provincial towns, Szeged, Debrecen, Miskolc, Győr, and others.

The central committee holds a meeting at night and decides on reshufflings in the government and party leadership. Imre Nagy, who has been taken back into the central committee, does not take part in this meeting.

Wednesday, October 24

The radio reports the events of the night and the shifts in the political leadership. The rebels are denounced as fascists; the street battles are played down. The workers go on strike. The government declares a state of emergency. Imre Nagy delivers a radio address calling for an end to the fighting.

Various officials, including János Kádár and Archbishop József Grösz, appeal to the populace to restore order.

Thursday, October 25

The fighting has died down. The government demands the resumption of work, but instead of going to their jobs the people go into the streets.

In the course of the morning a demonstration takes place; it had been summoned by leaflets distributed the night before. The demonstrators protest against the continuance in office of Gerő who is regarded as responsible for the bloodshed. Units of the Hungarian army do not intervene; some of them support the rebels. Some of the soviet troops fraternize with the rebels; others hold aloof but remain passive.

At the urging of Mikoyan, Gerő resigns. He is replaced by János Kádár. Radio appeals by Kádár and Imre Nagy do not succeed in checking the uprising, which is assuming ever greater proportions.

The struggle spreads in the large provincial towns also. The radio station of Miskolc falls into the hands of the rebels and begins broadcasting in their name.

Friday, October 26

Delegations from Budapest and all parts of the country pour into Parliament and urge Imre Nagy to take new measures to liberate the country.

The fighting in Budapest and the provinces continues. Throughout the country revolutionary committees are founded and try to bring the situation under control as rapidly as possible. Convoys of provisions from the country start toward the capital. The peasants try to supply the rebels with food. Workers' councils are formed in the factories to organize the fighting and to supervise the maintenance of the general strike. It is decided to continue to refuse to work until the Russians withdraw.

Saturday, October 27

The radio announces the formation of a new government from which the most notorious Stalinists are excluded and in which non-Communists are also represented. But public opinion is still not satisfied.

The workers' council of the Borsod district announces that it has taken control of the entire district, that the AVO has been dissolved and soviet troops have not intervened.

A similar report comes from the workers' council of Győr.

Sunday, October 28

The revolutionary committees that are being formed more and more gain the upper hand. Connections are established between the hitherto isolated centers of resistance.

As a result of a succession of compromises on the local level, the fighting dies down.

In a radio statement Imre Nagy announces the government's order to cease firing. He acknowledges the democratic and national nature of the uprising, holds out the prospect of dissolution of the AVO, and promises the withdrawal of the soviet troops.

Monday, October 29

After the ceasefire revolutionary committees organize in agencies and public institutions.

The Soviet troops begin their withdrawal from Budapest.

Thursday, October 30

New reshuffling of the government. A mixed cabinet is formed containing, in addition to the Communists, members of the newly reestablished Smallholders party and the likewise revived National Peasant party. The government intends to reintroduce the principle of coalition. The Social Democrats have not yet committed themselves on the possibility of participating.

Imre Nagy announces that he has begun discussions looking toward a complete withdrawal of the Soviet troops.

A revolutionary committee is formed in the core of the Hungarian Honvéd army. Cardinal Mindszenty is freed.

The representatives of the national councils of Transdanubia meet in Győr and found an independent national council there. It enters into negotiations with the government in Budapest, presenting a number of revolutionary demands.

Declaration of the Soviet government promising an examination of the relations between the USSR and the people's democracies.

Wednesday, October 31

A number of new newspapers appear as evidence of complete freedom of the press.

The Social Democratic party is once more permitted.

The government announces its intention to withdraw from the Warsaw Pact and begins negotiations to that effect with the soviet government. The military head of the uprising, Pál Maléter, is appointed deputy minister of national defense. Political prisoners are freed from jails. The revolutionary committee of university students issues leaflets supporting Imre Nagy.

According to information from the railroad men, transmitted orally by them and broadcast over the radio in the cities of western Hungary, soviet convoys are rolling toward the capital. Meanwhile the last Soviet troops leave Budapest.

Thursday, November 1

A new radio station appears on the scene. It calls itself Rádio Rójk, declares that its politics are communist, and criticizes the policies both of the government and the Russians.

Imre Nagy takes the post of foreign minister.

In view of the fact that the Soviet Union has broken the Warsaw Pact by sending troops to Hungary, the government denounces the pact, declares the country neutral, and appeals to the great powers and the United Nations to guarantee its neutrality.

János Kádár proclaims the abolition of the Hungarian Communist party and the formation of a Hungarian Socialist Workers party. In his statement he approves the revolution without reserve and hails its victory.

Friday, November 2

The Borsod workers council demands the establishment of a national revolutionary committee to replace Parliament.

The national workers council calls for an end to the strike. The government again protests the massed deployment of Soviet troops and sets up a military committee to negotiate with the Russians on withdrawal of their troops.

Saturday, November 3

Work is resumed in much of the country, and in the capital also.

In spite of the negotiations between the Nagy government and the Soviet representatives, the Russian troop movements continue, The Soviet authorities arrest the Hungarian delegation under Pál Maléter, which has been engaged in negotiating with them. In the evening Cardinal Mindszenty addresses an appeal to the Hungarian people and the world.

Sunday, November 4

General offensive by the Soviet army. Supported by parachute troops, the Russians simultaneously occupy all the strategically important points in the country.

Imre Nagy protests to the United Nations. Over a new radio station, Ferenc Münnich, János Kádár, and others announce that they have formed a new government and have called the Soviet army in to help suppress the counterrevolution. At 7:30 A.M. Radio Kossuth, the voice of the Nagy government, falls silent. At 10 P.M. that same day the station begins broadcasting the communiqués of the Kádár government.

Monday, November 5

Pope Pius XII addresses an apostolic epistle on the plight of the Hungarian people to the bishops of the world.

The Assembly of the United Nations condemns the Soviet Union.

Preface

WHEN YOU HAVE passed your sixtieth year, it is time to write your memoirs, should you have something you want to say to the world. In my own case, the destinies of my country and its Church prompt me to take up the pen. I cannot be a *laudator temporis acti,* praising the past like other, happier people. Suffering and imposed passivity occupy a greater part of my memories than the years spent in activity. In a dark period of my life I sat in wretchedness, like Job during his tribulations. Therefore I shall not be able to speak merely of edifying and joyful things. I must tell about life as it is, filled with suffering and grace. In short, I must speak of reality.

During my imprisonment a movie called *The Prisoner* was made. Bridget Roland is the author of the script; the lead was played by Alec Guiness, who has since been granted the grace of faith.

The story of *The Prisoner* is as follows: A cardinal, who is approximately as tall as I am and still in full possession of his strength, is arrested after divine services by policemen dressed in civilian clothes. The arrested man is led away, still in his vestments. His cell is a tiny room in an old castle. But it in no way resembles my cell. Only the barred windows and the peephole in the door remind me of that. But in the movie we have a glimpse of a divan. The furniture is actually luxurious, which it hardly is in Hungarian prisons.

In the movie the interrogation is conducted along the well-mannered lines of good society. The prisoner is even addressed as "Your Eminence." The mere fact that the guard so much as speaks to the prisoner must seem astonishing to anyone who has been interrogated by Hungarian Communists. In the film the conversations are quite pleasant and genial. Coffee is frequently served; it is first tasted by the interrogator and then drunk by the prisoner. The food is good, the table setting choice, the service gracious. Seconds are frequently offered—in one case twice within five minutes. Even the prisoner notices this, and avails himself of further helpings with a better appetite than prisoners generally have.

It is true, however, that the cardinal's wrists are handcuffed to make plain his hostility to the state. The interrogation itself is interrupted from time to time because of the prisoner's resistance.

During the trial strict security measures are taken; nevertheless, curious people force their way into the courtroom. But there are no other defendants. There is also no bench for the defendant. The defendant and the prosecutor pace back and forth, occasionally meeting in the course of these strolls. Later, the cardinal falls down unconscious, and afterwards makes a confession. He accuses himself of acts hostile to the state. He is condemned to death, but then his sentence is commuted. At the end his weeping mother appears.

After the verdict, the prosecutor commits suicide.

In my case, the minister of justice was later killed at the hands of the Communists.

This film was given a friendly reception by the critics and the public and was shown throughout the world. But I am sorry to say that the well-meaning script writer did not know Hungary's communist prisons, and so the movie failed to give any picture of reality. The one thing it had in common with events in Hungary is the presence of a cardinal.

In retrospect events often tend to be given quite a fantastic cast in yellow, white, and black books, or in films. Both on the left and on the right, many books dealing with my case have been published. After 1956, for example, I received one such book which had been published first in English and subsequently in Japanese, Chinese, Spanish, Portuguese, Arabic, and Burmese editions.

In my memoirs I want to show the reality as it was. This is the first time I am speaking after decades of silence.

The reader is entitled to ask whether I am telling everything. My answer is: I mean to tell everything and shall preserve silence only when it is required by decency, by manly and priestly honor. But I am not speaking out now to harvest the fruit of my sufferings and wounds. I am publishing all this only so that the world may see what fate communism has in store for mankind. I want to show that communism does not respect the dignity of man; I shall describe my cross only in order to direct the world's eyes to Hungary's cross and that of her Church.

Vienna, Easter Sunday, 1974

MEMOIRS

I. TWO WORLD WARS

☿ *Youth*

I WAS BORN on March 29, 1892, in Mindszent, Vas County. My parents, János Pehm and Borbála Kovács, owned a farm of some twenty-five acres. My father raised wine grapes and other crops. In the village important posts were entrusted to him. While still quite young he had been village magistrate, overseer of orphans, and head of the parish council and of the school committee. One of his forefathers had distinguished himself in the reconquest of the fortress of Kiskomárom from the Turks, and had therefore been elevated to the class of freemen in 1733. My mother's ancestors were indentured to Count Zrinyis in Zala County. Thus we all come from ancient Hungarian families and all our relations bear genuine Hungarian family names. Their occupations were extremely varied: artisans, farmers, shepherds, churchmen, businessmen, army officers, civil magistrates, parish priests, bank clerks.

There were six in our family. Two infants—twins—were taken home by God during the first few days of their lives. A third child died at the age of eight. The family's continuance was provided for by my two sisters. My mother saw grandchildren and great-grandchildren who were a consolation and a joy to her in times of anguish.

The love of a wise and kind mother presided over our home. She gave us warmth, a feeling of shelter, and together with father's active vigor, she offered a shining example. My parents, in their forethought and perseverance, also stimulated ambitious plans. I owe it to them that I was able to attend the classical secondary school after I finished elementary school.

☧ *Schooling*

IN MINDSZENT I attended elementary school for five years. There a good teacher laid the foundations for whatever knowledge I have. My parents supplemented that foundation at home, and often helped me with my lessons. Under the guidance of my mother, who was a deeply religious woman, I also learned to serve as altar boy, along with other village youngsters.

There were many gaps in the knowledge that the village school was able to give me. In 1903 I moved on to the intermediate school conducted by the Premonstratensians in Szombathely. It took almost three years before I caught up with the boys from urban schools. It was not until I reached the upper classes that I managed to work my way into the ranks of the better pupils. During this time I learned and read a great deal. Theology, literature, and history fascinated me. In the final examination I received the mark "very good" in all subjects except one (physics).

Shortly after I began my gimnázium studies I very nearly had to drop plans for a higher education. Toward the end of my first year my mother came to Szombathely to tell me, griefstricken, that my younger brother, who was then eight, had died. My father had intended him to inherit our farm; but now I ought to return home, learn farming, and later take over. I was able to change my mother's mind about this, and was allowed to stay.

During the time I was at the gimnázium I was also active in the Catholic Youth Movement and learned a great deal that was later useful to me in my pastoral duties. Ultimately I became prefect of the Marian Sodality.

After graduation I entered the seminary in Szombathely, where I soon fitted in quite well. The professors were capable and highly likable. Theological studies gave me great joy and satisfaction. But after only one year my diocesan bishop, Count János Mikes, wanted to send me to the University of Vienna. There was an institute for Hungarian students of theology there, the Pazmaneum, where I would be able to live. But the prospect worried me, and I declined the offer. The bishop was more than amazed by my refusal; he was quite annoyed and during the next few years let me feel his annoyance frequently. In fact, I visited the Pazmaneum for the first time in 1947, as Archbishop of Esztergom. Today, in exile, I am happy to have found a home in this very institute.

On June 12, 1915, on the Festival of the Sacred Heart of Jesus, Bishop János Mikes ordained me a priest.

☿ *My First Assignment*

IN THE MIDST of the First World War, I began my labors in the Lord's vineyard as assistant to the pastor of Felsőpáty, Béla Geiszlinger. I owe a great deal to this remarkable man. He conveyed to me profound insights into the lives of the people. The result was that I quickly made contact with all classes, concerned myself with the social and material problems of the souls entrusted to my care, and took part in the leadership of the credit and consumer cooperatives. During this period my first book on spiritual problems, *Az Édesanya* ("The Mother"), was published in two volumes. A second printing of it was issued during the same year.

The priestly office was a source of profound joy to me. My instruction was well received, my sermons evoked response, and many believers came to confession and Mass. I was especially happy when—even in cases of those who seemed to have hopelessly fallen out with God, the Church, and themselves—I was able to revive faith by persuasion and guidance.

To give just one example: In Jákfa there lived an eighty-year-old landowner, almost deaf, who was a liberal in religious and political matters. He got on rather badly with those who were close to him. That was understandable, for he constantly told the same stories. I too had to listen to them for an entire year; they came as a sort of dessert after a good many Sunday dinners. I knew that he had not come to divine service for a long time, pleading his various ailments; and after I had met with him frequently I asked him how he stood with God. He said that the last time he had confessed and had received communion was sixty years ago, before his wedding. I ventured to press him a little. His wife was afraid that I might forfeit his good will; I told her that his soul's salvation was more important than friendship. Contrary to expectations, the friendship was deepened and strengthened. The man received the holy sacrament and afterwards declared with deep emotion: "I have scarcely ever been so happy. Only now do I rightly understand what is meant by the parable of the workmen who are hired during the last hour of the day and nevertheless receive the same wages."

Two years later, in May 1919, when I returned to Zalaegerszeg from my first imprisonment by the Communists, I found a telegram on my desk reporting the landowner's death. His granddaughter wrote that his last wish had been for me to be at his burial. The telegram bore the date February 9, 1919—the same day that I had been arrested. I therefore could not have fulfilled his last wish, but I did what I could still do: I said the requiem Mass for the old gentleman, and thanked God that back in Jákfa I had been given the patience to listen to his tedious stories again and again, and that by so doing I had been able to win his confidence and lead him back to God.

☦ My First Imprisonment

I SPENT one and a half years as a curate. On February 1, 1917, I was asked to teach religion at the state gimnázium in Zalaegerszeg. This city is the county seat of Zala County and is an important cultural and economic center. Here I found myself confronting new and important tasks. Right from the start I was asked to take over not only the subject of religion but also to be a class teacher and to teach Latin, since part of the teaching staff was in the army because of the war. In addition I had two youth sodalities and the Marian Women's Sodality to supervise. That meant a great deal of work, but I was young. I quickly established a good relationship with my colleagues and struck up friendships with a good many of the higher officials in the county and city. They supported me in my work and opened the social and cultural life of the town to me. I became a member of the board of directors of the Credit Union, a town councilor, and an editor of the county's weekly newspaper. This last position gave me a great deal of trouble, but my pupils pitched in to help me with the editorial work and the distribution of the newspaper. One of these pupils, Jenő Kerkai, particularly distinguished himself; he later became a Jesuit, known and esteemed throughout the country.

Meanwhile, we had entered the fifth year of the war. Everywhere signs of uncertainty and exhaustion could be seen in the population and the machinery of government. A small liberal group consisting chiefly of intellectuals spread the slogan of "Peace and Revolution" in the capital. Such groups found their chances radically and rapidly spurred by the statements of President Wilson. Wilson spoke of the right of self-determination for the peoples of the Austro-Hungarian Empire. The enemy's press called upon the soldiers at the front to throw away their weapons. In October 1918, Hungary reached the point of total collapse. King Charles IV withdrew. Count Michael Károlyi took command of a revolutionary government in the Hungarian capital.

At first the people passively watched events and seemed impotent to affect the future. The disintegration of St. Stephen's country seemed to be proceeding inexorably. In Zala County, too, the upheavals produced a feeling of utter numbness. But then resistance began to grow. We gathered our forces. The newspaper which I helped edit sharply criticized the conduct of the new regime. In 1919, the Károlyi government prepared for elections. At the request of my friends and of many priests, I assumed the leadership in our area of the newly founded Christian Party. During the campaign I made speeches; at public meetings and in the County Council I frequently and insistently set forth our viewpoint. We managed to put up an effective fight against the socialistic Károlyi party in both the towns and the countryside.

In these circumstances it was not surprising that I, too, was the object of attacks, and that these were not always carried out along democratic lines. The general mood of the people protected me, but my opponents constantly spied on me. They must have learned that I had to go to Szombathely on February 9, 1919, to take care of some official church matters there. On the way back I was arrested by two policemen who told me that a warrant for my arrest had been issued in Zalaegerszeg. I was taken to the county courthouse and brought before Béla Obál, administrative commissioner of Vas County, who was a Lutheran pastor. His first question was: "What have you done, my friend?" My reply was: "That is exactly what I would like to know."

The commissioner informed me that there was a warrant out for my arrest wherever I was to be found. I was interned for the present in the episcopal palace. The bishop himself, who was considered hostile to the government, had earlier been placed under house arrest in the Benedictine Abbey of Celldőmőlk.

Two police sergeants from Zalaegerszeg were sent to guard me, with a police captain, István Zilahy, in charge of them. The supervision, however, was very loose. The captain spent his evenings in the Grand Hotel Szabaria, while the sergeants went to taverns. I was left alone, so that I had the opportunity to slip out of the episcopal palace and go to the offices of the daily newspaper *Vasvármegye* ("County Vas"), where we worked out a program for the spring elections.

At these offices the news reached me that the administrative commissioner was planning to have me transferred from my post in Zalaegerszeg.

This obviously was well meant, and I was afraid that my friend, Vicar-
general Dr. József Tóth, already might have tried to go along with this
suggestion in order to save me from worse treatment, from prison. I therefore slipped out again one evening and went to Celldőmőlk to see my
bishop. An officer who was guarding him allowed me to go in, and I was
able to persuade Bishop Mikes not to approve my transfer. "It shall be done
as you wish, my son," he said, well knowing that there was danger for me
involved in this decision. It was nearly midnight by the time I returned
from this outing. The police captain had already started a search for me.
He and his two sergeants were greatly relieved when I entered; they actually thanked me for having returned at all.

After ten days of this mild arrest, I was suddenly summoned to the telephone in the episcopal secretariat. The commissioner informed me that I
would be released if I would cease my opposition to the Károlyi government and prepare to withdraw from my parish in Zalaegerszeg. I would not
accept his terms, even when he threatened that I could be sentenced to up
to fifteen years in the penitentiary for opposing the power of the state. He
then asked me to hand the telephone over to my sergeant, and evidently
gave him a brief order. "Come along, Professor," the guard said. I had to
pack my things, was taken out to an alley behind the episcopal palace, and
here the sergeant told me: "You can go wherever you like, Reverend, only
you're not allowed to go to Zalaegerszeg."

I left him there. "Only the bishop has the right to give me orders," I
thought. "He alone decides where I work." And so I bought a ticket and
took the next train to Zalaegerszeg. But the police were waiting for me in
Zalalövő, where I had to change trains; they held me prisoner in the
railroad station all night. The next morning they sent me back to Szombathely. The annual fair was being held at the time. Groups of people were
standing around everywhere when the two gendarmes, flanking me with
bristling bayonets, led me through the town. People paused indignantly
and called out—loudly enough for me to hear—asking what kind of crime
this priest had committed. Had he killed someone, or stolen, or set a fire?

For the time being I was again held in the bishop's palace for several
weeks. On March 20, 1919, that day of shame in our history, Count Károlyi let the Communists seize power from him and proclaim the dictatorship
of the proletariat. The story of this Béla Kun uprising and the terror that
followed is well known. Throughout the country hostages were taken from
among the opponents of the regime. I was one of them. In the middle of the
night a police inspector, accompanied by two patrolmen, pulled me out of
bed and shouted in an official tone and with an officious look, but in bad
Hungarian: "You are under arrest." I replied that I had been so since February 9, 1919, and asked what this outlay of governmental authority was all
about. He said harshly, but with a touch of embarrassment, that the situation had changed. Actually very little had changed: the dog was the same,

but his collar was now redder. They led me down Szily Street from the episcopal palace to the police station, both policemen wearing fierce looks, as if they were accompanying a dangerous criminal. But in front of the police station one of them seized a moment's opportunity to turn to me, clearing his throat. I asked him what he wanted to say. In embarrassment he replied that he was not accustomed to transporting servants of God in this way. Formerly he had taken them about in a coach, for he had been a gentleman's coachman in Répceszentgyörgy. I had no choice but to try to comfort him. Then I was locked into a cell that had hitherto been used for prostitutes. The following evening I was transferred, together with all the newly arrested prisoners from Vas County, to the detention jail. There I met a good many acquaintances: the noted writer Pintér of Szombathely; the dean of Léka, Mátyás Heiss; the Cistercian superior, Guido Maurer; Staff Captain László Deme; a director of the state railroad lines, Ferenc Üveges; the tenant farmer Frigyes Riedinger; the landowner János Benrieder; and others.

Meanwhile the terror was raging in the capital. The cellar of Parliament in Budapest became an execution ground. Prisoners were brought there for execution even from other parts of the country. Bishop Mikes of Szombathely had likewise been ordered shipped to Budapest. But he managed to hide out in a lonely forest hut, and there he survived the brief dictatorship of the proletariat. The Communists also wanted to transport our fellow prisoner, Ferenc Üveges, to the capital. But we were able to save him with the aid of the guards themselves. Sergeant Talabér, whose name deserves to be recalled here, threw the prison keys through a window to us. We opened the doors, helped Üveges climb over the high wall, and he made his escape. To deceive the subsequent police check, we stuck my shoebutton hook into the lock; it was then confiscated as material evidence. By the time the guards came to take Üveges away, Talabér had his keys back, and no shadow of suspicion ever fell upon him.

Those days were extremely nerve-wracking. We knew all about the secret tribunals that were deciding the lives or deaths of prisoners. On the Saturday before Easter my fellow prisoners were released. I was the only one left. On May 15, 1919, two policemen took me to Zalaegerszeg. From Zalaszentiván Station we had to walk five miles, because such branch lines were not operating during the period of communist rule. We arrived at our destination dusty and exhausted. I was again taken to the county house, where a printer from Baja named Márkus Erdős reigned as president of the Directorate. He informed me that I was not allowed to return to the gimnázium again, that I must not associate with elements hostile to the state, and that I must not speak and preach publicly. "Was the regime bent on forcing people into idleness?" I asked. Furious at my sarcasm, he shouted: "We will force our enemies to obey."

I therefore returned home, donned my soutane, and went to the May devotions, which were just being celebrated. What joy I took in the privilege of once more praying in the community of the faithful. Afterwards, we greeted one another in the church garden, and I joined a smaller group of old friends. Evidently I was being watched and had overstepped the prescribed limits, for I was once more ordered to appear at the county house. There Erdős informed me that because of my public conduct I was regarded as incorrigible and was being expelled from the county. I had to leave town in Abbot Kálmán Legáth's carriage, take the train in Zalaszentiván, and return to my native village. There I remained with my parents for the two more months that the Béla Kun regime lasted.

☩ A Quarter of a Century in Zalaegerszeg

EARLY IN August 1919, after the collapse of the dictatorship of the proletariat, I returned to Zalaegerszeg. In the meantime the pastor, Abbot Kálmán Legáth, had retired. His parish now had no priest. On August 20, by unanimous decision of the parish delegates, I was proposed as his successor. Count János Mikes, the diocesan bishop, gave his approval, and on October 1, 1919, charged me with the parish of Zalaegerszeg. The appointment caused a good deal of surprise because of my youth—I was only twenty-seven. At the time of my installation the bishop jokingly responded to the surprise and to my own misgivings by remarking that my youth was "a fault that would diminish from day to day."

The region within which I exercised the care of souls embraced the county seat itself, with its sixteen thousand inhabitants, as well as five affiliated congregations. I knew the town well, having already been teacher of religion there for two and a half years. Nevertheless, I now became aware of impediments to an effective ministry and to any deepening of the religious life of the region. For example, the affiliated congregations with their four thousand inhabitants were located at considerable distances from the center of the parish; the nearest was two miles, the farthest five. Moreover, the faithful did not at all constitute a socially coherent community. All classes of Hungarian society were represented. Living in Zalaegerszeg were officials of the county and city governments, artisans, tradesmen, and factory workers. In the neighboring communities of Zalabesenyő and Szenterzsébethegy, Ebergény, Ságod, and Vorhota were peasants and farm-hands. I noted with regret that there was too little personal contact between the clergy and the laity and that the instruction in religion was inadequate. Church and cultural associations, which in other places offered laymen opportunities for participating in the life of the parish, were almost entirely lacking in this district. This and similar concerns troubled me daily. Once I was giving a bride and bridegroom from Szenterzsébethegy instruction in the principles of Christian marriage. Afterwards, when I presented the documents to them for their signature, it turned out that neither they nor the two witnesses were able to write. That surprised me, for in neighboring Vas County, where I had been born and raised, you seldom encountered anyone who did not know how to read and write. It was brought home to me that Zala County was one of the most backward counties in Transdanubia. Nor was Szenterzsébethegy the only community that had neither teacher nor school.

On one of the following Sundays I conducted Sunday mass in Szenterzsébethegy and discussed the question of a school with the villagers. I learned that only children who could spend a school year in another village, living with relatives or friends, would have the opportunity to learn reading and writing. I urged the parish community to embark at once on building a school for fifty to sixty pupils in Szenterzsébethegy.

In three other villages conditions were just as unsatisfactory; there were only one-room schools. With the support of the village magistrate and the communities concerned, I succeeded in the course of some six years in improving conditions and bringing in new teachers. In Ságod we even built a school chapel. Expansion of the school and the institution of thorough religious instruction soon tangibly improved the cultural and religious life of the community.

Later on, when I had time to look somewhat more closely into the history of the parish, I learned from the few and defective documents available that this, my first parish, was still suffering from a heritage of the period of Turkish rule. During the first half of the sixteenth century the Turks had conquered the southern and central parts of Hungary. An attempt was therefore made to protect the unoccupied areas by border fortifications—defenses that were frequently pierced by the enemy. When that happened, the inhabitants of the border villages fled—if they could—to avoid being dragged off into captivity or slaughtered. Houses, churches, rectories would be burned down. Thus within the area of my present huge parish several independent parishes had been destroyed in 1567, among them Szenterzsébethegy, Zalabesenyő, Ola, and Neszele. Zalaegerszeg had survived the Turks only thanks to its fortress. After the Turks had been driven back in the seventeenth century, the Church could not, of course, rebuild all the churches and parish houses. There were no funds, and the few remaining or returned inhabitants did not need a church organization on anything like the former scale. In Zalaegerszeg and the vicinity, therefore, only a single parish was reestablished where previously there had been four.

Around the middle of the eighteenth century Márton Biró, the bishop of Veszprém, completed the reconstruction of the county seat and built in it a spacious parish house and a handsome baroque parish church that remains to this day an ornament of the county seat. In 1777, the western part of the county was attached to the new diocese of Szombathely. Thus Zalaegerszeg became, after Szombathely, the most important town in the diocese. Nevertheless, during the following one hundred and fifty years up to the time I took office in 1919, there had been only slight changes in the parish. My aim was to create a contemporary parish life. The first task was to solve the problem of excessive distances; those who wanted to attend services often had much too far to go. In Ola, a working-class district on the outskirts of Zalaegerszeg, we built a large new monastic church that was placed in the charge of the Franciscans. We increased the number of Sunday Masses in the two big churches and in the local chapels, and also offered more opportunities for confession and more hours for religious instruction in the schools. Within the parish we set up religious and cultural associations. Through these measures and through an energetic program of visiting people in their homes—I placed particular stress on this—we created closer relations between the clergy and the flock. I ultimately came to know all the members of the communities within the parish—including those of other faiths—by name.

In all this work I was supported by zealous laymen. I remember them with great gratitude, especially those I had appointed "family apostles." They called priests to the sick, took care that no one died without having received the sacraments. They encouraged people to come to retreats, theological lectures, popular missions, and parish house events. Thanks to their efforts, the parish of Zalaegerszeg soon became noted within the diocese and throughout the country as a model of the religious life.

I became a member of the County and Town Council, and as a result, I naturally became more involved in public life. Nevertheless, I never became engaged in day-to-day politics, with the exception of that brief early period after the fall of the Béla Kún regime in which I assumed the leadership in the county of the Christian Party. Neither then nor later, however, did I take a seat as a parliamentary deputy, although it was common in Europe for priests to sit in the legislatures. Although I fully supported the political activities of Bishop Ottokár Prohászka and other clerics under exceptional circumstances. I myself firmly refused when my friends wanted to nominate me, because I had never thought very highly of the role of the priest-politician. I was all the more determined to fight the enemies of my country and Church with the written and spoken word, and to support all Christian politicians by giving clear and decisive directives to the faithful. But I myself wanted simply to remain a pastor. I regarded politics as a necessary evil in the life of a priest. But because politics can overturn the altar and imperil immortal souls, I have always felt it necessary for a minister to keep himself well informed about the realm of party politics. Knowledge alone enables the priest to give those entrusted to his care some political guidance, and to combat political movements hostile to the Church. It would certainly be a sign of great weakness if a priest were to leave vital political and moral decisions solely to the often misled consciences of the laity.

I took an active part in the cultural life of the town and the county and can claim to be the initiator of several cultural events, among them the jubilee of Bishop Márton Biró. That began in a quite simple fashion. In the course of pastoral visits on the street named after him, I discovered that the memory of this great benefactor of the city had been almost extinguished. I therefore proposed, together with Justice László Szalay, organizing a festival in honor of the memory of Márton Biró. This suggestion was gladly taken up by the city fathers, and I was asked to deliver the commemorative address. I prepared thoroughly by rummaging through the archives of both Egerszeg and Veszprém for documents and information about Biró. There was so much material that I could barely touch on it all in my address. The festival proved a great success. But since I did not want to let all my accumulated source material lie idle, I decided to write a biography of this bishop. Of course I could not devote all my leisure to this scholarly task, and consequently the book was not finished until 1934. Entitled *The Life and Times of Bishop of Veszprém Márton Biró*, it was published by our own press in Zalaegerszeg. I had the pleasure of favorable reviews by professionals, and it remains a satisfaction to me that even now—in the period of communism—the book is considered indispensable to scholars.

What I learned in the course of my research about the reconstruction after the Turkish occupation proved highly suggestive to me in my own work. I felt I had been summoned, after one hundred and fifty years, to launch a comparable campaign of reconstruction, first in Zalaegerszeg; and then, after 1927, in Zala County; and still later throughout the large diocese of Veszprém. At the diocesan synod in Szombathely I spoke out strongly concerning the lamentable ecclesiastical and cultural conditions in the Zala region. I did so in order to win support for our own underdeveloped section of the country. There were parishes with seventeen affiliates; parishes in which believers had to go fifteen to twenty miles to have a newborn baby baptized or to report a death. Many of the flock lived from five to ten miles from the center of the parish. There were not enough schools, and the existing ones were old and outmoded. Given this situation, it was natural that the people, who had to walk long distances to school, were poorly instructed in religion.

The diocesan bishop was present during my report. Afterwards, in 1927, he appointed me administrator of the Zala region of the diocese. Since I knew the conditions so well, he pointed out, I should be able to render good service. I was charged with founding new places for priests, establishing schools, removing stumbling blocks, and furthering pastoral activity in all areas.

It was with a heavy heart that I began the work of reconstruction after a century and a half of stagnation. Yet in the course of a decade, despite very limited funds, we were able by hard work to establish nine new parish churches and seven parish houses, nine temporary stations for divine services, eleven temporary parish houses, and, in addition, twelve new schools. Where there had previously been twenty-five places with priests, there were now forty-three, so that the average parish now contained twenty-five hundred faithful, rather than forty-three hundred. Soon, too, the blessed efforts of the teachers in the twelve parochial schools made itself felt in the improvement of the boys and girls in their charge. In the census of 1940 Zala County was no longer classified as last in Transdanubia, at least in regard to reading and writing; in literacy it now stood next to last, ahead of Baranya County.

I owed this success to generous and self-sacrificing associates, among whom was Prince Pál Esterházy, who contributed wood, bricks, lime, and roofing tiles for the buildings; Minister of Education and Religion Kunó Klebelsberg, who obtained government subsidies for the new schools; and Chief County Executive Zoltán Bődy, who secured the support of the county government.

Another strong contributing element to the cultural life of town and county was the newspaper *Zalamegyei Ujság* ("Journal of Zala County"), which we founded in 1919. During my time as head of the parish, the paper developed into a daily. We achieved this by setting up an independent printing plant which also allowed us to venture into book publication, since manufacturing costs were reduced. My Biró monograph was also published by this press, and my work *The Mother*, which I have already mentioned, was in its third printing.

Social and charitable work within the parish was also given a fresh spur. We had expert leadership in this field, provided by the sisters of the Society of Social Service. They sensibly organized the care of the poor, priestly work in the hospitals, and missions in railroad stations and prisons. With the aid of the family apostles and the members of the church associations, we tried to alleviate physical and moral distress in the parish. We also built an old-age home with thirty-five beds for those who had no one to care for them. We arranged for pupils from the country who had no resources to be boarded with families and admitted to intermediate schools in the towns. For girls we set up a convent school which comprised an institute for training teachers, a lycée, a junior high school, and several vocational and elementary schools. The convent school had a hundred girls boarding. The convent, with between seventy and eighty nuns, gave the southern part of the city a new look and had a beneficial influence upon mothers and wives as well as the girls.

Naturally we had to find funds to support these new institutions and organizations. Consequently the financial affairs of the parish had to be reorganized. I sold as building lots various parcels of land scattered throughout the town that belonged to the parish. With the proceeds I bought the estate of Ságod, in extent three times as large as the former property of the parish. This new and profitable property was modernized. In this way the pastor's income also increased. I used every last penny of the income from the parish's endowments to finance all these various activities of the church. Since the flock knew this and had confidence in how matters were being handled, they gave ampler donations and did not grumble about the tithes. Without the help of the parishioners we could not have built either the convent church or the school, nor would it have been possible to enlarge the community house and to rebuild the parish house into a two-story building. Expansion of the newspaper also cost money, and providing for pupils without means devoured sizable sums. We also needed large funds for charitable activities and for the care of the poor.

My work was vigorously supported by the bishops, who appointed me a titular abbot, and in 1937, nominated me for a Roman distinction. As a result I was awarded the title of papal prelate. I accepted this distinction not so much because I regarded it as a reward for my work but because it increased my personal prestige. And prestige facilitated working with agencies of the county and in some cases with the central government itself.

My former bishop, Count János Mikes, called the nuncio's attention to me, and at a period when three bishops were being appointed at once, Pope Pius XII offered a compromise which secured the government's consent to my appointment as bishop. On March 4, 1944, the Holy Father appointed me diocesan bishop of Veszprém. In my last sermon to my parishioners I rendered some account of my stewardship as their pastor for twenty-seven years.* I was consecrated bishop by Cardinal Serédi in Esztergom on March 25, 1944.

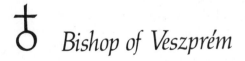

☩ *Bishop of Veszprém*

ON MARCH 29, 1944, my fifty-second birthday, I arrived in Veszprém. Hungary had been occupied by the Nazis for the past ten days. Tension

---

* See Document 1.

and uncertainty prevailed throughout the country. The county authorities in Zala had provided me with a travel pass, so that in spite of frequent checks by the troops of the occupying power I was able to reach my episcopal seat. Because of the unhappy times I dispensed with all ceremony, and entered the city quietly and almost unnoticed. The cathedral chapter received me at the episcopal palace, where a German general was also quartered at that time. I was quite annoyed by his presence. Once, when he came to me with a request for permission to hunt in the episcopal forest, I made my irritation quite plain. Ten days later he moved to new quarters.

Right at the beginning of my work as a bishop, I tried to establish close contact with the clergy. I promoted days of recollection for priests, retreats, conferences among pastors. I also supported the lay apostolate, the Catholic associations, and other organizations in the parishes. I particularly recommended systematic pastoral visits and special attentiveness toward the sick and the dying.

In the spring of 1944 I set out on my confirmation tour. This gave me the occasion to look into local conditions. Not that these were entirely unfamiliar to me, for Zalaegerszeg and all of Zala County had belonged to the diocese of Veszprém until 1777. My historical studies had taught me a good deal about the background of the area. I now tried to determine whether new parishes, schools, and ecclesiastical institutions were needed, and where. I regarded this as my primary task partly because four of my predecessors had entered office without previous experience as pastors. I also considered selling ten thousand of the twenty-four thousand acres of land that belonged to the diocese and distributing it among the peasantry with the idea of improving social conditions among a sizable portion of the population. With the proceeds from the sale of this land, new parishes could be set up.

At that time I was already well aware that the war would end badly for Hungary and that breakup of the large landed estates would follow hard upon the defeat. I reasoned that the Church's landholdings were in any case endangered, and that if they were sold in time, at least these parishes with their endowments could be retained. Unfortunately, developments frustrated my plans. On Hitler's orders the Sztójay government followed a policy declaring that in view of the necessity for producing food, any attempt to change property lines on the large estates would be regarded as a war crime. Even so, I succeeded within a short time in setting up thirty-four new parishes and eleven Catholic schools.

In June 1944 the Sztójay government ordered the confinement of the Jews in ghettos. The Hungarian bishops responded with a vigorous protest which they brought to the attention of the faithful and the public in a pastoral letter. In that letter they stated:

When innate rights, such as the right to life, human dignity, personal freedom, the free exercise of religion, freedom of work, livelihood, property, etc., or rights acquired by legal means, are unjustly prejudiced either by individuals, by associations, or even by the representatives of the government, the Hungarian bishops, as is their duty, raise their protesting voices and point out that these rights are conferred not by individuals, not by associations, not even by representatives of the government, but by God Himself. With the exception of a lawful and legally valid decision by a magistrate, these rights cannot be prejudiced or taken away by any person and any earthly power.

The Jews of Budapest owe to this intervention the fact that the majority of them were saved from death in the gas chambers. After the bishops had unequivocally announced their opposition, church institutions and many courageous individual Christians did their utmost to save baptized and unbaptized Jews alike from persecution. An inadvertent tribute to their endeavors came from the government commissioner for Jewish affairs, who stated in a report: "Unfortunately the clergy of all ranks have taken first place in the efforts to save the Jews. They justify their activities by appealing to the commandment to love one's neighbor."

In July 1944, Miklós Horthy formed a new government of generals. Headed by Premier Lakatos, it tried cautiously to offer some resistance to the German occupation troops and to lead the country out of the war. Secret negotiations were taken up with both the West and the Russians. As a consequence of these negotiations Horthy announced an armistice on October 15, 1944. After his radio address he was arrested on orders from Hitler, and Ferenc Szálasi, the tool of the Nazis, took over the government. The Russians were advancing on Budapest. The pillaging and rapes that took place in the course of their march created a panic. Tens of thousands of people fled westward.

I also took some security measures at the time. I sent some of the most precious possessions of the diocese—valuable chalices and vestments—to Mindszent. There they were hidden in the homes of my parents and sisters. I gave shelter in the episcopal palace to theology students, professors, nuns, and also to laymen. Only a single room was left for me, in which I received priests and members of the flock, discussed their problems, and tried to help them. In response to an order from Hitler, the Arrow Cross party (the Hungarian fascists) now conscripted the youth of the Hungarian lowlands and those from Transdanubia to take part in the battles. While the Red Army was preparing for the siege of Budapest, the Arrow Cross War Minister issued the slogan: "Annihilate or be annihilated!" He and his followers still believed that the German secret weapons would bring victory. The hour of darkness was descending upon Hungary. From the West the brown peril threatened us; and from the East, the red.

☿ The Memorandum of the Bishops of Transdanubia

IN THE COURSE of history Hungary has often been faced by grave crises. But the gravest of all were those that confronted us at the end of the Second World War. Throughout our history, it is true, great powers that threatened our independence stood to either side of us. But now the successors of these powers, Hitler and Stalin, were colliding on our soil for the decisive battle. Our homeland was to provide the stage for the bloody drama to be played out by the cruelest rulers in modern history.

It is understandable that I could not rest easy. I went to Budapest to find out what I could. On the way there and back I met huge bands of refugees who were trying to put themselves out of reach of the Red Army. All along the road there were evidences of the lost war: ruins, abandoned automobiles, shattered wagons, leaderless troops, frightened soldiers. In Budapest I toyed with the idea of having the Upper House of Parliament convoked to develop a new policy toward the Germans and the Russians, but in Budapest I found no other bishops, and the secular members of the Upper House were far too intimidated to take action. For in those days the Nazi and Arrow Cross party terror had reached its height.

I therefore drew up a memorandum* to the Arrow Cross government, which was completely dependent on the Germans, and took it to my friend in Győr, the diocesan bishop Baron Vilmos Apor, to inform him of its contents. I wanted to discuss the problems of our country with our primate, Justinian Cardinal Serédi. But Esztergom, his residence, was already in the center of the battle; moreover I was aware that the primate was ailing at the time.

Bishop Apor commented that we could scarcely count on any sort of hearing from the fanatical leaders of the Arrow Cross party. But he thought we ought to make the attempt anyway, in order to protect our flock insofar as we could and to carry out our responsibility to the country and the Church. We then were the first to sign our names to the memorandum. On the way back from Győr I called on Lajos Shvoy, the bishop of Székesfehérvár. He too signed, although he shared our doubts. A priest in my secre-

* See Document 2.

tariat, Dr. Lénárd Kögl, rode to Pannonhalma on a motorcycle and delivered the text to Abbot Chrysostom Kelemen, who likewise signed it. Then the memorandum was sent on to Szombathely. The bishop there was very fearful and did not sign. Because of the Russian advance, the messenger was not able to reach the diocese of Pécs.

I now personally brought the memorandum, signed by the four bishops, to Budapest, where I called on Deputy Premier Szőllősi. I had not wanted to give it to Premier Szálasi himself and was therefore not at all disappointed to hear that he was away at the moment. Szőllősi was unknown to me; I knew only that he had been the Arrow Cross party secretary in the Hungarian lowlands.

Our memorandum pointed out the perils to Hungary's cultural sites, and to the very survival of her remaining population, if western Hungary were made a battleground as Hitler and the fanatical Arrow Cross party men were insisting. I had counted on being arrested immediately when I handed in the document. Instead, Szőllősi merely asked me a few questions, which I evaded by replying that the memorandum was clear and that I had nothing to add to or subtract from it.

The expected arrest took place two weeks later—evidently the authorities needed that much time to frame their charge. Of course, they did not dare to publish the text of our memorandum, and in order to avoid making a stir, the dignitaries of the Church were not arrested all at the same time. As the deliverer of the memorandum, I was the first to be taken into custody. Administrative Commissioner Ferenc Schieberna of Veszprém was ordered to undertake my arrest.

☥ My Second Imprisonment

IN JUNE 1944, ignoring the bishops' protest, the Arrow Cross men, on Hitler's orders, carried off from Veszprém both baptized and unbaptized Jews. Ferenc Schieberna, at that time the Arrow Cross attorney, was the real author and leader of this operation. After he had completed his brutal work, he visited the Guardian of the Franciscans and, concealing his true motives, asked him to say a Mass and to have the Te Deum sung on the following Sunday. He then put up posters on all the walls announcing that divine services would he held in thanksgiving for the successful liberation of the town from the Jews. When I heard about this, I sent for the pious but unsuspecting Guardian and forbade him to have the Mass and Te Deum. Party Leader Schieberna—who had become administrative commissioner on October 15—thereupon sought an opportunity to avenge himself. Schieberna also had another score to settle: his younger brother, an agricultural official for the diocese, had been disciplined by the Church, although that had happened before my installation.

Soon afterward, the authorities obtained their desired pretext: space was required to quarter military personnel, and on instructions from the evacuation officer, the episcopal palace was to be inspected for available room. My economist, Szabolcs Szabadhegyi, informed Schieberna's men that the building was completely filled with refugees. A violent dispute followed. Schieberna now came in person and threatened to arrest the man. When I heard that, I went down to the ground-floor corridor, stepped to the front gate, and asked him: "My son, who is it that wants to arrest you?" Szabolcs Szabadhegyi pointed to Ferenc Schieberna, whom I had never seen before. I protested, and tried to offer a few arguments against such a move. Whereupon Schieberna uttered the decisive words: "And I am arresting you too, Bishop."

I quickly went back upstairs, dressed in my full episcopal robes, returned, and walked toward the policemen. They tried to force me into their car, but their attempt was brief. Sixteen of my theology students had been watching from the first floor window. They came down with their three instructors, gathered around me, and thus frustrated the intentions of the increasingly nervous police, who had no choice but to drive on ahead in their empty car. We followed on foot, I in my robes, and on either side of me, a row of theology students and their professors. Thus we walked in the autumnal twilight down the main street for about a mile. People came out of their houses; others poured out of the side streets. The growing throng knelt by the side of the street in consternation and asked for my blessing. A large, mournful procession accompanied us to police headquarters. Before I entered the building I asked everyone to return home and spend the night quietly. The police captain, whom I knew from the time I had been a teacher of religion there, was extremely embarrassed. He had a bed made up for me in his offices, and likewise provided for the three priests who had been arrested with me. The following day Schieberna also ordered the arrest of the seminarians who had prevented our being taken in the car. Thus the number of those arrested rose to twenty-six.

Next day the police waited until nightfall before taking us to the jail. In order to make room for so many persons, a number of minor malefactors—pickpockets and such—had to be released. Then a statement was issued to the effect that I had been arrested because I offered resistance to the authorities and their decisions, and to government officials, and because I had tried to organize a protest march in order to incite the populace to violence. Public order and safety had been gravely endangered by my actions.

On such pretexts, Schieberna ordered that we were to be held in jail for the present at the disposition of the prosecutor's office. The prosecutor, Dr. Visy, was a man committed to legal process. For an entire month, defying all the threats of the administrative commissioner, he refused to draw up an indictment. In the newspapers, meanwhile, and in deliberately fostered rumors, all sorts of reasons for my arrest were suggested. Oddly, however, nobody mentioned the main reason, the bishops' memorandum I had delivered. The occupation of the episcopal palace, which now went forward without hindrance, was likewise passed over in silence. Years later when the Communists were already in power and could not fit my arrest by the Arrow Cross people into their scheme of things, they circulated the story that I had been arrested for hoarding. Endre Sik, the foreign minister for the Communist government, was bold enough to peddle this fable in one of his books.

In jail the schedule imposed by the police governed our lives without, however, reducing us to inactivity. Mornings we had holy Mass, communion, and meditation. Theological lessons were given, and on December 7, 1944, in the catacomb-like darkness of a cell, I ordained nine students of theology. Only a single candle, a single surplice, a single chasuble, were available to us. There was an armed guard accompanying nearly every one of us. On the other hand the presiding judge of the court—himself an honest, religious man—was present at the ceremony, and several lay prisoners were also allowed to participate. There was an ever-present nervousness about whether the ceremony could be completed without interruption, for during this period we had to expect air raids, troop movements, or transports of prisoners at any moment. But we were spared.

In the middle of December we learned that the Russians had broken through at Bánhida. The Arrow Cross people in Veszprém now became intensely agitated. They threatened to shoot us if the Russians came near. But the Germans managed to hold the front for a while longer.

On December 23, 1944, we were transferred to Kőhida under close guard. The prosecutor had persisted in his refusal to draw up an indictment against us. But the prosecutors who were attached to the Arrow Cross party court in Kőhida had no such scruples. Our transfer may also have been due to the fact that Szálasi, who had confiscated my house for his own benefit, wished to have the rightful tenant as far away as possible. The prison in Kőhida had formerly been a factory. Next door to it the government had built a schoolhouse for the children of the staff in which the new military tribunal was now housed. In the school courtyard we stepped out of the police van. Women and children came running up to gaze in amazement on the captive bishop and his priests.

We were then quartered in the school building. Putting us up proved to be something of a problem for the jail administration. A bed was set up for me, but I refused to use it because I wanted to share the conditions of my companions. We were therefore all housed in a common room, but my priests set up a private sleeping cubicle for me made out of maps. In the morning we received only a single washbasin and very little water. We therefore went out to the pump to wash. All we had for drying ourselves were handkerchiefs. Again a curious throng gathered round us.

When Sunday morning dawned and we wanted to celebrate holy Mass, we lacked hosts for consecration. I used ordinary bread. The quiet of our service was broken by harsh commands and by the salvos of execution squads. At the holy sacrifice I thought of the unfortunate victims. Although it was Sunday—and the law forbade executions on Sunday—Endre Bajcsy-Zsilinsky was hanged that morning. His companions, Lieutenant General János Kiss, Colonel Jenő Nagy, and Captain Vilmos Tarcsay, had already been executed on December 8.

We were permitted to stay in the school building only that first night. Then we were assigned to an old, musty warehouse. Spiderwebs clung to posts and beams. Rats scurried in the corners. In these wretched conditions we celebrated Christmas Eve. The seminarians sang; I delivered the sermon. I spoke of the universality of redemption, and mentioned that on Christmas Day my mother always gave our pets food from the family table.

After the service, two large pots of potatoes were brought in; this was intended to be our supper. However, the wives of two of the guards appeared and in the name of all the other policemen's wives provided a festive Christmas meal for us. Thus we were their guests that Christmas Eve. In spite of the barrenness of our surroundings and the general distress, that Christmas has remained one of my loveliest memories. Those brave women selflessly risked their husbands' jobs, their families' livelihoods, to give us some Christmas cheer. We ate with great joy, but also remembered the vigil fasts and our hungry fellow prisoners, to whom we sent potatoes and many of the delicacies that had been brought to us.

I held the Christmas Mass in the prison chapel. My priests and the young seminarians assisted. The deep gloom of those days hung over the peacefulness of that holy night. Even as we walked to the Mass we were reminded of the suffering and death of patriots, for we passed the gallows and the fresh graves. I remembered that our head of state, Horthy, was imprisoned, that three premiers, a number of ministers, judges, members of the Upper House, deputies, high army officers, artists, priests, and many other unknown heroes were prisoners here as we were. Among them there were also members of the leftist parties, such as László Rajk, and even atheists whose praying and singing deeply moved me. The peril of death had brought them close to God. In common suffering we celebrated the memory of Our Lord's incarnation. Miklós Kállay, a former premier, had sent a request to me to include in the memento of the holy Mass the tribulations of all good and honest Hungarians. Thus our prayers and pleas reached far beyond the walls of the prison chapel, embracing Esztergom, Budapest, and the areas through which ran the front line between Germans and Russians, where the former pretended to be fighting to save us and the others claimed to be dying to liberate us. Weeping, we knelt and stood before the altar on which the body and blood of Christ were present. Never again, and nowhere else, has a Christmas Mass so moved me as did this one.

☦ *New Quarters*

AFTER THE CHRISTMAS Mass we went back to the unheated warehouse to sleep. I had slept for about two hours when I awoke and heard two young seminarians whispering: "I'm freezing like a dog." Softly, I called across to them: "My children, remember Saint Elizabeth's Christmas Eve, and her children in the stable of the inn at Eisenach. And do not forget the stable at Bethlehem either."

The afternoon of Christmas day brought visitors. Prelate Kálmán Papp, the curate of Sopron, had received permission to call on me. Dr. Aladár Krüger, an old friend, accompanied him. Dr. Krüger was a deputy who had fled to Sopron along with the rest of Parliament. He had also undertaken to defend us before the military tribunal. With his aid, a priest of my curia had also drawn up a petition to the government. Rather unwillingly, I gave permission for Prelate Géfin, rector of the Szombathely Theological Seminary, to present this petition to the Szálasi government. Afterwards, however, Géfin gave me the reassuring news that he had not done so. I was very glad about that.

Previously, in Veszprém, visits to prisoners had not been allowed. Both Bishop Apor and Abbot Kelemen had tried to see me, to make public their solidarity with me and to take co-responsibility for the memorandum, but their requests were turned down. Much later I learned that Bishop Apor had personally approached the leader of the Arrow Cross party as well as German Ambassador Weesenmayer in my behalf.

During the last days of the year many new prisoners arrived. To make room for them, we were transferred to Sopron, to the mother convent of the Daughters of the Divine Redeemer. Although we were considered prisoners, the sisters were allowed to care for us. A short time after our arrival Bishop Lajos Shvoy of Székesfehérvár and his brother General Kálmán Shvoy were brought there. The bishop had been arrested because he had forbidden priests to change their announcements and sermons as demanded

by the Arrow Cross party. I soon made friends with Bishop Shvoy, and
this was a friendship that stood the test of time.

In the middle of March 1945 my own former bishop and friend, Count
János Mikes, visited me. He was already living in retirement and wanted
me to save my life by escaping to the East. I could not, however, agree with
his well-meant proposal, for I had no doubt that one who went over to the
Bolshevists to save his life from the Nazis would sooner or later have to
repay his saviors. "A bishop can attach himself to communism only at the
expense of his own cause," I said. My experiences after the First World
War had made me certain of that. Bishop Mikes had listened to foreign
radio broadcasts and believed that Russian communism had changed and no
longer threatened the people and the Church. His remarks at the time were
proof of the unfortunate fact that responsible leaders of our people did not
know how to judge Soviet intentions correctly. They naively believed that
the western allies of the Soviet Union had the power to prevent ideological
and territorial expansion of bolshevism. Such a hope was natural enough,
for at the moment the country was suffering under Nazi rule and longing
for liberation from it. Probably the leading Hungarian politicians had not
studied the works of Lenin and Stalin sufficiently and had paid too little attention to the practices of bolshevism. I had always noted the lack of public
education on this score—even under the Horthy regime. Once, when a
campaign to remedy this situation was rather inadequately undertaken, it
was quickly discontinued out of consideration for the trade agreements with
the Soviet Union then being broached by Count Bethlen.

Immediately after my first imprisonment during the Hungarian "dictatorship of the proletariat," I had carefully studied the papal encyclicals and
pastoral letters dealing with this entire subject, and had further deepened
my knowledge of the materialist philosophy by studying both domestic and
foreign Marxist literature. Thus I early realized what kind of enemy the
Church was confronting, what sort of terrorism awaited us. "Every concept
of God is an unspeakable baseness, an abominable expression of self-
contempt," Lenin wrote to Gorki. He frankly admitted that part of the
Communists' program was to promote atheism. Just as they combat indi-
vidualism and private property, they try to reshape the family and marriage
in their own terms. The opposition is liquidated, although it is true that the
methods of persecuting Christians have changed in a good many details
since Nero and Julian the Apostate. One of the Bolshevist slogans goes:
"We do not take the churches from the people but the people from the
churches."

Historical studies had taught me that compromise with this enemy will
almost always play into his hands. I respected and continue to respect those
who bravely stand by the Church with full willingness to stake their lives if
necessary in the certain knowledge that, even though one persecutor of the
Church may succeed another, the Church always outlives her enemies.

Castles and fortresses fall, but the Church, despite all her human weakness, will never be destroyed. The blood of the martyrs has always been the seed of the Church, out of which she springs forth afresh toward her Easter Day. Such thoughts strengthened me during the visit from my old bishop, Count János Mikes, who at this time could only disappoint me precisely because he was a dear, paternal friend who wanted only what he thought would be best for me personally.

That meeting between Count Mikes and me in the wretched quarters of the Sopron jail was our last—the horrors of the so-called liberation resulted in his death. After the Russian troops reached the village where he lived, drunken soldiers tried to rape the women and girls. The bishop heard their wails and screams and came out of his house to help the hard-pressed women. At that moment his hand flew to his left side and he fell lifeless on the steps. His body was placed on a bier in the dining room. That evening the "liberators" entered the house, fetched sacramental wine from the cellar, dragged in girls, and drank and danced there all through the night.

In Győr, Bishop Apor was another victim of the troops. Terrified women and girls had hidden in the air raid shelter of his episcopal palace. When the bishop tried to keep out intruders, the Russian soldiers shot him down. "The good shepherd gave his life for his sheep."

At this moment the Russians were nearing our township also. We were now almost alone: there were two bishops with me; the brother of one of these, who was a retired general; and three priests who had chosen to remain behind with me. Their names should be remembered: Ladislas Lékay, Szabolcs Szabadhegyi, and Tibor Mészáros. About this same time Premier Szálasi was in a village near the Austrian border, and summoned the bishops of Transdanubia. I found an opportunity to send two priests to consult with Primate Cardinal Serédi, who sent word back that, like me, he was going to refuse any such meeting with our adversaries. But I was unable to send this rejection to Szálasi because he was already fleeing to the West. Suddenly, too, our guards disappeared without carrying out their threats against us.

II. RUSSIAN OCCUPATION

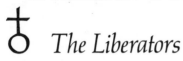 *The Liberators*

THE RED ARMY marched into Sopron on the night of Easter Sunday, 1945. Just before, the mayor called a meeting on how to prepare a worthy reception for our "liberators." The Bishop of Székesfehérvár, his brother, and I were invited to this meeting. I had been asked, as one of the liberated prisoners, to make a welcoming speech, but I replied that an inhabitant of Sopron should express its gratitude, and that besides I was not liberated but merely left behind by the fleeing police. We did not go to the reception and did not leave the building.

During the following days I watched through a window the looting in the neighborhood. The soldiers stood the men up against the wall, dragged women out of hiding, and made off with wine, food, family mementos, and peoples' valuables. The army commanders seemed disinclined to intervene, apparently because they wanted to humiliate the Hungarian nation, which had been compelled to fight against them under Nazi pressure. The idea seemed to be to make sure that the Hungarians understood who had won the war. The vicinity of Sopron was treated similarly, as plundering troops swarmed over it.

Beneath my window drunken soldiers divided up their booty. Naturally each soldier had not found exactly what he wanted or needed, and so they began quarreling with one another; invectives were shouted, submachine guns cocked, shots fired. The passion for private property shattered communist collectivism. Two dead men and a good many wounded were left behind as victims of the dispute. At last sober soldiers appeared on the scene, and took away their squabbling brethren, the booty, and the wounded. The corpses were left lying by the curb.

Soon after the Red Army settled, the Hungarian Communists arrived. Their posters announced agrarian reform as the first item on their program. Grandiloquently they promised that there would no longer be poor people in Hungary. The propaganda material had been brought in on Russian army trucks.

I have always regretted that no land reform had been carried out in Hungary—even before the First World War. Had we done that, it would not have been so easy in 1920 to shift Hungarian land into Czech, Rumanian, and Serbian hands on the pretext that only large landholdings were involved. The present reform, however, imposed by the enemy and his puppets, obviously served only the interests of the Communist party and the occupying power.

☦ *Homecoming*

DURING THE PERIOD of my imprisonment, many of the things I had feared happened. Cities and villages were destroyed, transportation collapsed, and the mails and telephone system ceased to operate. I had to reestablish contact with my episcopal see by sending a personal messenger, which, given the unpredictability of the Russians, had its dangers. At last, on April 20, 1945, a train of cattle cars, departing from the Sopron railroad station, offered the first chance I had had to leave. The Sopron railroad men warned us priests against making the attempt; they were afraid the Russians would fetch us out of the cars and take us away. Nevertheless, we decided to risk it. In a few hours we reached Pápa, the first town in my diocese. I inquired about the fate of my priests and flock, and heard frightful tales. I shall mention only this one detail: since the arrival of the Russians, approximately one thousand women and girls had been brought to the hospital; eight hundred of these women were infected with syphilis. Many women committed suicide at this time; others went mad.

We now tried to round up a vehicle. The acting mayor—his name was Dezső Sulyok—sent word to me that the Russian commander would surely be glad to place a car at the disposal of the Bishop of Veszprém who had just been liberated from Nazi imprisonment. All I had to do was to ask for it. I responded to this offer: "After what has been done to the wives and daughters here, the bishop would be ashamed to ask the commander for a car."

We finally succeeded in obtaining a wagon and team. The owner was worried about his animals, but nevertheless he went ahead and hitched them up to help "the bishop." I reassured him, saying that he need drive me only as far as Farkasgyepü where I could ask the diocesan forester for my own horses. But at Farkasgyepü we discovered that the liberators had also liberated the forester of the burden of caring for the horses. His wife served us a meager bean soup in their home which had been stripped bare, and we walked to Herend, where we spent the night with the parish priest. Next morning he told me that I had slept in the same bed as Marshal Tolbukhin, a Russian Army general.

The weekly market was going on when I arrived in Veszprém. A tall man was carrying a lamb on his shoulders—like the good shepherd. Some women asked him why he was carrying it, couldn't it walk. I had paused for a moment to witness the scene, and answered for him: "Perhaps he does so because otherwise this one might be taken away from him like the rest." The bystanders laughed; then they stared at me in consternation and realized that I was their bishop returned from prison.

The city was in an indescribable condition. The cathedral had been visited by a troop of women soldiers, and totally stripped. They had cut up vestments and altar cloths for their own uses. Like the houses of the citizenry, the church buildings and the episcopal palace had been thoroughly ransacked and plundered. We even found hacked-off parts of human bodies lying about. The pantry was empty, and I was weak with hunger. So I did what came most naturally: I went home to mother. She helped me get back on my feet somewhat; she also gave me provisions for my household. This she was able to do because my native village had suffered less than other places. The troops had marched through it comparatively quickly; it had been a rare and happy exception in the brown and the red storms.

The joy of reunion with my mother had to be brief. The distress in my diocese quickly summoned me back. In a one-horse carriage driven by my faithful priest Szabolcs Szabadhegyi, I toured Somogy County from Balaton to the Dráva River. Everywhere I found frightened people, pillaged and burned-out houses, deserted parishes. Nine priests in the county were among the civilian victims of the war. In Iszkáz the Russians had broken into the church, dressed up in ecclesiastical vestments, and mounted horses to hold a comic parade. The young priest from another village protested, and was shot. A notary's wife who had first been raped by seventeen soldiers was shot together with her son, who began to scream at the sight of these atrocious crimes. The husband, who had tried to protect his wife, was carried off as a "war criminal" because he had offered resistance to the Red Army. Everywhere on this tour I heard similar tales; everywhere there had been killings and rapes. Neither children nor old men were spared.

When the war ended in May 1945, the bishops of the twelve dioceses had only tales of horrors and bloody violence to report. Hundreds of thousands of persons were without shelter, wandering about homeless or being driven like so many cattle toward the east. In one village in Somogy County I asked an old day-laborer: "Well, Granddad, were you liberated too?" He replied: "Yes, I was liberated from my hat and my shoes."

☦ The Episcopal Conference, May 1945

DURING THE LAST year of the war there had not been an episcopal conference. Contact among bishops was maintained by means of personal messen-
gers. Now the longed-for end of the war had come, but everywhere the
people were more than ever weighed down by distress and misery. In May
1945 it at last became possible for us to form some picture of the state of
Hungarian Catholicism. Rarely had the Church in our native land bled
from so many and such grave wounds as it had in those days after the end
of the Second World War.

Angelo Rotta, the apostolic nuncio, had been expelled from the country
by the Russian high command. The occupying power obviously wanted no
witnesses to its work of annihilation. At this same time, unfortunately, the
primate's see became vacant. The failing health of Cardinal-Archbishop
Serédi had been shattered by agitation, and there was no medical help for
him. He died suddenly on March 29, 1945. In his place the ranking archbishop, Jószef Grösz of Kalocsa, presided over the conference of bishops.
As bishop of Szombathely he had formerly been my superior, and he now
asked me to compose the pastoral letter. I tried, with all due restraint, to
present a faithful picture of the Church's situation. I forbore to mention the
frightful devastation being wrought by the Soviet troops, and tried to show
some flexibility and understanding of the ordinances of the provisional government.*

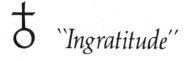

☦ "Ingratitude"

IN THE PASTORAL LETTER it had not been easy to show restraint, for
we were constantly hearing about acts of violence. Moreover, we were

* See Document 3.

forced to accept the imposition on us by the occupying power of a provisional government. Inveterate Hungarian Communists who had been living in Russia returned with the Russians. In Russian cars they drove over the Hungarian plains and those eastern territories that had already been occupied by the autumn of 1944. Using democratic slogans, they gathered supporters among the members of the provisional Parliament which was convoked to meet in Debrecen on December 21, 1944. Of the deputies, who were not so much elected as appointed, seventy-two belonged to the Communist party, thirty-five to the Social Democratic party, twelve to the Peasants party, and fifty-seven to the Smallholders party. In addition there were nineteen union members and thirty-five independents. The Parliament elected a provisional government from among these latter groups. At the request of the Russians, cabinet posts were assigned to three former generals and a count.

The National Assembly also turned over to the parties the administration in the provinces. In the counties, towns, districts, and villages, national committees were set up in place of the former local bodies. These committees were made up of delegates from the acknowledged parties and unions. The Marxist parties were, of course, influenced by Moscow. But the occupying power contrived from the start to infiltrate reliable men into the Smallholders party. Meanwhile the unions also held new elections. Massive pressure resulted in a selection of candidates taken from the ranks of the Communists or their sympathizers. All the above-mentioned parties now formed committees and tribunals which were supposed to convict members of "war crimes" and "crimes against the people." In reality their principal task was to exclude from the parties and organizations all those who seemed suspect to the Russians. Punishments were readily disregarded if a convicted person declared his willingness to collaborate with the Marxists. Theoretically it was possible to appeal from one of these local committees or tribunals to a "people's court"; in practice, however, it was not likely that an appeal would change a sentence or classification. Everyone had to be registered as a member of some party. Without a party book, advancement was impossible in community or in private affairs. It was the party book that opened doors. For that reason, when I first went to Budapest in conjunction with the pastoral letter, party passes of the Smallholders party were provided for me and my companions. On our return journey from the capital the Russian soldiers nevertheless objected to our papers. They would acknowledge only communist documents. We therefore had to return to the capital and try again. We managed to reach my episcopal seat by traveling on routes far from the main arteries.

Meanwhile the power of the political police, organized along the lines of the Russian pattern, was steadily growing. Soon they were taking action against innocent persons in all the larger towns. Their object was to intimidate the people and drive them into collaboration by forcing them to be informers.

In the spring of 1945 the provisional government moved from Debrecen to Budapest. That summer István Balogh and Béla Varga, two priests who were among the leaders of the Smallholders party, asked me to go to Budapest with them to express our thanks to the Red Army and its leadership for our liberation. During our conversation Balogh was the first to speak. While I was still in prison—at that time he was pastor of a church in a suburb near Szeged—he had joined the provisional government in Debrecen and had swiftly risen to the rank of a state secretary. At a press conference in Moscow he later declared: "Aside from the excesses inevitable in a war, there are hardly any major atrocities to be mentioned. We welcomed the Red Army, for the Germans had oppressed and exploited us for years."

For a while I looked at my two visitors in silence. Then I replied: "I am the youngest of the bishops. There are pastors who can better represent the Church of Hungary than I. Take your request to the bishop of Székesfehérvár or the archbishops of Kalocsa and Eger." But the two continued to press me. I then declared that this was no ordinary affair and I would have to think it over at my leisure. When I was visiting Budapest some time later, István Balogh met me in the street, perhaps by a chance that he had deliberately arranged, and reverted to his request. "I have thought it over," I told him, "and I cannot undertake what you ask."

Had I imagined that by performing such an ambiguous action I might have been able to alleviate suffering, I probably would have consented. But I feared rather that the people would inevitably be deceived about the nature and intentions of communism if their bishop took any such step.

☦ The Church and the New World

WHEN THE Red Army crossed the borders of historical Hungary, it attempted to show its best face to the nation. Thus a proclamation of the Russian high command issued in October 1944 had declared: "Hungarians! the Red Army calls upon you to remain where you are and continue your peaceable work. The clergy and the faithful can carry on the exercise of their religion unhindered."

This statement shows that by religious freedom the Communists mean only the free exercise of the cult, of divine services. They exclude all cultural, social, and charitable activity on the part of the Church. The Hungarian Communists, who knew Moscow's theory and practice, stressed that it was not their aim to drive the Church out of areas in which it had hitherto worked. They also declared that in all disputed questions between church and state, a solution would be sought in the spirit of true democracy. Within the party hierarchy, however, they continued to hold to the principle: "Religion is a pernicious ideological superstructure that serves to stupefy the oppressed and exploited people." But only party members were told the truth: that they were still following Lenin's views and that Marxism thus remained as ruthless an opponent of all religion as the materialism of the Encyclopedists had been in the eighteenth century or the materialism of Ludwig Feuerbach in the nineteenth. However, Lenin's further instruction was also acknowledged: for tactical reasons the battle against religion must in certain cases be so waged that religious groups do not take alarm. If possible, even clerics were to be enlisted in the service of communist goals.

For the time being, therefore, the Marxist parties obeyed these Leninist tactical instructions. Indeed, they had to, for otherwise they would have alienated large segments of the Hungarian population. Hardly ever before in the course of history had both Catholic and Protestant Hungarians held firmly to Christiantiy with such admirable loyalty as they did during this period. The good example of the previous period—the courage and resolution of their spiritual leaders during the time of Nazi rule—was now bearing fruit.

The dramatic statement issued by my predecessor had also had a powerful impact. Cardinal-Primate Serédi had admonished priests and monks not to abandon the faithful, to remain at their posts even at the price of martyrdom. Thanks to this, tens of thousand of persons were given refuge in institutions and buildings of the Church during the final phase of the war. Countless lives were saved. Later, women were offered protection from Russian soldiers by convents, monasteries, seminaries, and rectories. The Hungarian people did not forget.

Consequently the faithful everywhere became very closely attached to the Church. The most acute problems of our political and social crisis were solved with the Church's aid. Our Caritas organization provided the impoverished, emaciated, disease-threatened population with food, clothing, and fuel. Everywhere the faithful rebuilt destroyed churches, schools, monasteries, cultural centers, and rectories by voluntary labor. The number of those attending church and receiving the sacraments rose swiftly throughout the country. Parents registered their children in Catholic schools in greater numbers than ever before, and new life bloomed in the religious associations. Tens and hundreds of thousands of believers participated in processions and pilgrimages, eager to bear witness to their Christian convictions. Our publications, which were brought out in small editions, often merely in mimeographed form, were passed from hand to hand.

This steadily growing influence of the Church troubled the Communists, for they themselves could gather only insignificant groups. They realized that such close attachment to the Church also signified rejection of the materialist ideology. Thus our first great procession of August 20, 1945, was in itself an unmistakable repudiation of communism.

On that day five hundred thousand believers followed the uncorrupted right hand of Saint Stephen, while hundreds of thousands lined the route of the procession. Budapest was declaring in a thunderous voice: "The most precious possession of our nation is the heritage that the sainted king has left behind. Therefore we stand fast by Christianity and are not going to make a home in our country for atheism and materialism."

Faced with this situation, the Communists tried to infiltrate the congregations. Party members attended services, received the sacraments, and participated in the processions wearing their party badges. At the same time they tried to ingratiate themselves with the clergy. Communist brigades were sent to help with the restoration of bombed churches. They obtained written testimonials to the work they had done, and published these in the press as proof of their benevolent attitude toward religion. During these same months, however, the Communists inflicted three severe blows on the Church.

The agrarian reform removed the material basis that supported many ecclesiastical institutions. Although compensation for the expropriated property was promised, the question was never placed on the agenda of Parliament. Meanwhile the Church was given subsidies, but a final settlement of the matter was continually postponed, the aim being to better blackmail the Church in subsequent negotiations. Despite this violation of good faith, the episcopate accepted the land reform without protest. In its first postwar pastoral letter, the bishops gave the new owners their blessing and expressed the hope that the benefits to the peasantry from this measure would comfort the Church for its losses and its cares.

The second severe blow was the harassment of the Catholic press. Before the war the Church had had a flourishing press; but now licenses were granted solely by the Commander-in-chief of the Red Army, and he only permitted the publication of two Catholic weeklies, basing his decision on the paper shortage. At this same time, however, the Communists were putting out twenty-four daily newspapers, five weeklies, and a number of magazines. The Catholic papers were restricted to a small number of pages, could not be published regularly, and were also censored. The aim, of course, was to drive the Church out of public life, to diminish its influence as a source of information, and to paralyze its activities.

An additional great danger to the Church, and to religion in general, was the regulation governing the formation of political parties. That destroyed the basis for a specifically Christian party. In Hungary—as in the rest of Europe—Catholic-Christian parties had long played an important role in political life. The Hungarian Christian Party had exerted considerable influence in Parliament and among the people during the period between the two world wars. Now, while the government was still in Debrecen, the

Christian politicians asked to be allowed to reestablish the party. But the Marxists maneuvered things so that the permit applied only to a parliamentary fraction led by so-called "progressive Catholics" with whom the bishops could not collaborate.

In the summer of 1945 the Communists also revised the laws governing marriage. Mere separation was henceforth to be a sufficient ground for divorce, even when the couple themselves had not brought about the separation. Thus, if war service, captivity, or imprisonment had parted people for at least six months and they did not wish to rejoin one another, divorce would be possible. In August there followed a countrywide campaign dealing with the great historical personages of our nation. Their achievements for the country were reevaluated from the communist standpoint. The campaign was launched by the minister for public welfare, who published in the communist youth newspaper an article denouncing Saint Stephen. Teachers were required to make Marxism the basis for their educational work instead of "the outmoded Christian ideology." Catholic youth houses were turned over to the Marxist youth organizations. They were refurbished with government money, and their entire purpose was turned topsyturvy. Henceforth they were to help divert boys and girls from Christian ideals. It must be said that this whole process went forward quite slowly. The soldiers of the Red Army did not systematically destroy the institutions of the Church, and the Hungarian Communists avoided direct confrontations with the Church. The situation was described in the bishop's statement of May 24, 1945:

The rumor has been spread that the Russian Army intends to destroy the Church. The rumor has proved to be incorrect. On the contrary, we have been the recipients of much concern for the life of the Church on the part of the Russian command. Our churches still stand, our services are not hindered. But possibly more difficult times are to come for us.

In this last sentence we wanted to suggest, as a warning to the faithful, something of the equivocal nature of the Communists' conduct.

☩ My Appointment as Primate

ON SEPTEMBER 8, 1945, I returned from Somogy County to my episcopal seat in Veszprém. József Grősz, archbishop of Kalocsa, at that time president of the episcopal conference, was waiting for me. He informed me that the Holy Father wished me to take over the archdiocese of Esztergom and thus the Hungarian primateship. He wanted to convey an affirmative answer to Rome without delay.

I pondered until long after midnight. Then I asked for a postponement of twenty-four hours. There were many reasons, rooted in the history of the Hungarian Church, for my hesitancy. A hundred years earlier József Kopácsy had wrestled with himself for a long time before taking the same step of exchanging the position of bishop of Veszprém for that of archbishop of Esztergom. But it would be too involved to attempt to explain this matter to those unfamiliar with the conditions of the Hungarian Church. Suffice it to say that after two days of reflection I agreed. The decisive factor for me was the confidence of Pope Pius XII. He knew my character, knew that I was more concerned with the care of souls than politics, and it was he who had also proposed me for the diocese of Veszprém, although the government at the time had raised objections. The nuncio had fully informed the Holy Father about my administration of the diocese and also about my imprisonment. In addition, time was pressing. Archbishop Grősz pointed out to me that it would be highly disadvantageous to Hungarian Catholicism if the seat of the primate, which had already been orphaned for half a year, continued vacant.

When I gave my consent, I was trusting wholeheartedly in our people, brave defenders of their faith who had so often and so movingly proved their attachment to Christianity. But I confess that I was also hoping somewhat to obtain support from the Allied Control Commission, which after the Armistice became the supreme authority and highest power in our defeated nation. Representatives of the military missions of the Western Powers sat on this commission alongside the Russians.

During the week after my decision I undertook a confirmation tour in the vicinity of Pápa, visiting the parishes. I was especially concerned about the newly established parishes, which henceforth I would no longer be able to supervise personally. While I was on this tour, Pius XII's definite appointment of me as Hungarian primate arrived. Archbishop Grösz announced the news on the morning of September 15, 1945. In the course of that same day the provisional government thought fit, for my protection and in my honor, to place a flag-decked military automobile at my disposal. In this car I first drove to Pápa, where on September 16 I conferred the sacrament of confirmation on eight hundred boys and girls. After first addressing the candidates themselves in my sermon, I spoke briefly to the nation, admonishing all the faithful to try to reconcile differences and to carry out conscientiously their duties as citizens:

The Church wishes and requires of every Christian believer that he exercise his civil rights in accordance with his religion, disregarding all attempts at intimidation.

Every Christian Hungarian has the duty to make use of his rights as a citizen. Every Catholic Hungarian should be guided by conscience in the exercise of these rights and duties. Only in this way will Christian principles continue in the future to govern our public life.

I spoke with such directness because the parliamentary elections were impending, and the Communists were preparing for them with a great deal of political cunning and equivocation.

In the course of a thousand years in this land the Catholic Church has weathered many a storm. It does not go into hiding when storms are rising; it always stands in the forefront with the Hungarian people and for the Hungarian people. The Church asks for no secular protection; it seeks shelter under the protection of God alone.

The painting over the high altar in the church of Pápa shows the stoning of Saint Stephen. I pointed to this painting and asked Hungarians not to throw stones at one another, but to imitate the virtues of forgiveness and of love practiced by that other Stephen, the first martyr of our Holy Church.

Both friend and foe could gather from my words that the new primate was in no way deceived about the difficult situation in which both Church and nation found themselves, and that he knew well that in assuming the highest ecclesiastical and constitutional office in these times he had taken upon himself a task that would require more than human strength.

That afternoon I drove in the military car, chauffeured by a uniformed soldier, to see my parents in Mindszent. I was accompanied by a lieutenant who had been a pupil of mine and by the youngest priest in the episcopal curia. During those few hours I spent at home, my aged parents wept a great deal, tears more of anxiety than of joy. My mother promised me her prayers in the difficult times that lay ahead, and my father too, in parting, alluded to the impending perils.

These were truly not long in coming. We had driven barely ten minutes away from Mindszent when we found our lives in danger. In Csipkerek, near the main Budapest-Szentgotthárd highway, we came upon drunken, looting Soviet soldiers. They had just halted a truck and stripped it bare. Now they ordered us to stop also. Our driver braked briefly. Then I gave him a sign to speed on; he tramped down hard on the accelerator, and we raced past the Russians. They promptly wrenched their submachine guns from their backs and fired several salvos after us, they missed.

Next day, when I reported the incident to the Allied Control Commission, the Russian who happened to be presiding that day did not dignify my complaint with a reply. I had intervened not so much for my own sake as in the hope that my protest would help others by calling attention to intolerable conditions. How perilous it must be for everyone traveling around the country if not even the primate of Hungary could move in safety!

☩ My Installation in Esztergom

I NOW FINISHED UP the episcopal work in my diocese * and began preparing to take over the archdiocese of Esztergom. The date was fixed for October 7, 1945. On the evening of that day I arrived in my new see. My mother accompanied me from my native village. From Budapest came my cousin, Dr. Miklós Zrinyi, Justice of the Supreme Court; and there was also a delegation from Zalaegerszeg. Representatives of various Catholic organizations were also present.

Esztergom at this time was a depressing sight. The basilica, which looks down upon the city like a protecting mother and which had offered her children shelter under heavy shellfire, had suffered fearfully. All the windows were shattered. When I delivered my installation address, a near-tornado descended from the mountains of Upper Hungary. It raged across the country and howled through the empty windows of the cathedral. I hurled my words into the spacious church as if in competition with the blustering fury of the wind.

The episcopal palace, the world-famous Christian Museum, the seminary, the normal school, schools, monasteries and convents, rectories and private homes all showed the traces of the war. But in such a city with so great a past, life goes on even amid ruins.

Our forefathers called Esztergom the pearl of the country. Its natural beauty, its central position in the Carpathian basin above the Danube, the role it has played in the religious and constitutional history of the nation for a thousand years have earned it the right to such praise. Ottokár Prohászka called it the focal point of Christianity and Magyar consciousness, burning with pure flame. Here Stephen, our sainted king, was born. Here he was baptized and here crowned with the crown that was given us by Pope Sylvester. Here are the beginnings of Hungary's nationhood.

Esztergom had already been the capital of the country under Stephen's father, Prince Géza, who had the royal palace built on the hill above the city, and alongside it the three-aisled Romanesque basilica in honor of the saintly bishop and martyr Adalbert. And for two and a half centuries afterwards Esztergom remained the capital of Hungary. The court of Béla IV

---

* At this time I published an article in *Uj Ember* ("New Man"), which in some respects anticipated the spirit of the Second Vatican Council. See Document 4 for the text.

stayed there, although the king himself, warned by the experiences of the Tatar onslaught, sought out a more secure place and transferred the capital to Buda. At that time he presented the royal palace to the archbishop. The archiepiscopal residence, which I was now to move into, was badly scarred with the wounds of the war. Esztergom had been the capital of medieval Hungary. Here the laws were made. The city's culture, architecture, and art had been a model for the entire land. It was the center of Hungarian commerce and manufactures, the residence of architects, scholars, writers, and painters. Esztergom had also been the symbol of the medieval Christian concept of the state, in which *sacerdotium* and *imperium*, pope and emperor, collaborated. The Hungarian embodiments of this concept were the king of Hungary and the archbishop of Esztergom. The primate crowned the king with the crown that had been worn by Saint Stephen. Only after this coronation did the king become the head of the nation. The holy crown was regarded as the source of justice and of power in the land. The entire nation, the crowned king as well as his people, were subject to the holy crown. Uniting king and people, it was the symbolic origin of national sovereignty.

Because the right of crowning the king fell to him, the archbishop of Esztergom held the foremost place among the dignitaries of the state as well as the Church. When the king was absent from the country, the archbishop represented him. The king depended on him for advice. If the king violated the constitution, the archbishop of Esztergom was obliged to rebuke him and demand he obey the law of the land. In carrying out this duty the archbishops of Esztergom frequently suffered sore oppression and even imprisonment. The nation expected that of its primates; both Catholics and those of other faiths took it for granted that the archbishop of Esztergom would have frequent conflicts with the representatives of the state.

The dignity, the rights, and the duties of the primate had remained intact in the new constitution that was drawn up after the end of the First World War.* The provisional assembly that met in Debrecen in 1945 did not discuss the constitutional position of the primate at all, which signified that people and government acknowledged it as unchanged. In my response to the congratulatory telegram from the premier and the provisional government I was careful to refer to this fact. My telegram read:

MANY THANKS FOR THE WARM CONGRATULATIONS.

THE HIGHEST CONSTITUTIONAL AUTHORITY OF THE

COUNTRY STANDS READY TO SERVE HIS NATIVE LAND.

No one in the government, the parties, the press, or in public opinion made any objection. In my installation sermon I stressed the historical back-

* My predecessor, Cardinal Serédi, alluded to this fact in a radio message in 1942. See Document 5.

ground of the office and spoke of what the nation had a right to expect from its primate.*

☦ *Misery and Works of Mercy*

DURING THE HALF-YEAR that the primate's see had been vacant, Hungarian Catholicism had lacked central leadership during a highly critical period. Because of the war, moreover, Primate Serédi had been powerless to carry out his office effectively for a considerable time before he died. Communications with the countryside had been severed. He had not been able to make contact with the encircled capital, with the eastern regions, and with the Hungarian plain. Even Transdanubia had been closed to him when the Russians began military operations in the western part of the country. This situation had created previously unknown problems for the leadership of the Church. Planning, such as had been customary in peacetime, became an impossibility. All that could be done was more or less to take care of the concerns of the moment and of the locality. In the cities and industrial areas bitter misery prevailed. The people were starving. Conditions were worse in Budapest. During the fighting some 30 percent of the buildings in the capital were destroyed. Of the remaining houses, only a fourth could be partially inhabited. Buda with the royal castle was smashed to rubble.

A week after my installation I went to Budapest and addressed the people and the world in St. Stephen's cathedral.** I called for help for the Hungarian people in the hour of need. At the same time I sent personal emissaries with appeals to the Roman Catholic bishops and to various aid organizations in the West. In addition, on November 8, 1945, I made a radio appeal to Hungarian Catholics in the United States in which I pointed out that famine threatened Hungary.†

I had reason to be concerned about the distribution of the donations that began to flow into the country in response to these appeals. The Marxist parties wanted to check on the way these funds were handled. They alleged that they wanted to guard against the Church's supporting Arrow Cross partisans, enemies of the people, and war criminals. Their true concern,

---

* For the text of the sermon, see Document 6.
** For the text of this address, see Document 7.
† For the text, see Document 8.

however, was the fact that virtually no aid at all was coming from the Soviet area. Consequently, the shipments from the West were showing the Hungarian people where they might expect brotherly, Christian helpfulness to come from.

In order to wipe out this impression, the Communists felt obliged to speak of Soviet aid. Reports began appearing in the newspapers with references to generous gifts from the Red Army. For example, Diósgyőr, Miskolc, and Ózd had received 50,000 carloads of flour from the Red Army. The fact was in itself quite correct, but the reporter "forgot" to mention that this flour was a product of the Hungarian, not the Russian, soil. The same was true for the "donation of potatoes for Budapest," which was mentioned even more often in the press.

We did not only beg; we called on the people for self-help, and urged them to throw their maximum energy into the task. The small farmers had been able to save certain amounts of foodstuffs from confiscation; and by the united labors of many volunteers it proved possible—wherever the war had not prevented sowing—to reap a good harvest that first postwar summer. Consequently, before Christmas I issued an appeal to the farmers: "Give a package for hungry Budapest!" This appeal brought 165,000 pounds of food into Budapest in the winter of 1946, and provided 1,500 ill and starving children with a chance to stay in the country for a while.* When I addressed Caritas, the Budapest Catholic charitable organization, I reminded my listeners of the example of Saint Elizabeth of Hungary and called upon the population of the whole country to contribute vigorously to the work of aiding the needy.** The two Catholic weeklies printed my talks, and so my voice reached the whole country.

In December 1945, at the time of my trip to Rome, I was able to open up a generous source of help for the Hungarian Caritas. The Holy Father, Pope Pius XII, received me with wonderful graciousness. When I gave him an account of the difficult situation in Hungary, he helped me meet those who might be able to lend a hand. In the Vatican I learned that four American cardinals were in the city, staying at a hotel. I knew them only by name; the senior of the group was Cardinal Stritch, who was as distinguished as he was amiable. I telephoned to ask whether I might call on them in the evening. They invited me warmly and I had a two-hour meeting with them; speaking in Latin, I told them of the misery of Hungary and particularly of Budapest. Then the four cardinals stood up and thanked me for all the information. They promised me the support of the NCWC (National Catholic Welfare Conference), and emptied their wallets on the table in front of me. From their gifts I bought four trucks while I was still in

---

* For my expression of thanks, see Document 9. For another appeal to the central committee of the parish communities in Budapest, see Document 10.
** See Document 11.

Rome. These proved to be a true blessing for the Caritas work in Hungary, especially for the transport of supplies from the country to the city.

These American donations were a sign of the all-embracing solidarity of the world Church. World bolshevism did not like the idea at all. It was therefore scarcely surprising when the Marxist minister of transportation refused to allow a shipment of American aid goods from Vienna to Budapest on the transparent excuse that not enough railroad cars were available. Behind this obstructionism was an attempt at blackmail. The Hungarian Communists were demanding a share in the American gifts because they could not count on any help from the Soviet Union.* But the entire foreign Catholic press, alerted by the Budapest correspondent for *Osservatore Romano*, exposed these Communist maneuvers, and we were able to make our distributions.

Two years later the Communists, in order to block the work of our Catholic Caritas, charged the employees of the American aid organizations and the officials of Caritas with illegalities and espionage. Thus they forced the NCWC to cease its aid operations.

☩ *A Week in Budapest*

To RETURN to the days immediately following my installation: I then went to Budapest, as I have already mentioned, and spent a week there. My predecessors had largely governed the archdiocese from Esztergom. They were older than I at the time of their accession, for one thing, and illness frequently kept them at home. I myself later spent more time in the capital because the centers of the pastoral and cultural life of Hungarian Catholicism were located there. The majority of the faithful in the archdiocese lived in Budapest. The primate's palace, which in fact was only a largish ordinary house, had been gravely damaged during the war. In fact it had only two habitable rooms. Nevertheless, I could well be content with my own quarters, for living conditions in the capital at this time were still indescribably miserable. When Professor Mihály Marcell of the university expressed his sympathy, I replied: "It is only right that the primate of a country reduced to rubble should be living in a ruin."

---

* For the text of my statement on this question, published in the October 23, 1946, issue of *Magyar Kurir* ("Hungarian Courier"), see Document 12.

On October 14, 1945, I took part in a youth meeting. The Youth Secretariat of Catholic Action, with the vigorous support of the bishop, had issued a call for a countrywide youth day. Everywhere, Catholic youths paraded by the thousands. This manifestation of faith was an unmistakable profession of adherence to the Church and a rejection of communism. The youth, as well as their parents and teachers, were becoming aware of the dangers threatening us. For some time the Marxists had been trying to win over the youth with easy pleasures, and after the end of the war they succeeded to some extent here and there. I had touched on these questions in my installation address, and took them up again when I spoke to the youth of the capital who gathered by the tens of thousands in the vast cathedral square.*

On October 17 and 18, likewise in Budapest, we held the first episcopal conference over which I presided. We tried to deal with the multitude of problems that were affecting the entire country and the whole Catholic world. On Sunday, October 21, I took part in a Catholic doctors' conference of the Guild of St. Luke. I celebrated Holy Mass for these Budapest physicians, and had a welcome opportunity to express a few of my thoughts on the relationship between doctor and patient.**

☩ The Episcopal Conference, October 1945

ALL THE DIOCESAN bishops had come to the episcopal conference. They greeted me warmly and assured me of their brotherly cooperation. We discussed the usual administrative matters, but were largely concerned with measures for augmenting the welfare work of Caritas. Many of the plans we were later able to carry out originated at this conference. We also dealt in detail with the now urgent problem of how to assure a financial basis for the clergy and the institutions of the Church. The agrarian reform ordered by the Soviet commander-in-chief and being carried out along the most radical lines was placing the Church in a most difficult situation. After the agrarian reform, the dioceses and ecclesiastical institutions had only about 125 acres of land each for their support. Naturally cathedrals, episcopal offices, and

* See Document 13.
** See Document 14.

seminaries could not be supported by such small estates. We also now lacked all the other organs of pastoral activity and church administration, such as a press, publishing houses, and associations with a sound financial substructure.

We have never criticized the idea of land reform, but we did complain about the way in which a foreign power imposed it on us. We deplored the fact that, obviously, only partisan viewpoints were considered; and we censured the offhand attitude of the government on the question of compensation for church properties. I informed the members of the episcopal conference that in protest against the anti-Church posture of the Communists I had refused to accept my salary as bishop of Veszprém, and that as archbishop of Esztergom I had likewise rejected the government salary. All my brother bishops now wanted to do the same, but I advised them against such a step.

About a year later the central organ of the Communist party claimed that the finance ministry had provided very large sums for the reconstruction of the churches. In addition, the newspaper maintained, Mindszenty, the archbishop of Esztergom, who was an open enemy of democracy, was receiving from this democratic government a monthly salary that greatly exceeded the premier's. Only from my reply to this attack did the country learn that I had long ago refused the government salary.*

For the present the ecclesiastical institutions were not yet threatened with financial disaster. The faithful were supporting the parishes, monasteries, convents, seminaries, and above all the Catholic schools, with gifts in kind and contributions of money. May I hope that this book will serve as something of a testimonial to all those brave and self-sacrificing persons to whom I addressed my thanks at the end of the first school year after the war.**

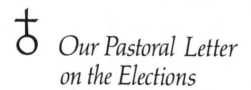

Our Pastoral Letter on the Elections

ON THE AGENDA for the second day of the episcopal conference was our pastoral letter in regard to the impending general elections. I had brought a

* See Document 15.
** See Document 16.

draft with me and presented it to the diocesan bishops for discussion section by section. All agreed with the firm tone and the references to abuses on the part of the Communists. The other bishops likewise assented to the frank language and to my call for a political program on the Christian foundation. The Russian commander, Marshal Voroshilov, was interfering radically in the domestic politics of the country in order to smooth the path for the Marxist parties. Right now, immediately before the parliamentary elections, he was trying to impose a joint list of all the parties upon us, because the Communists had come out badly in the preceding local elections in Budapest. The Smallholders party, which was the only middle-class agrarian party and was also supported by the Church, was offered first 40 percent, then 45 percent, and finally 47.5 percent of the seats. The Soviets exerted intense pressure. In fact, the leadership of the Smallholders party did not reject Voroshilov's offer until the Western press began criticizing this Russian intervention. In our pastoral letter we were concerned chiefly with explicating the situation to the faithful and putting an end to the widespread confusion. I therefore had the pastoral letter printed and on November 1, read aloud in all the churches in the country.* The letter decisively influenced the elections. I heard that even in Calvinist Debrecen the people gathered in the squares and at the marketplace to listen to the reading of the Catholic bishops' pastoral letter. Everywhere in the country it was regarded as the first courageous declaration on the abuses of the government and the Communists' covert endeavors to install a dictatorship.

The Smallholders party emerged as victor from the elections, with 57.7 percent of the votes. In its program it had committed itself to the defense and pursuance of Christian principles. The result of its campaign was a protest, erupting with elemental force, against the Communists' claims to leadership. The Communist party received only 17 percent of the votes and some of these had been gained by corruption, cheating, and terrorism.

Disappointed in their hopes, the Communists after the elections viciously attacked the bishops' pastoral letter. They accused the entire episcopate of trying to prevent a "democratic" reconstitution of the country. The bishops, they charged, were trying to take back the church estates, snatching the land out of the hands of the small farmers. To our amazement some leaders of the Smallholders party seconded these communist allegations. This weakness on the part of the Smallholders' leadership would be characteristic of it in the future.

* See Document 17.

III. COMMUNIST DOMINATION

☦ *The New Government*

PRESSED BY Voroshilov, the leaders of the Smallholders party had acquiesced to the formation of a coalition government after the elections of November 4. After the reorganization of Parliament the Russians declared that in view of this "agreement" they would accept only a government in which the Smallholders party and the Left divided the ministries half and half. They also demanded the post of minister of the interior for the Communists. This would give them control of the internal affairs of the country, above all of the police.

The Smallholders party yielded to the Russian pressure. Zoltán Tildy became premier. In the government with him were eight representatives of the Smallholders party, three Social Democrats, three Communists, and one member of the Peasants party. The composition of this cabinet surprised the whole country. Only now did people see how perilous the situation was because the leadership of the Smallholders party had been entrusted not to skilled politicians but to largely inexperienced men. Very soon information reached me that the "political police" was seeking— and "finding"—incriminating material in order to bring charges of "war crimes" and of being "enemies of the people" against some of the leaders of the Smallholders party. Soon these men became so intimidated by threats that they agreed to decrees that opened the road to power for the Communists.

On November 16, 1945, Premier Zoltán Tildy paid me his official visit. Béla Varga accompanied him. I received them rather coolly and alluded to the weakness of the party leadership and the dangers it might give rise to. They justified their conduct by referring to Voroshilov's threats. After a peace treaty had been concluded, they said, it might be possible to conduct somewhat freer policy.

Tildy asked when I would be going to Rome, and asked me to take to Pope Pius XII the government's wish for a resumption of diplomatic relations. He wanted me also to ask that Angelo Rotta, the former nuncio, who was generally esteemed throughout the country, be sent back to Hungary. This struck me as a strange request, since the Russians had expelled this very nuncio when they occupied Hungary. I could not help suspecting that they were trying to make a good impression on the Vatican and thus undercut whatever information I might be expected to give the Pope on the regime's hostility to religion. I did not let my feelings show, however, and promised to transmit the request. Tildy appeared visibly relieved. Then we changed the subject. I spoke of the rumors to the effect that the Marxists were planning to abolish the monarchical constitution and proclaim a republic. Tildy knew of these efforts. I urged him not to yield to Soviet pressure, pointing out that not a single party in the election had proposed any constitutional changes. But if the Communists wanted a decision on this question, the matter would have to be submitted to the people, I said. "They are demanding a republic only because they expect further advantages for themselves," I said, looking hard at Tildy. "I share your view," he replied. Both he and Béla Varga promised me that the leadership of the Smallholders party would lend every effort to oppose this communist project.

I therefore felt considerably reassured when I left for Rome on November 30. I stayed there for three weeks. During my absence Tildy, contrary to all his promises, recommended to the Smallholders party leadership a law making Hungary a republic. A group in Parliament protested, and many party organizations joined the protest.

As soon as I returned from Rome, I wrote a letter to Tildy and Béla Varga reminding them of their promise.* But my efforts were in vain, and the indignation throughout the country was ignored. Tildy wanted to become president of Hungary. Whatever constitutional scruples he may have had were now gone, and he was pursuing nothing but his personal ends.

♱ Campaign Against Prayer

THE STRUCTURE of communism is not simple; it is highly complex. Among the important aspects of the movement are its ideology, its party organization, its insistence upon loyalty to its principles. It is a kind of religion—but in the negative sense—with dogmas and a hierarchical leadership. The ideology might briefly be summed up as follows:

Matter is the sole reality, which has existed from the beginning and always will be. From it the universe, plants, animals have evolved. At the end of this evolution stands man. Communist philosophy knows no God,

* See Document 18.

no immortal soul. Matter is the source of its own being; it needs no creator. The order and purposiveness of the world is the consequence of a dialectical development, not the work of any kind of "world spirit." This development necessarily follows a constantly ascending line; it is based upon the dialectical tension that arises as a result of the contradictions inherent in matter. By using the adjective "dialectical" the Communists have sought to differentiate their materialism from what they call the "mechanical materialism" of the eighteenth-century Encyclopedists. According to the latters' theory, the universe and life in it, as well as man, evolved by slow, step-by-step quantitative and spatial metamorphoses of material particles. In contrast to the mechanical theory of the Determinists, the Marxists argue that matter has, in addition to quantitative and spatial extension, also the property of motion. Constant motion gives matter the ability to evolve and change. According to the nature of its composition, matter performs a variety of motions. On the lower stage it is capable of only chemical and physical movement. Then it becomes more highly differentiated and is alive. At a still higher stage it sustains consciousness of itself. But these new stages of being, life and consciousness, do not arise as a result of changes produced by slow, balanced evolution. Rather, they appear abruptly at a favorable moment, when accumulated quantitative change suddenly spills over into a qualitative change.

If we ask how the Communists go about justifying their dialectical materialism, we will find that they regard many of their assertions as incontrovertible axioms which need no proof. They also believe that their assertions are amply supported by science. But in this respect they do not ask for much by way of proof. They merely point out, for example, that many things can be made chemically, that boiling water turns to steam, and so on. Drawing on the experience of a century, the spokesmen of communism have learned the nature of human wishful thinking and turn it to good account. They promise workers nationalization of the factories, farmhands the division of large landholdings. They organize and propagate social assistance for the discontented and the oppressed. In every social class there are compassionate people who take the side of the poor and the suffering and who desire a just social order. Such people often become unwittingly the henchmen of the Communists. Their cooperation yields propagandistic gains for the Marxist movement. Often such sympathizers are won over by communism's empty promises of equality, the elimination of all earthly misery, the welfare state, and a happy, classless society in a free world. But the communist ideology can achieve lasting effects only where the religious foundations of a nation have been undermined so that reason, faith in God, and morality do not offer sufficient resistance to such ideas.

In Christian circles, Marxist tenets gain a foothold only when the religion has lost its place as the determinant force in social life. It is well known that people who have become uncertain about their beliefs will be on the lookout for new and stronger premises. In such cases Marxism seems like salvation. The waverer hopes that dialectical materialism will supply the answers to those questions religion and metaphysics leave as mysteries and do not answer. In a nation still rooted in its faith, communism therefore has little chance to accomplish its ends. Our communist fellow-countrymen who had been trained in Moscow and had just returned from Russia knew quite well that our people would take a dim view of their doctrines. They therefore concealed their plans for seizing control and maintained that they had no intention of imposing the Marxist doctrines on everyone. They spoke of human rights and freedom of conscience quite in the tone and style of Western bourgeois politicians.

Thus these Soviet emissaries succeeded in misleading even religious people. They masked communism as a genuine democratic party. Their speeches and writings made it seem that even strict Catholics might cooperate with the Communists and vote for them without the slightest pangs of conscience.

At our episcopal conferences we discussed the problem posed for us by these tactics. I also talked with the leaders of Catholic Action. The seductions of the Marxists had to be resisted and the parties of the extreme Left prevented from taking power. When, therefore, the composition of the government and the bill to transform Hungary into a republic became known, I decided to prepare our people for a difficult time of oppression and want. I asked Prelate Zsigmond Mihálovics, the leader of Catholic Action, to prepare plans for intensifying the religious life of the whole nation. Since God's hand lay heavily upon all of us, we wanted to do penance, to call upon Heaven for mercy, while also praying for the strength to bear the blows of fate. But it was also necessary to reply to unjust charges, some of which were also coming from abroad and being picked up by the Communists in order to justify Soviet high-handedness and oppression. On December 31, 1945, I tried, in a New Year's radio address to the nation, to save the honor of the Hungarian people from slanderers at home and abroad.* Three weeks later, on January 20, 1946, at a festival in honor of Saint Margaret of the House of the Árpáds, I again spoke of penance and called on the people to follow the example of this lovable saint who had made so many sacrifices for the nation.** My pastoral letter for Lent expressed similar ideas.†

I think I may say without boasting that the monitory voice of the Church was heard throughout the country. Many people, including non-Catholics, joined our movement of penance. The people were prepared to take upon themselves a heavy cross, like Christ, and to carry it. I recall that during

* For the text, see Document 19.
** See Document 20.
† See Document 21.

this period I often fell back on the simile of a hammer and anvil in my speeches. As a child I had frequently visited the village smithy, where I used to keep my attention fixed less on the hammer, which merely pounded, and more on the anvil, which never struck back and seemed to me harder and more resistant after every blow it had received. My phrase, "The harder the hammer, the tougher the anvil," became a household word in Hungary.

The response to our call for penance surpassed all expectations. Novenas were held in all the churches of the country between February 2 and 9, 1946. In many places the churches could not contain the swarms of the faithful. On the ninth I myself conducted the services in the Church of Eternal Worship in Budapest. I said:

Only a praying humanity can build a better world. I am not now thinking merely of such external things as houses, bridges, streets, cables, and the like, but I am thinking of relations with our fellow men and with our own inner selves. We must fit into our planning and our building self-sacrificing enthusiasm and the power of prayer. Prayer can intensify physical and spiritual forces; it is a power that can even overcome the laws of nature.

When I stepped out of the portal of the church after the services, I was warmly greeted by the waiting flock outside. But a few persons shouted the name of the Arrow Cross leader, "Szálasi, Szálasi!" The Political Police had sent its agents to mingle with the waiting crowd; these shouts were to provide a pretext for arrests. And promptly the newspapers reported that the primate, aided by Arrow Cross supporters, and under the guise of a Church ceremony, had organized an antidemocratic and antirepublican demonstration that had aroused indignation among the whole people.

The workers of the capital were required to march in a counterdemonstration. They tramped along silently, with a depressed air; but paid agitators mingled with them and shouted: "Work and bread—the rope for Mindszenty." Then the press published articles about the "spontaneous" demonstration brought on by my provocative antidemocratic attitude.

From that point on I was attacked incessantly in the press and in mass meetings. The real reason for this campaign was the upsurge of religious life, the growth of Christian consciousness. When the charges began appearing in foreign newspapers as well, I responded to them in our church newspaper *Uj Ember.**

* See Document 22.

☩ Meeting with Pius XII

IN EARLIER YEARS I had scarcely had any opportunities for visits abroad. As a young priest, in 1924, I had once been able to visit Lourdes, which had been a great experience for me. But my work as a parish priest kept me too busy for sightseeing tours. On the occasion of my appointment as a papal prelate in 1937 I would have liked to have gone to Rome, but the shadows of Nazism already hung over our country. And in 1944, when Pius XII appointed me bishop of Veszprém, the war had already been raging for five years. Moreover, the German occupying power controlled Hungary.

Now I had become primate and archbishop of Esztergom. In spite of all difficulties and in defiance of Russian suspicions, I was obliged by my new office to establish contacts with Rome as quickly as possible. General Key, the head of the American Military Mission, took me and my secretary with him by plane to Bari on November 30, 1945. From there we traveled by bus to Rome. We were delayed and arrived very late. The Holy Father had already begun his Advent retreat. But when he heard of our arrival, he interrupted the spiritual exercises and received me with great kindliness. I had always esteemed Pius XII as a towering personality; now I was able to see for myself what a kindly Holy Father God had given us. He was thoroughly familiar with Hungary's Church and the situation of Catholicism in our country. As papal legate to the Eucharistic Congress in 1938, he had come to Budapest and since that time had been warmly disposed toward us. I therefore looked forward to the prospect of reestablishing and deepening the relations between Rome and Hungary.

From my reports to the papal secretariat of state and to various congregations, the Holy Father was aware of the Hungarian Church's predicament. He showed concern and sympathy for our people and strong satisfaction at my coming. He also praised the Hungarian people for remaining true to their religion in the shadow of all suffering and distress. When I remarked that Hungary rejoiced because His Holiness and the Vatican, St. Peter's, and Rome had been spared the worst effects of the war, Pius XII asked: "You who have suffered so much still have the strength to rejoice at that?" I replied: "We truly do so, for we hope that help and salvation will come from here for wounded humanity and for shattered Hungary." Then I told him about the present life of the Church in Hungary. I also spoke about the filling of two vacant episcopal sees, and finally brought up Premier Tildy's request for the restoration of diplomatic relations.

The Pope was at once ready to send Nuncio Angelo Rotta back to Budapest. But I revealed my distrust and suspicions, and described to him the antireligious attitude of the Communists. I expressed my conviction that immediate dispatch of the nuncio would not reflect the situation. We therefore agreed that after my return I would first inform the country about my visit to Rome and the possibility of eventual resumption of diplomatic relations. Then I would wait to observe the effects of such an announcement.

Finally I asked the Holy Father for support for Hungarian citizens who were leading a miserable life in Austrian and German refugee camps. At the end of my audience the Holy Father had informed me that in the impending consistory my name would figure on the list of cardinals to be created.

In Rome I also met with Hungarian exiles and discussed their fate with Baron Gábor Apor and his associates. On December 9, I said Mass for our refugees in the chapel of the Papal Hungarian Institute. In the sermon I said to them: "Love one another; love the Church, the pillar of truth, the loving mother; love our country now bleeding from a thousand wounds. Let us help wherever we can. The storm that has swept over the world also lashed the branches of the Hungarian tree and scattered its leaves. Shelter every orphaned Hungarian."

These words were repeatedly quoted by refugees.

In February of the following year my nomination as cardinal did indeed come. I at once applied to the authorities for a passport. But the issuance was delayed. Almost daily we urged the appropriate government organs to take care of this formality quickly. It was almost time for me to leave for Rome. Finally word came that I would have to apply in person in the capital in order to obtain the passport. These delaying tactics were nothing but the expression of outrageous self-importance on the part of the officials. No government in the past would ever have ventured to treat one of my predecessors this way. I therefore did not go to Budapest, and would not alter my decision even after my episcopal vicar, János Drahos, tried to change my mind by arguing that if I failed to go to Rome I might be depriving the Hungarian Church of a great distinction. The announced day of departure, February 17, 1946, arrived. Since the passport had not yet come, I set out to visit parishes and schools in the vicinity of Esztergom. Meanwhile Premier Ferenc Nagy telephoned. Since he could not reach me, he asked Monsignor Drahos: "But tell me, isn't the primate going to Rome?"

"How could he? He has no passport."

Nagy responded: "Please send a messenger to the primate with word that the government begs him to leave for Rome at once. He will find the passport at hand when he reaches Esztergom."

Drahos could not forbear to ask, with gentle irony: "Doesn't he have to call for the papers personally in Budapest?"

"Not at all, but please see to it that he receives the message."

The messenger reached me in Visegrád. This sudden readiness on the part of the government was hardly surprising. At the last moment the Hungarian ambassador in Rome had telegraphed Budapest that of thirty-two newly appointed cardinals, thirty-one had already arrived in the Vatican. Only the primate of Hungary was missing, and the world press was already asking what this meant.

General Key, who had helped me on my first visit to Rome, had learned what was afoot with my passport. When I returned to Esztergom, he was already waiting with a plane in a field on the outskirts of the city. This plane flew me and my secretary, Monsignor Zakar, to Rome. We landed there at noon on February 18, 1946. Members of the Hungarian colony in the Vatican and many reporters were there to welcome us. We were quartered in the Papal Hungarian Institute. That afternoon I made several official visits. Next day the Holy Father received me in private audience. I had to tell him about the reason for my lateness. It may be that my description, which gave him insight into our situation, prompted him to embrace me at the consistory and to say: "Éljen Magyarország!" ("Long live Hungary!") When he placed the cardinal's hat on my head, he said in a deeply moved voice: "Among the thirty-two you will be the first to suffer the martyrdom whose symbol this red color is."

For my titular church—instead of Saint Gregory's Basilica, which the Holy Father had assigned to me—I asked for Santo Stefano Rotondo, which is dedicated to the memory of the deacon Saint Stephen and which in former times was the church of the Hungarians in Rome. Pius XII gladly fulfilled my request. On February 28 he personally handed me the archiepiscopal pallium—the symbol of my office. On March 4 he again received me in private audience. That was my last meeting with Pius XII. But his paternal kindness and his sympathy continued to accompany me. He constantly intervened in my behalf whenever difficulties arose for me. At every juncture he denounced the machinations of the Communists and also those of the so-called "progressive Catholics." I remember with great gratitude how he intervened for me when I was imprisoned and brought to trial, and I remember likewise the loving words of the telegram he sent me after my liberation in 1956.

While I was in Rome I negotiated several times with the leaders of the Hungarian colony there, discussing my own Roman plans and the affairs of Hungarian refugees. I visited refugee camps in Bologna, Regio Emilia, Rimini, and San Pastore. The homeless Hungarians received me with love and trust, and I pleaded their cause in my talks with authorities and aid organizations. Shaken, I tramped mile-wide Hungarian soldiers' cemeteries in the vicinity of Udine, where so many of our dead from World War I rest in the Italian earth, far from their native land and their families.

On March 18, 1946, an American plane flew me back home. It was an exhilarating feeling, after an absence of nearly a month, to fly over the blue mirror of Lake Balaton and return to Hungary.

The Persecuted

AT THE episcopal conference in autumn 1945, we also dealt with the lot of the so-called war criminals and enemies of the people who had been jailed. Many of those arrested were convicted by people's courts, others simply sent to camps without a trial. The majority of these people were innocent and were being locked up in order to intimidate them and soften them up for collaboration with the Communists. But of course the prisons also held unsavory figures from the previous regime who had abused their positions and carried out or passed on disastrous orders.

In the summer of 1945 the Big Three, meeting in the Potsdam Conference, had made arrangements for the resettlement of the German minority. Voroshilov was now pressing the provisional government for a decree ordering expulsion of the Germans. When word spread that action of this sort was impending, many Hungarian Swabians tried to escape deportation by joining the Marxist parties. Those who did not were immediately open to suspicion of being "war criminals" or Nazis. It was no long step from such suspicions to confiscation of property or internment or prison for the individual in question.

We bishops could not look on passively. It was our duty to call the nation's and the world's attention to such conditions, and we did so in our pastoral letter of October 17.* As it had been our Christian duty during the war to defend the Jews, we now felt that we had the same duty to defend innocent Germans.

After my return from Rome I accepted an invitation from the workers of Csepel, and on December 23 I said Holy Mass in the large parish church there. Csepel is a typical factory town of about 50,000 inhabitants. The

* See Document 23.

Communists regarded it as their citadel. My visit to the town and the ex-
ceptionally enthusiastic welcome by tens of thousands of workers was
therefore a bitter surprise to the Communists. Incidentally, the inhabitants
of Csepel have frequently manifested their attachment to Christianity. In
1945 a new Catholic high school was founded there, and the town asked
the Benedictines to take it over. Precisely because the Communists were
always insisting on their dominant position in this proletarian town, I
though Csepel was the right place to call the people's attention to the fate of
the persecuted. In my sermon, therefore, I contrasted Christian love with
blind hatred.*

At Christmas I visited two large internment camps in Buda and in Csepel. My purpose in going was that of a priest, but I also hoped my visits
would help alleviate suffering. I was also trying to express my own feelings
of sympathy and gratitude. Only a year ago, precisely at Christmas time, I
myself had been a prisoner together with my twenty-six priests and seminarians.

I had written beforehand to the officials of the camps announcing my
visits and the times of my arrival, and asking them to let me know if the
time I had selected was convenient, and, if not, to suggest a different time.
But I had received no reply. I therefore turned up at the camp gates, obviously an undesirable visitor, and declared I intended to wait until I was
admitted. News quickly spread in the vicinity that the primate of Hungary
was waiting outside the camp gate for admittance, and people swarmed to
the scene from all directions. The camp administration obviously found
that highly embarrassing, and they opened the gates to me. I first visited
the dormitories and then inspected many of the single cells. In Buda I asked
that the huge number of prisoners be assembled in the exercise ground so
that I could address a few words to them. Broken men raised their heads,
and a flash of joy and hope came into their eyes. In my person the Church
had come to them, to console them in their misery and humiliation. After
these camp visits the Marxist newspapers wrote that the archbishop of Esztergom was plainly making common cause with criminals, and maliciously
added that at Christmas the previous year he had neglected to visit the victims of the Nazis. But since everyone in the country knew that at that time
I myself had been a prisoner of the Nazis, I did not have to answer this silly
charge.

Wherever I could obtain permission, I visited the prisons in Budapest
and went from cell to cell. The prisoners often burst into tears, and
members of another denomination would sometimes ask me for my blessing. In one of these prison cells I came upon the aged former army bishop
István Zadravecz in a deplorable condition.

Warm human relationships sometimes resulted from these prison visits.

* For the text, see Document 20.

The relatives of a number of prisoners called on me in Esztergom or Buda to thank me, and although I had made the visits without the slightest thought of conversions, some prisoners became Catholics.

After these visits I wrote to the government requesting amnesty, parole, or at least somewhat more humane treatment for these prisoners, depending on the degree of their offenses. Since, of course, the prisons also held partisans of the former regime, collaborators with the Germans, and members of the Arrow Cross party, I was including such persons in my plea also. My letter was soon published in the press and a totally distorted interpretation put upon it.

☦ 6 *"Student Conspiracy"*

HUNGARY HAD OFFICIALLY become a republic on February 1, 1946. The new president was Zoltán Tildy; the premier was Ferenc Nagy. László Rajk replaced the more humane Imre Nagy as head of the ministry of the interior—a change fraught with grave significance. The three leftist parties now joined in Parliament to form a bloc. This was done in response to Russian pressure after the Social Democratic party and National Peasant party deputies initially refused to play the part of mere yes men in Parliament. After the formation of the bloc, party discipline hardened. Henceforth deputies could neither express their opinions nor take a position freely. The Communists initiated a bill for the protection of public order and the republic. Evidently they hoped it would provide a legal basis for their police operations and their blackmail. The people soon dubbed this bill the "Executioners' Law." It did indeed provide grounds for prosecuting a large number of people in public life. Later, when I myself came to trial, the prosecution based its indictment on this same law.

A resistance group under Dezső Sulyok tried to combat the new law. The proclamation of the Hungarian Republic had resulted in several bitter disappointments for Sulyok. At first he had been opposed to changing the form of government. Then the wily Communists had dangled before him the prospect of the premiership. This induced him to abandon his stand, and he then tried to persuade as many delegates as possible that in our predicament, given the pressure from the Russians, the change to a republican form of government was inevitable. He finally agreed to present the bill himself.

Once they had taken power, however, the Communists no longer felt bound by their pledge and backed Ferenc Nagy rather than Sulyok. Nagy, a modest Smallholder, was inexperienced in government. The Russians were able to persuade him to introduce the "Defense of the Republic Act." The growing opposition within the party was suppressed by the use of an old tactic: intimidation. The rumor was spread that if the law were not passed the Russians would inflict punishment, but that if we consented now, he would gain precious time and save the existence of the majority party, which would be able to act more freely in the better future. Once peace was concluded, we could get rid of all these measures that were being imposed on us today.

On the basis of such illusion, Ferenc Nagy succeeded in having the Executioners' Law passed on March 12, 1946. A small group under the leadership of Sulyok tried to oppose it. In the course of the debate they attacked László Rajk, responsible for the Political Police, and condemned his inhumane methods. The result was that Sulyok and twenty other deputies were expelled from the Smallholders party, on Soviet insistence.

It was becoming difficult to dig up any more real "war criminals" and "enemies of the people." New categories of antirepublican crimes had to be invented. At the end of April 1946 Interior Minister Rajk ordered searches of the intermediate schools. The police turned up during school hours, looked at the students' books and notebooks, and rummaged through their schoolbags. Then they arrested a dozen students and terrified them into denouncing various catechism instructors and teachers from the monastic orders as enemies of the government. During the searches the police also planted guns and ammunition in the school buildings, and then "discovered" these weapons in the presence of the school administrators. Reports of these "horrific conditions" in the schools promptly appeared in the left-oriented press, together with charges against the teachers. The parochial schools were branded "hotbeds of reaction."

As soon as I heard about these incidents, I ordered the directors of the Catholic schools to check every single case. Minister of Education Dezső Koresztury in person helped me with these investigations, with the result that I obtained official confirmation of what the public already fully realized: that the whole operation was nothing but an organized attack on the Catholic schools and on religious instruction. On May 4 we bishops then published a pastoral letter setting forth our stand on school questions and giving the lie to all those who pretended to see our church schools as a danger to democracy.*

There was intense and widespread indignation over the police action. Nevertheless, the police did not shrink from carrying out additional

* For the text of this letter, and a statement issued by the General Administration of Catholic Schools, see Documents 25 and 26.

searches and, of course, made further "discoveries." It became obvious that the Communists were determined to force the Smallholders party to consent to secularization of the schools and the suppression of compulsory religious instruction. But the collaboration of the newspapers and the Political Police had not yet been perfectly synchronized, so that in one case the Budapest newspapers published a report on a "conspiracy" uncovered in the search of a Cistercian secondary school at Baja before the search was conducted. The affair became a countrywide scandal because the report was extremely detailed and full of "precise" facts. Thereafter the subject of a "student conspiracy" vanished from the newspapers.

☩ *The Parents Association*

AFTER THEIR EXPOSURE in the Baja case, the police avoided that particular sort of trickery. But the school question was far from settled. From then on the necessity for unified education was urged, and the government propaganda insisted that reforms required new schoolbooks, the abolition of mandatory religious instruction, and a takeover of the church schools by the state. Such reforms had long ago been carried out in the Western democratic countries, it was argued. The same step was necessary in Hungary because the church schools, in contrast to the state schools, preferred an "antidemocratic, reactionary" educational system.

We had our reasons for fearing that the leadership of the Smallholders party would once again yield to pressure, and therefore mobilized the parents to defend our schools. We organized lectures, conferences, and courses for the parents and teachers of the conventual schools. We held large mass meetings to answer the charges of the parties and the press. This parents movement forced the Communists to change their tactics. They now made the school question an internal problem for the political parties. In this way they succeeded in shaking the structure of the Smallholders party. More and more they insisted that certain governmental questions should be settled by discussions among the leaders of the parties. The idea was to circumvent Parliament and run the government by negotiations among the parties. The leaders of the Smallholders failed to realize the dangerous part the collaborators in their own ranks were playing, nor did they grasp the machinations of the politically skilled Marxists. But the voters were outraged by the wheeling and dealing. Grassroots organizations of the

Smallholders party demanded that such negotiations stop and that government affairs be dealt with by Parliament, which was the sole proper body for them. These demands intensified when it became known that the parents association had rejected the Communists' demands for a new educational policy.

The parents association had spoken up when the first accusations of student conspiracies were raised. Its representatives insisted on taking part in all investigations and emphatically rejected the groundless charges. I myself frequently attended the parents association's protest meetings, and addressed it on such subjects as the educational rights of the Church, the value of Christian schools, and so on. On May 21, 1946, speaking in St. Stephen's Academy, the forum of Christian artists, scientists, and writers, I suggested the possibility of acting in conjunction with the Protestants on the school question.* I had previously called on the Calvinist bishop László Ravasz, and we had reached complete agreement on our desire to oppose the Communists' educational aims. Bishop Ravasz also approved the efforts of the Catholic parents association. The Protestants understood my words and my intentions, and began appearing at our meetings and our congresses, and even participated in our pilgrimages during the Marian Year.

On May 30, 1946, I took part in the mass meeting of the parents association in Kalocsa. In my address I answered the charges that the church schools neglected the lower classes.** The demonstration sent a statement to Premier Ferenc Nagy protesting the systematic attacks on the parochial schools.† A delegation of the parents association followed this up by delivering a memorandum to Dezső Keresztury, my former pupil from Zalaegerszeg, who in the interval had become minister of education as well as an important writer. We knew he was opposed to the Marxists' educational policies, contrary to the instructions of his party, and thought the parents association statement might back him in his stand.††

By all this activity the parents association succeeded in calling public attention to the dangers threatening the church schools and the Christian education of their children. The result was that in the following school year more Hungarian parents than ever before had their children registered in the church schools. It was like a plebiscite in favor of our slandered schools and our allegedly outmoded educational methods. Resistance within the Smallholders party to the concessions of its leadership increased, and for the time being the party deputies were able to block the plans of the Communists. During the struggle Minister of Education Keresztúry took an admirable position, and ultimately resigned rather than play the part of a puppet in the coalition government.

* For the address see Document 27. For another address on the subject of interdenominational cooperation, see Document 28.
** See Document 29.
† See Document 30.
†† See Document 31.

☿ *Murder on the Boulevard*

IN THE MIDDLE of the summer of 1946 a Russian soldier was killed in the capital. The news was first broadcast on the radio. Next day the newspapers published a story under sensational headlines. The reports stated that a "murdered" Russian soldier had been found on the Teréz-Kőrút (Budapest's Ring Boulevard) and that immediately afterwards, in the attic of a bombed-out house, the corpse of a young man in the uniform of KALOT, the Catholic youth association, had been discovered. The investigation had concluded that "the shot which killed the brave soldier was fired from a window of the bombed house; the assailant had fled to the attic after his criminal act, and when the police tracked him there he shot himself to avoid capture."

At the time it happened I was told the true story. On the busy boulevard a Russian soldier had been shot down by his own comrades in the presence of a number of bystanders. At about the same time a young man died in the prison on Andrássy Street; the Secret Police had gone too far in an interrogation. Because of the proximity of both bodies it was possible for the Secret Police to establish a connection, brand the unfortunate young man as an assailant, and make the Russian soldier a victim. The claim that the "murderer" was a member of the "reactionary Catholic youth organization" provided a pretext for liquidating the Youth Association. The public, of course, was soon aware that the story was a texture of crude lies. It was generally known that KALOT members had never worn uniforms. The Russians, however, used the fiction as a basis for demanding the dissolution of all youth organizations. The government complied, issuing Ordinance No. 7330/1946 ME, empowering Interior Minister László Rajk to carry out all measures necessary for that dissolution.

On July 20, 1946, we held an episcopal conference to discuss the situation created by this ordinance. We decided to protest vigorously. I thereupon wrote to Premier Ferenc Nagy pointing out the illegality of such executive decrees and requesting that the matter be dealt with in a proper and legal manner.* Throughout the country no one doubted that the whole campaign was the communist reaction to the fact that the Hungarian youth

* See Document 32.

had stayed away in droves from the organizations founded by the Marxists and supported by government funds. Nevertheless our clubs and organizations were dissolved, their property and centers expropriated and turned over to the Marxist youth organizations. The leaders of our associations were forced to collaborate in all of this.

At this same episcopal conference we also dealt with the fate of the inmates of internment camps. On behalf of the episcopate I wrote still another letter to Premier Ferenc Nagy demanding general amnesty and urging the government to seek national unity rather than to continue to pit Hungarians against Hungarians.* When the Russian commander-in-chief learned of our letters, he demanded that the premier reprimand the clergy publicly. Ferenc Nagy complied. He held a press conference and, without mentioning our arguments, charged the clergy with refusing to assist in the peaceful development of the country, with tolerating anti-Soviet and antidemocratic elements in their ranks, and with showing no gratitude to the Red Army. I answered each of his charges in a letter ** of August 10, which was never published in the government press, although I had asked for it.

In our letters to the premier we characterized the attacks on the youth organizations as a serious violation of the freedom of religion. The leftist press and the Marxist party leaderships claimed that their measures were urgently needed social and political reforms. Such claims were, of course, intended to influence the free world and the Western powers, whose military missions were still in Hungary. But from the summer of 1946 on, the life of the Church was restricted in a number of other areas. On June 20, 1946, for example, we found we had to call off the usual Corpus Christi Day procession. The authorities would not permit us to use the customary route; at the last moment only the side streets around the cathedral were thrown open to us. Evidently the authorities feared a demonstrative profession of faith on the part of the masses, who had always joined in the procession.

I mentioned this religious persecution in my speech to the plenary session of the Society of St. Stephen on November 7, 1946. For tactical reasons, I reminded my listeners not so much of the Soviet practices as of those of the Nazis. Nevertheless my address opened the eyes of many deputies of the Smallholders party and their local party chiefs. It turned out that even some members of the Social Democrats party and of the National Peasant party were impressed by the truth of my arguments.†

* See Document 33.
** See Document 34.
† See Document 35.

☦ *Collective Responsibility*

WHEN THE SECOND WORLD WAR ended, the ancient city of Kassa became the temporary seat of the Czechoslovak government. President Benes soon issued a declaration that Czechoslovakia was to be exclusively the native land of the Czechs and the Slovaks. This statement was followed up by systematic expulsion of the Hungarians and the Sudeten Germans. At that time there were living in southern Slovakia, in a broad border zone that had formerly been a part of Hungary, some 650,000 Hungarians. The government in Kassa now decided to Slovakize some 200,000 of them. About 100,000 were to be exchanged for Slovaks who had hitherto lived among us in central Hungary, and the remaining 400,000 were to be scattered throughout all of Czechoslovakia in order to promote their assimilation.

First the Hungarians were stripped of their citizenship. There followed the dismissal of all Hungarians from the central and the municipal civil service jobs. Their salaries and pensions were cut off, their businesses expropriated without compensation. Henceforth they were not allowed to work in industry or in commerce. They had to turn their houses and other property over to Slovak partisans. All Hungarian elementary and intermediate schools were closed. A decree prohibited the giving of religious instruction in the Hungarian language. In many places even the singing of Hungarian hymns was forbidden. In the churches the gospel could not be read in our language. No Hungarian newspapers and books could be printed. Many Hungarian priests were expelled, so that the people were a flock without shepherds. Only those who were prepared to deny or renounce their Hungarian background and accepted "Slovakization" could count on forbearance.

In the summer of 1945 the Czechoslovak government requested the great powers at Potsdam to approve its plans for resettlement. The conference approved the resettlement of the Sudeten Germans, but not of the Hungarians. Nevertheless, shortly afterward some 20,000 of them were expelled. Our government did not dare intervene in behalf of the persecuted minority, for the Russians approved the attitude of the Czech authorities. Therefore the Hungarian Communists would have countermanded any intervention in favor of the refugees. The behavior of the Soviet Union is easy to understand: it was bent on keeping alive the antagonism among the nationalities in its satellite states. It was following the ancient principle of "divide and conquer."

All these circumstances imposed on the Church alone the task of helping the hard-pressed refugees, and those who were not yet refugees but threatened with expulsion. In the summer of 1945, when I was still in Veszprém, I wrote a letter to the Slovak bishops at the request of Vince Tomek, a Piarist professor who later became general of his order in Rome; it appealed to them to intervene in favor of the Hungarians. I never received any reply. Some time later, however, expelled priests informed me that the heads of the Slovak churches had provided help for the refugees in a number of cases. After I took office in Esztergom I issued a pastoral letter in which I referred to the unhappy fate of the expelled Hungarians.*

Toward the end of the year the Czechoslovak government at last began negotiating in regard to the population exchange. Thereafter the situation improved somewhat. It was agreed that Slovaks from Hungary equal in numbers to the expelled Hungarians from Slovakia would be sent to settle in Czechoslovakia. But it soon turned out that comparatively few Slovaks were willing to leave Hungary. Thereupon Czechoslovakia once again appealed to the great powers, and at the Paris Peace Conference asked permission for a major resettlement of 200,000 Hungarians. This request was not granted. But it was set forth in the Hungarian Peace Treaty of 1947 that the interested countries were to settle these questions by negotiations among themselves. Meanwhile the Czech government began transferring the Hungarians in the regions abandoned by the Sudeten Germans. This forcible resettlement resulted in hordes of refugees streaming across the Czech-Hungarian border. As a result we had many eyewitness accounts of what was going on, and we used two of our weekly newspapers to keep the populace informed. In order to call the attention of the free world to the distress of these people, I sent telegrams to Cardinal Griffin in London and Cardinal Spellman in New York, and gave the texts to a news agency. In this way some word of the tragic fate of the Hungarians from Slovakia reached the world public through the international press. The Czech government lamely alleged that the mass movements of people represented not deportations but public works projects.**

In the meantime I had asked for a visa to enter Czechoslovakia. I wanted to intercede for the persecuted people with the ecclesiastical and secular authorities in that country. I waited a long time, but received no answer. At last I wrote to Archbishop Beran of Prague, who informed me on December 21, 1946, of the position the Czech government was taking. They would grant me a visa only if my visit dealt exclusively with affairs of the Church and if I refrained from any statements that were not purely religious in nature. I had counted on that. It meant that the government did not want me to establish contact with Hungarians who had been resettled

* See Document 36.
** I answered this falsehood in a statement. See Document 37.

in the Sudetenland. I would also not be permitted to enter the formerly Hungarian villages. But at least I had succeeded in directing the world's attention once more to the fate of the suffering Hungarians. The world could condemn the cynical, inhumane conduct of their persecutors.

On February 5, 1947, I sent a telegram to King George VI and also to President Truman, calling their attention to the cruel persecution of 650,000 Hungarians in Czechoslovakia, in violation of all the human rights guaranteed by the United Nations.* But in spite of the most forthright condemnation by public opinion throughout the world, the harassments and resettlements did not cease. Once more thousands sought refuge in what was left of Hungary. It was no easy task to provide so many people without resources with shelter, food, and places to work. For the time being the Church's Caritas organization was their only hope. Efforts by civil servants in the foreign ministry, combined with the pressure of publicity, later forced the Hungarian government to show more concern for these persecuted Hungarians. On February 27, 1946, negotiations were initiated which led to an agreement on population exchange and brought temporary relief after the uncertainties. But by next year the Russians had succeeded in weakening the Smallholders party fraction significantly. They brought about a reshuffling inside the government which gave more power to the Communists. The Hungarians in Slovakia felt the effects at once. As early as the summer of 1947 large numbers of them were again harried across the frontier, and our government did not dare to protest this procedure, but instead deported Hungarian Germans—with the Soviet Union's "permission"—to East Germany to make room. The wickedness and cynicism with which this campaign was carried out spread terror throughout Hungary. All I could do was to send a telegram of protest to the new premier, Lajos Dinnyés,** and to follow this up two weeks later by a public declaration.†

The Communist party took power in Czechoslovakia in 1948. The Communists in Prague and Budapest now treated the problem exclusively on the party basis—which meant grim suffering for the deportees and the Hungarian nation. At the end of August 1948 I once again sent a telegram of protest in the name of the Hungarian bishops, directing it this time to our foreign minister.†† The Communists then issued a statement from the cabinet asserting that but for my chauvinism and interference the whole matter would have reached a "favorable solution." In reply we pointed out that the Communists were afraid to make public the relevant documents.†††

It was after this exchange that the Communists began preparing the way for my arrest.

---

* See Document 38.   †† See Document 41.
** See Document 39.   ††† See Document 42.
† See Document 40.

☦ My Visitations in the Dioceses

IT SEEMED to me that the most effective defense against atheistic materialism was a deepening of the religious life throughout the country. I therefore gladly participated in the festivities of other dioceses whenever their bishops invited me. These occasions gave me the chance to discuss questions of the religious life with the priests. I was able to go into the problems of Hungarian Catholicism with them and to offer them my guidelines for a solution. Moreover, I had the opportunity to present personally to thousands and even tens of thousands of persons the Church's views on ideological questions and questions of Church policy. These talks influenced public opinion in the country. The whole population realized what the problems were, and learned how the Church regarded them. My visits strengthened cooperation between the flock and the clergy in defense of the faith and of the institutions of the Church.

The Communists soon realized how effective my pastoral tours were. Rákosi complained that I was spending more time among the faithful in the capital than in Esztergom. Whereupon, speaking to thousands of workers in Csepel, I answered him: "I am also at home among you here, as for nearly a thousand years seventy-eight of my predecessors in the office of primate have been at home on every patch of Hungarian soil."

In 1946 I carried out various ecclesiastical functions in other dioceses ten times. On April 28, for example, after my journey to Rome, I brought back to József Pétery, the bishop of Vác, the pallium I had received for him from the hand of the Holy Father; since 1754 the pallium had been conceded to bishops of this diocese as a special privilege (it is usually reserved for an archbishop with the rank of a metropolitan). The faithful filled the cathedral to the very last place, and I addressed them on the subject of loyalty to the Church and the Church's role in ransoming prisoners from the Turks.*

Without directing my remarks explicitly to the Marxists, I answered their charge that the Church had been little concerned for the people and had always stood on the side of the exploiters. In my reply I had facts to fall back on. During my years as a parish priest I had become convinced that in apologetic and ideological discussions it was always best to argue on the

* See Document 43.

basis of facts. I therefore spent much of my free time studying historical references and narratives. This work proved very worthwhile; the knowledge I obtained served me splendidly in carrying out my tasks and duties. Moreover, these historical researches taught me that in the struggle of ideas abstract reasoning and dry theory are of little use. I also realized that uncertain leadership and perpetual weighing of every contingency stood in the way of success. Especially when dealing with determined Communists, a hesitant, irresolute attitude could prove disastrous. And I think to this hour that our position is seriously weakened by those Christians whose primary concern seems to be worrying about whether any of the charges brought against the Church may not sometime, someplace have been justified. The excesses of modern "self-criticism" often serve only the interests of our bitter enemies. It takes people with carefully trained minds to see the "faults and weaknesses" of the Church in the proper proportions and to fit them into the circumstances of the times. Even a good many theologians and intellectuals cannot do that, for they lack the historian's eye.

On June 16, 1946, I consecrated Kalmán Papp as the new bishop of Győr. In my address I spoke of St. Ambrose as a beacon light for our stormy times,* stressing his forthrightness and truthfulness. For my part, I regarded love of truth as a bishop's most important virtue, which he must not part with out of fear or for praise and advantage; which, in fact, he must cling to even at the peril of his life. The liturgy of consecration also stresses that the bishop may in no circumstances pretend that the light is shadow, the shadow light, or call good bad and bad good. These admonitions rang in my ears when I took charge of the Hungarian Church. When the struggle against the Church began—the Hungarian *Kulturkampf*—I realized at once that Christianity and communism were about to measure their strength in a decisive contest. We could not ask whether the Christian spirit would win. It seemed to me, rather, that our principal task was to hold out where we stood, to alarm Christendom, to call the attention of the whole human race to the danger of communism. I was convinced that we had been called to bear witness. Within the Church we had to maintain the hope that better times in the future would restore to us all that was being taken from us. Come what might, we must never act opportunistically, disregarding religious interests.

On May 30, 1946, I took part in the demonstration of the Catholic Parents Association, which I have already mentioned; on August 25 in the St. Stephen celebration in Székesfehérvár; and on September 8 in the pilgrimage of 250,000 Greek Rite Roman Catholics to Máriapócs. On September 15 I was in Zalaegerszeg and on September 23 in Szeged. There we celebrated the nine hundredth anniversary of the founder of the diocese, the sainted Bishop Gerardus (Gellért). A tremendous crowd had assembled in

---

* See Document 44.

the cathedral square of Szeged, where I was greeted by Bishop Endre Hamvas. In his cordial welcoming words he forthrightly dismissed the slanders
that had been spread about me. I replied:

As long as the faith lives in the Hungarian people, it will give the nation the
strength to rise again. As for myself, I am nothing but the servant of my nation and
my people. But I intend to carry out my duties, no matter what price they demand
of me. To you I say: Be unshakable in your attachment to the Church, in your respect for moral principles, and in clinging to your Magyar virtues.

In the course of a thousand years Hungarian tradition and Christianity
have become closely bound to one another. In times of stress their unity
could always be counted on. For that reason we incorporated national holidays into the life of the Church. The people knew that the leaders of the
nation were simultaneously engaged in the defense of the Church even as
they furthered the interests, the welfare, and the prosperity of the country.
Anyone who assumed suffering for the sake of our deeply rooted Christian
religion was also doing his part for his native land. As I pointed out in my
address in Pécs on October 20, 1946, religion is not in fact the private matter it is often said to be.*

Many of our intellectuals imagine that in questions of public life it is possible to take a neutral stand. The historian who has learned the lessons of
history will think differently. The fact remains that in human society the
most important factor is belief in a transcendental God and in a life in the
hereafter. History also proves that no power exists that can more deeply affect human life, can more deeply stir the souls of men, than religion. In
keeping with its nature, religion influences the whole life of the individual.
It guides his actions in society. It shapes his conscience. Hence not even
partisan politics can be free of the influence of religion, especially not when
parties are competing and fighting on the ideological front. The attitude
most suited to man is one that corresponds with the dictates of conscience.

There is another perspective that the experienced shepherd of souls must
keep constantly in mind. He must realize that the institutions of state and
society surrounding his flock, and in which the faithful move, can influence
their religious life for good or ill. A pastor who judges this situation in real-
istic terms will be very cautious in counting on the "maturity" and immunity of his flock. The true priest engaged in the cure of souls—even if he is
held to be an outmoded type—considers himself responsible for the souls
entrusted to him. His sense of responsibility weighs heavily upon him, and
he will try to protect his flock from all perils and all obstacles.

* See Document 45.

☦ Reviving the Christian Past

BOTH NAZISM and Bolshevism insisted that they had to penetrate our country in order to replace a faulty past by a happy new world. The Communists, in keeping with their doctrine, announced that the past had to be uncompromisingly liquidated. It was in response to that prospect that I had said in my installation address: "I wish to be the conscience of my people. As the appointed guardian, I knock upon the doors of your souls. Contrary to the errors that are now springing up, I proclaim to my people and my nation the eternal truths. I want to resurrect the sanctified tradition of our people. Individuals, perhaps, can live without it, but never the whole nation."

The Marxists considered the whole of Hungarian history one grand mistake. They presented this view to the inexperienced youth of the nation, with the obvious purpose of making our youth more pliable by taking away their patriotism and their self-confidence. For my part, I fervently desired, in this time of national disaster, proud, self-confident young people who stood firmly on the religious and ethical foundations of the Hungarian past. In the seventeenth century Cardinal Pázmány and his priests had reared the young men who reconquered Buda and who rebuilt the country after the withdrawal of the Turks. Similarly, it now seemed to me a vital task of the Church to prepare our young people for the defense of our native land and of our Christian culture.*

In town and countryside I constantly pointed out the local historical events that held some lesson. It is a very human trait for everyone to be proud of the history of his family, his place, or his nation. The historian knows that an organic tie exists between the present and the past of all social organisms. For this reason history can also be used to awaken religious awareness and to deepen the religious life. In earlier times, of course, social conditions were different and the premises of secular and ecclesiastical institutions were not what they are today. But the fundamental problems of the human spirit have remained the same through the ages. Interestingly, the Communists attacked me for my frequent references to his-

* A week after my installation I seized the first favorable opportunity to address tens of thousands of young people on this subject in front of the basilica in Budapest. I raised the question, "What path should Hungarian youth take?" See Document 46.

torical events and historic sites. On that account they called me a leftover from the feudal age, a narrow-minded, reactionary bishop operating with medieval arguments. My adversaries' propaganda even affected Christian groups because those who did not hear my remarks were unable to read the actual texts of them. For that reason, not so much for my defense as to set the record straight, I am appending examples of two of my sermons that were based on historical parallels.*

☿ Smashing the Smallholders Party

AS A CONSEQUENCE of the pastoral work of the Church, our flock stood ready to fend off attacks on the institutions of religion. I have mentioned how the protests of the Hungarian Parents Association frustrated the Communists' plans to abolish religious instruction and to introduce uniform textbooks into the schools. We were also helped by the hardening attitude of the Smallholders party. From February 1946 on, under pressure of public opinion and the leadership of its courageous new secretary-general, Béla Kovács, the deputies of the Smallholders party more and more openly opposed the Communists.

At first the communist cadres behaved with restraint. The tougher stand of the majority party seemed to take them by surprise. In Parliament they merely grumbled mildly for the time being. But behind the scenes they tried to alter the situation by a variety of intrigues. Fellow travelers and troublemakers pressed the interests of the Left. Efforts were made to expel deputies, thereby undermining the unity of the bourgeois parties and reducing their majority. When these tactics proved insufficient, the Communists resorted to force. In December 1946 representatives of the Smallholders party and army officers who had close relations with that party were arrested. When the premier and the defense minister attempted to look into the cases of the arrested men, the Russian commander, Sviridov, forbade any investigation. He declared, since the pretext for the arrests had been an antistate conspiracy, that the affair was solely a matter for the Secret Police. It was László Rajk who blocked the efforts of Premier Nagy to intervene. Meanwhile the "confessions" of the arrested men were noisily

* See Documents 47 and 48.

publicized. These so-called confessions alleged that an antistate conspiracy had been organized within the Smallholders party. Various leading members of the party, among them a cabinet minister, were then arrested. With the consent of Tildy and Ferenc Nagy, the immunity committee of Parliament stripped the arrested persons of their parliamentary immunity. When some American and West European newspapers and periodicals expressed doubts of the credibility of the confessions, Zoltán Tildy, the president of the Republic, was forced to confirm the police accounts. On January 16, 1947, Tildy publicly stated: "The police have done their duty and worked well. I am certain that a Hungarian court, acting in the interests of the Hungarian people, will come to a just verdict."

It was obvious that a show trial on the soviet pattern was being prepared. Tildy's easy compliance had horrified me. Three days after he made his statement, I spoke to the nation on the hatred prevalent throughout the country, on the spirit of revenge and punishment, on the ruthless application of the principle of an eye for an eye and a tooth for a tooth. I stressed that the result could only be the "putting out of innocent eyes and the breaking of teeth that do not bite." Meanwhile, basing their charges on the "confessions" already extracted, the Communists involved the secretary-general of the Smallholders party, Béla Kovács, in the "conspiracy." Rákosi paid a personal call on Premier Ferenc Nagy and handed him "proofs" implicating Kovács. Rákosi demanded the dismissal of the secretary-general and a public reprimand of the Smallholders party. Nagy yielded to the latter demand, and on January 28, 1947, he issued the following statement: "I must admit that a conspiracy against democracy and against the government was actually in progress. The conspirators created an extensive organization and infiltrated into the large political and social organizations, especially the Smallholders Party."

On the basis of this statement the Communist party shortly afterwards called for the lifting of immunity from an additional number of deputies of the Smallholders party. Ferenc Nagy also gave in to this demand, although with the hope, as he said, that the court would acquit the men. The Secret Police, under the personal supervision of Gábor Péter, placed handcuffs on the deputies right outside the gate of Parliament. Only Béla Kovács still retained immunity. With the courage of despair one member of the Smallholders party made a motion that a parliamentary committee consisting of twenty-five members should investigate the alleged conspiracy. Rákosi saw clearly that this would make the show trial impossible. He therefore had the motion removed from the agenda, claiming that the Russians insisted on this procedure. He even urged that Béla Kovács, while retaining his rights of immunity, should voluntarily report to the police so that he could be questioned about the conspiracy. When Kovács, on the advice of Tildy and Ferenc Nagy, did so, he was received not by the Hungarian police but by the Russian military authorities, who arrested him. On March 2 the following statement was published:

In Budapest on February 25, 1947, the Soviet Occupation Authority arrested Béla Kovács, the former secretary-general of the independent Smallholders party for complicity in the recruiting of secret anti-Soviet armed terrorist groups and collaboration in espionage against the Soviet army. Béla Kovács participated actively in the recruiting of such secret anti-Soviet armed troops, whose members committed terrorist acts on Hungarian soil and murders of members of the Soviet army.

At this point General Weems, the American member of the Allied Control Commission, intervened. On March 5, 1947, he handed a note to Soviet General Sviridov protesting "foreign intervention" in Hungarian internal affairs.* In his note General Weems also proposed that representatives of the three Great Powers should collaborate with the premier of Hungary, the president of Parliament, the minister of the interior, and the minister of justice in a joint investigation of the "conspiracy."

Publication of the American note in the Hungarian newspapers was forbidden. But Sviridov replied at length on March 9, charging the Americans in turn with interference in the internal affairs of Hungary.**

The "conspirators" were brought to trial before a people's court. The exhausted, intimidated, and evidently tortured defendants testified against themselves. On the basis of extorted confessions three innocent men were condemned to death, the rest to more than ten years at forced labor. Once more the Americans protested, but in vain.† Sviridov answered the second American note as cynically as he had the first.

Shortly afterwards, Ferenc Nagy restructured his government. He was forced to take two "fellow travelers" into his cabinet. In order to insure that a Communist would not be charged with carrying out an attack on the Catholic schools, Gyula Ortutay was appointed minister of education. Lajos Dinnyés filled the post of defense minister. Only two months later, however, Dinnyés succeeded Ferenc Nagy as premier. The Secret Police made the remarkable discovery that Premier Nagy himself had participated in a conspiracy against his own government. However, probably with the intention of avoiding a trial, he was not informed of this until he happened to be abroad. While he was on a lengthy vacation in Zurich, word reached him from Budapest on May 29, 1947, that he too—as it appeared from a communication of the Soviet commander-in-chief—had taken part in the conspiracy organized by Béla Kovács. That same day he talked on the telephone with Rákosi. After this conversation he resigned, and Dinnyés succeeded him on June 1, 1947.

After these events many leading members of the Smallholders party fled

* See Document 49.
** See Document 50.
† See Document 51.

the country. With the help of the Russians the Hungarian Marxists had succeeded in reducing the Smallholders in Parliament from 57.7 percent to 44.2 percent. Thus the Smallholders party had been deprived of its majority position.

☦ *Horse=trading on Religious Instruction*

THE PRETEXT of conspiracy enabled the police to arrest ordinary members as well as leaders of the Smallholders party. Week after week came new arrests. The incriminating "confessions" led in a chain reaction to further arrests. It was up to the Communists who remained at large and who was taken off to prison. Within two months everyone was numbed by fear. Resistance collapsed, and on March 11, 1947, the leaders of the Smallholders party came to an agreement with the Marxists. The main points of this agreement were:

1. Abolition of obligatory religious instruction and introduction of new textbooks in all schools.
2. Preparation of an agreement between Church and state in which all remaining questions would be settled.
3. The party leaders undertook to purge the party of all those who would hinder peaceful collaboration among the parties.
4. A planned economy was to be instituted and a three-year economic plan devised.

The two ecclesiastical leaders of the Smallholders party, Béla Varga and István Balogh, promised—probably after intense pressure from the Marxists—to bring the conference of bishops around to approving the first point. Bishop László Bánáss, a man who liked to push to the forefront, was asked his opinion. He said he thought the conference of bishops would be reasonable for the sake of the new democratic order of things. The follow-informed a party conference yesterday that the entire episcopate has accepted the introduction of optional religious instruction without opposition."

As soon as I heard about this I wrote to the president of Parliament to say that this was inaccurate, that in fact the conference of bishops had opposed the plan, not accepted it, and I asked him to make a public statement correcting the misstatement.

In our ranks there was only one unimportant group, the so-called progressive Catholics, who accepted the abolition of obligatory religious instruction in the schools. Now they also recommended an accommodation with the Communists for the sake of "peace." I recall how at this time the superior of an order visited me and repeated to me Béla Varga's arguments. He said it would be for the best of the entire country if the bishops in their entirety would consent to the government decision. He was much surprised when I explained to him the unanimous opinion of the bishops and told him:

The bishops may not surrender their lawfully assigned task of religious instruction. They are strengthened in their attitude by the clearly expressed will of the faithful and by repeated demonstrations of public opinion. The conference of bishops can only note with distaste that the question of education has been dragged into the arena of political struggle and has become an issue in the tug of war between the parties. Such discussions profit the Communists alone and bring their assumption of a dictatorship closer every day.

Meanwhile protest was gathering all over the country. Thousands of telegrams demanding the retention of obligatory religious education poured into the offices of Catholic Action every day. These were signed by Catholics and Protestants, priests and laymen, students and professors, Church associations and various social organizations. Quite often the protests were sent to my address with the request that they be passed on to the government. For example, from Szarvas, a predominantly Protestant town, I received a telegram declaring: "In regard to your official position on the church matters at issue the Evangelical Christians stand behind you as one man."

I took occasion, during the anniversary celebrations of the city of Győr, to condemn the irresponsible haggling over the religious and ethical education of youth. Speaking to sixty thousand persons, who encouraged me by hearty applause, I warned that "promising freedom of religion while creating institutions of irreligiousness" was the height of hypocrisy.* And on April 12, 1947, I issued a pastoral letter in the name of the conference of bishops. In this letter I carefully examined the communist arguments against obligatory religious instruction, pointed out the motives behind those arguments, and made clear the viewpoint of the Church, which is based on many centuries of experience.**

In the face of this opposition the leftist parties for the time being had to put aside the plan for optional religious instruction and uniform textbooks.

* See Document 52.
** See Document 53.

Two years passed before the law concerning obligatory religious instruction was rescinded. The Church's resistance had plainly shown how deeply rooted religion is in the souls of the Hungarian people. Rákosi realized that the Church had won, temporarily. Mendaciously, he now maintained that the Smallholders party—not at all the Communists—had concocted the plan. All the Communists wanted was "free" religious instruction, in keeping with the democratic principles of freedom of conscience. But as long as the Hungarian people were "bleeding from a hundred wounds, we should avoid raising such questions, since they might sow the seeds of fresh unrest and dissension." The secretary-general of the Communist party made this statement at the start of the campaign for new parliamentary elections. In the following section, which deals with the elections of 1947, the reader will be able to see how much cunning hypocrisy was concealed in this declaration.

☦ The Second Parliamentary Elections

AFTER THE DECIMATION of the Smallholders party, the Communists dominated Parliament. They were therefore able to push through a new electoral law on June 25, 1947. It was prepared and presented by the communist minister of the interior and amounted to a method for controlling the outcome of the elections to be held on August 31. The elections were arranged because the Communists wanted to give at least the semblance of legality to the power they had now achieved illegally. In this way they hoped that they would be able more quickly to institute communism on the Soviet pattern, which was their goal. The new electoral law required reissuance of lists of eligible voters. The communist minister of the interior "supervised" the new registry of voters and saw to the omission of vast numbers of citizens who could not be counted on to vote for Marxists. In this way nearly a million persons were disenfranchised. Among those affected were many priests, monks, and nuns. In addition, immediately before the call for elections the Freedom party was dissolved; during the winter and spring, when the crisis in the Smallholders party was in full swing, this Freedom party had been organized and consolidated with great success throughout the country. Enthusiastic masses everywhere joined it. The evidence was that it would win a victory of 60–65 percent in the new elections. Even the bishops, in consideration of public opinion, were inclined to recommend to their flocks support of the Freedom party. The popularity of this party was evidenced by 300,000-copy editions of its newspaper, *Holnap*. But one day, on instructions from the union, the printers refused to print it. This was a threat to the party's existence. Its chairman, Member of Parliament Dezső Sulyok, protested in vain. Although a wave of indignation ran through the country, the Communists demanded that Sulyok dissolve his party before the elections. Neither he nor the party leadership was prepared to bow. At this point the police intervened, as they had done in the case of the Small-holders party, and began arresting innocent people. Dezső Sulyok gave up the struggle; in order to avoid further mass arrests he disbanded the party. Once more the Communists had had their way.

Once this was done, the Communists cunningly arranged for six other opposition parties to participate in the elections in place of the Freedom party. Four of these had a more or less Christian program. The Russian commandant, in sharp contrast to his previous behavior, gave every peti-tioner permission to found a new party and to participate in the elections. I heard of cases in which individuals were requested to found a party even against their own will. Thus the Communists prepared the ground for splintering the votes of a numerically overwhelming opposition. But at the same time the Marxist parties, under pressure from the Communists, united and presented a single slate. Then, because they knew that the Marxist parties in spite of all these maneuvers still could not obtain an absolute majority, the Communists applied pressure to the Smallholders party to join this electoral union. The four government parties (Commu-nist, Social Democratic, National Peasant, and Smallholders) founded the Hungarian Independence Front. On July 30, 1947, they published a pro-gram promising religious freedom, rejecting foreign intervention in Hungary's internal affairs, and guaranteeing freedom and the inviolability of private property.*

Faced with this situation, the conference of bishops decided not to sup-port any party in the elections.**

Before election day the Communists first diminished their attacks on the Church and at last stopped them completely. To the surprise of the public, they even began to display a measure of benevolence toward the Church and religion. At their mass meetings and in their newspapers as well, they began emphasizing that in carrying out the land reform they had given land to a great many members of the clergy, that Communists who had gone out to the villages had helped with the rebuilding of many Church buildings, schools, churches, and rectories. In one village Rákosi, the secretary-general of the Communist party, told a mass meeting: "We are bringing back the

* See Document 54.
** See Document 55.

bells that were stolen by the Fascists; for the bell, by its ringing, is meant to summon the souls of the faithful to the praise of the Lord. I am happy that I personally have been able to help regain your bells." That same day a reporter took a photograph in another village showing Rákosi shaking hands with a Catholic parish priest. The picture was made into a postcard and sent all over the country. It was intended to symbolize the good relations between the Church and the Communist party.

We felt obliged to point out to the faithful the contradiction between the Communists' earlier actions and their present behavior, and the reasons for it. Our newspaper *Uj Ember* raised the question of whether this change in attitude was merely temporary and tactical. The Communist daily newspaper promptly responded: "There can be no question of tactics here, but rather of recognition of the fact that the churches and the people's democracy must find the way that leads to compromise, to mutual understanding, and to the building of a lasting good relationship."

In our weekly we answered this by listing the unsolved questions that cast a shadow on the relations between Church and state. We mentioned the harassment of the Catholic press. We had been given back only a fraction of our former press, and the paper quota for our two weekly papers was inadequate. We also pointed to the efforts to prevent processions. Our charitable organizations had been crippled and church leaders, institutions, and schools subject to constant attacks and slanders. We summed up our view: "The difference between the former and the present attitude is so great that most Catholic circles have concluded that the conduct displayed for several months past is merely a tactic."

In a good many of my speeches I alluded to this hypocritical good will and allowed more than a note of sarcasm to creep into my remarks. Speaking to the workers in Angyalföld, for example, I said:

The Savior warned us against those false prophets who come in sheep's clothing but are inwardly as ravening wolves. The hour of temptation has dawned, when the wolves change their costume. Only yesterday they rent and devoured the wicked lamb, but today they try to prove how kind and good they are by wearing the lambskin for camouflage. We do not need any wolf's hide, but we also need no lambskin under which wolves are hiding.

The Hungarian bishops were very soon to test the seeming change of heart. Gyula Czapik, the archbishop of Eger, acting for the conference of bishops, conducted informative conversations with representatives of the government. Pointing to the conciliatory attitude of the Communist party, he requested approval of a Catholic daily newspaper. The government representatives declared that within a week both the permit and a larger paper quota would be granted. But the bishops waited in vain for this promise to be kept. The Communists refused their consent. Meanwhile, the new registration lists were made public. It was at once clear to all what crude illegal acts had been involved in the drawing up of these lists. The people themselves, deprived as they were of their political rights, had no way of making their indignation heard. I therefore took it upon myself to protest these abuses in a letter to the premier.*

Sometimes, in order to deceive the faithful, priests were put up as candidates of the Marxist parties without their knowledge or consent. In order to deceive people in this election year, the government sent representatives to the great annual procession following the relic of St. Stephen's right hand. Even the Soviet ambassador offered his congratulations to the Hungarian nation on St. Stephen's Day. Then came August 31, the day of the election. Embittered as people were, many wanted to express their protest by boycotting the election. But in response to our appeal, a majority of the faithful voted after all, giving their votes to one or another of the opposition parties. We considered participation in the election an urgent necessity because there was no other way, in the political confusion, amid so much intrigue, to express the vital fact that the nation was not inclined to introduce communism voluntarily.

The new electoral law provided that voters who had registration cards issued by the proper authority could cast their votes even if they were away from their homes. This innovation played neatly into the plans of the Communists. Their partisans spent the day busily racing from place to place, casting their votes in different election districts. From early morning to late at night they drove about in groups of forty to fifty, disguised as vacationers on outings, carrying all necessary papers with them; they used government buses and factory trucks for these expeditions, and went from place to place to vote in specified election districts. But if any election board in a village or town raised objections, the Political Police promptly appeared on the scene and enforced this illegal multiplication of votes.

This sort of trickery, and the use of election registration cards forged within the ministry of the interior, brought the Communists fake votes by the thousands. In addition, representatives of the Political Police were present at the counts and tried to make sure that the final result met the expectations of the Communists. If because of the number of touring voters the number of votes did not correspond with the number of those registered in the district, the discrepancy was "corrected" by the exclusion and destruction of oppositional ballots.

When the result was published, the Communist party had received 22 percent of five million votes. The four government parties taken together had received 60 percent: Communists 22 percent, Social Democrats 14 percent, National Peasant party 9 percent, Smallholders party 15 percent. The opposition parties had managed to win 40 percent. The non-Marxist parties (if the Smallholders party is included in these) therefore still had

* See Document 56.

more than 55 percent of the total vote. But the Communist illegalities had stirred anger even among the parties of the government coalition. Throughout the country investigations were launched of electoral fraud and the abuses in voter registration. The leadership of the most important opposition party, the Hungarian Independence party, demanded that the election be declared invalid. The Communists thereupon accused the independents of having put up candidates on the basis of forged signatures in several election districts. This charge was likewise based on the new electoral law, which required candidates of new parties to submit a certain number of voter signatures. Five hundred men of the Secret Police were assigned to check the signatures on the petitions of the accused party. And sure enough, 11,000 forged signatures were "discovered." On the basis of this police report, the four government parties, on a communist motion, called upon the electoral court to void all the seats won by the Hungarian Independence party. This electoral court was also a "present" of the new election law. It was made up not of independent judges but of delegates from the parties in proportion to their representation in Parliament. Thus the four government parties held a 60 percent majority in this court also. No one was surprised, therefore, when the court largely granted the Communist motion and voided the seats of the deputies of the Hungarian Independence party, except for four.

Thus Parliament became a docile tool in the hands of the totalitarian Communists.*

☿ The Marian Year

On August 15, 1038, as he lay dying, King Stephen, the future saint, had dedicated the land of Hungary to the mother of our Lord. I had long regarded that act as a contract to which all of us were bound, and it was my urgent desire to strengthen the historic *regnum Marianum*. I frequently alluded to this in my sermons and pastoral letters; and I hailed the announcement by the country's bishops on August 14, 1947, appointing the Hungarian Marian Year.** The following day I inaugurated the Holy Year in Esztergom. All the bishops of Hungary and 60,000 pilgrims attended the

* A short survey of Hungarian history will provide the basis in historical events and explains my position. See Document 57.
** See Document 58.

ceremony. Two days later Czomgrád in Vác diocese held its Mary Day. I celebrated the pontifical Mass there, where no less than 70,000 persons from the villages of the Great Hungarian Plain assembled in a community of supplication and hope.

Then I went on to Szombathely. I arrived there on September 2 and participated in the two-day Marian congress. More than 100,000 persons assembled for the ceremonies here; and I addressed the huge crowd on matters concerning the education of the youth. I now encouraged the clergy to lead pilgrimages to places dedicated to Our Lady. There was a tremendous response. On August 18, 1947, the *Magyar Kurir* reported nearly 1.5 million pilgrims at the various sites. On September 8, 1947, on the festival of the birth of Mary, 1,768,000 persons were counted at these holy places; 1,112,000 took Holy Communion. On September 14 I accompanied 100,000 men from the capital on a pilgrimage to Máriaremete.* In Eger on September 20, 120,000 persons commended themselves to the protection of the mother of Jesus. Once again I admonished, comforted, and tried to encourage the faithful to courageously maintain their Christian bearing. Their hope and their readiness for sacrifice increased my own strength manyfold. Thus all of us, under the protection of Our Lady, daily grew more and more together into a community that indeed knew suffering but was nevertheless joyous in God.

The beginning of October brought the inspiring celebrations of the national Marian congress in Budapest. On October 4 I addressed 150,000 young people there, and that same evening 90,000 workers. No less than 250,000 of the faithful assembled on October 5. On the following day I addressed representatives of the 3,000 Catholic parishes. I told them: "Our times are very grave. . . . The Catholic parishes must be on the alert in such times of struggle. . . . We harm no one, and will not do so in the future. But if there be an attempt made to destroy justice and love, the foundations that sustain us, we then have the right of legitimate self-defense."

On the last day of the congress 200,000 Catholic parents met in the square in front of St. Stephen's basilica, impressively affirming the will of the people to seek refuge in the protection of the Madonna.**

These celebrations of Mary produced a torrent of blessings that resulted in a rich efflorescence of our religious life. The winter months did not lend themselves to mass demonstrations. But there was a great deal of praying in private and at the Marian year ceremonies in churches throughout the country. And when the weather improved in the spring, thousands of pilgrims poured out to the celebrations at various cities and sanctuaries. Whenever possible, I attended, preached, and celebrated holy Mass.

But the opposition was now beginning to speak out. Two days after the

* For brief extracts from sermons on these occasions, see Documents 59–62.

** For my joyful New Year message on these wonderful demonstrations of devotion to Mary, see Document 63.

celebration held in Törökszentmiklós on May 9, 1948, I had to send a protest note to the minister of religion and education. I pointed out that three rural meetings had been disturbed by violence, and demanded that such incidents be curbed. But in spite of the obstacles placed in our way, the masses of devout pilgrims grew ever larger. It was with profound joy in my heart that I said at Baja, addressing 150,000 of the faithful on June 12, 1948: "Never before have people so hungered and thirsted for the truth. Never before have so many come to the table of the Lord as today. We sense that the sacrament of the altar is the vitality of Hungary. Earthly bread can be taken from us, but the bread of the angels remains with us." In this holy year the Corpus Christi processions became a tremendous shout of prayer on the part of our whole country. No less than 2,356,000 persons took part in them. Finally, the tenth anniversary of the Budapest Eucharistic World Congress on May 30, 1948, united some 250,000 of the faithful. At that time Pope Pius XII addressed a radio message to us.

The Communists did not dare to prohibit these ceremonies, but they tried to interfere with them. The usual lowered fares for such public occasions were refused, and the number of trains deliberately reduced. Here and there we were not allowed to install public address systems. In some areas mass meetings and travel were banned on the pretext that there was danger of epidemics. Occasionally veterinary examinations of horses were staged on the same day as a pilgrimage in order to prevent the use of wagons and carriages. On June 13, 1948, the police actually broke up the Fatima procession in Budapest.

The following incident was characteristic of the situation. On September 12, 1948, the Benedictine Church of Celldömölk was to celebrate its two hundredth anniversary. Two days before, the government issued a notice that cases of epidemic encephalitis had occurred in various parts of the country. All travel from place to place was therefore forbidden. The people were outraged. The authorities repeated their ban, announcing however that worship inside the church would not be affected by the ordinance. On the day of the festival itself, armed police checked those attending church. All those whose papers showed they came from elsewhere were turned away. A police cordon encircled the church. During the services the fire department sprayed a yellow fluid around the vicinity of the monastery. When, at the end of the solemn ceremonies, the monks came out of the portal in procession, they too were sprayed with these "antiseptics."

Mary's banner was being carried through the hard-pressed land. Hungary's Great Lady watched over us. But her opponents did not mean to cede the field. They were forging their plans.

☩ *Nationalization of the Catholic Schools*

THE LAST STAGE in the struggle over the schools began with a coordinated onslaught in the press. All the charges that had long since been proved untenable were trotted out once more. Simultaneously, the Communist press loudly demanded an immediate remedy to existing abuses. The Church naturally tried to justify and defend itself. It answered the calumnies clearly and unequivocally. But its attempts at self-defense were termed hostility to the people. Both in Hungary and abroad the government authorities spread the word that the bishops were not willing to accept peaceful coexistence; that they would sit down to negotiate only under preconditions that could scarcely be met, whereas the republic was trying to find a suitable compromise.

After an extended bout of such propaganda, in April 1948 Minister of Religion and Education Gyula Ortutay came forth with a proposal for the nationalization of the Catholic schools. I gave our preliminary response in the pastoral letter of May 11. I noted that the fears I had expressed two years ago were now, unfortunately, being proved correct. I asked teachers and parents to stand by their Catholic schools, to stand behind the Church, and I thanked them all for their loyalty hitherto.

Nevertheless, at a press conference on May 15 Minister Ortutay declared that the government's decision was irrevocable. At the same time he announced that in the old as well as in the new government schools, religious instruction would remain an obligatory subject. Then he accused the ecclesiastical authorities of exerting terroristic pressure on the "progressive priests" and on the teachers. In my pastoral letter of May 23 * I pointed out that it was the government that terrorized its citizens. Teachers were being induced for "thirty pieces of silver" to violate their oaths. Believers were being forced to join the Communist party. Students who advocated the continuance of obligatory religious education were being arrested.

The government reacted at once to my pastoral letter. The employees of offices and factories were compelled, under threat of dismissal, to sign petitions supporting the government plan for secularization of the schools. And the rumor was spread that the bishops were not united on the question.

* See Document 64.

Radio and newspapers asserted that a number of priests resisted and refused to publish the pastoral letters; that priests who had tried to read them aloud had been interrupted by heckling shouts from the faithful; that the teachers would heartily welcome nationalization; and that negotiations with the Church had already been started. In a pastoral letter of May 29, 1948, the conference of bishops rebutted these assertions.* On that same day I sent two letters to Minister Ortutay denouncing the government campaign against our schools.**

On instructions from the Marxists, "local national committees" all over the country were supposed to send resolutions to the government demanding secularization of the church schools. These committees consisted almost entirely of members of the government coalition parties. Under the watchful eye of the Political Police they carried out their orders.

Naturally, once again all sorts of "stories" and rumors were collected and published in order to libel the clergy and their schools. One particularly ugly charge was published in the newspapers under the headline, "The Murder of Pócspetri." According to the testimony of eyewitnesses, what had happened was this:

At 8:00 P.M. on June 3, 1948, in the village of Pócspetri the political municipal council held a meeting to discuss the question of secularization. Since this was the eve of the first Friday of the month, the local priest had been hearing confessions during the afternoon. At seven o'clock in the evening he held his services, but without a sermon. After these services many members of the parish went to the town hall to hear what decisions would be taken. The police promptly appeared and demanded that the street be cleared. The people refused to leave. From minute to minute the excitement increased. Someone fetched the pastor so that he could calm the people. But before he could address the crowd, the police were surrounded. One of the police brandished the butt of his rifle. The crowd shrank back, the rifle butt hit the ground, and the weapon discharged. The policeman himself was fatally wounded.

Subsequently, the reports of the police and of the ministry of the interior maintained that the policeman had been the victim of an assault. The town clerk, Miklós Királyfalvy, was branded the killer; the priest was charged with incitement to murder. The clerk was later executed, the priest condemned to death and then pardoned.

After the events in Pócspetri, Minister Ortutay sent me a letter. He declared that the whole affair could be traced to the provocative sermon of the village priest. "The case of Pócspetri is a serious warning to the Church," he wrote. "I scarcely think that Roman Catholic bishops wish to assume the responsibility for further bloodshed. . . ." †

* See Document 65.
** See Document 66.
† For my reply to this letter on June 4, 1948, see Document 67.

Popular tension increased steadily. On June 7, 1948, the *Magyar Kurir* reported: "Millions of Hungarians are protesting secularization. . . . Catholic Action has transmitted to *Magyar Kurir* a list of the telegrams and letters of protests which are daily arriving in huge numbers at Catholic Action headquarters." The newspaper mentioned three hundred towns and villages from which protests had come. On June 10, another 257 were listed, and on June 13, 350 more localities. In addition, the paper published the texts of many strongly worded telegrams.

On June 14, 1948, the cabinet decided on secularization. On June 16, the bill was submitted to Parliament, declared urgent, and voted in the course of a single session, 230 votes in favor, 60 against, with 70 abstentions. For a correct reading of this vote, however, it must be realized that this Parliament had been elected in 1947 by the methods previously described.

The new law nationalized 4,885 schools, of which 3,148 belonged to the Catholic Church. We bishops protested, but, predictably, without the slightest success.

☿ *Agreement at Any Cost?*

THE ATTACK on the Catholic schools had unfavorable consequences for the Communists. People everywhere realized that such a law could have been passed only by a Parliament that had been hand-picked as the result of all kinds of electoral manipulation. Moreover, the Iron Curtain was not yet completely closed; foreign countries were still aware of what was going on in Hungary. We too, of course, took care that the Catholic press in the West obtained documentary evidence of what had really happened. It was still possible for me to receive many Western correspondents and to inform them in detail. Thus the world obtained a truthful view of the methods employed in Bolshevist persecution of the churches. Such information, together with dismay over the coup in Czechoslovakia that had just taken place, gave the anticommunist movement in the free world a tremendous impetus. That, in turn, prompted world communism to camouflage its assault on the churches. Since I kept pointing out the reality underneath the camouflage, both Hungarian and foreign Communists came to look upon me as one of their chief enemies, who had to be got out of the way. They realized that I would persist in the struggle, with God's help, even if it cost me my life. Immediately after the nationalization of the schools, therefore, plans were hatched to remove me from my post as head of the Hungarian Church. In fact, in the summer of 1948, I was told, a directive had gone out to the new minister of the interior, János Kádár.

From now on the attacks on me personally increased in frequency and intensity. Almost everywhere and at almost any hour of the day loudspeakers in streets, squares, and factories, speakers at mass meetings, and newspaper reporters repeated the refrain: "The hostile, antidemocratic attitude of the primate is the reason for the disunity and misery of our people. He is demanding the return of the confiscated estates, refuses to recognize the republic, is organizing counterrevolution, and is blocking a compromise between Church and state."

In reality the bishops were perfectly willing to discuss the various problems between Church and state. They desired a restoration of diplomatic relations with the Holy See, an agreement in regard to ecclesiastical clubs, associations, and newspapers. As things stood, the bishops even thought of accepting separation of Church and state, if in return the state would acknowledge the internal freedom of the Church, not interfere with it, and respect its administrative independence.

The Communists, however, were thinking of an agreement on the Soviet pattern. The bishops were to acknowledge the illegal position of power held by the Communist party, tamely surrender their schools and cultural institutions, and subordinate themselves to the interests of the communist state. By this time, however, we had become only too familiar with Bolshevist church policy and with the situation of the Church in the Soviet Union to allow ourselves to be hoodwinked. We knew about the methods used to destroy the Greek Rite Catholic Church in the annexed territories of the western Ukraine and in the sub-Carpathian region, which had once been part of historic Hungary.* I was well informed on the predicament into which the Church in the Soviet Union had been forced.

We ourselves had, therefore, no illusions, and gave little credence to the "good tidings" that spoke of a democratization of bolshevism. We therefore tried with all our might to deepen the religious life within our flock and to strengthen their Christian principles. We Hungarian bishops had no intention of entrusting Hungarian Catholicism to the mercies of an arrangement on the Soviet pattern. On the urging of the Communists we sent delegates, in February 1948, to preliminary conferences which were to prepare the way for actual negotiations. But we insisted on the following conditions as warrant of the seriousness and sincerity of the negotiations:

* See Document 68 for a summary of the struggle that had raged for a quarter of a century between bolshevism and the Church. The story of that struggle should help the reader understand the position that the Hungarian bishops took.

1. Establishment of diplomatic relations between the Holy See and Hungary.

2. Approval of the publication of a Christian daily newspaper, and distribution of the requisite quota of paper.

3. Restoration of the disbanded clubs and associations. Return of their confiscated buildings and funds.

4. Cessation of the Marxist parties' attacks on religion and the Church.

When Mátyás Rákosi was informed of these conditions, he himself appeared at the preliminary negotiations as the representative of the regime. The government, he told the bishops, would send an invitation to discussions at the appropriate time. But no invitation arrived. Instead the government set about organizing a movement, within the lower clergy and the youth, for the unification of state and Church. A great deal of energy and intrigue went into this movement, but it made no headway at all.

On April 26, 1948, I made a public statement to the effect that the Communists—in the newspapers, on the radio, in propaganda addressed particularly to the university students—spread the slogan that peace between Church and state must be restored at any cost.

Certainly no one has any objections to peace, if it is real peace. From the very start the Church has always regarded peace as desirable. But empty words and dubious signatures on petitions are not enough to attain it; serious intentions and practices are needed. There was no discussion at all of the Church's demands, as listed above, or of the abolition of censorship. The tactics already used for smashing our organizations were hardly evidence of a desire for peace.

Again, peace is not served by defamatory statements such as: "Most of the parochial schools are preparing a pitiless crackdown on the worker and peasant youth"; or "Let us drive out the reactionaries who are hiding under the cloak of the Church." It was even claimed that the Church was guilty of spiritual terrorism, when in fact it was merely the anguished witness of acts of terrorism. The constant slandering of the Pope was also not calculated to bring about peace. Instead of such calumnies the Hungarian people wanted to see acts—improvement of the general conditions of life; the elimination of corruption; an end to the harassment of the Hungarian population in Slovakia, which had been going on for three years; and the return of our fathers, sons, and brothers from Soviet imprisonment.

After an interval of three months—secularization of the schools had already been announced—the bishops on May 15, 1948, at last received the invitation to the abovementioned negotiations. On May 19 we informed the minister of religion and education that we were "in principle prepared for negotiations, and if the conditions for them are met, we will appoint our delegates without delay." But we demanded that secularization of the schools be dropped from the agenda.

Minister Ortutay waited until June 14 to reply. By that time the cabinet had already accepted the bill for secularization of the schools. In his letter the minister evaded meeting our conditions, calling them "essential matter" for the negotiations. But he also made a counterdemand. He expected the conference of bishops to issue a declaration similar to that made by the heads of the Protestant churches, wherein recognition of the Hungarian Republic was acknowledged even before the negotiations started. "The government of the Republic holds," he wrote in his letter, "that at the beginning of the negotiations no conditions can be directed at the state, but that recognition of the Hungarian Republic must be acknowledged first of all."

They had forced the desired declaration out of the Hungarian Reformed Church by removing all the legitimate heads of that Church from their offices (including Bishop László Ravasz) and replacing them with intimidated or status-seeking renegades. Even so, pressure had to be exerted upon these new men also before they could consent, on May 21, 1948, to the "agreement" between the Reformed Church and the Republic. But in the Catholic Church bishops could not be replaced simply by holding "new elections." Consequently, the government had no willing partners to sign an agreement. We therefore refused such recognition, which would have been tantamount to accepting the illegal power the Communist party had won by intrigue and violence. In taking this stand we were following the course of Pope Pius XI, who in 1922 had refused to grant diplomatic character to a Vatican mission dispatched to the Soviet Union, as the Soviet government had demanded. For that would have meant recognition.*

Later, by which time I was already imprisoned, an agreement was after all reached. It subjected the Church to supervision by the state.

IV. ARREST AND INTERROGATION

☩ *My Arrest*

THE ATTACKS on me and the slanders directed against me continued throughout the summer of 1948. In the autumn, as an immediate preliminary to my arrest, a new campaign was launched under the slogan: "We will annihilate Mindszentyism! The well-being of the Hungarian people

---

* For my formal reply to Ortutay, see Document 69.

and peace between Church and state depend on it." School children and the factory workers were ordered into the streets to demonstrate against me. Communist agents led the demonstrators to the episcopal palace and demanded that the bishops help remove me, "the obstinate and politically short-sighted" cardinal-primate from his position as head of the Church. The bishops rejected these demands. But disregarding their response, the newspapers reported that some of the bishops also condemned my "antidemocratic attitude of enmity toward the people." In my absence the bishops issued a statement stressing their identity of views with me.*

As had happened previously, before the secularization of the schools, armies of agents appeared in offices and factories to extract signatures to petitions demanding that I be removed from office and tried before a people's court. Village, town, and county governments, all of them under Communist direction, sent letters to the cabinet and Parliament declaring that it was the people's wish that I be punished. On November 18 I responded to this shameless falsification of public opinion in an appeal to the people in which I pointed out, among other things, that free elections had not taken place since the end of the Second World War, except in the capital.** I ended with a reminder that some of my predecessors in the office of primate had been martyrs, and added a word of forgiveness for my persecutors.

The edition of the *Magyar Kurir* that carried my appeal was confiscated. Parish priests were forbidden by the police to read it aloud. But the press reported, contrary to the truth, that the clergy had been unwilling to read it because they disagreed with me and would condemn my position.

On the morning of November 19, 1948, my secretary, Dr. András Zakar, was arrested in the street as he was about to return from holy Mass to the archiepiscopal palace. The police carried him off directly to the notorious No. 60 Andrássy Street. Preparations for my arrest were now rushed through. Collaborating and "progressive" Catholics were made to sign so-called open letters. To my sorrow I discovered that even Zoltán Kodály had been persuaded to sign with Gyula Skekfű and József Cavallier. Moreover, after the publication of their letter the three were sent to me in Esztergom. I received them on December 8 in the presence of my vicar-general, Dr. János Drahos.

As soon as they had entered, Kodály silently withdrew to the window niche at the farther end of the room. By that he meant me to understand that he had nothing to do with this sad spectacle. He was playing the role of an extra, and obviously not of his own free will.

József Cavallier, who between the two world wars had been associated with the Catholic newspaper *Új Nemzedék* ("New Generation"), acted as

* See Document 70.
** See Document 71.

spokesman of the three in explaining the motives that had brought them to Esztergom. As good Catholics, he said, they were not prepared to make common cause with the other signers who had been excommunicated by the Church because of the secularization of the schools. I wondered that this man, who had already been appointed Hungarian "ambassador to the Holy See" should have been so uninformed about canon law, and remarked: "Excommunication also follows for participating in an intrigue against a cardinal of the Catholic Church." Cavallier, the former journalist, now a puppet in the hands of the Communists, never actually took up his ambassadorial post, but I imagine he drew the salary.

After my barbed comment he said no more, but gave the floor to Gyula Szekfű, a Catholic historian and associate of Bálint Hómans, who was languishing in a Communist prison. During the Nazi period Szekfű had been driven farther to the left. Rákosi had managed to make him acceptable to the Russians as ambassador to Moscow. He published a small book glorifying the Soviet Union—to the detriment, in the world's eyes, of his scholarly reputation.

Szekfű now asserted that the future of Catholicism and of the nation demanded an honest recognition of the present power-relationships—in other words, acknowledgment of the dictatorship that the Communist party had attained by illegal means. Hungarian Catholicism need not scruple to take this view because communism was no longer an enemy of religion. Religious persecution had also ceased in the Soviet Union, and the Orthodox Church was serving the welfare of the people in happy concord with the atheistic state.

I replied that we knew perfectly well the kind of dependency the Orthodox Church was subjected to in spite of the loyalty it had shown during the war. We also knew, how the Soviet Union had used all the old methods of religious persecution to subjugate the Greek Rite Catholic Church in the western Ukraine and in the sub-Carpathian region. I also presented my arguments in regard to the Hungarian situation. That same December 8 I thought it wise to set down my views in writing and to publish my reply to the open letters.* In my answer I pointed out that archbishops and cardinals in other "people's democracies" were likewise being persecuted; that religious persecution had nothing to do with my personality or our Church, but with the nature of materialistic atheism.

After this I expected arrest. I therefore asked my seventy-four-year-old mother to come to Esztergom, thinking she might be able to bear the blow of my imprisonment more easily if she were near me at the time than if the news were brought to her in her distant home. I knew what it would cost her and was searching for some way of easing her pain. For that reason I had already discussed with her several times the threat of arrest that hung

* See Document 72.

over me. And I felt greatly reassured when she declared she would go the way of the cross in the footsteps of the *Mater dolorosa*. Perhaps she was hoping, as others among my relatives and friends were, that I would go abroad to escape arrest. But in the end she became accustomed to the idea that a shepherd may not abandon his flock.

In preparation for arrest I made my final arrangements. I issued orders on the succession in which, after my imprisonment, the three vicars-general appointed from the cathedral chapter should take over my duties. I declared that even in prison I would never voluntarily abdicate or make a "confession" of any kind of wrongdoing. If, subsequently, such a confession should nevertheless be produced, it would have to be regarded as either forged or the consequence of torture and the shattering of my personality. Having made this statement in November 1948, I hoped in this way to diminish the effects of any show trial and to unmask its directors.

I also arranged that my statement should be delivered both to the bishops and the cathedral chapter after my arrest.

In Esztergom, on December 16, we held the last conference of bishops with me in the chair. The police had for some time been posting informers along the route to my house, and my visitors had to identify themselves.

It was, therefore, with the feeling that we were being guarded almost like prisoners that we met for our episcopal conference. We published a joint declaration explaining why no concordat between Church and state had been arranged. I asked the bishops not to sign any such agreement after my arrest. I also recommended to them that they not accept the government subsidies that were to pay the salaries of the priests, and to trust that the Hungarian people would not leave its priests without a pittance. "We may be poor, but we must remain independent. In an atheistic state a church that is not independent can only play the part of a slave."

After a lunch, which my mother shared, the bishops left one after the other. When their cars started away, the police blocked the road. Each car was searched; the passengers had to identify themselves. Obviously the police thought the primate would be attempting to escape in one of these cars.

So I was already a prisoner.

About 1:30 P.M. on December 23, 1948, squads of policemen surrounded my house. They had driven up in a long column of cars under the command of Police Colonel Gyula Décsi. Without permission, in fact without a warrant, they forced their way into the archiepiscopal palace and conducted a search. When the director of my secretariat demanded to see their warrant, they alleged that this search was in connection with the case of my secretary, Dr. Zakar, who had already been in custody for more than a month. Nevertheless they took over the entire house; and in addition to Dr.

Zakar's room on the first floor, they went through the two upper floors, the ground floor and the entire basement. They rummaged through all the offices, the archives, the library, all my residential rooms. The search lasted five hours. During this period they locked me, together with my mother and three priests of the archiepiscopal curia, in one of the smaller dining rooms. There, in all stillness, we prayed, saying the rosary several times.

Why were they going to all this trouble? Why were they wasting so much time? Any documents they needed for their show trial were surely in their hands already. Possibly they wanted to give the impression that the subsequently famous cylinder was hard to find. This "mystical" object lingered in the memories of many persons as a mysterious piece of evidence, in the form of a photograph showing two priests of the curia standing beside a long metal container from the archives.

In the archiepiscopal archives on the second floor of the palace there were many such containers of various lengths and diameters. In these cylinders deeds to the archiepiscopal estates were preserved to protect them from dust and decay. Blueprints and photographs of buildings and rented estates were likewise kept in them. And, of course, there were also empty containers in stock for future use. After the search the police reported that in one such capsule, hidden in the basement, documents of the "conspiracy" had been found. They had brought my secretary, in a twilight state of semiconsciousness, into the palace with them, and they now maintained that his information had enabled them to discover the place where I had collected and hidden the dangerous papers.

This whole metal container episode was, of course, nothing but a diversionary maneuver. Months earlier the police had provided themselves with "documents of the conspiracy." We knew that by intimidation and blackmail the police had attempted to make spies of our secretariat assistants, our typists, and our couriers. The director of my secretariat discovered that one typist was providing the police with copies of documents she had typed. The handwriting expert László Sulner and his wife made it known after their flight to the West that several copies of the documents allegedly found in the metal cylinder had been given to them months before the search of the archiepiscopal palace. The Political Police had turned these documents over to them for "editing." Among the "found documents" were some that I had ordered destroyed in October because I did not want to involve others in my own impending misfortunes. I had long been expecting a search of the premises and had therefore given my secretary timely instructions to destroy all letters, notes, memoranda, and anything else that might prove awkward for the writers after my arrest. There is no reason to assume that my secretary did not carry out this order. I never ordered mere concealment of written matter.

At the end of the search I was asked to sign a record of it. I refused and protested, basing my protest on the international legal position of a cardinal in the Roman Catholic Church. I likewise protested the arrest of two priests of the archdiocese, Treasurer Imre Bóka and Archivist János Fábián.

After the police had left, Dr. Gyula Mátrai, the chief of the secretariat, reported that our arrested secretary András Zakar had in fact led the police through the house, and that he had shown them everything they wanted to see. But the strange thing was, Mátrai told us at supper, that throughout the "conducted tour" Zakar had laughed constantly. His face and his eyes had been utterly different from normal. The police officers treated him like a madman, and emphasized that Dr. Zakar was their particular friend, that they treated him very well, and that he had meat to eat twice a week. Zakar seemed to be having a very good time with them. He ran down the halls, which he had never done before. His ordinarily grave demeanor had changed to an entirely new manner, said Mátrai.

I was deeply distressed by this bizarre story, and during our meal and later in the solitude of the night, I could think of nothing but Dr. Zakar and the change in him. My poor secretary! He was only thirty-five years old, in the fullness of his strength; and now, after only five weeks in prison, his personality had been shattered. What had been a strong, resolute man was now a wreck.

But from the Communists' point of view the secretary was only an incidental figure. They meant to strike at the primate through him.

Prepared for the worst, I now donned my oldest, most threadbare cassock, put on the simplest of my episcopal rings, and chose the plainest chain with crucifix. My idea was that when they took me away they would be robbing the Church only of these less precious objects. I also prepared to take with me a picture sent me in November by a monk I did not know. It showed Christ with the crown of thorns and bore the inscription: *Devictus vincit* ("Defeated, he is victorious"). I thought I would take this picture with me to Secret Police headquarters on Andrássy Street, and keep it with me in prison if that were allowed. Actually I still had it at the time of my trial; and when in prison I was given permission to celebrate Mass, I chose this for my altar picture. It accompanied me later on in house arrest; and when the liberators came to free me in 1956, the first thing I did was to take this picture into my hands. In the American Embassy, too, I always celebrated holy Mass before this picture of Christ defeated and victorious. It is still my constant companion. The first half of the inscription, "defeated," has been the reality of my life; the hope of victory lies in the future, in God's hands.

Christmas Eve came. The day took its usual course. I said midnight Mass in grief and depression, heavier-hearted than I had been in 1944 in the Sopronkőhida prison. My mother was present. I did not know what sorrows she might be confronted with in the next few hours; perhaps my arrest and summary execution.

At five o'clock in the afternoon on December 26 I took a last walk in the garden with the head of my secretariat. Our wolfhound accompanied us. When we returned to the house, the dog came up as far as the first floor. In front of my room he rose on his hind legs and placed his forepaws and his head on my shoulders. He had never done that before, for I had not devoted much time to him. I remarked: "Perhaps this faithful dog senses that this has been my last walk in Esztergom."

On the eve of the feast of St. Stephen, the first martyr, in whose honor was built my titular church in Rome, Santo Stefano Rotondo, I was arrested. Once again an unusually large police squadron came to the house under the direction of Police Colonel Décsi. They drove into the yard and turned their whole column of cars around, ready for instant departure. They noisily tramped into the house and with thudding boots approached my apartment on the first floor. I was kneeling on the prie-dieu, praying and meditating. The door flew open. Décsi entered. In a state of high agitation he confronted me and declared: "We have come to arrest you." Eight or ten police officers thronged after him into the room. I was surrounded by them. When I demanded that they show the warrant for arrest, they bawled brashly: "We don't need anything like that." One of them added that the democratic police were alert and could find traitors, spies, and currency smugglers even when they wore a cardinal's robes.

There would have been no point to resistance. I took my winter coat and then my breviary. We left the room. More policemen were waiting in the hall. None of my officials was anywhere in the vicinity. Eighty policemen had occupied the building and kept my officials and staff away from me.

But my mother, who had heard the noise, came out of the guest room. She screamed. I turned to her to bid her good-bye. The police tried to prevent me. I broke through the ranks of them and went to my mother. She threw her arms around me. "Where are they taking you, my son? I am going with you!" I calmed her, kissed her hand and cheeks. She sobbed heartrendingly.

The police wrenched me away, dragged me down to the gate, and forced me into a big car with curtained windows. On my right sat Colonel Décsi, on my left a major. Beside the driver, and facing me, sat policemen with submachine guns. In this way I was taken from my archiepiscopal see and driven through the night to Budapest.

I tried to say the rosary. But I could not. I remembered the words of Scripture:

> He reached down from heaven, caught hold of me, rescued me from that flood, saved me from triumphant malice, from the enemies that held me at their mercy. Evil days, when they faced me at every turn! Yet the Lord stood by me. . . . (Psalms 17, 17–19)

> Your time has come now, and darkness has its will. (Luke 22, 53)

I want to set down here the words that, foreseeing what was to come, I had already spoken to my priests in farewell:

Always and everywhere, nothing can happen to us except what the Lord commands or permits. Not a sparrow falls without His knowledge. The world can take a great deal from us, but never our faith in Jesus Christ. Who can part us from Christ? Neither life nor death nor any created thing can separate us from the love of God. . . . We are not like those who have no hope and no faith. . . . Rather, we must now more than ever feel that we have become exemplars for the world, the angels, and men. . . . As long as we are able, let us strive for the Kingdom of Christ, a kingdom of justice and mercy. But on the way thither let us recall the words of Tertullian: "The accusations of certain accusers are our glory."

☦ In 60 Andrássy Street

THE COLUMN of police cars stopped in front of 60 Andrássy Street. I was ordered to get out of the car. Then I was led between two closely packed rows of policemen into the notorious building. Here Hungarians who had been taught their trade by Hitler's Gestapo had already created, during the period of the German occupation, a gruesome place of torture, a true center of terror. Even then passers-by who had business in the vicinity gave the building as wide a berth as possible, or turned their heads if they had to pass in front of it. Now the whole neighborhood was given its character by the movement of prisoners and police cars. The number of arrests was rising to a fearful extent, so that all the buildings in the neighborhood had been made into jails. I thought of the good Hungarians who in former days had been led by Turkish pashas across the bridge of Eszék into the misery of the Seven-Towered Fortress of Istanbul. In the same way, at the present time, so many were crossing a bridge of sighs into this Chekist inferno. I thought of the labyrinth of Minos, in whose depths destruction awaited prisoners.

Andrássy Street also had its bloodthirsty pashas. One of them was Lieutenant General Gábor Péter, the supreme master of the entire system of organized terror. I did not know Gábor Péter, but I was now to have the opportunity to become thoroughly acquainted with him. In his youth he had learned tailoring, and along with this had evidently learned how to appear quiet, well-mannered and tactful—or in other words, to present himself as quite human. He could be obliging and grant requests that his comrades rejected.

After these apprentice years he trained in the party school and was thoroughly prepared for his new occupation. This short man manifested a self-importance far beyond that of the other "Moscow aristocrats." Moreover he was, according to György Pálóci-Horváth, married to Jolanda Simon, who for a long time was Rákosi's private secretary. He served the regime successfully. The Russians probably knew this, and therefore placed him at the top of the regime's most notorious institution.

Toward me he tried dissimulation, endeavored to present his amiable side. With a great deal of emotion he told me about his poor mother, and how he used to split wood for her when he was a boy, so she could start the stove in their cold apartment. But Dezső Sulyok has sketched a truer picture of Gábor Péter:

> When in the winter of 1947 the National Assembly, in response to pressure from the Russians, revoked the immunity of those deputies who had been accused of a "conspiracy against the Republic," Gábor Péter personally appeared in Parliament. Slavering for his prey, he awaited the moment to fall upon the unfortunates who were leaving the Parliament building. With hate-filled, vengeful looks, he stood at the entrance of the building personally handcuffing these men who had been abandoned to his mercies. He was no longer the courageous tailor, but a sadistic beast hurling itself at its victims to destroy them.

After the Rajk trial Rákosi said of Péter: "He's done a pretty good job of work." Later, however, when pressed by Tito, Rákosi, like Pilate washing his hands, declared: "That gang of Gábor Péter's has to take the responsibility."

Gábor Péter's office was at 60 Andrássy Street. At night in his room he no doubt heard the screams of the tormented prisoners, their groans, their death rattles. He knew that defendants were beaten with clubs on their kidneys and genitals; that needles were driven under their fingernails and burning cigarettes used to singe their eyebrows; that special drugs were administered to turn them into nervous wrecks; that they were not allowed to fall asleep. He knew that all this was done to them to force them to make whatever confession the regime wanted of them.

But Andrássy Street was not the only place in which Hungarian patriots were tortured to death. The military-political department had several barracks and prisons. In Budapest alone there were many. The Russians had devised the system and introduced Hungarian torturers to their diabolic science. I have no doubt that behind the scenes the Russians directed many of the specific measures.

☿ *The First Night*

ANYONE WHO HAS not been interrogated or held captive in Andrássy Street cannot imagine the horrors that took place there. Even the policemen who were on duty in the building did not know about everything. Too many initiates might, in case of flight, reveal too much about the cruel reality. And those who were released from the dungeons (though that seldom happened) kept silent for obvious reasons. Among the people, however, stories of the horrors were told, which the government tried to offset by planting quite different stories. Thus an account in a book published in English (the author was Hungarian) reported that we were first taken to a hotel on Csokonai Street where we were well treated, wined and dined for two days, and only then brought to Andrássy Street. The author purported to have learned this from a police official who was stationed in Andrássy Street and later fled.

Now and then it did actually happen that if a prisoner showed "good behavior" and made a satisfactory confession he would be released to serve as an informer. In such cases the government would occasionally reward him with a meal in a hotel. But the regime also knew how to impose involuntary fasts. (I heard from Archbishop Grősz that during his imprisonment the guards "forgot" to feed him for a period of forty-eight hours.)

At any rate, I was taken directly to Andrássy Street. There I was led to a cold room on the ground floor, where a sizable crowd had gathered to watch my clothes being changed. The police major and a lame secret policeman grabbed me and pulled off my gown, while the bystanders bleated with laughter, and finally stripped me of my underwear. I was given a wide, particolored, Oriental clown's outfit. Several of the onlookers danced around me, and the major bellowed: "You dog, how long we have been waiting for this moment. A good thing we don't have to wait any longer." This stocky, paunchy officer boasted to me during one "treatment" that in the last twenty or twenty-five years he had seen the inside of a church only twice, and then very briefly. He could ingratiate himself like a cat, but his nature was that of a hyena. He had been nicknamed "Uncle Gyula." Those who had been given the "treatment" by him might have called him "Little Usakov." Incidently, we were quite often unsure about the real names of the officers and torturers, for false names and false insignia of rank were frequently used as camouflage.

When Maurice Thorez, secretary-general of the Communist party in France, was once ordered by the French police to undress during an interrogation, he began to protest and likewise objected to their addressing him with the familiar pronoun *tu*. But in this encounter with his Hungarian comrades, I saw at once that protest would be pointless. I remained silent, thinking that my fate was only that of so many martyrs and prisoners over the centuries. I remembered the cardinal-primate of England, John Fisher, who suffered in the prison of Henry VIII, and Pius VII in the hands of Napoleon, or Polish Cardinal Ledochowsky in the power of Bismarck. In the twentieth century I was sharing a fate similar to that of Cardinals Stephan Wyszynski, Alois Stepinac, and Archbishop Beran. It was my special cross to be an imprisoned cardinal in the land of the Virgin Mary. Thus there rose before my mind's eye the image of Pilate and his *"Ecce home!"*

In 60 Andrássy Street they took from me not only my breviary, my rosary, my *Imitatio Christi*, and my Marian medallion, but also my watch and the penal codebook. I had taken this last with me so that, lacking a lawyer, I could throw the appropriate articles into their faces and expose their injustices. For I fully realized that I would be dependent upon myself alone for my defense.

For a priest his clerical robes mean a great deal, especially in that kind of surroundings. Ever since becoming a priest, I have very rarely worn ordinary dress. Therefore I found it very painful when my cassock was taken from me. The cassock serves as a kind of bodyguard for a priest.

After I had been thus deprived of everything I had brought with me, I was taken to an upper story. A door off a narrow, low-ceilinged corridor led into a room that was about twelve by fifteen feet and fairly dark, although a window looked out on a courtyard. Instead of a bed there was only a battered couch. But there was no opportunity for sleep in any case, for in this building most of the activity went on at night. My cell, in which there were almost always several persons, was at first not aired at all, later twice a week for a short time. The jailers were afraid it would be possible to see into the cell from the opposite wing of the building, and thus someone over there could find out who was kept in the cell. The overseer of the cell, a former mason, stayed in the room almost continually. In the days after the First World War he had proved himself a stalwart Communist. In 1920 he had been sent to the penal camp of Zalaegerszeg, and he now wanted to take out on me, who had then been the parish priest of that town, what he had suffered. He had enrolled in Communist party courses, and like a graying professor talked ponderously about the superiority of materialist philosophy and the inadequacy of idealistic philosophical systems. (I met him once later on in the prison at Vác; by then he had become a major.) He had a number of youthful companions who kept up a steady stream of brash talk and filthy jokes. The youngest of these boasted that since he had stopped going to confession and church he always had money in his pocket for the "best" entertainment, by which he meant his visits to the brothel.

Outside the cell all was funereally quiet. Only now and again would screams from the torture chambers carry through the door of our room. It would have been about 11:00 P.M. that pounding footsteps rang in the corridor. I was taken to my first interrogation, in a room angling off one of the corridors. Behind the desk the "jurist" of bolshevism, Police Colonel Gyula Décsi, had taken his seat. Beside him sat five other police officers; at the typewriters were two female comrades, cigarettes in their mouths. All of them had an air of confidential intimacy and used first names with one another.

Gyula Décsi lit a cigarette also, and asked: "What is your name?"

I told him.

"Where and when were you born?"

I replied.

"What is your occupation, what were you before, when did you part ways with the Hungarian people, how did you become an enemy of our country?"

I replied: "I am a Catholic priest and served as chaplain in Felsőpáty, where I worked among the common people during the First World War. Afterwards I became a teacher of religion in Zalaegerszeg, later parish priest there. All my work has been solely for the sake of the Hungarian people. I have always tried to serve its welfare. Neither as bishop of Veszprém nor as cardinal-primate of Esztergom have I parted ways with the Hungarian people. To my knowledge I have committed no acts against the people."

Décsi: "If that were true you would not be here."

I: "Only one real reason is needed for a person to be brought here—that he is objectionable to the regime."

Décsi: "You are obstructing the progress of the Hungarian people."

I: "I have never, nowhere, attempted to hinder progress. But I haven't noticed any signs of progress. I regret that the actions of your regime stand in contradiction to your words."

Décsi: "You have tried to establish communications with the imperialists against the interests of your country. You wanted to persuade them to intervene in the internal affairs of Hungary and stir up a war."

I: "The regime itself forced me to attempt to communicate with American authorities. I did so only after I had repeatedly and vainly requested the Hungarian government to oppose infringements by the Soviet occupying power."

Décsi: "You provided the Americans with information about the Red Army."

I: "That is not even a falsehood. For example, when the levies of money and goods for the Red Army were collected twice in the same year in the counties of Komáron and Esztergom, I did inform the Americans. The vice-commissioner of the county complained to me about it. In the interests

of the suffering people I asked the American member of the Allied Control
Commission to do something about such abuses. At that time Hungary had
only an armistice with the United States. The country was considered one
of the occupied regions. The United States was one of the legal occupying
powers and had a seat on the Allied Control Commission. Any Hungarian
citizen could have appealed to them as I did. Your assertion that I was trying to incite the United States of America to make war on my country
makes no sense at all. When I wrote my letter, the United States was actually still in a state of war with Hungary. When I turned to the Americans,
it was only to ask them to use their influence in the Control Commission to
stop the frightful excesses of the other occupying power. That is what you
now call treason."

While I was talking, the minutes of the session were being prepared. But
they did not contain what I had actually said. I therefore refused my signature. At that point Décsi commented: "Remember this: The defendants
here have to make a confession in the form that *we* want." He waved his
hand, as if to say: "Teach him to confess his guilt!"

The major brought me back to the cell. It was about three o'clock in the
morning. Two guards pushed the table away from the middle of the room.
The major shouted at me to undress. I did not obey. He beckoned to his assistants. Together with them, he pulled off my clown's jacket and trousers.
Then they went out and searched feverishly around the corridor. Suddenly
a massively built lieutenant entered. "I was a partisan," he said. His language was Hungarian, but not his savage, hate-filled face. I turned away; he
drew back, but suddenly came charging at me and kicked me with all his
might. Both of us fell against the wall. Laughing diabolically, he exclaimed:
"This is the happiest moment in my life." The words were unnecessary; I
could read his feelings in his distorted, sadistic features.

The major returned and the partisan was sent out again. The major
produced a rubber truncheon, forced me to the floor, and began beating
me, first only on the soles of my feet, but then raining blows on my whole
body. In the corridor and in the adjacent rooms raucous laughing of sadistic
delight accompanied the blows. The men and women who had been at the
interrogation were apparently nearby, and probably Gábor Péter was
among them. The major was soon breathing heavily, but he did not slacken
his blows. In spite of his exertions the beating obviously gave him sheer
pleasure.

I clenched my teeth, but did not succeed in remaining wholly mute. And
so I whimpered softly from pain. Then I lost consciousness, and came to
only after water had been splashed on me. I was then lifted and laid on the
couch. How long this ordeal lasted, I cannot say. My watch had been taken
away, and if I had had one, I would scarcely have been able to read the
numerals. I thought about the fate and feelings of innumerable honest Hungarian girls, nuns, and mothers who had been raped. Within them, too, a

world must have collapsed. I recalled the noble figure of Baron Vilmos
Apor, the bishop of Győr. I would gladly have changed places with him.
The psalms I had prayed in the breviary for so many years came to my lips:

"Now it was my turn to reel under fortune's blows . . . Gleeful they met, and
plotted to attack me unawares; tore at me without ceasing, baited and mocked me,
gnashing their teeth in hatred. (Psalms 34, 16–16)

"(I might) as well lie among the dead, men laid low in the grave, men thou
rememberest no longer, cast away, now, from thy protecting hand. Such is the
place where thou hast laid me, in a deep pit where the dark waters swirl; heavily thy
anger weighs me down, and thou dost overwhelm me with its full flood. Thou hast
estranged all my acquaintance from me, so that they treat me as a thing accursed; I
lie in a prison where there is no escape, my eyes grow dim with tears. On thee I
call, to thee stretch out my hands, each day that passes. (Psalms 87, 6–10)

Then I was dressed and taken back to interrogation. Once more my signature was demanded. I refused it again, saying: "That is not my confession."
    Furious, Décsi ordered: "Take him back." And once more I was beaten.
For the third time they demanded my signature—without success. For the
third time they tried to thrash it out of me with the rubber truncheon,
wielded with undiminished force, to the accompaniment of yammering
laughter from the spectators. Then they again demanded that I sign. I
replied again: "As soon as I am shown a record that contains only what I really said, I will do as you ask." And once more I was told: "Here the police
decide what is confessed, not the defendant."
    Meanwhile a great deal of time had passed, and day was breaking. The
interrogators also seemed exhausted. For this night I was brought back to
the cell.

☦ The First Day

THE MAJOR in person led me back from the interrogation room to the cell in
which, aside from myself, the five-man squad of guards—the mason and his
four fellows—stood about in the thick tobacco smoke and evil-smelling,
stale air. I stretched out in my striped clown's outfit on the couch, but
could not fall asleep. The others went on talking about me in the most obscene terms; I tried not to hear them, but to think back on the frightful

The cardinal's birthplace in Mindszent, a village in Vas County to which his ancestors had immigrated four centuries before.

Formal portrait of the cardinal's family taken on the occasion of his parents' golden wedding anniversary in 1941. In the middle row, from left to right: his two sisters Anna and Thérèse, his mother, his father, himself.

The cardinal's mother and two sisters: a photograph taken while he was in prison and successfully smuggled into him.

Veszprém. Mindszenty became bishop of Veszprém in 1944.

Esztergom as seen from the Danube. The city was the original capital of King Stephen's domain; it is also the primatial see of Hungary.

Baron Vilmos Apor, bishop of Győr.

Lajos Shvoy, bishop of Székesfehérvár.

Chrysostom Kelemen, chief abbot of the monastery at Pannonhalma. Apor, Shvoy, and Mindszenty joined Kelemen in signing the letter of protest against the persecutions of the Jews. The document was submitted to the Arrow Cross government.

Jusztinian Cardinal Serédi, Mindszenty's predecessor as primate of Hungary.

Count János Mikes, bishop of Szombathely.

Mindszenty in 1946, the year in which Pope Pius XII created him a cardinal.

(LEFT) Mindszenty in 1924, the year in which Bishop Mikes appointed him titular abbot of Pornó; the appointment was in recognition of Mindszenty's extraordinary service to the Church.

German soldiers marching past fallen Red Army men, January 1945. (*Süddeutscher Verlag, Bilderdienst, München.*)

The Russian army advancing.

Battered Budapest. (*Süddeutscher Verlag, Bilderdienst, München.*)

Trainload of people heading out into the countryside in search of food. (*Süddeutscher Verlag, Bilderdienst, München.*)

The May 1 demonstration in 1945. The banner hails agrarian reform. The new rulers used such pictures as this one to create the impression that the majority of the Hungarian people were strongly opposed to the views of Cardinal Mindszenty. (*Ullstein Bilderdienst, Berlin.*)

Parade in Budapest on the occasion of the fusion of the Communist and Social Democratic parties in 1948. Secularization of the schools soon followed. (*Ullstein Bilderdienst, Berlin.*)

(LEFT) Matyas Rákosi addressing demonstrators in Budapest on May 1, 1945. (*Ullstein Bilderdienst, Berlin*)

Cardinal Mindszenty during the cross-examination at his three-day trial in 1949. (*Associated Press, Frankfurt/ M.*)

(LEFT) Cardinal Mindszenty during an outdoor Mass, 1948. (*Religious News Service Photo.*)

Cardinal Mindszenty in the prisoner's dock at his trial before the Budapest People's Court, February 3, 1949. (*Deutsche Presse Agentur, Frankfurt/M.—Berlin.*)

Abbaye Grande Trappe (Orne)   Fr. Marie Bernard, sculp.

TU SERAS AVEC MOI
DANS LE PARADIS.

Luc XXIII. 43.

Devictus vincit...
November, 1948.

This picture of Christ, bearing the words *devictus vincit* ("once overwhelmed himself, he now overcomes all"), Cardinal Mindszenty put in his pocket the day he was arrested. It proved to be a source of continuous consolation through the years of his imprisonment and later through the years of his asylum in the American Embassy.

Cardinal Mindszenty listens to co-defendant Juzstin Baranyay reading a statement; Baranyay was charged with attempting to found a pro-monarchist government. (*Associated Press, Frankfurt/M.*)

Cardinal Mindszenty consulting with the state-appointed defense counsel, Kálmán Kiczko. (*Religious News Service Photo.*)

Having been pronounced guilty as charged, Cardinal Mindszenty is led off to prison. (*Deutsche Presse Agentur, Frankfurt/M.—Berlin.*)

Yielding to government pressure, the Catholic bishops of Hungary take the loyalty oath on July 22, 1951. Archbishop Gyula Czapik, who became chairman of the conference of bishops after the arrests of Cardinal Mindszenty and Archbishop Grősz, reads a statement for journalists after taking the oath of loyalty. (*International News Photos, London.*)

night now behind me. There was a small gladness in the thought that at least this first night they had not succeeded in making me sign their record with its innumerable lies and distortions.

At eight o'clock they brought water for washing, and they themselves stripped to the skin and washed in front of me. I took care of my morning ablutions in my harlequin's suit. When I was finished, they ordered me to carry out the wash water. One of the men went with me, while the room chief and the others shouted after me, their yammering mockery echoing down the corridor.

Then they came with breakfast and insisted that I eat it all. But I took only a little, to moisten my dry, cracked lips. Several times more they urged me to eat, but finally carried the tray out when they saw that I did not touch it. The smoking went on, likewise the obscene conversation directed at me, this time under the leadership of another rough fellow. The major of the rubber truncheon also looked in, apparently to make sure I would not forget him. Later, when sleep overpowered some of the guards, the room became quiet. I too continued to think quietly and to meditate. There are many things I can meditate on.

Ill-wishers that grudge me life itself lay snares about me, threaten me with ruin; relentlessly their malaice plots against me. And I, all the while, am deaf to their threats, dumb before my accusers; mine the unheeding ear, and the tongue that utters no defence. On thee, Lord, my hopes are set; thou, O Lord my God, wilt listen to me. Such is the prayer I make, Do not let my enemies triumph over me, boast of my downfall. Fall full well I may; misery clouds my view; I am ever ready to publish my guilt, ever anxious over my sin. Unprovoked, their malice still prevails; so many that bear me a grudge so wantonly, rewarding good with evil, and for the very rightness of my cause assailing me. (Psalms 37, 13–21)

It occurred to me that Rákosi would ask for and receive a report on the past night, that from this report possibly a telegram to Stalin would be drawn up. I imagined how feverishly the ministry of the interior under Kádár was working, and what vigorous activity there must be in the ministry of justice under István Riesz, and how Gábor Péter and his henchmen would be given additional powers and encouragement to use them against me. Red totalitarianism was venting its fury on me. I was being made to feel in my soul, my body, my nerves, and my bones the power of bolshevism which is now taking over the country.

This was going to be a show trial that the world would watch with fascination. Therefore there could not possibly be any halfway measures, any sparing of the victim. I would have to go this route to the end, and so too would they.

Toward noon I was asked what I wanted for lunch. I answered curtly that I was not interested. As if they were acting in the theater, they repeated again and again that for me the meal would be brought from a restaurant. I did not believe that, of course. On the contrary, I had no doubt that the food was prepared in Andrássy Street and that stupefying drugs would be mixed with it to numb the will. I had previously heard how strong men were broken in this place. It was public knowledge that two sorts of drugs were employed. One loosened the prisoner's tongue; the other made him totally apathetic. Aware of this, and filled with intense suspicion, at the beginning I hardly took any of the food that was placed before me.

My first meal consisted of soup, meat, and vegetables. I took very little, since after my treatment the previous night I was convinced that I was being prepared for the interrogations and the subsequent show trial. My suspicion became a certainty when, unannounced and unexpected, three doctors appeared. After lunch they entered my room and without introducing themselves and without asking me or the guards any questions they began to examine me. They felt my thyroid gland, for which I had previously had surgery, examined my eyes, listened to my heart and lungs, took my pulse and blood pressure. A rather earnest man of between fifty-five and sixty directed the examination; the two younger men, around thirty-five, respectfully and attentively followed his instructions.

The doctors left medicines, and at the following meals the guards gave me the prescribed doses. There is hardly any doubt that the guards were supposed to make sure I took the tablets. But whenever I had the chance I destroyed them. Most of the time I crushed them between my fingers and disposed of the powder in the leftover food. At other times, when the guard was standing close by me, I took the tablet, but with so little water that I was able to press the dry tablet against my palate. Afterwards I spat it out unobserved. If the remains of the food had already been taken out, I hid it in my shoes.

After a while, of course, hunger forced me to eat something, and so they finally succeeded in mixing the drugs into the food I was given. I concluded that because the doctors, always the team of three, came to see me every day either at mealtimes or immediately after. There were, however, some days on which I was examined again between meals. They did not speak to me at all, asked me no questions, and gave me no information. But from their conduct and their presence I concluded that in addition to the effects of the drugs, they were supposed to determine whether I could endure the beatings, how far they could go with their physical torture, whether my heart would give out. They had to balance the dosage of the drugs and the physical and psychological torture in such a way that they could bring me to the show trial and expose me without its making a bad impression. The goiter operation, which had impaired my heart, must have particularly concerned them.

After the three doctors left I stretched out on the couch again, but I still could not fall asleep. In any case, the noise around me had resumed. Nevertheless, I closed my eyes for a few minutes and dozed off. Almost at once the room commandant was at my side, waking me up. Not being allowed to sleep is in itself a mode of torture, and was part of the diabolical technique by which a defendant's willpower was broken. In my case the guards had strict instructions not to let the prisoner rest or sleep.

The afternoon in that evil-smelling atmosphere passed with agonizing slowness. With my fingers I tried to pray the rosary. When they noticed that I might be praying, the mason began speaking in even filthier terms than before. He basked in his own disrespect and the bleating laughter of the young men. Their rudeness and depravity cut me to the quick. What will become of Hungarian youth if communism can infect them as it wishes? I thought. What a disaster that would be for the nation. For just now, when so dark a future seemed in the offing, the nation would need spiritually strong, heroic young people. The same dark and godless power that was robbing the land of its independence and thrusting the nation into slavery was also corrupting and destroying our young people, so that no one would make the effort to save our country and Christianity. In the time of the Turks there were selfless, heroic guardians of the frontiers. But would young people ruined by bolshevism be willing and ready to undertake the necessary efforts? The picture of a mournful future entered into my soul. I told the rosary on my fingers and implored the Virgin Mary, Hungary's patroness, to spare Christian Hungary this terrible fate.

It would have been well if I could also have become absorbed in my breviary, but it had been taken from me. I began to go through the prayers for the canonical hours from memory. I recited the psalms and meditated on the meaning of Christmas. The martyrdom of the first Saint Stephen and the life of the holy apostle John offered me ample material for meditation.

Toward evening I was asked what I wanted for supper. As at noon, I replied that I was not interested. Once again I was told that the meal would be fetched for me from a restaurant. At six o'clock a bowl of vegetables with a pair of sausages was brought to me. I ate only a little, which did not satisfy them. I also destroyed the medicine before the doctors arrived. As at noon, they went through their examination without a word.

Afterwards, things were quiet in the cell until the beginning of the interrogation.

☼ Charge—Evidence— Refutation

ONCE AGAIN the interrogation began at eleven o'clock at night. I was taken to the same room as the previous night and was with the same persons.

Colonel Décsi looked me over carefully. Then, in a dry, colorless voice he read a prepared statement. It contained, in verbose elaboration, my so-called "confessions," the individual items of which were as follows:

1. My protest to Premier Zoltán Tildy against the founding of the Republic.
2. My contacts with and meeting with Otto von Habsburg in the United States in the summer of 1947.
3. Drawing up a cabinet list for the future kingdom of Hungary.
4. Initiating contacts with the American Embassy in Budapest in order to stir up a Third World War.
5. Preventing the Crown of St. Stephen from being brought home to Hungary because I meant to use it to crown Otto von Habsburg when the proper time came.

Midnight was past before Décsi had finished his reading. He requested me to sign this statement. I said I would not:

"The text is full of falsehoods and misinterpretations. I know nothing about a conspiracy and an organized attempt to overthrow the government, nothing about a coup or seditious activity in the army, which alone would make a coup possible. The fact that I am being held here in Andrássy Street, as well as the events of last night, indicate that there is no evidence for these charges. If you had evidence, my secretary, András Zakar, Professor Jusztin Baranyay, and myself would be immediately transferred to the prosecutor's jail. Neither prefabricated statements nor kicks and blows would then be needed to force the defendants to confess. The rubber truncheon would be superfluous. You would not have to extort a confession from us by torture, because the police would be able to make public facts proved beyond the possibility of denial by documents. 'Confessions' that are extracted from beaten, half-dead prisoners prove nothing whatsoever. The authorities pretend that they have to protect the security of the state. But their real aim is to drive someone from a high position merely because this person justifiably criticized the methods and the despotism of the Communists."

Décsi did not allow me to continue. He beckoned to the major. I was taken back to the cell and had to undress again, for the rubber truncheon to resume its work. As on the preceding night, the mocking laughter of the guards inspired the torturer to aim fierce blows at especially sensitive spots. I collapsed. When I picked myself up after the beating, and put on my underclothes and that harlequin's costume, I was again brought before Décsi. Cursing, he once more demanded my signature, and once more I replied that I was prepared to sign a statement that really contained what I had said. This time I succeeded in making the following points, which of course I was not permitted to speak all in one breath. I am not quoting word for word, but summarizing what I then said:

"It is true that I warned against the proposed law making our country a republic. It was my right and my duty to do so. Any ordinary citizen would have been permitted to do the same; the Constitution guaranteed him that freedom. Even today anyone, assuming that we live under a democratic government, is legally entitled to found a party that aims at restoring the monarchy.

"Otto von Habsburg once asked György Pallavicini to transmit his greetings, and asked me through Cardinal van Roey whether he could meet me in Rome. I accepted the greetings but refused to meet with him. Any fair-minded person would find it ridiculous that organs of the security apparatus should try to construct an antirepublican plot on such flimsy grounds.

"In 1947, after the Marian congress in Ottawa, I in fact received Otto von Habsburg, as can be seen from your own prepared statement. I did so at his, not my request, in Chicago. If my traveling to the congress in Ottawa was really for the purpose you assert, and if my real business had been to plot the destruction of the republic, it is very strange that I saw Otto just once during the twenty-six days I spent in America, and then only for a half-hour audience. Your conjecture is correct that I spoke with him about the sad predicament of the country and the problem of the Church. I did so because I knew that he has good connections with important persons in public and ecclesiastical life in America. I therefore asked him to help us in obtaining and transporting charitable gifts from America. I was glad when he did promise his help and told me that Americans had great respect for Hungarian Christians and that Hungarian Catholicism could count on support from Catholic Americans.

"The statement you have presented to me mentions a written commission from me to Otto von Habsburg. Cardinal Spellman, the archbishop of New York, who is very well disposed toward us, asked me to prepare such a commission for Otto von Habsburg. The cardinal, like many others, feared that sooner or later I might be arrested. In that case he wanted some well-known and well-informed personage to be authorized as the spokesman for persecuted Hungarians in my stead. My own reason for executing that written commission was solely concern that the collection and sending of

American gifts would be safely under the direction of a well-known personage of unchallenged probity.

"Again, I have not drawn up any 'cabinet list.' The truth behind that charge is that I asked Professor Baranyay to give me a list of those patriotic men who were formerly active in public and political life and who were now, after the great purges, living in freedom. Professor Baranyay also prepared a study for me on the primate's constitutional position. In the letter accompanying it he mentioned that in a perplexing and dangerous national predicament, which he called a 'legal vacuum,' the primate is obligated to play the part of a political arbitrator. Possibly he was thinking of an international conflict, but certainly not of any attempt to persuade the United States to make war on Hungary. I have already stated my opinion on that matter during the interrogation last night.

"Your record of my interrogation refers to documents allegedly found in a metal container in the basement of the archiepiscopal palace. I must tell you that I learned of the existence of this container for the first time during the search of the palace in Esztergom, and now it is mentioned again. I believe that this container and its contents represent about the same sort of evidence as the guns and cartridges allegedly discovered in Catholic schools.

"As for the charges concerning the Holy Crown, I should like to make the following statement: From my letters—which have evidently been in the hands of the police for some time—it is apparent that I wished to bring Hungary's most precious ecclesiastical and national relic to Rome in order to have it in a safe place, during a difficult period of tribulations and vicissitudes. For I had heard of a plan to use the crown for archeological research. That is why I wanted to return it to Rome, whence we received it a thousand years ago. I wanted it entrusted to the care of Pius XII, who is a great friend of Hungary."

At this point Décsi roared at me that he had already told me the police did not want to hear such rot, but a confession that answered their questions. This was followed by the well rehearsed ritual: refusal of my signature, return to the cell, a beating, and at dawn another brief interview in the interrogation room. Once again Décsi cursed and demanded. This second night, too, he had no success to record.

☧ The Daily Grind

At last I was brought back to the smoke-filled unventilated room. Utterly exhausted, I lay down on the battered couch and turned toward the wall.

Then I noticed a small glass of wine on the stand. So even in this place of horror there was still a humane person who considered what a blessing Holy Mass is for a priest in such a situation. I took a small piece of the bread I was brought for breakfast and concealed it. When the guards left me alone for a moment, I poured half of the wine into my water glass, spoke the words of consecration over the bread and wine, and communicated. In this way I was able to celebrate Mass twice. Thereafter no more wine was put out for me. On the third morning the "partisan" reappeared. He searched the entire room and carried off the wine and water glass. Obviously they were counting on being able to bargain with me on this matter. But during the thirty-nine days I spent in that room I took care to make no requests, for I was certain that in "gratitude" my signature would be expected.

The routine remained unchanged. I had not slept for forty-eight hours. If I ever did close my eyes, one of the guards would immediately come over to shake me awake. In the afternoon Colonel Décsi appeared and "complained" that I was so hostile to him. After all, he said, my case was almost entirely in his hands. I replied that I wanted no exceptional treatment, but that I insisted on procedures in accordance with the penal code. According to the penal code I had the right to a lawyer during interrogation, and I had already appointed Dr. József Gróh, the attorney for the diocese to conduct my defense. Moreover, only the state prosecutor could indict me, and his indictment had to be based on evidence as required by law, not on mere suspicion. If such evidence was lacking—as it was in my case—the defendant had to be released. If I were going to be held any longer, I wanted to be transferred at once to the regular state prosecutor's prison.

Décsi merely shrugged and started to turn away. I remarked that Gábor Péter would be informed of the situation. He made no objection; in fact, he ordered two guards to take me at once to Gábor Péter's office, which was on the ground floor. With my whole body bruised from the beatings, I found climbing the stairs difficult. A policeman opened the door. The master of Andrássy Street sat at a desk in a spacious, well-furnished office. He scrutinized me and then invited me to sit down opposite him. In a pleasant voice he asked: "How are you? How do you feel?"

I replied: "Exactly the way anyone would feel in this place of yours."

Péter: "You are very unfriendly to us and show no spirit of compromise in your conduct."

I: "Everywhere in Hungary nowadays lip-service is paid to the rights and liberties of the citizen. But under your aegis not much is said about that. Here the defendant is kicked and beaten, is deprived of sleep, is forced to take drugs, is ordered to sign statements prepared before the interrogation. The examiners stress that the confession must correspond to the wishes of the authorities, not to reality. Permission to have a defending lawyer present is not granted. Minister Béla Kovács at least was allowed to have Dr. Zoltán Pfeiffer, then state secretary in the ministry of justice, accompany him."

Gábor Péter looked sharply at me and said threateningly: "You will learn a great deal more if you go on being so obstinate."

I stood up and left his room.

Years have passed since this scene, and at present I sometimes think that Décsi and Péter may have regarded my wish to see the chief of the Secret Police as signifying that my judgment was already breaking down. The request might be interpreted as illogical and contrary to my conduct and character, since I should have told myself that Péter had ordered all the measures being taken against me. In reality, what motivated me to see Gábor Péter was something akin to boredom, the desire for change, a certain weariness with the monotony of the interrogation ritual as it had been practiced up to this point. He and Gyula Décsi were of course annoyed by my continued resistance. Nevertheless, the following day Minister of the Interior János Kádár issued a press release stating that the evidence had persuaded me to confess to conspiracy, espionage, and also to currency speculation in foreign exchange, and that I had then collapsed.

At one of the next interrogations I took up the matter of this release and pointed out that the newspapers were publishing lies about me. Décsi correctly guessed that I knew of this because the guards had been reading their newspaper carelessly, so that I was able to see some of it. Thereafter the guards were forbidden to read any newspapers in my presence.

Torture can bring about the collapse of any prisoner after a few days. Two weeks passed before I was brought to the point of signing the minutes of an interrogation, and this one contained no confession of guilt in the sense of the indictment, and no acknowledgement of and no expression of gratitude for the regime. Even after thirty-nine days of imprisonment my tormentors did not obtain any such document from me. But then I must say that physical torture was applied to me much more restrainedly and circumspectly than in the case of many other prisoners. Their primary aim was to break me psychologically because I had to play my predetermined role in the show trial. My adversaries did not consider the illogical aspect of the matter—that everyone would have to ask himself why I was kept for more than a month in Andrássy Street if in the face of the "incriminating evidence" I had already made my "confession of guilt" only two days after I was arrested.

When darkness fell, my supper was brought in a bowl, but I would eat hardly any of it. I merely broke a piece off the bread and chewed on that. The very sight of the food made me wonder what kind of narcotic or will-enfeebling drug might be in the food. If I became aware of any odd, suspicious smell, I did not touch the soup or vegetables at all. Later, too, I ate only soups that were clear and transparent, with nothing suspicious floating on the surface. But sometimes in my anxiety I even passed up the meat broth, which otherwise I would eat. As I now recall my state of mind, so many years later, I cannot forbear to smile at my naïveté. For in Andrássy Street the broth was, of course, no less dangerous than any other soup or any other food that was offered to me.

Seventy-two hours without sleep had passed when I was taken to the fourth nocturnal interrogation. The scene and the participants were the same. Once more I was charged with conspiracy and espionage. The idea was to pound the charges into the prisoner's mind, so that he gradually became convinced he actually had fomented a plot, that he really had had nothing in mind but the planning of an uprising, that he had lived and acted solely for the purpose of overthrowing the Republic. Unknown names were mentioned, dates and places cited that the prisoner scarcely knew, until he began to feel like a marionette with the police pulling now one string and now another. The curtain in his marionette theater was lowered and then raised again. The stage could also rotate; the defendant could be placed in any desired position. Ultimately the prisoner became so confused that he himself helped to spin the yarn, to elaborate the scenes, to confess the wildest crimes, which he would never have dreamed of committing.

When I entered the interrogation room I had already resolved to answer all questions as calmly and matter-of-factly as possible. For a while I did so. But I lost patience when my tormentors arrived at an entirely nonsensical declaration built up by twisting facts. The colonel bellowed at me: "Your business is to confess to what we want to hear."

I replied: "If facts don't count here, if the minutes, the interrogation, and the charge are only pretense, untenable nonsense without any basis in fact, a confession shouldn't be necessary either."

I was promptly turned over to the major again for "disrespectful" remarks. He took me again. Again the rubber truncheon thumped my naked body, while outside in the corridor the usual scornful laughter accompanied the torture.

I was brought back to the room. They threw the record of the proceedings in front of me and bellowed: "Sign!"

"I will not sign until the passages I objected to are removed."

"What are your objections?"

"Let us go over the details, and I will bring up my objections."

They read through the record again and tried to word some passages differently or to change the text slightly. But no significant changes were made. Fury mounted and became general; again I was beaten. The brutalities did not end until daybreak. I suppose they ended then because the policemen who were on duty here during the day were not supposed to see what had gone on during the night.

The day renewed the already familiar scene. Filthy jokes, raucous laughter, acrid smoke filled the room. During his visit the doctor looked concerned, but said nothing. In the afternoon a lieutenant from the interrogation board visited me, bringing grapes. When I refused to accept them, he put them down for me and once more asked me to make at least a partial confession. He was depressed to have to work on clarifying my case, he said; he was a religious man but had a large family, depended on his job, and would surely be dismissed if the interrogation failed because of my obstinacy. I was sorry that I could not help him.

The whole scene was obviously staged, for later Décsi sent another member of the examining commission to inform me that my secretary and Professor Baranyay in their hearings had made incriminating statements about me, so that further denials were pointless. Their statements were read to me and I was shown the signatures of both accused men. I took note, but gave no reply. Décsi's representative left; the angelus from a nearby church reached my ears. I prayed the rosary. Evening came, and with it the doctors' visit. Lying on the battered couch, I thought over my situation and tried to collect my thoughts in preparation for the nocturnal interrogation.

☧ Currency Manipulations

THESE INTERROGATIONS continued to be a part of the unvarying routine, and by day I dozed in the foul-aired prison room in the company of the noisy, five-man guard detachment. Sometimes there would be a change when the police officers conducting the interrogation would relieve one another. Even Décsi permitted the major to deputize for him one night. Then I had two nights in succession in which only my tormentor was with me; during the frequent beatings with the rubber truncheon he asked repeatedly who my "accomplices" were. The interrogations I am able to remember took place during the first two weeks of my imprisonment. At that time I still knew what was going on around me, and I tried to resist all influences, those I recognized clearly and those I only sensed. A terrible abyss yawned, of course, between my tormentors and myself. I did not hate them, but I dreaded them and tried to keep them from getting to me. I looked over their heads and made them feel how contemptible they were in their depravity, in their wicked conspiracy with Moscow against the Hungarian people and the Catholic Church.

Much less of what happened after the first two weeks remains in my memory, and most of that is not clear.

During the first two weeks of my imprisonment Décsi had already accused me of violation of the laws regulating currency. He mentioned large sums in dollars and Swiss francs, spoke of checks from America and from the Vatican. At the time there was no way I could determine whether any of his statements were correct. Many years later, when the documents of the "Mindszenty Trial" finally came into my hands, I saw that the figures in the charges were different. The *Yellow Book* gives different sums from the *Black Book*. The record of the interrogations, the indictment, and the justification for the verdict again mentioned sums that did not agree. In the interval, however, I have grasped the reason for this charge of currency manipulation. It was one that had become customary especially as a weapon against the Catholic Church with its international involvements—so much so that during the Hitler period as well as under Communist rule this became a standard item in trials. The Communists were aiming if possible to charge me together with Prince Pál Esterházy, head of the wealthiest noble family in the country. By identifying the two of us in this way they wanted to persuade the Hungarian and the world public that the primate of the country, allied with the largest landowner, meant to appropriate the land that the regime had assigned the small farmers. What is more, the primate intended to restore the monarchy under Otto von Habsburg and revoke the "democratic" liberties of the Republic.

During the interrogation I could not state precisely from memory what sums we had received from foreign benefactors in the course of three years. My habit was to send the money and checks that came to me to whatever institution particularly needed support at the moment. When, for example, American Ambassador Chapin brought me a gift from Cardinal Spellman of $30,000, I handed the check in the ambassador's presence to Mihálovics, the prelate who was in charge of the soup kitchens and other charitable works in Budapest. It was these sums that Décsi brought up. He charged me with not having exchanged this foreign money at the official exchange rate, thus harming the country's economic interests. Bishops, priests, and church institutions had changed funds at black market prices and thus brought foreign currency into circulation, Décsi said. And I was responsible for all that, he charged. He mentioned various specific sums. I strained my memory to the utmost in the effort to answer this cunning, treacherous accusation.

First of all I referred to the multifarious activities of the Church's Caritas organization in Budapest and in the large cities and industrial areas. I mentioned the miseries of the inflation years, 1945–46, and reminded Décsi that at the time the entire nation—except the occupying power and the Communists—was able to survive only by engaging in barter for all sorts of goods. The Church had been maintaining 126 soup kitchens in the capital alone. Buying food was possible only if we had valuables or foreign currencies to offer. Our kitchens would have had to close forthwith if we had had no American or Swiss money at our disposal. With the donated money we had

been able to supply tens of thousands of persons with a warm meal, clothing, fuel, and medicine regularly for more than two years. We alone had
cared for the poor and the sick when the government by and large could do
nothing at all to alleviate the tremendous misery.

Naturally, physical and human aids were needed for such works of
mercy. We had to have cars, warehouses, offices, staffs. During a period in
which all plants and factories were compelled to pay their employees in
kind, Catholic Action had to do likewise. Anyone who exchanged a U.S.
dollar for Hungarian currency would find by the next day that his money
could buy at most a couple of pounds of salt or a box of matches. It would
have been absurd if we had handed over our foreign currency in this way.
The donors rightly expected us to get the most for the money they gave and
to keep our charitable activities going as long and as well as possible for the
benefit of hundreds of thousands of persons. Moreover, I added, it would
scarcely have been moral if the government had skimmed off a profit of
70–75 percent out of the alms from abroad. But my crowning point was
that the ordinance controlling foreign currency, to which Décsi alluded,
had not been introduced until after the end of the inflation, and the exchange value of the dollar had been kept so low—in the interests of certain
partisan aims—that the Church would have received no more than 25–30
percent of the real value of the foreign gifts of money. With emphasis I
added: "If normal political conditions existed in Hungary today, the government would thank Hungarian Catholicism rather than practice torments
and tortures here in Andrássy Street that future generations will feel
ashamed of."

I also pointed out that it would have been quite impossible for me personally to study every government ordinance, but that my finance department had experienced experts who had informed me in November, after
the trial of Lutheran Bishop Layòs Ordas, that their exchanges of foreign
currencies were always undertaken in accordance with the law because they
had bank officials keep them up to date on changes in the regulations. Décsi
replied that he had a confession of speculation from my bookkeeper, Imre
Bóka, and my secretary, András Zakar. At this point I again requested the
right to consult my lawyer and to an evidential hearing of the bankers in my
lawyer's presence. Décsi replied that my lawyer, Dr. József Gróh, was "fas-
cistic" and "an enemy of the people," and therefore not worthy of pleading
before a people's court. (Years passed before I learned that Dr. Gróh had
been arrested at the same time as myself, obviously to prevent his appearing
in my defense.) After this refusal I asked to speak to the president of the bar
association.

When I regained my freedom I learned about a declaration by former Finance Minister Miklós Nyárádi that the Supreme Economic Council had
decided, in the spring of 1947, to grant churches and other charitable organizations a higher exchange rate than the official one for foreign currency.

This "humanitarian" regulation sprang from the understandable desire not to stop the influx of such money but to bring as much of it as possible into the country. According to Nyárádi, this exceptional exchange rate actually exceeded that of the black market, where the dollar was quoted at four or five times the official rate. The regulation was, however, not published; it was merely communicated privately to the interested parties. Mihálovics, the bankers, and my experts in the finance department undoubtedly knew of the special regulation.

In order to cut short the arguments back and forth, I finally declared that the decisive factor was that I had used none of the sums mentioned for my personal needs. At this point I was shown a promissory note made out by me to pay for work on the vineyard of the archiepiscopal estate, thus assuring the archbishop and his priests their wine for Mass. But this was clearly not a private expense.

Another fragment from the interrogation probably should be mentioned in conjunction with this line of questioning. In the course of a later interrogation conducted by the major he suddenly asked me: "Have you made out a testament? What is in it?"

I replied: "Everything a cardinal and primate has to say to the faithful, to the priests, and to the people. I state in it that many things that have been done in our country under the threadbare cloak of legality were in reality illegal. I admonish the Hungarian people to remain true to their history, to love their country, and to respect the religious and moral foundations of life. I also dispose of my few personal possessions and give instructions for my funeral."

This reply seemed to stimulate interest in the document. I was asked to instruct the Esztergom Cathedral chapter to hand over my testament to the police for safekeeping. A typewritten message to this effect was presented to me for signature. Because I was already worn out and wanted to escape a fresh round of battering with the rubber truncheon, I submitted to this demand. The police then sent for my testament. But it was neither cited nor mentioned at the trial. Apparently the authorities were disappointed that it contained no listing of large sums, no references to personal wealth.

That interrogation ended, as usual, at daybreak. I recall that Décsi repeatedly shrugged and that virtually none of my statements were recorded in the minutes of the hearing.

☿ Shattering the Personality

THE NOCTURNAL INTERROGATIONS also tired the examiners. They were therefore relieved frequently. Only the major, his truncheon, and I were present night after night. My physical strength perceptibly declined. I began worrying about my health and my life. Terrible visions beset me; it seemed to me that there were brightly colored hoops all over the walls; they whirled rapidly and also came spinning out into the room. My goiter, which had been checked by an operation ten years ago, once more became acute. My heart flagged; a sense of being utterly abandoned and defenseless weighed upon me. Often I spent whole days considering: "Is there truly no way out, no protection?" In vain I asked for a defense attorney and inquired during the interrogation why the president of the bar association had not come. Décsi said condescendingly that he could not be reached; later he stated bluntly that in such an unequivocal case he was not going to have a defense lawyer appear. There was nothing I could do. Worn out, exhausted, I went on fighting and arguing alone. Again and again I forcefully refused when they tried to persuade me to sign their prepared confession. And again and again the major took over, dragged me back to the cell where I was stripped, thrown down, and beaten. Just as regularly the guards afterwards tried to intensify the effect of this torture by preventing me from sinking into a sleep of exhaustion.

During these hours of pain I often thought of our saintly bishop, Ottokár Prohászka, one of the great leaders in Hungary's Church, who had suffered from natural insomnia and had remarked that during his dreary nights he had even been able to understand the impulse of suicide. I also thought of the methods of torture in ancient China, where prisoners condemned to death were subjected to the additional penalty of not being allowed to sleep. The idea was to force the condemned to suffer their impending deaths in their minds without pause.

My powers of resistance gradually faded. Apathy and indifference grew. More and more the boundaries between true and false, reality and unreality, seemed blurred to me. I became insecure in my judgment. Day and night my alleged "sins" had been hammered into me, and now I myself began to think that somehow I might very well be guilty. Again and again the same theme was repeated in innumerable variations; they always steered the dialogue in the same direction. I was left with only one certainty, that there was no longer any way out of this situation. My shaken nervous system weakened the resistance of my mind, clouded my memory, undermined my self-confidence, unhinged my will—in short undid all the capacities that are most human in man.

While I lay in such states of lethargy, I heard screams from other cells. But sometimes my own apathy was such that I scarcely listened to them any longer. I ate almost nothing because of my fear that mind-impairing drugs would be smuggled into the food. As usual, the three prison doctors visited me after every meal. And though they could not help noting my deteriorating condition, during the thirty-nine days I spent in detention they never once prescribed even a brief exposure to or walk in fresh air.

An anxiety I had never felt before now began to oppress me. I was frightened for the Church and trembled for all those others who might be dragged down into misery because of my "affair." This pathological feeling of anxiety was in all probability the effect of drugs. With medical means, the police succeeded in producing an intense dread that more and more dominated my acts and decisions.

One gloomy January evening the inquisitors brought me down into the basement again. I was taken to a dimly lit hall. There, in theatrical poses, Lieutenant General Gábor Péter and Gyula Décsi awaited me. To one side of the room, weary, unshaven, and seedy, in the posture of humble sinners, stood my curia officials who had been arrested before me—my archives director, my secretary, and my bookkeeper. It was not hard to see what these three priests had gone through. Obviously they had been given the same treatment as I had received, or even worse.

Gábor Péter, who had seated himself on a sort of dais, gestured to them, and my secretary—standing in an awkward posture that was not at all like him—for ten minutes recited a text learned by heart. His voice kept breaking; he trembled nervously. The idea was that all resistance was pointless, that the examiners knew everything, that total power was theirs and they would use it mercilessly. In conclusion my secretary asked me to testify as the authorities wished and to answer every question.

I thought: "My poor secretary, what suffering they must have inflicted on you before you consented to play this part!" It was perfectly plain to me that he was not speaking for himself but delivering a speech pounded into him by the truncheon or worse. But I showed no sign of my awareness of this, merely looked at my unfortunate assistant with deep sympathy and made no comment. Then they took me back to my cell. The tin bowl with my supper was placed on the table, and the doctors appeared as usual. I was left with some time in which to reflect on what I had seen, and imagine what sort of ordeals my priests must have undergone.

Then I was again taken to interrogation, and Décsi promptly threatened me: "If you behave as you did yesterday, the truncheon will make you talk." Nevertheless I remained silent, with the result that by daybreak that night I had been beaten twice.

The following nights they did not bother interrogating me; only the torturer dealt with me. I was taken into a large, empty room where there were just the two of us. Total silence surrounded us. Someone might have been listening behind the door, but not a soul was visible. After I had been stripped of my clothes, the major took up his position in front of me and asked: "Who worked on the ideological and political points of your program?"

This new question took me by surprise. It occurred to me he was trying to find out something about Provost Pál Bozsik. In order not to harm the provost, I said nothing. What he had "done" was permissible in every democratic country, and was even considered a duty to Church, country, and nation. The tormentor raged, roared, and in response to my silence took the implements of torture into his hands. This time he held the truncheon in one hand, a long sharp knife in the other. And then he drove me like a horse in training, forcing me to trot and gallop. The truncheon lashed down on my back repeatedly—for some time without a pause. Then we stood still and he brutally threatened: "I'll kill you; by morning I'll tear you to pieces and throw the remains of your corpse to the dogs or into the canal. We are the masters here now." Then he forced me to begin running again. Although I was gasping for breath and the splinters of the wooden floor stabbed painfully into my bare feet, I ran as fast as I could to escape his blows.

It was approaching two o'clock in the morning before the torturer realized that although this procedure gave me great pain and might lead to my physical collapse, it was not going to produce the desired result of a confession and my betrayal of fellow defendants. At the time he arrested me he had observed my mother's grief at parting. Now he recalled the scene, for he bellowed: "If you don't confess I'll have your mother brought here tomorrow morning. You'll stand naked before her. She'll probably have a stroke. Rightly so, she deserves it, since she brought you into the world. And you will be responsible for her death."

Again the truncheon fell, again I ran around the room, and again I remained silent. In my pain and fear I momentarily believed that this threat would be carried out. To conceive of my mother in this place was unbearable. But gradually I realized that it was altogether impossible for them to bring her here by morning; Mindszent was one hundred twenty-five miles away. With that insight, I calmed down somewhat, but I was totally exhausted from the brutalities. No one who had seen me a month earlier would have recognized me after these scenes of repeated physical agony. But in the course of the following day I collapsed into so shattered a psychological state that I decided to give in on some of their demands. Thus the following night, in response to their questioning, I mentioned three names of "fellow conspirators" of whom I knew that two were dead and the third had left the country. Hesitantly, I let them drag these names out of me, hoping that at least a week would pass before they had discovered that the persons in question could no longer be interrogated. But I was mistaken. The major at first rejoiced; but my "deception" was quickly discovered, and the following night I was subjected to the same round of tortures. Later, especially in prison, when I happened to step on a nail or a splinter, the painful memory of those horrible nights would instantly come flooding back.

As it turned out, my efforts to protect Provost Pál Bozsik were in vain. Later, in the hospital, when I read the book about the trial of the archbishop of Kalocs, I learned that Bozsik had been dragged into the Grősz trial and given a severe sentence. Later still, after my liberation, I learned that he had died in prison under circumstances that were never disclosed. I always esteemed him highly as a man loyal to his convictions.

But the torturers eventually achieved their aim of forcing me to corroborate a crude falsehood. In spite of my broken condition I at first drew back; but I was no longer able to fight. The thought of the rubber truncheon made me shake in advance, and at last I signed—though employing one last little trick, as the captive Hungarians in Turkey had once done. It was this: after my signature I placed the initials C.F., meaning *coactus feci*, "I have done this under coercion." The colonel asked suspiciously: "What does József Mindszenty, C.F. mean?" I replied that it was the abbreviation for *cardinalis foraneus*, the term used for a provincial and not a curial cardinal. He accepted that. Delighted at having obtained a signature from me, he ordered me taken back to the cell. I well understood his gladness. No doubt his superiors had already reprimanded him for his failures; probably Rákosi and perhaps Stalin had expressed their dissatisfaction. But my little trick had nasty consequences for me. The following night the colonel, accompanied by five men, came rushing into my cell. They pounded me with their fists and with bundles of documents. "You swine," the colonel screamed at me. "You've made fools of us. You're not allowed to add anything after or under or before your name. You're not a cardinal, not an archbishop anymore; you're nothing but a convict!"

That was the last incident of this period of my detention that has remained clearly in my memory. What happened later, after the end of the second week of detention, January 10–24, 1949, remains in my memory only in fragmentary form. A good deal of it came back to me only when I read the *Yellow Book* and the *Black Book*. It is possible that during this second period I was beaten less but increasingly treated with drugs. The doctors turned up with ominous regularity to check my health. And I could feel my resistance ebbing. I was no longer able to argue cogently; I no longer rejected coarse lies and distortions. Now and then I resignedly said things like: "There's no need to say anything more about it; maybe it happened the way others maintain."

I usually gave such replies when they read to me from the "interrogation records" of "accomplices" and "witnesses." I would ask to have certain documents revised before I signed them, but was unaware that the records of sessions were always prepared in various versions and that the documents I signed often contained different dates and facts from the texts that were read aloud to me. I also had no opportunity to read through the texts again before signing them, and I was usually so exhausted and revolted that I no longer paid attention to whether the written document corresponded exactly to my statements. Without knowing what had happened to me, I had become a different person.

☿ *The Documents*

YEARS LATER, in the American Embassy, *Sárga Könyv* (the "Yellow Book"), subtitled "Documents of the Mindszenty Criminal Case," came to my notice. The minutes of the interrogations reproduced there were in themselves a great surprise to me. I was even more surprised at the publication of my "holograph" confession. It seemed to me that anyone should at once have recognized this document as a crude forgery, since it is the product of a bungling, uncultivated mind. But when I subsequently went through foreign books, newspapers, and magazines that dealt with my case and commented on my "confession," I realized that the public must have concluded that the "confession" had actually been composed by me, although in a semiconscious state and under the influence of brainwashing. This was the explanation offered for the many spelling errors and the confused language of the document. It was also assumed that the police had had handwriting experts retouch parts of the text; but that the police would have published a document they had themselves manufactured seemed altogether too brazen to be believed.

The *Yellow Book* was published in the middle of January 1949, that is, during my third week in detention. Certainly I was a broken man by that time, but nevertheless not yet ready either to compose such a "confession" or to write it down on dictation. Granted that I signed things, as I have said; but even during the second half of my detention I went on rejecting documents that contained lies and falsifications far less incriminating than those of the "confession." Quite possibly a special application of the rubber truncheon would have reduced me to a state where, not responsible for my actions, I might have given my signature; but then I simply would not have had the physical strength to write out such a long document from dictation.

But there is nothing whatsoever in my recollections that relates to the writing out of any such handwritten confession. The whole thing must have been produced by the police and their handwriting experts. Obviously they had to work quickly, and they did their job clumsily and nervously, looking anxiously over their shoulders at their superiors. In the American Embassy, years later, when conversation came around to these questions, an embassy official informed me that the evidence of forgery was conclusive. A couple named Sulner had discussed the matter in detail in a series of articles published in the New York *Herald Tribune* in July 1950. The American Embassy displayed these articles in its library and word of them soon got around Budapest. Hundreds of people poured into the library, especially on Sundays, to read articles about me and my conduct without the intervention of the Hungarian censorship. I was told that the copies were soon read to tatters. The people wanted at least to see the illustrations. Those who knew English and could translate the text always found a large circle of listeners gathered around them. Soon Rákosi was informed of these library visits and their significance. He sent word to the embassy that it was not authorized to run a library. Thus this source of information had to be shut down; the embassy also complied because it did not want to endanger those who came to the library.

The *Tribune* had obtained a great deal of significant information from the handwriting specialists Hanna and László Sulner. Mrs. Sulner, born Hanna Fischof, operated a handwriting bureau she had inherited from her father. Her father had also constructed a device that made it possible to take letters, words, and fragments of sentences out of a manuscript and put them together as desired to make a new manuscript. Her husband developed this device to such a point that he was able to manufacture documents that even experts could not tell from originals. The author himself, shown a document that was in fact in his handwriting, could only recognize a forgery by the use of unaccustomed phrases—in other words, by the contents.

In September 1948 Sulner gave a talk to a group of experts in Budapest, among whom were some police officials, on the Fischof apparatus invented by his father-in-law. A few days later two secret police officers from Andrássy Street visited the laboratory. They had been sent by József Száberszky, Péter's aide, and brought documents for examination. One of these allegedly came from my fellow defendant Jusztin Baranyay; it contained a list of cabinet ministers I was supposed to appoint after the overthrow of the government. Sulner promptly recognized it as a forgery. He declared he could make a much better forgery than that. Whereupon he was challenged to prove his skill. The result satisfied the officials, and in September 1948 he prepared an even more complete "document" in Baranyay's handwriting. On December 30 the newspapers reported for the first time that Cardinal Mindszenty, in the face of overwhelming evidence, had made a confession. To his surprise Sulner learned that the fabrication he had produced was cited among the documents proving the cardinal's guilt.

On January 4, 1949, two police officers again paid Sulner a visit. They brought him several bundles of confiscated documents and asked him to produce a "holograph" confession by me corresponding to a typewritten draft they had drawn up. Sulner was taken aback by the potentialities of his craft; at first he refused, but under threat of liquidation he finally had to obey.

In the New York *Herald Tribune* articles Sulner further attested that the "document" on land reform reproduced in the *Yellow Book* was also a forgery from his hand. The document was obviously designed by the Communists to turn the rural populace against me. Among other things, I am supposed to have written:

The rural populace was bribed by the gift of land reform. The harm done by this measure is already perceptible. So much has become clear not only to those who suffered loss, but to those who received the gift. In Parliament the distributors of the land themselves have declared that the yield from the divided land (500,000 acres) is steadily diminishing as a result of insufficient expertise in economic planning. The fruit is being destroyed by aphids.

The *Yellow Book* published the following comment by the prosecution on my alleged statement:

According to Mindszenty's own words, the land reform was a blow such as the Hungarian people had never before suffered. That is how this haughty feudal lord judges the reform which helped 600,000 Hungarian peasant families obtain land of their own. He calls the Hungarian peasant lazy and ignorant, and thus tries to challenge his right to the land.

The Sulners also reported that they were required to insert forged signatures and marginal notations in the cardinal's handwriting on typewritten documents. These signatures and glosses were supposed to create the impression that I had had these documents, which dealt with espionage and conspiracy, in my possession and had studied and edited them.

The police functionaries kept pressing the Sulners to speed up on their work. The Sulners, however, wanted to proceed carefully and precisely; they were by profession highly painstaking. The police therefore tried to take over the process themselves. Finally Commissar Szaberszky ordered that the entire Sulner apparatus and operation be moved to police headquarters. All assignments henceforth were to be carried out there. For two weeks in January the Fischof device was to be exclusively at the disposition of the police. Thus forgery was placed on an assembly-line basis, and the harried couple were kept busy day and night. A steady stream of police officials came to the Sulners' private laboratory and to their office in Andrássy Street, bringing instructions, drafts, supplements and revisions for documents, as new ideas occurred to those who stage-managed the show trials. "Documents" manufactured with great effort suddenly had to be replaced by new ones. Together with Sulner, but quite often without his help or even knowledge, ignorant, inexperienced people used his apparatus. Such efforts often resulted in products of outlandish form and spelling, such as my "confession."

On February 6, 1949, the Sulners succeeded in escaping abroad. They took with them microfilms that enabled them to prove their statements. As soon as they published their story, the Hungarian press launched savage attacks on them. When László Sulner suddenly died under obscure circumstances it was whispered that the police had taken their revenge.

Such "texts" were the basis of the prosecution's argument in my trial. It was on them that my sentence to life imprisonment was based.

V. TRIAL

☿ *Preparation for the Show Trial*

I HAVE ALREADY said that during the period that followed my first four weeks in detention, I lived in a kind of twilight state. Many years earlier I had undergone several operations under anesthesia. I can compare my state at the end of those four weeks in Andrássy Street with the insecurity and confusion I felt when waking up from anesthesia. I had the feeling that my spine and other important parts of my body were simply not there. To this day I cannot remember whether or not I was beaten during this period.

I can be certain that no physical abuse was inflicted on me during the last two days of this period, February 1 and 2. Obviously this forbearance was in consideration of the trial that was to begin in the People's Court on February 3. Probably, too, no more drugs were given to me. Nevertheless the doctors appeared as usual to examine me. It seemed to me that they were more concerned than they had been and that they stayed longer. Probably they were under orders to prevent my collapsing completely. Both Stalin and Rákosi no doubt wanted me to play my proper part in their drama, the part that would result in my total humiliation. On the other hand, I undoubtedly owe it to this desire on their part that I was able to leave Andrássy Street alive and without any fatal damage to my health. Even today, a quarter of a century later, it is true that I still suffer from painful cramps which at times affect my whole body—the aftereffects of those days of torture.

When I had the opportunity to read *Fekere Könyv* (the "Black Book"), the following reminiscence came to mind:

January 23, 1949: A lieutenant of the investigation commission entered my cell, sat down, introduced himself as a Catholic, and stated that his faith and his Christian convictions were unshakable. Only concern for his own and his family's livelihood kept him in this sinister company in Andrássy Street and forced him to take part in the interrogations, he said; he sympathized with me, worried because he had observed that my life was now at stake, that it was no longer a matter of a prison sentence of four or five years. For days he had been considering ways to free me, and was all the more eager to do this because he himself had suffered many sorts of injuries from his superior, Colonel Décsi.

The lieutenant told me all this in a sincere tone. I was deeply affected. In my loneliness his show of sympathy deceived me, and I began to hope again. In the light of that hope I even found the man likable. Thus I wondered whether it might not have been he who brought me the wine for consecration that morning. He had once brought me some grapes; his tone during the interrogations had always been friendlier than that of his associates; and once when all of them were beating me at once, his blows had been the mildest. Therefore his good will seemed honest, and I was less suspicious. "Can you give me your word of honor that you sincerely mean your proposals?" I asked. Whereupon the man stood up and solemnly gave his word on his honor as an officer. He also gave me his card with his name, László Jámbor. Then he sat down again and explained his plan of rescue: I was to flee abroad in the same American plane that had once taken me to Rome. He himself would accompany me. He suggested, therefore, that I get in touch with the American ambassador as quickly as possible by writing a letter to him. The lieutenant had brought paper with him for me, and he helped me to compose a suitable text. I can no longer tell whether the text printed on page 97 of the *Black Book* is identical with that letter. The lieutenant took the letter with him. Next day he brought a verbal reply from the Americans. They were willing to carry out my request, although— he explained—they had made unkind remarks about me because I had previously not asked for the embassy's support. The lieutenant expressed the opinion that it would have been better for me to have fled before arrest; now he would have to figure out ways to deal with the obstacles that had accumulated in the meantime. Nevertheless he promised me to do his best so that I would be able to set foot on free soil in forty-eight hours. He would find some suitable area for takeoff. We would leave the building here unnoticed and take a cab to the plane. On his honor as an officer he guaranteed the success of the plan, he said.

During the nocturnal interrogations of the next few days, this officer was no longer present. But one day he suddenly reappeared in the cell, in uniform. He wanted to apologize; he had not been able to do anything, he said, because he had unexpectedly been sent off to the border with a police detail. He had just returned and wanted to tell me that his contacts with the Americans were going well.

Shortly afterwards it turned out that the whole idea of this flight had been conceived not by this "religious and kind-hearted" officer but by the stage managers of my show trial. I have mentioned the episode only to give the reader some idea of the intrigues into which a person could be maneuvered once he found himself caught in the machinery of Andrássy Street.

The "escape plan" played an important part in the show trial. My court-appointed defense attorney hypocritically argued that I had penitently confessed my sins and promised to make amends; in the light of this the People's Court ought not to punish me according to the strictness of the law, but should pass a mild sentence. After this plea, the prosecutor replied that the escape plan indicated not penitence but obduracy.

In the fourth week of my detention I was required to choose a defense attorney. Right from the start I had demanded one, and as I have mentioned I wanted to entrust my friend József Gróh with this task. But he himself was already under arrest. I therefore asked the president of the bar association to take the case. Colonel Décsi informed me, however, that he had refused. Later I learned that in the meantime my mother had asked Endre Farkas, a well-known Budapest lawyer, to defend me. But he was not allowed to see me at all during the investigation. Finally, during the fourth week Décsi spoke of the necessity for defense counsel and recommended Dr. Kálmán Kiczkó. "Do as you like," I said, for my spirit was already broken, and I signed a letter authorizing Kiczkó to take the case. That must have been some time around January 20. The lawyer did not come to see me until the end of the month, after the interrogation was over. I did not know him, but later heard that he had played a part in Hungary's first period of communism in 1919. There could be no doubt concerning what side he was on.

I met with this "defense" attorney in a room on the first floor of the prison. A guard was present at our conference. The conversation lasted for no more than fifteen minutes. Kálmán Kiczkó told me that he came from Transylvania, had served as a magistrate, and was now a lawyer in Budapest. The Cistercians in Zirc knew him very well, he said. From this capsule biography I was supposed to conclude that he was a Hungarian and a good Christian. I told him about the nocturnal interrogations, about the demand that I sign statements already drawn up, about the beatings and the torture of sleeplessness.

He promptly declared: "If you want to bring up such matters at the trial, I won't take your case. None of that can be proved. Talking about it would only worsen your situation. The only hope of obtaining a more lenient sentence is to keep quiet about such incidents. That is much wiser." In other words, a defense counsel's function in a show trial is to further the interests of the authorities. I imagine that Kiczkó never even read the records of my interrogation. He was simply given a text for the part he was to play, so that he could quickly get it letter-perfect in time for the trial. The files on my case were by now so vast that it would in any case have been impossible for him to look the material over in so short a time.

During this period Colonel Décsi in person "visited" me. He said he was fairly sure that at most I would be sentenced to four to five years imprisonment. He was in a position to tell, he said, because of the close relations between the departments of justice and the police. Nevertheless he was worried about me, he went on, because the prosecutor, who acted on party instructions, was an uncertain factor. I had done myself a great deal of harm because I had proved to be an obstinate enemy of a "compromise between Church and state." If I were ready to cooperate now, the police might be able to turn things in my favor. "Don't forget," he declared, "that the Vatican will relieve you of your office once you have been convicted of the charge. You know what St. Paul has written: the bishop must be without reproach."

I listened calmly and gave no reply. For a moment I felt as if I were confronting the "Temptor" himself. It seemed to me that a colored light in a frame was plainly dancing above Décsi's head. This phenomenon lasted two or three minutes. It happened again in prison later on, and several times more in the hospital. Décsi left me without my having said a word to him.

Probably it was the very next day that I was taken to see Gábor Péter.

The general received me with an air of cordiality and mild reproach He observed that I was cold to him and would not even look at him. Since we were not going to be together much longer, he hoped I would change my attitude, so that we could part in a conciliatory spirit. I sensed the hypocrisy and menace in his voice as he continued: "Remember that your fate is in my hands. I can see to it that in spite of the grave charges you will be sentenced to only four or five years in prison. Moreover, an exchange might be arranged so that you could be sent to Rome after only eight months or so."

Again, as in my talk with Colonel Décsi, Péter brought up the possibility of a "compromise between Church and state." He informed me that negotiations between the government and the conference of bishops were in progress, and that if I wished I would have the opportunity to participate in them. However, he asserted, the delegation from the conference of bishops seemed to take only the slightest interest in my case. It had declared that it would leave the verdict upon me, and my fate, to the wisdom of the government. "Confidentially," Gábor Péter added, "it seems that several bishops have taken positions against you."

He mentioned several names. Obviously, all these points were drawn from the department of "psychological preparation." The idea was to make me feel that I had been abandoned by one and all. I also remained silent with Gábor Péter.

I was taken back to my cell, and Décsi reappeared. "I have an idea," he announced. "File a motion, in consideration of your position in the Church, for removal of your case from the docket of the People's Court. But you yourself must put in this plea."

The feeling of repugnance that I had earlier felt for this man was no longer so distinct, but my cautious attitude about him had not vanished. Like every prisoner my overwhelming desire was to be free once more. Therefore his proposal seemed to me worth looking into. But at the same time I was beset by the cautionary thought: "What will my fellow defendants say if my case is given exceptional treatment?" I expressed this concern. Décsi replied: "You can ask the opinion of Professor Jusztin Baranyay on that score." And I was taken to the professor. Jusztin Baranyay, whom I had always known as a friendly, kind-hearted monk, stood before me with a look of apathy in his eyes, his face emaciated, marked by suffering. I put the plan to him, pretending that I myself had already accepted it. He said nothing against it, even approved it, remarking that there was always something good in a conciliatory gesture. My codefendants could scarcely feel betrayed or injured. Rather, my release might well help them, since the removal of the chief defendant would surely prove advantageous to all the others. While we talked, our minds were only on the recourse seemingly being offered by Décsi, without realizing that this smooth article was merely setting another trap.

We parted. Décsi came to see me again. He had already arranged for my motion to be forwarded without delay to the minister of justice.

✝ 8 The Show Trial

PARTLY FROM my own experiences during my first imprisonment by Communists, I knew a good deal about the nature of totalitarian justice. As primate after 1945 I had seen and been deeply moved by the fate of many condemned persons, whether these had been pro-Nazi or merely "bourgeois" conservatives. From the human standpoint I understood their situation, their suffering. And because I had frequently raised my voice in the interests of all the persecuted, I had found it necessary to study all the new regulations and laws promulgated by the government. I soon realized that most of them had been invented solely to further the interests of a single party. That was officially called "socialist justice." From my own sources of information, too, I knew how statements and confessions were manufactured in Andrássy Street. Consequently, I had not been surprised by what I encountered there; but it took about five weeks before I resigned myself to my fate and accepted punishment and humiliation as the sacrifices I must make. At the time of my arrest I was entirely aware of the trials that awaited me; but later on everything became blurred. I was ultimately so shattered by the "systematic treatment" that I was scarcely able to realize what was happening to me. Therefore I could not always take a position promptly and accurately.

During the trial my thought and action, as far as I can recall, were guided by the following intentions:

1. I would defend my Church and its influence with all my strength. Thus I considered all the possibilities for an agreement between Church and state, though there were many hidden dangers here. Colonel Décsi with his various arts of persuasion kept urging me to think along these lines.

2. I would harm no individual. It was chiefly for this reason that I forebore to mention the tortures that had been inflicted on me in Andrássy Street. I was afraid that if I spoke of this, the police would retaliate by making new arrests, and the sufferings of my associates and other priests would increase.

3. I would at all costs avoid confrontations with my own clerics and with "confessions" by other members of the clergy. For I did not wish to contribute to shaking the people's confidence in their Church and their priests. Hence I took the entire responsibility in regard to the charge of currency manipulations.

Political trials were held not in the ordinary courts but in "People's Courts," as in fascist countries. They were patterned after the Soviet model. My own case was set before a special branch of the Budapest People's Court. The body of judges consisted of one professional justice and four people's judges. The president of the court was appointed by the minister of justice; the people's judges obtained their appointments from the political parties. In my case the president of the court was Vilmos Olti, a former Arrow Cross party man who had now become a member of the Communist party. Because of his past, he had to show special zealousness. He became the willing instrument of his new comrades. Since he had belonged to the Marian Congregation as a student, the prosecution tried, by referring to this fact, to arouse the impression that the cardinal-primate's trial was being conducted by a religious judge.

Along with the president, Gyula Alapi played a spectacular part. He had only recently become chief state prosecutor; and the government also laid stress on his Catholic past. He came from a good religious family and had spent his schooldays in Catholic schools supported by church groups. But he soon proved to be a light-minded and opportunistic young man who during the postwar years turned to the Communist party. There he rose rapidly. At the time of my trial he was perhaps thirty, and even my defense attorney hailed him during the trial as a "new star" in the juristic firmament. With an air of complacency he sat enthroned in his place between the bench and the police.

We defendants sat opposite the judges. To our right were the places for the defense attorneys, to our left the police, headed by Décsi. The stenographers had their seats behind the judges. Alongside them, separated by a glass wall, were the radio technicians who took care of the microphones and passed on the "confessions" to the reporters. These confessions must all have been prepared beforehand, for the tape recordings and the newspaper stories frequently contained contradictory statements and invariably showed great differences.

☩ Change of Clothing

THE STAGE MANAGERS of the show trial were greatly concerned about the world's opinion. They therefore made an effort to win over the world press beforehand, and hoped to make use of me for that purpose.

On one of the last days I spent in Andrássy Street I was unexpectedly required to don my cardinal's robes again. Thus dressed, I was taken to General Gábor Péter's lavishly appointed reception room on the ground floor. There I found Senator Ottavio Pastore, a member of the Italian Senate. He was introduced to me as a representative of the Italian press. He had come from Rome, he told me, to find out whether I was still alive and still in Hungary, for rumors were circulating in the West that I had already been deported to Siberia. I was now supposed to issue a statement denying these rumors, which, though inaccurate, did have an element of underlying truth about them. I did not want to, and so I evaded the question and made no statement in favor of my persecutors. The fact that I was not yet in Siberia was something the senator could see for himself. The doctor, whom I already knew from his daily visits, was recommended to me as interpreter for any statement I cared to make. But I refused to be drawn out of my reserve.

Later I heard that the senator was also a correspondent for the communist newspaper *L'Unitá*. He showed his annoyance with me quite plainly, and on February 6, 1949, he published in *L'Unitá*, the central organ of the Italian Communist Party, the following "report from Budapest":

The primate of Hungary is no hero, and the explanation for his confessions is not to be found in the lying protestations of his friends, who claim that he has been coerced. Mindszenty is simply a cowardly person. He has even been dropped by the Americans. . . . Moreover, Mindszenty is being rejected by his own people: by the peasants, who hardly want the land that has been distributed to them to be taken away again; by the workers, who no longer want to be exploited. . . . There is nothing left for him to do but to resign his office and admit his failures.

The senator also referred to his meeting with me and asserted that he had seen no signs that would indicate physical or mental torture. He also stated, in blatant contradiction to the reality, that he had met me in a well-furnished room where I had been pacing back and forth, saying the breviary.

After this meeting with the Italian senator I was brought back to the cell, my cassock was pulled off, and I was given a black suit. It had been custom made for me on orders from the "well-meaning" police. The true reason was that they did not want me appearing on the street or in court in my priest's gown.

A large detachment of police, with Décsi and Péter among them, conducted me from Andrássy Street to the court on Markó Street. Except for Décsi and a few of the patrolmen, they wore civilian clothes. The idea obviously was not to attract attention. The uniformed men carried submachine guns, and as we descended the stairs they took care that I remained in the middle of them. I might well have asked: "Why all this protection if the people, as you say, no longer care about their primate?"

The transfer took place on February 2, under cover of twilight. As soon as the motorcade arrived in Markó Street, the guards hurried me into a room on the second floor. The prison on Markó Street, a nineteenth-century building, normally has room for 300 inmates. But at this time between 800 and 900 were housed there. I heard later that on the day of my arrival the number of prisoners was exactly 773; probably some had been removed shortly before.

In my youth I had heard with horror about this penal institution, where murderers, robbers, burglars, arsonists, and counterfeiters were housed. Now I myself was a prisoner in the notorious place, charged with a "capital crime," breathing the stale air of a filthy cell furnished only with an ancient bed on which lay a musty straw pallet and a threadbare blanket.

After thirty-eight almost sleepless nights, another sleepless night began here, during which I asked myself whether I already stood in the shadow of the gallows. For a brief moment my eyes closed; then sudden noise awoke me. My cell window looked out on a courtyard, from which sounded a roll of drums, followed by the reading of a sentence. I became wide awake and listened: "The sentence of death is now being executed upon so-and-so, who murdered his mistress for the sake of money." I sat up in bed, thinking: "An immortal soul is entering eternity." And then I wondered whether the man had asked for a priest, whether the priest had been summoned.

I meditated and prayed. About two hours after midnight I heard a dull thud; it seemed as if the body had been dropped from the gallows. Then the thought came to me: "Has this all been a dream? That can be my fate, too; my tormentors have told me often enough that my crime is among the worst."

Early in the morning of February 3 there was a knock at my door. I had to get up and get ready for court. The barber came to shave me and make me more presentable. Apparently my new black suit alone was not enough to do the trick.

I stepped out into the corridor and noted with astonishment that the number of "conspirators" being brought to trial with me had risen from four to seven. The three additions were László Tóth, Béla Ispánky, and Miklós Nagy. During the interrogations no one had ever mentioned their names, and now here they suddenly were part of the "general staff of a worldwide conspiracy." Later, however, it was stated in the *Black Book* that their case had no relationship to my trial. Presumably they had to be present because seven defendants made more of an impression than four.

Prince Pál Esterházy, who was likewise indicted, also had nothing to do with my "conspiracy." I had not so much as spoken to him or exchanged a letter with him since my appointment as archbishop of Esztergom. Evidently he had been arrested because a rich magnate had to be in the cast of characters.

The entire group of "conspirators" therefore consisted of only three persons: the cardinal-primate, his secretary, and a monk whose health had been shattered. These three had no weapons, no weapons carriers, no secret fund, no intelligence service, no couriers, and not even a password.

We set out toward the courtroom. In front of me strode my torturer, this time without his truncheon, in gala uniform, beaming with pride. Contentedly, he looked over his victims. I followed him, then the policemen; the other defendants brought up the rear. Since the trial lasted several days, the ritual of this procession had to be repeated frequently; back and forth, however, the arrangement varied somewhat.

In a loud voice the major called out, "Clear the corridor," although it was almost empty. Then we entered the courtroom and were shown to the defendants' bench. Without turning my head I whispered in Latin to Professor Baranyay: *"Circus incipit"* ("the circus begins"). The policemen instantly threatened me: prisoners were not allowed to talk; they were allowed only to answer questions!

✝ *The First Scene*

ON FEBRUARY 3, 1949, the president of the People's Court opened the proceedings. First, as usual, personal data were recorded and the "defense" counsel's letters of authorization were examined. Then the indictment was read. The prosecution accused me of three major charges:

1. Of being the leader of an organization that was planning the overthrow of the government.
2. Of having engaged in espionage against the Hungarian state.
3. Of having illegally used foreign currencies.

I suspect that the indictment had already been drawn up by the police and had been transmitted to the newly appointed chief prosecutor only a short time before the trial opened. According to law, it should have been read aloud to me beforehand, in order to enable me to obtain exculpatory documents, to have my witnesses called, and to orient my defense attorney.

After the indictment Olti read out the letter that I had sent to the minister of justice at the instigation of Décsi. I have already mentioned that the police composed this letter, not I. The handwritten version that was published in facsimile was a forgery prepared by the Fischof process. I myself would not have been capable of writing it down. The content and style, moreover, indicate that I cannot have been the author of it.*

It was undoubtedly the intention of the police to use this letter to humiliate me. It was meant to give the impression in court that the indictment had been handed to me in good time, and that I was willing to relinquish my responsibilities and leave my priests in the lurch. Perhaps the letter was also supposed to indicate my "inexperience and ignorance" in legal matters. The presiding judge construed the letter as a "motion to adjourn" and gave the floor to Alapi, asking him to comment on my petition. Alapi declared that he could see no way for the prosecution to accept this motion to adjourn on the part of the principal defendant; no doubt the defendant was making it only in order to delay the proceedings; he therefore demanded continuance of the trial.

Alapi's arguments had also been prepared beforehand. The point was to avoid the impression of illegality and to forestall anything being said about

---

* For the text as published in the *Black Book*, see Document 73.

the tortures the defendants had undergone. As the regime saw it, everyone would say: a defendant who makes a motion to adjourn certainly has not been deprived of his wits. If, moreover, the defendants were allowed to write up such petitions, obviously the rules of legal procedure were being scrupulously observed. To underline this impression, my defense counsel declared: "the defendant's request for adjournment of the case is, as far as it affects himself alone, well founded. . . . There is no obstacle to granting this adjournment on the basis of the primate's letter."

This statement by my "defender," Attorney Kiczkó, was likewise prefabricated. The idea was to convince the public that he really was acting in the interests of the defendants. The police also wanted "my" letter to offset or negate the statement I had made before my arrest. For in the petition ascribed to me were the words: ". . . I voluntarily confess that I did in fact commit the offences with which I am charged." In the statement I had earlier issued, however, I had said: "I will not renounce my archiepiscopal see. I have nothing to confess, and I will sign nothing. If nevertheless I should some day do so, that will only be a consequence of the human body's weakness, and I declare it in advance null and void."

The People's Court now dealt with the question of adjournment. My "motion" was rejected. The questioning was interrupted; I was led out of the courtroom, and the questioning of my codefendant, Professor Jusztin Baranyay, began. During this time I had to remain in another room under close guard.

☦ Charges and "Crimes"

AS I HAVE MENTIONED, I was charged with treason, misuse of foreign currency, and conspiracy. I wish to explain how the prosecution succeeded in ascribing to me not merely infractions of the law, but crimes punishable by death or life imprisonment.

Article VII of the criminal code of 1946, specifically drafted "for the protection of the Republic" and to meet the needs of "socialist justice," provided considerable leeway for the drawing up of the indictment and the conduct of the trial. The significance of that article is quite simple: the judge is no longer obliged to ascertain objective truths; his business is solely to serve the Communist party's interests. The court is there to help the police eliminate dangerous or merely troublesome opposition. The sole purpose of my trial was to clear the way for communist despotism.

The "hangman's law" was employed for show trials from the very start. Article VII had been adopted on the insistence of the Russians. The leader of the Smallholders party, Ferenc Nagy, a man without legal experience, had actually been in favor of its adoption at the time. I have spoken of this law earlier in my account, in connection with the "students' plot" and the crackdown by the police. With its sanction the government could carry through every kind of injustice and tyranny. The very newness of the law, or the new amendments to older laws, allowed for amazing acrobatic feats of interpretation.

From the start I faced grave disadvantages, first because of my physical weakness, and then because I was not allowed to make any detailed statement. The judge asked questions based on the records of the police interrogations, and I was allowed to answer only yes or no. Inevitably that gave a distorted picture of all the facts and produced the impression of at least a partial confession.

By their nature, show trials are always rushed through in great haste. In my case the People's Court took three days, in which it examined the most complex charges, involving actions that extended over two continents. It drew upon all pertinent articles in the criminal code, found forty-one illegal actions, interrogated seven defendants and all the witnesses, and examined the written evidence and the transcript of the court proceedings. What is more, during these same three days the summations of the prosecution and the defense were heard, as well as the defendants' last objections, and the verdicts were handed down.

Truly, this would represent an incredible performance for a court; and on fact it was possible only because discovering the truth was the one thing not desired in such a show trial. All probing questions that might help reveal the truth, and that would be required by simple justice, were never even asked. No one, including the defense counsel, raised the question of the defendants' guilt or innocence. If our defense attorney had taken the trouble to analyze the "hangman's law," he would at once have seen that my actions bore no relation to the crimes defined in it, that they merely violated the concept of justice as defined by the dominant political party.

But of course no such study was undertaken. The court, the prosecution, and the defense were pursuing the same goal. All of them were subordinates of the state security service. The defense counsel should have pointed out infractions of the rules governing trial procedures. It should have been his business to interpret the law correctly, especially in arguments with the prosecutor. It should have been his task to show that the actions I was charged with were not criminal in the sense of the law either by their nature or their intention. He should have carried out his duties as a defender all the more faithfully because the chief defendant was prevented by weakness and exhaustion from undertaking his own defense. But he paid scarcely any regard to such tasks, though these were prescribed by his official position. Instead, he cooperated with the prosecutor, the judges, and the police in a judicial comedy (or rather, a judicial tragedy), playing his assigned role. The editors of the *Black Book* give the following scene (the subject was my letter to the chapter of Esztergom Cathedral, which the president of the court read aloud):

PRESIDENT: Among other things your letter contains the following statement: "A plan is afoot to assassinate me. . . . If any announcement is made that I have resigned my office as primate, this is either a deception or else the declaration was coerced." Did you write these words?

MINDSZENTY: Yes, I wrote them.

PRESIDENT: Then was your confession forced or were you coerced to make a statement?

MINDSZENTY (decisively): Certainly not.

PRESIDENT: When did you write the letter?

MINDSZENTY: Long before my arrest.

PRESIDENT: In November 1948?

MINDSZENTY: In November 1948 I arranged for the letter to be transmitted only if I were arrested. That is the reason it bears no date. I gave instructions for the letter to be called to the attention of the chapter of Esztergom, of two archbishops, and of two bishops. In that connection I now make the following statement: When I wrote the words that have been read aloud here I did not know many things that I am aware of today. My present standpoint is expressed by the letter that I addressed to the minister of justice and which you did me the honor of reading aloud here yesterday. I now regard my former declaration as inapplicable.

PRESIDENT: The letter addressed to the chapter is a grave insult to this court. For after all you have been perfectly free to defend yourself.

MINDSZENTY: Yes, for that reason I am making this new statement now.

I can no longer reconstruct the exact course of this scene, but I can certainly say that it did not unfold in the manner represented in the *Black Book*. Possibly this was the version being broadcast over the radio from behind the glass wall. My conjecture is based on the fact that President Olti's question in the radio broadcast went as follows: "Did anyone prevent you from making any statement during the court proceedings, or on the other hand were you compelled to make any such statement?"

Had I really replied, "Certainly not," I could have done so only in response to the question that was asked me (according to the radio broadcast)—namely, whether I had been subject to coercion during the court proceedings. To such a general question as the one quoted in the *Black Book*, without the restriction to what was happening in court, I would not have answered "certainly not," not even in a state of total exhaustion and apathy. For that would have been untrue, and I know I could not have confirmed an untruth. I can therefore assert that the *Black Book* published a cunning distortion. The answer ascribed to me in it was a falsification.

There were, of course, people who preferred to believe my adversaries and who themselves insisted that the trial took place under conditions of complete freedom, with the requirements of due process scrupulously observed. They bolstered this view by referring to the introductory words of my defense attorney: "First of all I feel obliged to declare that I was freely chosen and empowered by the defendant to act in his behalf. . . . All the defendants had the opportunity to conduct their defense in full freedom. On this point I fully concur with the opinion of the honorable representative of the prosecution."

Perhaps the situation can best be summed up with an ironic quotation:

"There was indeed a conspiracy in the Mindszenty trial, not of defendants conspiring against the Republic, but of the police, the prosecution, the judge, and the defense attorney conspiring against the defendants."

☿ The Evidence

IN THE COURSE of normal judicial proceedings the defense has the opportunity to present its arguments, to raise objections, to cross-examine witnesses. Only by such means can the judge formulate his own opinion of the adversary disputes between the parties. The judge therefore takes care that each of the two parties enjoys the liberties assured him by law. The defense is also afforded the opportunity to present evidence, to name witnesses, to examine the *corpora delicti*, if such exist. This extremely important aspect of a trial takes place in public before the judge. Moreover the defense is allowed to equip itself beforehand with affidavits from experts and similar documents.

The judge can convict a defendant only after he is convinced beyond a doubt that the defendant in fact committed the punishable acts defined by law. Should the judge believe that the arguments advanced have not adequately proved the defendant's guilt he is supposed to acquit him. According to the fundamental principles of jurisprudence, the primary task and duty of the judge is to seek the truth. He can dispense justice only when the truth has been brought to light. Both defense and prosecution are also obliged to examine all the evidence presented and all extenuating circumstances. When this fundamental right is not granted to the defense, and when the defense is not allowed to speak freely, this can only be because the prosecution is bent on obtaining a conviction by force rather than by argument. The court is being used to approve a predetermined verdict.

Strictly speaking, a totalitarian government may well be in a better position than a liberal one to employ all possible means for determining the truth. If a government does not do so, we can assume that it has no interest in the truth, that it simply wants a conviction.

My defense, therefore, was first of all hampered by the fact that no witnesses in my favor were allowed to testify. But all witnesses on the other side had their say. They, too, however, were not allowed to testify freely, for they were either in jail or under police pressure. Such was the case with my archivist, János Fábián and my treasurer, Imre Bóka. Both had been arrested after the archiepiscopal palace was searched on December 23, 1948, and they were taken to Andrássy Street. The "confessions" of Professor Jusztin Baranyay and of my secretary Andras Zakár, which formally implicated me, had been extracted by torture.

The prosecution had certain confiscated documents that were apparently intended to be their prime exhibits. These were read aloud to prove that I had entertained the wild, not to say insane, notion of inciting the American government to make war on Hungary. That crazy charge had already been made in Andrássy Street, and at the time I had called it the spawn of a morbid imagination. At the time I wrote the letters in question, America had only agreed to an armistice with Hungary; together with England and Russia the United States exercised the rights of an occupying power in the Allied Control Commission in our defeated country. Nevertheless the indictment charged:

> According to the testimony of a large number of documents introduced in evidence, József Mindszenty established contact with Arthur Schoenfeld, the American ambassador in Budapest, and, after the latter's recall, with Ambassador Selden Chapin for the purpose of persuading the government of the United States of America to undertake hostile action against Hungary and influence the Hungarian government by force, in fact to bring about the realization of reactionary aims by forcible intervention.
>
> (*Black Book*, p.26.)

Further:

> According to the testimony of the impounded documents, Mindszenty fully realized that the overthrow of the democratic Republic would be possibly only by means of a war. Therefore he incited various leading personalities in American political life to take action with the end in view.
>
> (*Black Book*, p. 24.)

The prosecutor quoted only two brief snatches from my "incriminating" letters, and the letters themselves were never subsequently published anywhere. They did not appear in either the *Yellow Book* or the *Black Book*. Since the texts are therefore unknown in the free world, I have included them in this book; see Document 74.

I had written these letters not in order to overthrow the Republic, but in the hope of curbing the Communist party from blatantly acting entirely in its own interests. My reasoning was as follows: Those countries that had, according to the agreements at the Yalta conference, guaranteed the liberated countries of Eastern and Central Europe free elections and free governments could surely not permit Hungary, Christian for a thousand years, to be turned into a communist colony. But I was to find out that where Yalta was concerned, theory and practice were often miles apart.

During the trial Olti insisted that I confirm my authorship of these letters, but he read out only two half-sentences wrenched out of context. Then he declared that writing such letters was nothing less than warmongering.*

Such evidentiary logic can be regarded as typical of "socialist justice." The prosecution went so far as to characterize my stand against the Communist party as a crime against the democratic system—that is, against the Republic. That was tantamount to saying that "the democratic system" means the same as the Communist party. Such manipulation of jurisprudence is surely almost without parallel.

☦ The Defense

As is apparent from the *Black Book*, my defense counsel participated in four separate incidents that greatly enlivened proceedings in the court. The first time was at the very beginning of the trial, when Kiczkó was invited to take part in a consultation concerning the abovementioned letter to the minister of justice. The role he played consisted chiefly in speaking in behalf of the police and helping them conceal what had gone on in Andrássy Street.

He suddenly spoke up for the second time during a long, wearisome interrogation and asked that a seat be provided for me. His intervention led to the following little scene:

PRESIDENT (turning to me): Please say so if you are tired.
MINDSZENTY: Yes, I am.
PRESIDENT: Bring a chair! (A prison guard brings a chair; Mindszenty sits down.)
PRESIDENT: If you are by any chance mentally tired also, please say so and I'll order a recess. Can we continue the proceedings?
MINDSZENTY: Yes.

* See the quotation from the prosecution's presentation, Document 75.

The defense attorney's interjection was probably due less to his sympathetic heart than to his desire to serve the regime. Kiczkó waited until it was quite plain that I was on the point of collapse. Some members of the press corps had already noticed my exhaustion. Consequently, some of the news stories expressed suspicion that I must have been "prepared" for the trial in Andrássy Street. Others laid stress on "the humane treatment of the accused," and some accounts even referred to the "compassionate staff of the court" against whom slanders were being irresponsibly circulated.

Kiczkó's third bold stroke occurred toward the end of my testimony. The prosecutor once again was asking questions about my confession and the evidence for it. Suddenly—as though the matter had just happened to come to his mind—he spoke of the planned escape from Andrássy Street. "There was a discussion with Chapin in the course of which you declared you wanted to stay in the country. Do you, in this connection, now recognize your handwriting in a letter whose text I shall read aloud to you?" And he read:

> Dear Mr. Ambassador:
> We must act by Thursday. I ask you to do so because there is talk of the death penalty and because the proceedings are beginning to turn against America. They are asking me for a confirmation that I received money from America in return for revealing state secrets. Please provide an automobile and a plane. There is no longer any other way out.
> Mindszenty. January 23, 1949

PROSECUTOR: Did you write this letter?

MINDSZENTY: Yes. (Prolonged stir and noise in the courtroom.)

PRESIDENT: Are there any other questions? (He turns to the defense attorney.) Will you please question the defendant in the interests of the defense.

KICZKÓ: Does the primate identify himself with the plan proposed by Jusztin Baranyay in the sense that he completely grasped and thoroughly thought through every single sentence in it, or did he merely accept it as a plan?

MINDSZENTY: Since I did not pursue the matter . . .

KICZKÓ: Yes.

MINDSZENTY: . . . and did nothing further . . . it is obvious that I did not identify myself with it.

PRESIDENT: But you did not say this earlier. Earlier you said that before this document was drawn up you discussed it with Baranyay; that after several weeks, perhaps even after a month, Baranyay came and handed it over to you. It was studied and you once again discussed it. You agreed with it. Afterwards Baranyay drew up the cabinet list; before that was done you negotiated once more and made arrangements that Baranyay was also to prepare a list of administration officials. There were specific discussions of some names. Baranyay, then, made this list, had it sent to you, and on the whole you were in agreement with it. You said that only two hours ago, didn't you?

MINDSZENTY: Yes.

KICZKÓ: You studied it carefully but perhaps did not quite understand the matter.

PRESIDENT: That is not what he said.

KICZKÓ: But he is saying it now.
PRESIDENT: That is precisely why I am calling attention to the statements made during the earlier testimony.

This scene, too, proves to what extent the police, the prosecution, the judge, and the counsel for the defense were collaborating in the judicial farce. The police invented the plan of escape; a police lieutenant craftily obtained my consent to it when I was no longer in possession of my mental faculties. He himself wrote the letter, and during the trial the letter remained in the hand of the prosecutor, who read it aloud to the judge and the counsel for defense. But the so-called counsel—whose duty it should have been to ask how the plan had arisen, who had composed the letter, and how it came to be in the prosecutor's possession—passed over these details as if he had to use the time at his disposal for the other, more important question regarding the matter of the Baranyay "plot." His discussion of this "plot," moreover, was an exercise in hypocrisy. His attitude was plainly revealed when he attempted to have me say that I had subscribed to but had not wholly understood the affair.

Of course, the whole little scene was also intended to show that the "honorable" and "capable" counsel had done his best for a hopelessly lost cause.

Kiczkó demonstrated his talents for the last time when he answered the prosecution's summation. I scarcely think any of his colleagues abroad is likely to match this particular "masterpiece" of his. For to my disadvantage, but to the great advantage of those who staged the trial, my counsel stated:

1. At all times, including the period he was in Andrássy Street and during the trial itself, the defendant had the opportunity to conduct his defense without interference.
2. He confessed fully to all the charges.
3. He must be regarded as a victim of the Vatican.
4. The Church is an enemy of the state because the latter deprived it of land and took away its schools. "My client erred when he thought that the secularization of the schools would promote religious and moral decadence among the youth."
5. The defendant lived in a kind of ivory tower and therefore failed to observe the great progress and reconstruction in the country.
6. He was an inexperienced cleric who rose to the highest office in the church.
7. He confirms what the prosecutor has frequently stressed: There is no religious persecution in Hungary.
8. He affirms the necessity of an agreement between Church and state.
9. In view of extenuating circumstances the defense moves that the sentence of life imprisonment be granted instead of the death penalty demanded by the prosecution.

Kiczkó several times referred to my "repentance." Before this altogether astonishing defense summation the prosecutor had delivered his summation, demanding the defendant's execution.*

* See Document 76.

I want to mention two sidelights on the trial. When the police were leading us out after the close of the session, Colonel Décsi walked alongside me. He expressed his regret that the letter to the minister of justice had been of no avail and that my case had not been treated separately and adjourned. As for the failure of the plan of escape, Koczak, an official at the embassy, was responsible for that. He had left Budapest at the end of January, forgetting the letter to the ambassador, which had been handed over to him to pass on, in a drawer of his desk. After Koczak someone else moved into the apartment, found the letter, and promptly turned it over to the police for fear of being implicated.

(Years later, in the American Embassy, I learned that Koczak had not left Budapest and the country until February 11, 1949, when he was expelled.)

I also want to add that during a recess Kiczkó tried to persuade me to make a statement to the effect that I had not been tortured and influenced, but had been able to defend myself freely in Andrássy Street and in Markó Street also. My defense counsel wanted such a statement, he said, because the foreign imperialist newspapers were carrying articles about torture and drugs, and were going so far as to impugn his own integrity, the "honorable and conscientious" counsel.

☿ The Verdict

THE PUBLIC PROCEEDINGS lasted for three days. At their end the court was convinced we were all guilty and imposed severe prison sentences on all of us.

I was sentenced to life imprisonment and Jusztin Baranyay to fifteen years, since we were regarded as the leaders of the organization that had aimed at overthrowing the Republic—the crime specified in the notorious "hangman's law." András Zakár was sentenced to six years for participation in the organization. Pál Esterházy was given fifteen years because he had provided the organization with financial aid.

As I now see from the documents published in the *Black Book*, the question of how Esterházy supported the conspiracy was raised erroneously from the start. From his own confession and that of his secretary and my treasurer it appeared only that his secretary had bought dollars and checks on foreign currencies from my treasurer, paying for them in forint. Allegedly these sums were payments for "certain purposes." My treasurer gave the forint thus received to the poor and needy, in keeping with the donor's request. The People's Court nevertheless sentenced Esterházy to fifteen years imprisonment for giving financial support to an organization that intended the overthrow of the Republic.

According to the court, there was not the slightest doubt that we were guilty. No evidence of armed uprisings or riot was required, for any opposition to the Republic was regarded as an infraction of the law. Thus any attempt to change the form of government by peaceful and legal means was also a criminal offense. In reality we had not aimed at overthrowing the Republic either by peaceable or by violent means. The prosecution had only cunningly twisted some of my acts to make it seem so. My actual crimes consisted in having fought against the illegalities of the communist rulers, in having defended the religious freedom the laws solemnly guaranteed, and in having attempted to preserve the Catholic schools and religious instruction and to prevent the introduction of atavist monopoly in education.

In drafting the text of their law the Communists had already been thinking of future show trials. But the deputies who accepted the new law, especially the members of the Smallholders party, did not perceive these designs on the part of the Communists. To those who still recalled the show trials under Hitler and Stalin, and who therefore wanted a law that specified more precisely what crimes were involved, the authors of the "hangman's law" stressed the word "overthrow," implying that only acts of direct violence were in question.

When I first discovered in Andrássy Street that I was to be charged with conspiracy on the basis of Article VII of the law of 1946, I pointed to this word "overthrow" in the text and reasoned that my actions were all outside of the scope of the statute. Moreover, in invoking this law against me, the People's Court was violating two principles of the Constitution.

Article I of 1946, which proclaimed a republican form of government, had guaranteed every citizen the free exercise of fundamental human rights. Among these it explicitly named free expression of ideas and opinions, the rights of organization and assembly, and the right of participation in the governing process. In 1947 the Hungarian Parliament ratified the Peace Treaty of Paris. In Article XVIII it solemnly pledged itself to respect the rights of man.

Accordingly, no illegality could be imputed to any movement or organization seeking a change in the republican form of government. Theoretically and constitutionally Parliament could at any time repeal Article I of 1946; and members of Parliament can start a movement to do so. So can any individual citizen. In handing down our verdicts, therefore, the People's Court was citing Article VII of 1946 in an unconstitutional manner. In purely formal terms, conviction of the group of us was a grave violation of the law.

I consider this view of mine confirmed by a proclamation of Imre Nagy's government during the Revolution of 1956. The statement read:

The government of Hungary solemnly declares that the charges made in 1948 against Primate József Mindszenty lacked all legal foundation. We declare null and void all legal actions taken against him. The primate is free to resume his office and to exercise all his civil and ecclesiastical duties.

The authorities tried to cover up their lack of evidence and legality by shrill propaganda. From the moment of my arrest to the last scene in the judicial spectacle, the controlled press kept up its ranting about "traitors" who meant to rob the Hungarian people of their newly won democratic freedoms.*

The *Black Book* also published my "final statement"; legally I was entitled to one, but I was not at all the author of the printed statement. Anyone who is even casually acquainted with me will recognize that neither the tone nor the content of this speech, nor the self-accusation contained in it, are consonant with my character and my way of thinking. The accompanying address to the episcopate, with its expression of a wish for a concordat between Church and state, was intended to bring the "intimidated" bishops to the negotiating table, but it failed in its purpose. The Holy See promptly declared that it would not countenance any negotiations under the present circumstances and that willingness to negotiate was "incompatible" with the treatment that had been visited upon me.

Consequently, no discussions were held. I, however, did not know that this was the position taken by the bishops. My only information was the lie Gábor Péter had told me in Andrássy Street, that the majority of the bishops were against me. On the eve of the trial I had heard only the false report that "the bishops are leaving the settlement of the Mindszenty case to the wise judgment of the government."

On January 2, 1949, Pope Pius XII sent a letter to the bishops of Hungary decrying my arrest. In a secret consistory held on February 14, 1949, the Holy Father denounced my conviction in the strongest possible terms.** What a consolation it would have been to me in Andrássy Street and in Markó Street if I had heard about the pope's loving concern. But not a gleam of his kind, bright words penetrated into the darkness in which I dwelt.

In the later era of coexistence, the events surrounding this show trial, and also the convictions of Rákosi and his successors, caused some problems. The Kádár regime found itself forced by the mood in the country to rehabilitate some of the victims of the political trials. The principle of "socialist justice" guided the decisions. Consequently, the victims of the Mindszenty trial were not rehabilitated. They were merely given the opportunity to ask for a humiliating pardon.

I myself always demanded rehabilitation as a precondition to my agreeing to leave the country. After the Vatican's negotiations with the Hungarian

* See Document 77 for a sample of government rhetoric.
** See Document 78.

authorities in 1971 I was unable to leave my country rehabilitated; I was still a convict. It was only after I was out of the country that the news reached me that I had been pardoned. Evidently the authorities had not dared to hand me the documents of this procedure in Hungary. As soon as I heard about them abroad, I wrote to the minister of justice:

A few days after leaving my native land I learned that the regime had sent me notice of a pardon. Throughout fifteen years I made no application for any such pardon, did not accept one, and now reject it on the grounds that amends can be made for the judicial crime committed against me only by an act of rehabilitation, nothing less.

VI. IMPRISONMENT

☿ The Reception Prison

ON FEBRUARY 8, 1949, after the announcement of the verdict and sentence, I was taken to a car with draped windows. Three servants and three police officers accompanied me. While I kept silent, they lauded the achievements of the communist movement for the good of the country. No doubt one of its greatest achievements was my incarceration. After an hour's drive we arrived at Köbánya Prison, which was used as a distribution point from which prisoners were sent to their final destinations. I was taken to Room No. 10 in the prison hospital. Here I was held from February 8 to September 27, 1949.

It struck me that I had been sentenced to the penitentiary but had been taken to an ordinary prison. Perhaps this was because my battered body would not have stood the hardships of a penitentiary after the mistreatment I had undergone in Andrássy Street. But it may also have been that they wanted me near a hospital because I needed medical treatment after the drugs that had been administered to me.

The doctor who had visited me three times a day in Andrássy Street also came to see me here—daily during the first two weeks. He examined me without a word in the same strange fashion that he had practiced in Andrássy Street, checking my heart, breathing, pulse, eyes, thyroid gland, and blood pressure. Probably at this time medicines were being given to me in my food to restore gradually my organism's shattered equilibrium. I imagine that the government also wanted to hoodwink the public by having me in a somewhat better place than an ordinary penitentiary. From my mother's visits the world would be able to find out that I was not in the penitentiary, but in a prison. Not that it was any the better place to be. A convict can be treated with penitentiary methods even when he is in a prison. This prison was an old building intended for about 1,000 persons. After the end of the Second World War the number of persons regularly held there by the Communists always amounted to several thousands. Death sentences were frequently carried out there. We lived in the shadow of the gallows.

Convicts were not left alone in their prison. Every three months commissioners arrived from the ministry of the interior to ferret out any hidden accomplices of the political prisoners. Listening devices were installed in the cells. Informers were at work. Earlier confessions extracted by torture were compared with the evidence obtained from the "bugs." By favors or threats prisoners were persuaded to denounce other persons. Those who proved stubborn found the quality or quantity of their food diminished. If they still resisted, there was always the threat of transfer to insane asylums.

The prison was a one-story building in the vicinity of a desecrated church and a police barracks; one side was surrounded by the high stone wall of the Rákoskeresztur cemetery. Our warden was Police First Lieutenant Károly Kiss. Maybe he shifted from the gendarmerie to the new department of the Secret Police, and was trying to make a career by a policy of harshness toward the prisoners. But there were also humanely minded persons in the prison, among whom I want to remember the name of First Lieutenant Fülöp. These men, however, had to suffer reprisals for their decency and for every act of kindness toward me.

My room was not entirely without its comforts. In length it was somewhat over twenty-two feet, in breadth about twelve feet. The furniture consisted of bed, table, and chairs; there was even a built-in toilet, and also central heating, which, however, was seldom turned on, so that I often suffered from cold. The room, but especially the bed and bedding, was a paradise for bedbugs. When I called Lieutenant Kiss's attention to this, he replied brazenly: "I would be surprised if there weren't any." Airing the room was forbidden, although even Kiss himself once clapped his hands and exclaimed: "Ugh, what a stink!" Nevertheless opening the window continued to be banned by the prison regulations. It was permissible to open only the door, through which entered nothing but stale hospital air.

Every day I was allowed a short walk in the garden, but only when there was no danger of my meeting or being seen by other prisoners, patients, or outsiders. Usually I was fetched for this refreshment only after twilight had fallen. If the comrade guards were having a particularly good time with the comrade nurses, it would not be before ten or eleven o'clock at night that I was taken out to the open air. If I had already gone to sleep by that time, I would be awakened, for the government was very concerned about my health, I was told. Kiss, who often accompanied me, was never content with the way I behaved on my walks. If I walked too slow, he nagged; if too fast, he also objected to that. Sometimes he would simply break off the walk and order me back into the building.

Outbreaks of sudden frenzy occurred frequently in the prison hospital. The guards tried to explain these to me as the result of advanced syphilis. After my liberation, however, I learned that the cases of mental illness had greatly increased during the years of my imprisonment. Hundreds upon hundreds of political prisoners had been brought to this particular prison hospital. By "special treatment" the police had first ruined their minds and nerves, and then did not dare to send their victims to ordinary mental hospitals where it would have been more difficult to hide the facts from the public.

Aside from the regimented organization, which dominated the everyday life of the place, I was struck by the prevailing filthy and ugly tone. Employees and guards both male and female outdid one another in this, and the worst of all was the chief physician whom I never saw, thank God, but heard all too frequently.

The secrets of the adjacent cemetery weighed heavily on my mind. It held the graves of many fine Hungarians who had risked their lives for God and country. Stretcher bearers were constantly carrying dead fellow prisoners across the courts and out through the garden to this last resting place, past whatever prisoners happened to be having their exercise in the open air. Later, during the days of the 1956 struggle for freedom, many a young hero was buried here.

☩ Confirmation of the Verdict

THE VERDICT and sentence of the court had been pronounced. I myself, however, was not given the opportunity to see it in writing. The prosecutor applied to the Supreme Court for imposition of the death sentence. Evidently it did not occur to my counsel that he too might have challenged the verdict. When I became somewhat more accustomed to my new surroundings, the prison hospital, I therefore decided to turn to the court of appeals, which in this case was the National Council of People's Courts, asking that the verdict against me be overturned on the grounds that I had been treated in Andrássy Street with drugs that paralyzed my will. I therefore asked for a lawyer to draw up my petition, and wrote several letters, some of them to the minister of justice. Probably my letters never reached their destinations, but were held by the police.

I also turned to the archbishop of Kalocsa and asked him to help me, as well as to send a copy of my letter to the archbishop of Eger. Only after my release did I learn that the police had confected, from my short note, a much longer letter which they turned over to the Hungarian news agency. The main theme of this forged letter was my insistence on an "agreement" between Church and state and an expression of my "regret" for my former conduct. Fortunately the bishops promptly recognized this foregery for what it was and paid no attention to it.

During the first part of July 1949, even before the decision of the court of appeals, I recanted in writing the "confessions" that had been extorted from me in Andrássy Street, referring to the tortures inflicted by the police and the use of drugs. This recantation, however, seems to have been completely ignored. As a matter of custom, convicted men were not allowed to appear in person before a court of appeals. I therefore knew almost nothing about the status of my case. The court of appeals took it up on July 6. Since the first verdict was pronounced I had not seen my counsel, Kálmán Kiczkó. I was informed of the decision of the court of appeals on August 14. Thus I lived for half a year in uncertainty as to my fate, frequently wondering whether the prosecutor's appeal would be granted and whether I would be condemned to death or would be able to go on living. I certainly wanted to go on living, among other reasons because I did not give up hope of some time again being able to work for my Church and my country. Later on there were times when I thought death would be better.

On August 14 I was handed the decision to read, but required to return the document and never had another chance to see it until 1954. In August I saw only that the death penalty had been rejected and the sentence to life imprisonment in the penitentiary confirmed—only because my case was no longer regarded as of much significance.

☦ My Mother's Visits

MY MOTHER was allowed to visit me three times in the prison hospital. Her first visit came two weeks after the trial. The authorities waited that long after the judicial farce because my health still left a good deal to be desired. The authorities ruled that the conversation must be confined to family matters. Gábor Péter informed my mother that this, her first visit to me, would likewise be her last if she did not keep to this condition.

My mother drove out to the prison in a police car, accompanied by a secret policeman and a policewoman. We met in Room No. 10 in the presence of Károly Kiss. A chair was brought for my mother, but I had to remain standing. My mother then asked Kiss to give me a chair also. He thought this needless and declared that it was forbidden. So we talked standing for about twelve minutes.

My mother had counted on my being in such ill health that she happily took note of my relatively good condition.

Before her second visit my mother had attended a baptism in Márianosztra. A family of believers wanted to express their sympathy for me by choosing me as the godfather for their newborn child. My mother took my place, acting as godmother. After the baptism, then, she came for her second visit, and informed me that she had just been in Máriaremete to pray at that place of pilgrimage to the Virgin Mary for me. And she added: "My son, you have a large family who prays for you everywhere."

At that Károly Kiss interrupted to remind us that we were allowed to speak only of family affairs. I replied: "You can hear that my mother is talking only about the family," and I went on to ask also about our blood-relations and whether they were also praying for me. But when my mother began telling about the newborn baby's family, Kiss again protested, and my mother informed him that "among religious people like us not only relatives by blood belong to the family, but our spiritual children also." The "dutiful" lieutenant did not reply.

My mother visited me for the third time on September 25, 1949. She talked to my former doctor and to friends about this last meeting, describing me as tired and low in spirits and suffering from a noticeable enlargement of the thyroid gland. I later learned from Dr. József Vecsey's memoirs that at the time my mother had the impression that the Communists were trying to prepare the ground for my dying a "natural" death; and that they were doing so not only by negligent medical treatment, but by deliberately speeding the process. Perhaps they wanted to use my mother's visits for the purpose of slowly preparing the public mind to expect my death.

This seems all the more probable since after her third visit I was after all transferred to the penitentiary on, I believe, Conti Street. Under former regimes, it had also served as the prison for political offenders. Usually a "natural" death followed rapidly, thus solving all the problems associated with such persons.

At her last visit in the reception prison my mother insisted that I be given the medical treatment my condition required. But instead the following day brought the news that I was soon to be transferred to the penitentiary. The pretext for this order was an "infraction" that I had allegedly been guilty of during her visit. It seems I had asked my mother to arrange in Esztergom for a Mass stipend to be set up for the Masses I daily celebrated, and to distribute the sum thus accumulated among the poor from time to time. I had also asked her to send me a coat which I could wear in prison. This was also called an infraction of the rules. On September 27, therefore, I was transferred to "stricter incarceration."

I had spent half a year in the reception prison. This span of time had sufficed to let me and my cause fall into oblivion in the outside world. Thus my enemies could now send me to the penitentiary without fear of any criticism.

☩ *The Penitentiary*

ONCE MORE I sat behind draped windows in the transport car. The officials with me refused to give me any information on the destination. I conjectured, however, that we had only driven a short distance and could not be very far from the reception prison. By way of a dirt road that wound through fields and groves of trees, we reached my new home. There at the gate, to my great surprise, Károly Kiss awaited me again. Evidently he enjoyed the favor of my former torturer in Andrássy Street, who was now his superior and had made him acting warden of the penitentiary.

A major led me straight to the clothing center. There the black civilian suit and my underclothes were roughly stripped from me. When I protested against this form of undressing, the lame policeman whom I had encountered on my first night in Andrássy Street made filthy remarks. Everything I possessed was taken from me, even my shoelaces and suspenders. I was allowed neither a drinking glass nor a fork and knife; there was a general fear here that the convicts might use such implements to commit suicide. The usual convict clothing was then distributed to me: old, yellowed underclothes, trousers and a smock of cotton twill, a cap of the same material. There were no gloves, handkerchiefs, or nightshirt in this wardrobe.

Nevertheless a special kindness was shown to me: I was given a volume of the breviary. This one was, however, intended for the spring, although we were already deep into the fall. When I remarked on this, Kiss replied: "Don't be choosy, prayer is prayer." In spite of my pleas I was refused any other book. I was also not allowed to have a watch, writing materials, and my rosary. Nor was I permitted to say Mass anymore.

Károly Kiss obviously enjoyed his power. His face beamed when he could appear in gala uniform. He loved his boots, but even more the heels of his boots, thanks to which he could settle a good many questions rapidly and drastically. The humiliation of prisoners gave him pleasure, in keeping with his view that a convict could never be right and was always insolent.

Apparently his health was none too good; he had a sound stomach, but there seemed to be things wrong with his lungs and heart. Fresh air was the medicine for these, he believed; and he had become a passionate walker. The remarkable fact is, however, that he did not regard the air in the interior court, in the street, or in the fields—available to him at all times—as the right medicine for him. The only air that suited him was that along the prisoners' walk. He was already out on that walk at six in the morning. At first he gave himself a limited time to exercise; but later on he often continued right on to noon, so that the prisoners' hours for walking had to be curtailed and frequently eliminated entirely.

Only the "lieutenant with the whistle" could compete with Kiss in making the lives of the prisoners miserable. The lieutenant's speciality was search and confiscation. He rummaged through everything, from the straw pallet to the last page in the breviary. At such times he enjoyed stationing me in the corner, face to the wall, so that I would hear nothing and see nothing. If I permitted myself a remark, he informed me: "You talk only when I ask you a question!" Once he tried to involve me in talk of such filthy vileness that I showed him the door. It is relatively to his credit that he went out at once. A professional villain, as Oscar Wilde would have said. While Rákosi was still flourishing, the man vanished from the institution. Major Vékási, who succeeded Kiss, was an entirely different sort of man. He proved to be much more humane. Although he was not always objective, he never committed acts of cruelty or coarseness.

The guards at that time observed the change of climate and adjusted to it. A prisoner could distinctly feel how the guards behaved precisely in keeping with the warden's mentality. How often I had to listen to blasphemous curses using Christ's name. I thought at such times: "No Hungarian mother bore you, and if one did, the fruit belies the tree." Some of my fellow prisoners seemed to think that the cardinal's guard had been recruited from the worst elements of the prison staff. For quite often I would hear prisoners remark of violent guards and other personnel: "I suppose they were used to guard Cardinal Mindszenty."

Between September 27, 1949, and May 13, 1954, the period I spent under penitentiary conditions, I often asked myself where I actually was. When we got out of the car at the time of my arrival, I asked a lieutenant in my escort whether we were in Harta. He nodded mutely. I therefore thought I was in that penitentiary, where Nádossy had once been a prisoner after he was convicted in the Frank forgery trial. But in 1955 when I had the opportunity to talk to a priest, he did not know where I had been imprisoned for all those years. From my description he was inclined to think I had been held in Kistarcsa. But there was no penitentiary there. From official documents I was later able to see, I learned that I was deliberately kept uncertain of the place. There was one unclear passage in the documents which seemed to suggest Conti Penitentiary in Budapest.

There is a penitentiary on Conti Street in the VIIIth District of Budapest. It has room for 200 prisoners, but 300 were held there. During the last century the building served as headquarters for the garrison and for the military court. In the 1940s military spies were held there before being sent to the dungeons. The rooms were damp, close, and moldy. Generally the prisoners died within six months. On the whole only those political prisoners were sent to Conti Street whom the authorities wanted to get rid of by a "natural" death. Next door to the building was a tavern where gypsy music was played all summer long. There also seems to have been a police barracks with offices and living quarters in the vicinity; many children would be playing in the garden. If wrangles broke out among the women, the husbands and fathers—policemen all—had to hurry over to straighten things out. There were also idyllic times, on Sundays and after meals, when someone would be playing the familiar song on a guitar: "I hitch my horse to my yellow carriage . . ."

In the distance I heard the bells of several churches. During the first year of my imprisonment the Easter parade and also the Corpus Christi procession were allowed in the streets; and I always joined these in spirit.

☧ The Cell

THE DOOR of my penitentiary cell opened on the main corridor; the window gave on a rectangular courtyard partly paved, partly lawn. The cell was smaller than the one adjacent to the cemetery had been. Nevertheless, it was not altogether an ordinary cell. There were rather good murals on the walls. That surprised me; and I was more surprised that the murals had not yet been effaced. For they were not at all in keeping with the new ideology.

There was a peephole in the wooden door, but of course it was not there for the convict's entertainment. And yet so many interesting things might have been seen in the corridor outside: large numbers of guards in ordinary clothes and in uniform! There were often more of them than prisoners.

Guards repeatedly peered in through the judas, enjoying the sight of the new arrival, cracking their jokes. I made no response to any of it. Suddenly the warden appeared and shouted: "Don't you be impertinent! Forget who and what you were before. There are worse cells than this one—in the dungeons."

The "livestock" I found already present in the gloomy, damp room was not especially edifying. A whole colony of spiders seemed to be living by the window. Other small creatures dwelt on the floor and in the filthy bedding. Facilities were completed by a bucket, an aluminum washbasin, two threadbare blankets, a towel, table and chair, and a multicolored sheet that may once have served the painter of the murals as a cloth on which he wiped his brushes. There was a slip of paper on the wall that announced, in wretched Hungarian, the daily routine. I still remember it fairly well:

A.M. 5:00 Rise, collect refuse, wash, brush teeth [without toothbrush or toothpaste], make bed.
6:00 Dust [the towel serves as dustcloth]. Then free time.
7:00 Breakfast.
8:00 to 4:00 P.M. Waiting to take a walk, with time out for:
P.M. 1:00 Lunch.
6:00 Supper.
7:00 Bed.

This entire schedule was enveloped in boredom and garnished by the curses of the guards.

This cell was, however, not destined to be my permanent quarters. Forcible removals are reckoned among the duties and the amusements of jailers. Thus a "change of lodgings" came for me as early as the middle of the night on November 18, 1949. Surrounded by policemen, I carried my possessions (washbowl, tin mug, etc.) to a new cell. It was a close, damp room next to the noisy toilet. Here, too, the wall had been decorated, although this mural did not show a historical scene, but some common obscenities. Perhaps for that very reason I was being assigned to this cell.

I thought of the day's patron saint, St. Elizabeth, who after her expulsion from the Wartburg had withdrawn to a stable. At the time she had begun to sing a Te Deum; and so I too did not want to complain. I prayed to God for the grace of being able to say:

Be gracious to thy servants. For us thy timely mercies, for us abiding happiness and content; happiness that shall atone for the time when thou didst afflict us, for the long years of ill fortune. Psalms 89, 13–15

And in my thoughts I looked up to the saints. Asked what he expected for his struggle and for the sacrifice of his life, St. John of the Cross replied: "To suffer and to be despised for thee, Lord."

We are small, but we can grow taller. The saints always walked upon the highest heights when they descended into the deepest depths of human wretchedness and human suffering. Lord, give me only a little of the bearing of the saints!

I stayed in that room for three nights. Then I was taken to another on the ground floor and told: "Hereafter this good cell will be permanently yours."

In December work began on the ground-floor cells, renovating and installing stoves—evidently there had been no time for such repairs in the summer and fall. During the operations, but possibly also because the number of prisoners had increased, we had to move up to the first floor. The warden appeared with his retinue. The "lieutenant with the whistle" ordered: "Pack up, you're moving!" In front of me strode a policeman; behind me, in high good spirits, the warden. He showed me my new cell and said mockingly: "This will be your new private apartment—until death do you part." In the short span of a month I was placed successively in eight different cells. How many I lived in during the eight years I can no longer say.

At seven o'clock in the evening on New Year's Eve came the order: "Back to the ground floor." I was given strict orders not to lie down until I received special permission to do so.

When I entered, I found myself in an unheated dungeon. (The stoves never had a fire in them during the entire winter.) The cell was icy cold, probably in part because the newly plastered walls were still damp. What is more, this room was deep below the ground level, and water seeped incessantly through the walls. There was little hope that the dampness would ever improve, for the sun never entered here, not even in summer.

My teeth chattered and I wished at least that I could be back on my cold, moldy straw pallet—while I continued to pace back and forth waiting for the announced permission. But no one came. And so dressed, without permission, I slipped into bed. Immediately the guard appeared and bawled at me that I had plenty of time to wait. It was true, the "lifer" has time to wait until death.

From a book by Father Walter Ciszek, S.J., I have learned that this procedure of making the convict change places frequently is a Soviet invention. In the span of twenty-three years Father Ciszek was transferred from Moscow to Norilsk, Krasnojarsk, and Abakan. In the larger towns he repeatedly had to change prisons, and in each prison he was moved from cell to cell.

Such shifts are quite often an amusement for the jailer, but they are also undertaken as a precaution. The idea is to make it impossible for the prisoner to form lasting relationships with any of the individuals in his environment.

☦ 8 *Convict Humor*

EVEN A CONVICT is not always mournful. A prisoner's heart is surely the cradle for gallow's humor, as the term suggests. There are many tales to bear this out. A gypsy being led to the gallows on a Monday sighs: "Well, this sure is a good start for the week." Another story has come down to us from the Middle Ages. Markalf, who had just been condemned to death, asked the king to grant him one last wish. The king promised. Whereupon Markalf asked permission to go into the forest and himself choose the tree on which he was to be hanged. He never found it.

Lifers, too, retain a dash of humor. My jailer was a thorough representative of the regime. Now and then, when he came in to see me, I felt the need to amuse myself at his expense. I therefore presented him with complicated legal questions and let him decide them. I would pretend that I did not know what course of action to take. For example:

"Is a convict priest who has been sentenced to life imprisonment and therefore will never see his congregation again still required to go through the prayers of the breviary for them? And is he still required if he does not have the book corresponding to the season? Is he required to say Mass for the faithful when he is not allowed to celebrate?"

The warden took the trouble to reflect and then pronounced the "wise" opinion: "I dispense you from all of it."

Once he asked: "Is there anything you wish?"

I replied: "There is only one thing I wish. When I was arrested, forty-nine forint were taken from me. I suppose that was the very least I have been deprived of. This money has been set aside, I imagine. Even lifers can be released after fifteen years. By then, however, there may have been an inflation. If the money were returned to me now, however, I could use it to buy clothes for some of my godchildren."

The warden actually fell for my allusion; he flushed red as a turkey and exclaimed furiously:

"What? You think the Hungarian forint will lose value? Let me tell you something, it cannot lose its value. It is the best currency in the world; on all the money markets it is marked up."

"Please don't be angry. I'm delighted to hear that our Hungarian currency is so highly esteemed these days," I said. "It doesn't matter really; it has no materiality and therefore can't disintegrate the way all material things do."

In 1955 the sum actually was returned to me without my having asked again. When my mother visited I was able to give her the money for my two godchildren. My mother merely smiled, and I could guess that she was thinking: "He no longer knows the real value of the forint."

The proverb says: "Weeping, the Hungarian amuses himself." That is even more true for Hungarian prisoners. The convict's humor is like that of the exiled Mides, who wrote: "We are in such high spirits that we are almost dying in our grief."

☦ *Gábor Péter Visits Me*

ONE DAY the guard informed me that the lieutenant general in person was at the prison and was going to visit me. I received this announcement in silence. Shortly afterwards, the door opened and the feared, almighty lord of Andrássy Street entered my cell. He greeted me and asked how I was.

"In the usual state of a person in such a place," I replied.

To that he answered: "I have always held that the conviction of the primate was a major political error. It has done nothing but harm to the state as well as the Church. Your connections should instead have been used to obtain foreign exchange for us, which we need."

I said nothing.

He told me that László Rajk had been convicted and sentenced to several years at hard labor. Then he returned to the subject of dollars. I could be helpful to the government now, he said, and if I cooperated I would be released.

I thought over this strange offer. Was I to go to America and beg dollars for the Communists? What a perverse idea: I was being asked to abandon my principles and obtain money for the Communists.

Gábor Péter likewise remained silent. He waited for my answer. But I could not let such a good opportunity pass, and commented sarcastically:

"But you know I'm in this dark cell just because I brought foreign exchange into the country."

The general pretended that he had not rightly understood the reply. He took up the idea once again, offering the argument that such action on my part would help our country, myself, and the Catholic Church. I did not show sufficient interest in the proposition for Gábor Péter even to discuss what ideas he might have about "release."

It may be that he had come simply to see for himself how I was getting along in the penitentiary and what the state of my health was. After he left it occurred to me that the Red Cross might have inquired about me. It was good policy to give reassuring answers to such inquiries from abroad—that the prisoner had made a good adjustment; that the higher authorities were concerned about him and had checked his conditions; and that he was receiving whatever medical treatment he needed.

Years later I learned that the chief of the police had not even told me the truth about Rajk. For Rajk was executed on October 15, 1949. That was during Kádár's period in office as minister of the interior. Like me, Rajk was convicted under the "hangman's law." It is said that the minister of the interior persuaded him, on a friendly basis, to make a confession of guilt, holding out the prospect that after the end of the judicial spectacle—Rajk was perfectly familiar with the technique of show trials, after all—he would soon be released.

Later, after I learned that he had been hanged, my mind dwelt a good deal on Rajk's fate. For on that same October 15, 1949, I had had to watch an execution from my window, so that later I conjectured that he may at that time have been executed in the prisoners' yard. In the early morning hours there had been considerable hammering as the carpenters set up the gallows. The normal hour of waking passed without the usual command to get up. Suddenly there was a great deal of movement in the courtyard. Through the small window I could not make out much, but I saw parts of a viewing stand and the gallows. A large crowd was assembled down below.

I pounded on my door. Luckily one of the friendly guards responded. I asked him why we had not been wakened.

"We have orders to allow a long rest period today."

"Is there a hanging?"

"Yes, there is an execution. But I'm risking my neck, talking to a convict."

"My son, I have no connections with those who could possibly harm you. Is it an officer, an enlisted man, or a civilian being hanged?"

"Not an ordinary man, an officer."

I returned to the window and wished I could stand on a chair, but there was none in the cell. There was a fairly large nail in my shoe, and I managed to pull it out. With the nail I broke some of the wires from the grating over the window, so that I could see out rather more clearly through the small gap. Drawing myself up by the sill, I peered out. On the platform stood a man I did not know, but who had the important look of someone high in government. Gábor Péter was there, and several of the policemen who had interrogated me in Andrássy Street. The warden of my present penitentiary was there likewise, and some men I took, from their pads and pencils, to be reporters. All wore dark suits. Beneath the gallows stood a middle-aged man clad only in underwear. The hangman knotted the noose on the rope; the party of spectators seemed to let that in no way diminish their good humor. But suddenly the babble of conversation stopped as the condemned man screamed: "I die an innocent man!" I spoke the prayers of absolution for him, and the execution was carried out. Shortly afterwards, the dead body was let down and carried away.

There is nothing more depressing than a convict's funeral and a convict's grave. In many large cities there are well-cared-for cemeteries for dogs and cats with marble gravestones bearing tender sentiments; there are grave mounds, wreaths, ivy, hot tears, choking sobs. "We will never forget this beloved animal," the bereft owners say; and they mean it, for throughout their lives they will remember their grief. But nothing of the sort is accorded the prisoner when he closes his eyes and the noose is tightened around his neck. Neither his mother nor his wife and children will be informed of the time or place of his burial. No tears will be shed, no flowers strewn or prayers said over his grave. No stone or other marker will tell who lies there. Only the trumpet of the Last Judgment can reach such a grave. No one ever even sees the prisoners' graves.

After the execution, breakfast was evidently provided, and when the participants were satiated with food and drink they wanted to "see Mindszenty." Thus, on the same morning of October 15, 1949, two officers entered my cell and one of them said:

"Comrade state secretary has ordered you to be brought to the rooms on the first floor. Follow us. I remind you that you are to behave like a prisoner; otherwise you will receive a punishment."

I decided to remain silent—but not because I feared their threat. For that was what my Lord and Master had done before Herod when he was arrayed in gorgeous apparel. The disciple does not stand above his teacher, nor the servant above his master.

We walked down the narrow corridor, my spiked shoes making a loud clatter, the guards in front and behind me. I found climbing the stairs hard, but they hurried me on.

We entered an empty office with the familiar pictures of Lenin, Stalin, Zhukov, and Rákosi. Then the door to the adjoining room was opened. I entered and stood there in my convict's uniform, emaciated and pale. In front of me in the center of the room was the high official I had seen on the platform. Gábor Péter and his men were there, and also a brace of reporters. All broke into laughter when I entered. The high official also laughed and then asked: "Are you Mindszenty?"

I did not reply.

"This uniform is very becoming to you." The bystanders gurgled with laughter.

"Have you any wishes?"

I did not reply.

"This is just as it should be; the people are the masters now. We'll soon have the pope behind bars too."

We stood confronting one another for a while, each mute. I thought of Herod's banquet and his victim, John the Baptist.

Then the official gave a sign and I was taken out.

Back in my cell I knelt and thanked the Lord that He had found me worthy to share shame with Him, our Savior and Redeemer.

☿ *Moods in Solitary*

NOISE INDUCES nervousness, but the quiet of solitary confinement also destroys the nerves gradually. The mere question: "How late is it really?" can wear down the prisoner. He no longer has a watch; it is therefore difficult for him to follow the passage of time. There are only a few clues to the course of the day. The time for getting up and going to bed alone are usually signaled punctually. But even these fixed points are occasionally advanced or retarded, as in the case of an execution, or when prisoners are moved to different cells in the evening.

Inactivity makes solitude worse. I have come to understand the poet Ferenc Verseghy (1757–1822) who was so bored in Austrian prison that he translated the *Marseillaise* into Hungarian, and for that act was sentenced to an additional nine years imprisonment.

In the stillness of the cell, the solitary prisoner feels like the polar explorer Nansen, who wrote of his own experience with being cut off from the world: "I wander aimlessly about the wasteland of the icefields. I am downcast; I don't feel like doing anything. Day and night I am depressed, physically and psychically drained, shattered."

Only the pictures on the wall, their captions, and the scribbles on the doors stimulate the imagination. In these graffiti former prisoners speak to present and future prisoners. The messages often seem to be coded in secret symbols. The prisoner knows that these were born out of suffering, like the pearl in the oyster.

Nevertheless the days pass. First there are only a hundred, then two hundred, then five hundred days. Soon they number a thousand. There is something very strange about these prison anniversaries, these round figures.

The time continues to pass. Slowly you become a veteran prisoner, a witness to the past, only waiting for death to devour all these days, months, and years. The years pass irrevocably, but the captive human being has been unable to lead a human life. Every day means sinking further into the abyss, a new fall.

The convict in solitary confinement never sees God's green fields, woods, flowery meadows, acres of ripening grain scattered with poppies; he never sees the bubbling spring, let alone the mighty Danube, or the retting of hemp, or the sea, silvery moonlight, the Milky Way, the stars, the graves of his loved ones, seminarians in their surplices, the host of the faithful before the countenance of the Lord, the glow of the Eternal Light, the altar, the pulpit and confessional, the baptismal font, the processions, a Christian family, or the innocent eyes of children, which our Lord Jesus so dearly loved. He never sees first communicants; he never sees his bride again, whether she is a girl, a church, or a cathedral. The sole portion of his beloved native land that he is able to see is the one accursed little spot within it. He cannot see any of those things that people think they could not possibly live without.

In the institution in which I was confined the prisoner was not even allowed to see another prisoner. It was as hard for him to catch a glimpse of a fellow convict as of a white raven; and yet at this time almost one out of two Hungarians was imprisoned. If regulations had been followed with absolute strictness, in those eight years I would not have seen a single one of my fellow sufferers. I would have had to find out from self-analysis alone what a prisoner was. However, I did manage to meet at least one fellow inmate. One day, as we were returning from my walk, the guard intended to take me back to my cell as usual. But instead of locking me into No. 105, he stopped at the door of the adjacent cell. The lock squeaked, and he told me to enter. I noticed his mistake at once, but never before had I more willingly obeyed a jailer. We two convicts looked probingly into each other's eyes.

The "owner" of the cell lay undressed on his cot—it was in the heat of the dog days. He had stretched out with the confidence that he would not be disturbed. But now he was receiving unexpected visitors.

Our guard did not spend much time in reflection. He looked horrified for a moment, then wrenched me out again. In the corridor and back in my cell I attempted to console him; people made mistakes in every job, I said; maybe even Rákosi did; and I promised that I would say nothing about the matter. Actually I was grateful to him for this single opportunity to see a comrade in misery.

That evening, after the guard's footsteps faded out down the corridor, I tapped on the neighbor's wall. He answered. I certainly do not mean to claim, as convicts are wont to do in their journals, that we held whole conferences through the wall and organized a news service. I was not up to that sort of thing, and my neighbor also seemed to be inexperienced in such arts. Nevertheless we were able to communicate somewhat by means of this wall "telephone." We could exchange signs of life, and two human beings were able to show their compassion for each other. Of course we would have been punished if the guards had discovered these expressions of mutual sympathy.

For many nights, weeks, and months we talked to each other in this way, until one evening I found to my dismay that there was no longer any response to my tapping. I brooded painfully about this: "Have I said something wrong?" It can hardly be that. Last night he was as friendly as ever, and nothing has happened since. Has he suddenly become obedient and decided to observe the prison regulations? That is even more unlikely. My thoughts groped toward more serious possibilities: Could he have died? Had he been killed? It is remarkably easy for convicts to die. Had he been transfered to another cell, or even another prison? Or had he fallen ill and been taken to a hospital? That would be a luxury for a prisoner. Had he been given his freedom by the mercy of Rákosi? Even such things had been known to happen. But where in Hungary today could anyone really find freedom?

All night long I turned over the various possibilities. But it was not possible for me to solve the mystery. Only one fact was certain, that my neighbor in the adjoining cell was no longer there.

Shortly afterwards some small repair was carried out in my cell, and for a little while I was put in the empty neighboring cell. I stayed there a few hours, sat at his table, lay on his bed, thought about him and tried to imagine who he might have been.

☿ Daily Life in the Penitentiary

THE GREATEST TORMENT in prison is the monotony, which sooner or later shatters the nervous system and wears the soul thin, for it is monotony that seems to have no possible end. Anything that makes even a small breach in this monotony is felt as an enormous relief.

FOOD

I had worked hard most of my life and never paid much attention to food. Moderation was not difficult for me. I had no particular fondness for choice dishes. In prison, however, interest in the meals naturally became more marked, for three daily meals filled out some three hours of my time. The unappetizing bowl, the aluminum spoon, the dirty table, the sameness of the food, its sparseness, and the general difficulty of my situation were all good reasons for my stretching out each meal.

In prison I read a book by László Somogyis entitled "On Rational and Economical Nutrition."

Although the prison authorities always made the point that the food contained the requisite quantity of calories, this was certainly not the case, if I may judge on the basis of that book. There was, for example, hardly ever any sugar. Packages from my mother reached me at intervals of six to nine months; but whatever sugar she had included did not reach me. Similarly, the lemons she sent disappeared.

The food was virtually thrown down in front of us. If, while the guards were talking out in the corridor, something fell to the floor, slices of meat or bread, say, the soiled food was simply picked up and handed out. The guard at the door badgered the prisoners to eat as quickly as possible so that he could be finished with his job the sooner. Cleanliness was the least concern. Traces of breakfast often clung to the spoon that was brought for lunch. Variety was provided by serving potatoes after potato soup, beans after bean soup.

Each week's menu hardly differed from the previous week's. We rarely received milk, butter, cheese, or eggs. Fresh fruit was even rarer, and if it ever was served it arrived in a shriveled condition. In winter, at any rate, there was usually some preserved fruit. Green peppers, that staple of the Hungarian diet, never appeared on the table all the while I was in prison.

THE WALK

Walks are included in the routine of all penitentiaries. They are meant to provide the prisoner with some essential exercise. But in the limited space allowed him the prisoner cannot help feeling like a bird in a cage, like a tiger behind bars, or like a dancing bear being led around on a nose ring by a gypsy.

Our prison exercise yard—a paved area surrounded by four high walls— was about 130 feet long. For my benefit it was kept even shorter. One guard always walked in front of me, one behind, and a third watched from the corner tower. Frequently I involuntarily collided with my escorts; the man in front would suddenly stop and say I was walking too fast; or then again the man behind would urge me on, insisting that my pace was too slow.

For an hour I had to march back and forth in silence. It made me think of a mill idling because the millers had forgotten to pour the grain into it. It may be that when groups from the dormitory cells were out walking, things would be somewhat livelier. The men might be able to nod to one another now and then, or whisper a few words. The walks were a torment to even these prisoners. But they had a better chance to relieve their feelings by grousing than the solitary prisoner had. The complaints of a group are always more satisfying as well as more effective than those of an individual.

I added to my exercise by walking back and forth in my cell. In the course of five years I paced many miles in solitude. István Széchenyi, the great Hungarian statesman and patriot, once calculated the miles he had traversed in his cell in Döbling. Enough, he reckoned, to have tramped twice around Europe.

CHORES

In every orderly household there must be a routine and certain chores to be done. So it was with us. After washing up in the morning, the convict was required to clean his room. That meant shaking up his straw bolster and draping his blanket over his straw pallet. He must be sure the bed was wrinklefree. Then, using his one towel since he had no dustcloth, he had to wipe the bedspread, the deal table, the inside of the door, which was covered with prisoners' paintings, the bench (which was made of a single plank), and the spiderwebs on the window.

Every day the cell had to be swept, and every so often the floor had to be scrubbed on hands and knees. At such times it was also usual to carry out the straw pallet and fill it with fresh straw, while the guards bellowed commands. The guards also liked to blow their cigarette smoke into our faces, or play other practical jokes on us.

The convict is required to do his chores even when he is sick.

SHAVES AND HAIRCUTS

Once a week we were shaved. That was no pleasure. The barber in policeman's uniform does not wield a gentle razor. He is not allowed to talk with the convict while he works. If the prisoner tempts him into talking, he is supposed to report the man.

The general opinion of our barber was: "Only his instrument is worse than he is."

The words of the old song, "Short the convict's locks are shorn," are no longer applicable. In our prison hair was allowed to grow. With "kind" forethought, orders were issued as early as August to leave the hair untouched so that the prisoners would not catch cold in winter. It would be dishonest if I were to conceal the fact that there was one barber in the lot who behaved decently.

EVENING OCCUPATION

There is also an evening occupation in prison. The prisoner lives a largely autarchic existence; he is himself the maid of all work, so that he must learn how to sew even if he has never before taken a stitch. Convict's clothing is made of heavy material. Nevertheless, it wears and tears, and buttons come off. The prison as a whole has a tailor, but the prisoner has none. He must be master, journeyman, and apprentice all rolled into one— this is what is called collectivism.

A record must be kept of the wear-and-tear of clothing, the buttons that come off, the consumption of thread. For patches, the color and quality of the material did not matter at all. Black cloth would be provided for patching white, or red or white cloth for twill as brown as beer. Often the thread was too thick for the eye of the needle. Then it became necessary to split the thread lengthwise—hairsplitting in the literal sense.

Such work often took hours. The prisoner found out that tailoring is a toilsome occupation. While he wiped the sweat from his brow, the guards sitting around puffed their cigarettes into the air. For they were supposed to be present as long as there was a needle in the cell. When the work was done, the guard retrieved the implement and delivered his report: "The prisoner did not carry out a suicide attempt with the needle; he neither opened his arteries nor attempted to swallow the needle."

My own tailoring was just an ordinary prison experience. I could not reproduce the famous trick of two Czech mercenaries in the prison at Melk, who asked for clothing to mend because work would make the time pass more quickly. They then made ropes out of the clothes and vanished through the window one night.

The prisoner was not allowed to do any cobbling. He was issued such tough shoes that, what with his limited exercise and much sitting, they rarely needed repair. One pair generally sufficed a convict for his whole life. But in our penitentiary if on occasion a pair of shoes did have to be soled, we often received them back with the points of the nails poking through the inner sole. Nevertheless the convict walked in them. He was not supposed to be oversensitive. If he had the effrontery to begin to limp, the guard inspected the shoes, and then the prisoner would not be allowed any walks for some time, because the shoes would be placed in a corner and for the time being would be left there.

CELEBRATING MASS

It was only after nine months in prison that I received permission to celebrate for the first time. During the Holy Sacrifice the guards peered through the peep hole to see how far along in the Mass I had come. It frequently happened that I was summoned to the weekly bath when, after the consecration of the bread I was just about to speak the words of transformation over the wine. Of course I did not go to the bath, but continued Holy Mass, although the guards said threatening things.

THE PRISON LIBRARY

The convict never actually sees the prison library. He has been convicted of a crime and therefore is no longer worthy of participating in the culture of the "new" world. But he can scarcely encounter the old world, since most of the books dealing with it have been removed from the shelves.

After nine months of imprisonment the guard, as a special favor, would occasionally bring me a book without my having asked for it. The principle of "reeducation" was beginning to be applied. Prisoners were given the chance to acquaint themselves with propaganda literature: communist books.

But paradoxical as it seems, in a prison there is little time for reading.

Ten hours are provided for sleep, two hours in the morning for the walk and cleaning the cell. With meals taking three hours, fifteen of the day's twenty-four are already accounted for. Few of the remaining nine hours can be used for reading. Between seven and ten o'clock in the morning it is still too dark. On foggy days the cell is dusky all day long. Not every warden allows the electric light to be switched on during the day. Thus I was once praying with the light on when the major came rushing in, saw my breviary, and bellowed:

"I won't have you wasting current. It's bad enough the workers already have to bear the expense of your imprisonment." I replied that I had not asked to be sent to this fine hotel, and that the Hungarian people also did not want to keep me in this luxury, whereupon he left the cell without another word.

After those many months I was given permission to borrow one book a week from the library. Choices, however, were very limited. The former prison library had for the most part been pulped or burned. The books of the St. Stephen Society, for example, had been destroyed without exception. For other books, such as Antal Schütz's *Dogmatics*, reactionary pages had been cut out. Even such popular books as the adventure tales of Karl May were on the list of forbidden books, as were the stories of Ferenc Herczeg and several of our other Hungarian writers.

Other classics were spared—so that the works of such Communists as Rákosi, Révai, and Andics could be slipped in among them—but certain passages were inked over to the point of illegibility. This was done, for example, in the works of Lajos Kossuth, who was otherwise hailed by the regime for tactical reasons. Even the writings of Ambassador Szekfű, the Moscow envoy, were censored. It is understandable that Victor Hugo, Balzac, Zola, and Anatole France were acceptable, also that Zsigmond Móricz met with favor. Less understandable was the sympathy for Kálmán Mikszáth. The bulk of the prison library consisted of Russian, Hungarian, German, and Danish literature, both older and more modern books: works by Marx, Engels, Lenin, Stalin, Mayakovsky, Zhdanov, Gorky, Makarenko, Fadeyev, Tolstoy, Martin Andersen Nexö, Rákosi, Révai, Andics, Lukács, Erik Molnár, Háy, and, proliferating like mushrooms, two or three dozen contemporary poets. The library's accent was as distinctly Russian as it was communist.

First of all I read what was left in the library in the way of scholarly literature. Later, however, I read the published speeches and articles by the leaders of neighboring people's democracies (Gottwald, Georghiu Dej, etc.). That was a wearisome study! Whatever the Czech Gottwald said in 1953 was invariably proclaimed by the Rumanian Georghiu Dej and the Pole Berman in almost the same words. Tito alone struck a different note.

Naturally communist pretenders to the throne were also there: Thorez, Togliatti, and so on. Works on the materialistic philosophy were likewise richly represented in the prison library.

I chose the best works of Russian literature, Belinsky, Pushkin, Lermontov, Gogol, Turgenev, Tolstoy, Dostoevsky, and so on. In English literature I read through all of Shakespeare's plays, most of them several times. I also read Milton and Dickens, whom I especially loved. Shaw and Ibsen appealed to me less. Carlyle's great work on the French Revolution made a tremendous impression on me. I read Goethe and Molière. I read all the American novels that were available, but these were very few. I also read Dante, and the Polish novel *Quo Vadis?* In Hungarian literature I read Zrinyi, Gyöngyösi, Széchenyi, Kossuth, the two Kisfaludys, Arany, Petőfi, Vörösmarty, Czuczor, Tompa, and magnificent Beőthy. The struggle between Széchenyi and Kossuth especially intrigued me. As I read I felt amazement that the communist censors had shown mercy to such writers as Dante, Zrinyi, and Sienkievicz.

I was particularly interested, of course, in all writings about prisoners and prisons. Consequently I read Tolstoy, Gogol, and Dostoevsky from an entirely different point of view, and likewise the descriptions of prisons in Dickens. In the course of the years I read something like seven hundred books. Among them were also political pamphlets on the Grősz conspiracy, the Rajk trial, the church "conspiracy" in Prague, some denunciations of the Vatican, and some anti-American articles. The works of Rákosi were also lent by the library. I had the opportunity to leaf through the new Hungarian schoolbooks, especially the textbooks in literature and history.

After the twentieth Communist party congress in Moscow, there was a new leaf turned over in Hungary also. A rapprochement with Tito took place. The consequences could be observed in the prisoners' library. Virtually overnight the numerous works of Stalin and Rákosi disappeared, likewise the pamphlets on the Grősz and Rajk trial, the anti-American articles, and so on. The library had by this time grown to approximately 1,500 books; now about 20 percent were sacrificed to this "reform."

☿ Imprisoned Writers

GREAT BOOKS have been written in prison from antiquity through the Middle Ages, modern times, and right up to the present. The Holy Spirit inspired Paul the Apostle to compose several of his letters while he was held in Roman captivity. During the first three centuries of Christianity twenty-two martyred popes wrote their pastoral letters in prison. (The pagan emperors allowed them to do so; our modern tribunes of the people are not so lenient to the four cardinals and the many bishops they have locked away.) The late Roman philosopher Boethius wrote his *De consolatione philosophiae* in prison. Imprisonment made a writer of the Transylvanian János Haller (1626–97). Count István Koháry (1649–1731) wrote his "Songs from Prison" while incarcerated. But there are also examples to the contrary: many writers fell silent in prison. For captivity is worse than war for throttling the creative spirit.

I have always loved books and writing. Often, after a wearisome day of much work, I would sit down with pleasure to read or to write. In prison I could do so only by overcoming many blocks and obstacles. The secret police bothered me; the pointlessness of what I was doing depressed me; and during the early period I simply lacked writing materials. When I succeeded in obtaining these secretly I felt strengthened in my belief that everything I was undergoing was happening solely for the glory of God.

One day I found the stub of a pencil and managed to hide it in my jacket pocket. I acquired a little paper in the same way. I could now set to work. But then came a search of the cell. My notes were found and taken away, although with the consoling assurance that "the literary works of prisoners are kept under seal in the secretariat." Later, without my having asked for it, I was given a pencil and a small notebook.

Those outside prison walls might think that doing nothing can have no history. But it can. I later kept a diary, and in the course of time filled five notebooks.

I also took extensive notes on my reading, and even wrote some detailed critiques on communist books. I became absorbed in studies of art history and wrote six long treatises on the subject of "Religion and Art" alone. Years later, during my house arrest and my stay in the American embassy, I was able to get books and much source material; and I was able to continue my research and writing on various subjects.

I also wrote a paper on philosophy and its responsibility, drawing on very sparse source materials, it is true, but based all the more on reflection of my own. In addition I put together a reader on apologetics. A. Schütz's *Lives of the Saints* occupied my mind a great deal, because I was gathering material for a book on the lives of the Hungarian saints. I took notes on world literature, or Hungarian literature, on history, and on sociology.

☦ Convict Nights and Convict Dreams

I SUSPECT that one of our worst punishments consisted in our having to go to bed immediately after supper. A person who has passed his sixtieth year needs little sleep, not even half of ten full hours. The result was that all my bones ached from lying still. It was impossible to switch on the light so that I could read, because the switch was out in the corridor under the control of the comrade guard. Not many convicts, I think, would have dared to appeal through the peephole for the light to be turned on.

What then is a convict to do during the five or six hours in which he lies sleepless? Perhaps he probes his conscience, goes on a tour through his own life, listens to the other inhabitants of his cell gnawing and scurrying. Or he imagines he sees his mother's face and, by contrast, the diabolic mask on so many other faces. His mind dwells on his "crime," with the taking of fingerprints, and so on.

Absolutely none of the charges against me troubled my mind in the least. But there were other cares that weighed terribly upon me: the fate of the Church, of the country, of the archdiocese, of all the faithful and renegade priests and believers. And I also reviewed my life. Many things appeared to me in a new light. I envisioned my home parish with its church and its cemetery. I looked back on my studies in the gimnázium, recalled my consecration as a priest. My employees and coworkers passed before my mind's eye. I thought over my decades of struggle, the achievements of which were now being extinguished. I also asked myself what were the faults and sins of our country. How could all this have come about? What form should the rebuilding—with God's help—take? How could so many wounds be healed? Where would the work have to begin? Those sleepless nights brought somber thoughts that ultimately summoned me to prayer.

The ever-repeated fight with insomnia exhausted me, and if I did manage finally to doze off, the guard frequently came in and shook me awake, shouting: "You're not sleeping according to regulations. Head and hands must be visible to the guard at all times." They insisted on this idiocy with unrelenting cruelty. I would then try to fall asleep again in the proper position. But I would be awakened again and again. The *nox quieta*, the restful night called for by Vespers, was unknown in prison.

But there was something even worse than the convict's nights: the bed rest prescribed by the doctor. One day the doctor discovered an irregularity in my heartbeat. He therefore ordered thirty days of bed rest. During those thirty days the guard clung to the peephole like a leech to the body. I had to take even my meals in bed, and woe if I made an "unnecessary movement" or allowed myself to "needlessly turn around." The first week passed at a snail's pace, then ten days, then two weeks. My unsteady heart only became unsteadier. Faith alone helped me to get through this foretaste of purgatory. Now not only the prison walls but also the prison bed was a source of torment. Like a child before Christmas I counted the days until I would be permitted to get up again. On the thirty-first morning I sprang happily out of bed at five o'clock and at once set to work sweeping and dusting the room (it was high time for this to be done). The simplest objects on my rough, unplaned table, the eating bowl, the spoon, seemed to have acquired beauty. Almost dreamily I paced back and forth in the cell. I hoped I could catch a glimpse of a green leaf through the window; I hoped for a walk. Then the lightning crashed into my paradise. The chief of the guards suddenly confronted me: "Who gave you permission to get up?"

"The thirty days are over."

"When the doctor so determines and I inform you of his determination, then and then only do you have permission to get up. Discipline must be preserved. Back to bed."

The doctor came, and another thirty days of bed rest were imposed on me. When this second spell came to an end, I was already apathetic. I remained in bed, immobile, until the guard berated me:

"How long do you mean to stay in bed?"

This time, however, I got to my feet joylessly and without strength.

Too much importance should not be attributed to dreams. But they also should not be entirely disregarded. God has often used dreams for instruction, as we know from the testimonies of Revelation and from ecclesiastical history.

The typical school dream can be depressing and frightening: even in the dream the arithmetic problem is never solved. But the typical convict's dream is full of horror and a consciousness of being utterly trapped. The events of the convict's life merge into a nightmare.

Psychology has taught us that usually it is not our most recent experiences that recur in dreams, but things that happened to us much earlier.

Twice I dreamed that I was visiting with the Holy Father. Then, in my dreams, I met bishops Mikes, Grősz, Czapik, Shvoy, and Rogács. Once I also encountered a former Hungarian premier. Likewise I saw my parents in my dreams. They came toward me young and cheerful. Rarely did my mother appear old and in mourning in my dreams. I also dreamed of Rector Géfim, my successor in Zalaegerszeg, of the mayor, and of my former chaplains. In my dreams I also joined Hungarian exiles in the West. Then the jailer entered my dreamland; but now and again a dream would be pierced by a faint ray of hope.

After my liberation the worst nightmares at once vanished from my dream world. A free man ceases to have a convict's dream; they seem to afflict only the prisoner. During my first nights in freedom I hardly dreamed at all. But in the following days of semi-imprisonment (from November 4, 1956, on), the events in Hungary filled my dreams once more with agonizing visions.

When shall I ever again have peaceful, calm, comforting dreams?

♀ Religious Life in Prison

MEN OUGHT to venture out more often on the stormy seas to learn how to pray. Penal institutions are scarcely inferior to the battlefield and the wild ocean as a school of prayer. Supercilious Oscar Wilde converted in prison to our crucified Lord. Paul Verlaine, the great French poet, began writing religious poetry of the strongest reverence and sincerity while in prison. "They were prisoners of sensuality, but now penitence and Christian humility dwelt in them."

A stay in prison can direct men's minds toward God. Solitude often revives memories of long-forgotten religious truths. Even lukewarm Christians and people indifferent to religion, who have forgotten how to pray and no longer perceive the needs of their souls and who have neglected the commandment to keep the Lord's day holy, are reunited with their Creator by attendance at the prison chapel, perhaps for ever after.

It is well known that in 1945 the Budapest prison chapels would be filled to capacity during services. Many striking conversions took place; great numbers of prisoners found their way back to the Catholic Church. Many a condemned man crossed into eternity wonderfully strengthened and composed.

Even Marxists in prison quite often found their way to the services. The communist functionaries objected to such behavior, of course, and maintained that the Church had caught their comrades in its toils. But this charge was altogether false. Each person came of his own accord, although perhaps some were persuaded by the example of others.

In the outside world many of these persons had not set foot inside a church for a long time. Now the chapel, and in it Christ in the Holiest Sacrament, became the very heart of the prison, for the longing for God arises with especial force within prisoners. Even the revolutionary Rosa Luxemburg admitted: "I don't know why, but I cannot help humming along with Gounod's *Ave Maria.*" And at Christmas she set up a Christmas tree with eight candles.

But once the Communists had finished taking power into their hands in Hungary, religion in the prisons was condemned to death. The chapels were closed or made over into cells. The prison chaplains were dismissed. Henceforth it was not possible for the prisoners to attend Mass; no priest could bring them the viaticum or extreme unction. Even in the last hours before an execution the condemned person must do without any spiritual consolation. Hungarian Communists have adopted *in toto* Lenin's hatred for religion. Ardent in their hostility, they have tried to extirpate every expression of the religious life as being "against science" and against their conception of the welfare of the people.

I myself experienced that from the very first in Andrássy Street, when I was changing to the prison clothes. All objects that had any religious reference were taken from me. After my second sleepless night I nevertheless communicated, whereupon one of the policemen muttered the comment: "That claptrap won't help you."

In the penitentiary I was not allowed to celebrate for the first nine months. Attending Mass was not permitted, not even at Christmas and Easter. I could not receive the sacrament of penance during those feast days either.

In the first week of December 1949 and 1950 groups of children went about the nearby police barracks and the neighboring homes singing Christmas carols. I listened to their singing with deep emotion. But 1951 marked the end of even this tenderest kind of annunciation of the glad tidings.

And so, at Christmas, I participated only in spirit in the Midnight Mass. Under my breath—so that the guards could not hear and spoil things—I lay in bed humming the Christmas carols.

From 1950, however, I had permission to celebrate the Midnight Mass. On December 24, all through my life as a priest, I had never lain down for a nap or a rest before Midnight Mass. But here in the penitentiary I had to go to bed at seven o'clock. I then meditated until half past eleven. Then I got up and offered the Holy Sacrifice. I shall never forget these Midnight Masses in prison. During the hours of my first prison Christmas I thought of the solemn High Mass in Zalaegerszeg and of the beautiful folksinging there. Sobs rose in my throat. Meanwhile, outside my cell door the guards were talking about a lecture they had just attended, the theme of which was that Jesus had been a swindler. Listening, I broke into tears.

On New Year's Eve there appeared before my mind's eye the tremendous church of Zalaegerszeg, filled to the very last space. Similarly, I felt strongly my ties with Zalaegerszeg when the singing of the Easter and Corpus Christi processions reached my cell. On the feast of the Sacred Heart of Jesus in 1950 I was allowed to celebrate for the first time after nine months of prison. I was also given the proper breviary for this time of the church year and a rosary. I rejoiced, although there was bitter wormwood in my gladness, for I had to include in my memento Dr. Drahos, my vicar-general, of whose death I had just heard. I did not know who was responsible for his unexpected death.

For an altar I was given the smallest imaginable telephone table. My altar image was a tiny saint's picture, the lid of my chalice a communist book. On the walls to either side were pictures like those in pagan Pompei. While I celebrated, the guards took turns at the peephole in the door, chatted, and made remarks. Then breakfast was brought. As I have already mentioned in an early chapter, they wanted to have me go for my bath at any time between the consecration and the communion. But then and later I ignored this summons.

My religious life certainly suffered from my surroundings, but it was not destroyed. There was a great deal I lacked that I had earlier possessed, but many of my religious exercises became all the more intensive. It was, of course, impossible for me to practice the spiritual and corporal works of mercy, and that always means a tremendous impoverishment of the religious life. By giving to others we are ourselves enriched. But there remained fasting—which, strangely enough, is a difficult matter in prison of all places. I also missed weekly confession; in place of it I practiced detailed probing of my conscience twice a day. I regularly held novenas and triduums. I prayed daily to my guardian angel, St. Joseph, and to the saints of an easy death, the apostles John and Judas Thaddeus. I also prayed to the saint of the Little Way, Thérèse of Lisieux, who has rained a shower of roses upon earth, to the saints of each day, and to my twin brothers who had died in childhood. I prayed to Hungarian saints, to the saints of the world Church, and to all servants of God, including those in whose canonization I myself had assisted. While meditating I prayed the breviary. This procedure took up three hours. When I summoned my fellows to mind, my act of recollection was so vivid that I literally saw these faithful souls before me in the flesh, not only colleagues in Esztergom but also those in Veszprém and Zalaegerszeg.

I included the concerns of the entire world in my rosary prayers. Praying the rosary on one's fingers is still customary in a great many places; prisoners pray that way from the Iron Curtain to Norilsk. Every day I prayed six rosaries: in the morning for the Church in general, for my country, and for the archdiocese; in the afternoon and evening for my fellow prisoners, for the youth, for my mother, for myself, and for the poor souls in purgatory. "Not to us, Lord, not to us the glory; let Thy name alone be honored. (Psalms 113, 9.)

It is hardly surprising that my jailers deliberately thwarted me over the Friday abstinence. On Friday they provided meat; on Sundays and at Christmas there was none to be had. Since the prisoner has no choice of foods the Church gave him dispensation to eat meat on Fridays. Nevertheless I refused to touch it, and the guards reported that. Whereupon the warden came rushing in, furious.

"Do you think the convicts give orders here?"

"No, I do not think so."

"Then eat what is set before you."

"On Friday I eat no meat."

"I'm not giving you anything else."

"I am not asking for anything else."

"I'll put you in the hole."

"I'm beyond caring about that."

The meal remained on the table. They did not carry it out until shortly before supper time. And for supper they again brought meat.

A blasé, twenty-year-old policeman set the food down before me. I did not eat it. Whereupon he threatened: "I'll put you in chains if you don't obey.

"The warden has already told me what will happen," I replied.

Finally he carried the food out, slamming the door behind him. The same scenes were repeated four Fridays in a row, until they served me meat on Sunday instead of Friday.

I have always been fond of praying on my knees, and so I continued this habit in prison. At first the guards were extremely annoyed. However, they did not quite dare to forbid me explicitly to pray on my knees. But they told the doctor whose visits had now been reduced to once or twice a week, and he forbade me to kneel "in consideration of your health" and especially the condition of my heart. I said nothing, but continued my practice of kneeling. The truncheon, sentence, cell, scrubbing floors, and carrying pails were certainly not good for my heart, and yet I had been put through these strains. So why should I not kneel at the accustomed times? The guards observed me and pounded on the door. But I merely asked them what all the noise was about, and went on praying on my knees, even though they disturbed me at my prayers several times a day. The second, more humane warden made no objection; after he took over I was disturbed only occasionally when one guard or the other of the old staff wanted to be obstreperous.

My saying grace was also a thorn in their flesh. If they saw me praying, they would bellow that the food was growing cold. After the meal they regularly came in during my thanksgiving, on the grounds that they could not delay cleaning up any longer. During my walks in prison I also quite often prayed under my breath. This infraction was also reported to the higher authorities. With clanking spurs the warden (the first warden) appeared, and even before he crossed the threshold he roared at me:

"I forbid praying during the walk!"

"That is none of the government's concern," I replied.

During my next walk the guards paid even closer attention to me than usual. One watched me from the tower, one preceded me, one followed me. Nevertheless I again prayed.

I said above that imprisonment could lead to more intense spirituality and to God. But it can also lead men away from God. Prisoners are human, and wherever human beings dwell the Temptor dwells also, and weakness and sin are close by. Tolstoy says in his novel *Resurrection:* "The prisoner undergoes a profound moral shock; he is plunged into the abyss of sin and depravity." In Tolstoy's opinion the principal sins of the convict are drunkenness, card playing, and cruelty, these being the inevitable consequences of imprisonment, but he does not say how the prisoner has the opportunity for such sins. In any case it is certain that pious Christians in prison sometimes bid good-bye to their Christianity and go over to the side of vice.

For decades the political Left has been given to hero worship of prisoners. The theme of imprisonment has always played a great part in Russian novels. Western writing also hailed criminals and outcasts so long as they were behind bars. The year 1945, with its revelations of what happened at Dachau and Szeged, lent prestige to many a prisoner, the result being that certain ex-inmates were able to rise to high honors and posts even though many aspects of their earlier lives might not have justified such promotions. The truth is that someone who has done time in prison becomes neither a villain nor a hero. Prison walls are certainly no bulwark against sin; only grace and good will are that. Nevertheless I do believe that in prisons the heavenly Father confers His Grace more generously; He knows best all the things we need in our situation.

In the cell, as everywhere, the spiritual life grew and flourished only if the prisoner himself tended it. But if there were several men together, and perhaps a priest among them, the religious life did attain a high point in prison; and that was certainly not because the regime guaranteed "religious freedom," but because of the strength the priests and their fellow religious displayed, frequently against the wishes of the authorities. After our imprisonment a wise man said to me: "The bearing of many prisoners exalted my soul. It encouraged me to trust in the future of our nation." Here was corroboration of the words Dostoevsky wrote about the prisons in Siberia: "In prison, too, one can lead a great life."

☧ The Abysses of Prison

ASIDE FROM WAR and general dissipation, penal institutions produce the greatest number of mental patients and suicides. Behind the barbed wire in the prison camps of Siberia during the First World War, nervous breakdowns and insanity proliferated on a gigantic scale. Any kind of prison existence is inhuman. No one knows how many individuals in Andrássy Street, in Markó Street, or in other prisons went out of their minds. In the reception prison I frequently heard the penetrating screams and roars of human souls on the brink of madness. Outside the police barracks shrill whistles could frequently be heard. Cars drove up, blows thudded, and people were dragged away or led away. The next morning the man who brought me water whispered that two prisoners cracked up, that the guards had had a tough time subduing them.

Such fits of madness frequently occurred in the cells. For half a year I kept records in my diary—writing in Latin—of the beatings and outbreaks of madness around me. I set down the exact details of the day, hour, and duration, and was horrified by the frequency of such fits. Those who had broken down this way were transferred from the prison to mental hospitals. But a good many individuals were unjustifiably labeled mentally ill so that the prison authorities could get rid of them.

The excessive precautions taken against suicide certainly do not speak for the rarity of suicides in Hungarian prisons. We were given neither fork, knife, comb, razor blade, nor even a drinking glass. Mirrors were not tolerated anywhere in a convict's vicinity. I suppose the fear was that the prisoner, seeing himself, might attempt to smash the mirror in order to cut the artery of his wrist with one of the splinters.

On June 16, 1950, when I was permitted to celebrate Mass for the first time, wine was brought to me in a glass and the glass afterwards put down in a corner of the cell. Two weeks later the warden happened to come into the cell; he saw the glass and cried out in alarm at this careless violation of regulations. He himself at once picked up the glass and took it away. From then on I received the wine necessary for Mass in an aluminum cup.

However, when, the authorities would find a suicide attempt expedient, they did not hesitate to supply the objects that would be needed for the act.

Beatings of prisoners were an almost daily occurrence. I remember one occasion when the cries of pain reached my cell. How could I have remained indifferent? The sense of community among convicts is very strong. I therefore began drumming on my door with both fists. The protest was taken up at ten or a dozen other doors in the corridor. The guards who were administering the beating stopped and ran back and forth trying to find who had started this "reactionary" protest. They found me.

I expected them to continue where they had left off, using me as the whipping boy. But at least on this occasion they did not touch me. If they had, it is fairly certain that the enraged prisoners would have resumed their drumming in sympathy and protest.

Those who suffer in communist prisons because they are opponents of the regime at least have the satisfaction of feeling that their struggle is justified. But how terrible must be the state of mind of those who for decades strove to bring about the victory of this "new world" only to be charged in the end with crimes against the regime. There were many such cases under Stalin.

The Hungarian "Authority for the Protection of the State" (AVH) possesses a grim notoriety for us Hungarians. Premier Imre Nagy announced after the Revolution of 1956 that this secret police was being dissolved. The Kádár regime also declared that it did not wish to retain the AVH. The leaders of that regime knew how much hatred and abhorrence the people felt for this organ of state security, which expressed the very soul of the regime. Kádár's declaration was obviously disingenuous. The fact is that after November 4, 1956, the AVH men turned up once more, appearing on the side of the Russians in the capital and in the countryside, to make arrests and forcibly carry off patriots. "The fox leaves his tail in the trap to save his skin."

Kádár had recognized, and publicly admitted, that the work of the secret police was criminal and that the members of this body were bitterly hated by the people. The official party organ of the Kádár regime, *Népszabadság* (*People's Freedom*), even stated on December 28, 1956, that abuses by the AVH during interrogations had been steadily increasing and that the AVH as an organization had committed injustices. But four months later Károly Kiss, a minister of the same party and the same government, sounded a different note at a public meeting in Diósgyőr: "The AVH displayed heroic courage in the months of October and November side by side with the Popular Front."

In Rákosi's book, in which his speech after the Rajk trial is given, we find: "Tito gang, Rajk gang. . . . The AVH with Comrade Gábor Péter at its head has done a fine job." That is praise for crimes, tortures, mass murders; we cannot even estimate the number of those executed. I myself could cite many names—but for obvious reasons will not do so—of persons who suffered nervous breakdowns or went mad in the hands of the AVH. It is highly revealing of the temper of Rákosi's successors, Gerő and Kádár, that they sent Rákosi off on an extended vacation instead of bringing him to trial.

✝ Joys and Consolations in Prison

IN PRISON there is not only evil but also goodness. Prison shields the individual from many sorts of danger and temptation. Thus, it shielded me from having to swear an oath of allegiance to the destroyers of my people, who have trampled upon the Church. The various sins of a loose tongue will not be committed in solitary confinement. Controlling the senses becomes far easier; in regard to our threefold concupiscence, the man in prison is well protected. Could a prisoner *in profundis* continue to be proud? Nowhere is it more patent than in prison that "man's life is like the grass, he blooms and dies like a flower in the fields" (Psalms 102, 15). For self-examination, for repentance, for looking into one's own heart and exalting the soul, the time in prison is fruitful; the days of captivity are days of salvation. We have faults of which we have never become aware in the bustle of life. How many of the good resolutions we take of the sort that begin: "My Lord, if I ever again . . ."? I too did this sort of thing; I vowed: "I shall take up the cause of prisoners; I shall go to the Holy Land."

When I was allowed to offer the Holy Sacrifice of the Mass, that act became for me the center of the day. I devoted from two and a half to three and a half hours to it. I meditated; I prayed for our distressed Hungarian Church and my native district. I never failed to include in my prayers the pope, the cardinals and bishops, the priests, the sick, my mother, my sister, my seminarians who lived in temptation and harassment, and also our enemies, the guards, the prisoners, my country, the Hungarian refugees, Hungarian fathers and mothers, the youth, Hungarian family life.

St. Philip Neri used to celebrate very slowly, for he always wanted to make the Holy Sacrifice unassisted. Those who celebrate Mass alone take their time and do it with greater awareness.

I secreted on my person or in my clothing the consecrated host, and I frequently worshiped before it, especially during the long nights. The breviary became a true source of joy for me. I had the time, but I also hungered and thirsted for it, like the stag crying for the spring. For me a breviary prayer frequently took two and a half to three hours instead of the usual hour and a quarter. For a long time this book was my Holy Scriptures, my dogmatic theology, my mystical theology, my spiritual guide.

The prisoner's life also helps one arrive at a true understanding of the psalms. It becomes apparent that the psalmist, in most cases a prisoner, speaks of the world of the imprisoned, speaks and sings of and for the prisoner. The *De Profundis* (Psalm 129) is universally known; but there are also many other prison psalms, such as 21, 25, 29, 37, 53–56, 68, 69, 70, 85, 87, 90, 101, 102, 108, 142, 145 and so on. In addition there are the scenes of Joseph, Job, and Daniel as prisoners.

The "O's" of Advent ("O root of David . . ." etc.), the anthems sung during Advent, touch upon man's imprisonment in sin. The prisoner prays them from the heart when he sings: "To bring out the prisoners from the dungeon and them that sit in darkness and the shadow of death." The captive's soul clings, during Advent, to the words of the psalm: "What blessings, Lord, thou hast granted to this land of thine, restoring Jacob from captivity" (Psalm 84, 2). The liturgical prayer of Good Friday: *Aperiat carceres, vincula dissolvat* ("May He open the dungeons and break the fetters") speaks directly to the prisoner; he feels the words directed straight to him. In the Passion, Jesus stands before us fettered and abused, so that He may raise up each prisoner's soul. The twin mysteries of the rosary, the scourging and the crowning with thorns, are also relevant to the prisoner.

I found a telling personal text: Before long, the devil will throw . . . you into prison, to have your Faith tested there" (Apocalypse 2, 10). Bede tells us prison is a testing place for the innocent captive and redounds to his honor. Blessings upon the Church whose motherly pedagogy has included the true prayer of prisoners in its breviary: "Could but the groaning of the captive reach thy presence! Thy arm has not lost its strength; claim for thine own the children of the slain!" (Psalms, 78, 11).

The *Imitatio Christi* of Thomas à Kempis also gave me fresh strength, as did meditating on the lives of the saints and making the stations of the cross in my cell. Of the saints I could ask myself who among them had not been a prisoner. The martyrs of the first three centuries, indeed of all centuries, were all thrown into prison. St. Athanasius was sent into exile five times, and in the course of four of these banishments he hid in cisterns or in his father's tomb. St. Hilary and St. John Chrysostom, the future doctors of the Church, were familiar with banishment and dungeons, as was St. Anselm.

In this connection I might also mention the saints who founded orders for prisoners. Many saints pronounced a fourth vow: voluntarily entering imprisonment in order to liberate Christian prisoners.

In the peaceful atmosphere at the end of the nineteenth and the beginning of the twentieth centuries we in the Church tended to think that the age of martyrs was over. But it will never be over. The number of martyrs in the Roman Empire during the first three centuries of the Christian era is estimated at from three to six million. The number of martyrs in the first four decades of the twentieth century approaches or exceeds the higher of these

two figures. According to data from the Vatican and other official ecclesiastical sources, in China alone there have been 14,000 martyrs among priests,
nuns, and laity. This calculation is based on figures supplied by Cardinal-
archbishop Tien.

In prison you learn to feel with every fiber of your being that this world
in its essence is not a place of joy but a vale of tears. Such is the reality. All
ties, no matter how strong and good, are eventually torn. Only the Gospel
continues to give us a true answer to the ultimate questions: "Whence?
Whither? Why?" We grow more and more remote from those who are still
living; those who dwell on the other side come ever closer to us. On the eve
of an All Saints Day we feel closer to the blessed in heaven, but also to the
suffering souls in purgatory.

In prison one also comes closer to redeeming grace in the sense that Saint
Augustine meant when he spoke of *gratia liberans:* "It was in mercy thou
didst chasten me, schooling me to thy obedience" (Psalms 118, 71).

I was convinced that the pope was praying for me, and that gave me
strength. I could also assume that Catholic Eskimos, the inhabitants of Pat-
agonia, of France, of Africa, and of Malaysia were praying for me, and that
I participated in the sacrifices of the Mass throughout the entire world.

It became a cherished habit of mine in prison, every Sunday at ten
o'clock—the time of parish services in villages throughout the land—to join
in spirit the churchgoers, to sing the psalms with them, to be present with
them at so many churches dear to me within and outside my native land. In
spirit I also joined Hungarians in America, peoples of other races all over
the world, sons and daughters of all the continents, in attendance at Holy
Mass. Although I had come to know the horror of hatred, the grimace of
the devil, prison also taught me to see love as the underlying principle of
life.

Dostoevsky had his death sentence commuted and spent several years as
a prisoner in Siberia. For a long time he preferred to remain silent about his
experiences, but ultimately he wrote *The House of the Dead*. He left prison
strengthened; he had experienced the meaning and the purifying power of
suffering. In prison he had come to know his own people and the human
soul.

Even in Hungarian communist prisons things happened that wrenched
the heart. In 1949, at the very time that hatred was dominant, an auxiliary
policeman slipped into my cell when the others were already asleep, looked
around cautiously, and whispered: "Father, trust in God! He helps!" Later
he came to comfort me a second time. The third time he came to bid good-
bye, for he was being transferred.

In 1954, toward the end of my stay in the penitentiary, the stocky little
sergeant whose duty it was to take me to the bath, looked at me one day,
peered anxiously at the door, then murmured: "I am a Christian too." A

barber in the prison hospital proudly told me that his daughter was receiving religious instruction and that he had gone to Midnight Mass with her.

Faith and love must be reinforced, that they may ever and again outlive hatred.

☩ *My Health*

FROM MARKÓ STREET, as I have related, I was taken to the hospital of the reception prison. Evidently this was done to remove some of the traces of what had been done to me in Andrássy Street. As I have already mentioned, I was visited by the same doctor who had treated me in Andrássy Street, along with two others. My fatigue had vanished, but my face and my entire body showed clear marks of grave abuse. Naturally, these signs could not remain hidden from my mother's eyes when she came to visit. On September 25, 1949, observing my exhaustion and lethargy, she asked:

"My son, aren't you glad I've come to visit you?"

I replied that I felt ill. My thyroid gland was swelling, producing a nervous state of the heart. My mother wanted to report the condition to our regular physician, Dr. Ernő Pethő. She therefore opened my shirt collar and felt the area of the thyroid gland. Then she asked whether I was receiving medical treatment. I replied that the medical supervision and care was of prison quality—that is, superficial.

At that my mother turned to the police officer who was present at the visit and asked him to inform his superior that she herself would assume the costs of having Dr. Pethő treat me, if he were permitted to enter the prison.

"Mother, what are you thinking of?" I said. "They certainly won't allow an outside doctor access to the prisoners."

Nevertheless, she returned to Szombathely at once and gave our doctor a report on the state of my health. Pethő declared his willingness to examine me and if necessary to operate. My mother then appealed in writing to the ministry of justice. Archbishop Grősz made a similar application to the ministry in my behalf. Both his appeal and my mother's were rejected.

I was therefore a sick man when I arrived at the penitentiary. But the two doctors there were scarcely ever rude to me. If a certain roughness of tone did prevail, that was probably because the doctors were conscious of the ever-present police. Several times I was summoned to the X-ray room for pictures to be taken. A large quantity of medication was prescribed for me. Never in my whole previous life had I swallowed so many medicines. I always had to take them in the presence of witnesses. But I tried to reject the water and fluids that were given along with them, just as I refused the liquid foods that were offered. In the penitentiary I was not so much worried about the possibility that the food and the medicines might contain poisons that would ultimately cause death. I was, rather, still afraid that drugs would be added, drugs that would shatter my nerves, weaken my judgment, numb my courage.

The doctors were seriously concerned about my health. Now and then my goiter would seem to diminish; but suddenly the condition would flare up again. I continually lost weight. A careful examination showed that I was also suffering from shingles. Cramps, fever, fatigue, and depression were among the symptoms that accompanied and followed it. Later, when I was out of the penitentiary, I learned that this disease, though usually starting from an infection, is also frequently caused by chemicals in foods. In Andrássy Street, at any rate, I constantly thought I detected admixtures of chemicals in my food during the thirty-nine days of my stay. No doubt a vitamin deficiency was also partly responsible for my condition. Resistance is lowered when food is poor in vitamins. But above all I suppose the rule applies that a prisoner's nervous system is constantly exposed to an excessive burden.

The inadequate nutrition, my voluntary abstention from certain foods, the isolation, the inactivity, the dreary atmosphere, the treatment, and my intense anxiety about the Church and the country gradually sapped the vitality of my organism. Sickness and infections finally brought low an already weakened body.

My condition did not escape the doctors' notice. They asked whether I had any particular wishes about food. "I don't want to be an exception," I said. "I'll eat whatever is given to the other prisoners here."

During the first half of 1954 my weight dropped nearly half, from 170 to 97 pounds. I was literally nothing but skin and bones. Once, when in spite of the ban I secretly caught a glimpse of myself in a mirror, I was alarmed at the change. What I saw was only the shadow of myself. On walks I could scarcely keep my lightweight body going. Getting up in the mornings became harder and harder.

One winter afternoon in 1954 I made the discovery that my sight was failing to an extraordinary degree. Even when I held the book as close as possible to the electric bulb, I could scarcely read my prayers. Nevertheless I went on reading, with the greatest effort. Suddenly it seemed to me that the cell, in fact the whole world, was spinning around me. Colored circles danced in the book and on the wall. That is all I remember. When I gradually came to I found myself lying on the floor, the breviary and a pool of blood beside me. I felt myself. My hair was soaked with blood. Laboriously, I picked myself up and considered the situation. I had been standing with my back against the tile stove; probably I had had a dizzy spell and in falling struck my head against the stove. I must have been unconscious for some time.

At this point I sank back on the bed. My trembling legs could no longer support me. With a dampened towel I wiped the blood from my neck, hair, and the floor. Then I bound the towel around my head so that the bedding would not be soaked with blood during the night. Nevertheless it trickled through. The guards noticed nothing. That was amazing, considering that ordinarily they were so watchful when it was a matter of serving meat to me on a Friday or getting me up from my knees when I was praying. They casually overlooked the wound and continued to do so when they brought my supper at six o'clock.

Not until the time came to change towels, on the weekend, did they examine the bed and find the bloodstained bolster. They then also inspected my shirt. The warden appeared; he interrogated me almost as if he had begun to suspect an attempt at suicide. That the towel which also served as my dustcloth might have infected me apparently did not worry him.

Around this time my mother had once again been granted permission for a visit. As usual, I had to meet with her in Vác. When she saw me, she was so stunned by my condition that she turned on the guard indignantly: "Aren't you ashamed to have prisoners look this way? What are we paying taxes for? If you can't or won't pay for his keep, let me take care of my son myself. I'll send money for food; just tell me how much it will cost!" The police officer who was there to supervise the interview was taken aback. He did not answer, but reported her remarks to the ministry. And wonder of wonders, the ministry acceded to my mother's proposal.

Naturally my mother asked at her next visit whether decent food had been brought to me in return for her money. I said that I had unfortunately not noticed much difference in the fare, and asked her not to send any more money to the ministry; after all, she needed it for her own household, and the institution was supposed to take care of me.

The officer who overheard all this did not like it at all. After my mother's departure the warden came to see me and asked what I would like to eat. I replied that I had no favorite dishes; but thereafter I received somewhat heartier and tastier food. Moreover, I was repeatedly examined. The doctors held a conference in which the warden also participated. As for myself, I had by now become indifferent to whether I lived or died.

After all this, on May 13, 1954, I was taken to the hospital at the reception prison. There I remained uninterruptedly until July 17 of the following year.

On the eve of my departure the new warden of the penitentiary came to my cell. He admitted that a good many things had happened to me and around me that were not strictly in accordance with the laws. I was quite amazed, for I knew nothing about the new winds that were blowing in the country. My mother belatedly informed me about Stalin's death some time later. I could only guess that great events must have produced significant changes, which by now were even reaching my cell. But I could not imagine as yet that Imre Nagy was at the helm.

Cell No. 20 in the prison hospital was right near the entrance. Henceforth this was to be my cell. The adjacent room was intended as a guardroom for the guards who accompanied me from the penitentiary. Nearby there were operating rooms and doctors' rooms. The cell was larger, more healthful and less gloomy than the one I had occupied in the penitentiary. On orders from the doctors the upper part of the window had to be left open all the time. Here there were plates instead of an eating bowl; there were spoons, knives, forks, and even a drinking glass. The food was nourishing and tasty. Some of the credit for this change must surely go to the chief physician of the hospital, a warmhearted, humane person whom everyone respected. At first my penitentiary guards insisted that they had to be on hand each time he came to see me. But he declared that under such conditions he could not assume the medical responsibility that had been assigned to him. At that, they yielded.

With the ampler and better food, I slowly began gaining weight. I was also permitted to wear my black civilian suit as my everyday clothes. The days of the prison stripes were over.

Major Vékási, the deputy warden of the penitentiary, was transferred to the hospital. He was not a bad fellow at all. Nevertheless I was still accompanied by my "escort" whenever I was taken from one point to another. I was now also permitted to sit out in the garden behind screens which served the dual purpose of providing shade and concealing me. Occasionally I would also be taken for walks on the grounds. But at such times strict instructions were issued to close all the windows of the building and to keep the curious at a distance.

In good weather I could see the swallows flying about, and I thought: "They come in the spring and depart in the fall; fate has given them two native lands. We have had only one and have lost it. But perhaps not forever."

After a temporary improvement in my condition, I suffered a relapse. The doctor was disturbed and broached the possibility of an operation. I said I would consent only if Dr. Pethö were to operate. But that suggestion was not approved.

I now received various injections which the head doctor administered in person. For several weeks I took them from him without anxiety. But once, when he was absent for two days, the sergeant of the prison health department turned up with the syringes all ready. I turned him away because I did not trust him. Sure enough, the chief informed me after his return that he had given the sergeant no such assignment.

In general I suffered considerably from the injections. At night I was tormented by itching; then swellings and rashes developed all over my body, so that the doctor had to stop the course of injections. My weight began dropping once again. My eyes became so weak that I could no longer read the text of the breviary. For three weeks I was unable to recite office. I could scarcely make out the large letters of the Mass book although the doctor had given me stronger glasses.

The words of the psalm were becoming true for me: "Thy arrows pierce me, the hand presses me hard. . . . Restless my heart, gone my strength; the very light that shone in my eyes is mine no longer" (Psalms, 37:3, 10).

On July 16, 1955, I had a visitor. Colonel Rajnai appeared and informed me that the government, in consideration of the state of my health and at the request of the episcopate, was mitigating my penitentiary sentence. I should hold myself in readiness; by the following day I would be taken to Püspökszentlászló. He added that he might have brought me even better news if in the interval I had shown somewhat more willingness to meet the authorities halfway.

Obviously the government feared the reaction in the outside world if, after the deaths of so many priests and loyal Catholic laymen, the head of the Hungarian Church were also to die in prison.

At dawn on July 17, 1955, a Sunday, Colonel Rajnai and I left the prison hospital. The warden accompanied the car as far as the gate.

I rejoiced at this change, for my own sake and partly for the doctor's also. The deterioration of my condition had given him grave concern. He had been caught between two millstones. His physician's oath obligated him to help me; but the regime wanted him to play the part of a policeman. Perhaps he may also have thought that it would cause him less trouble if I did not die on his hands.

☦ *In Püspökszentlászló*

WE DROVE OFF with Colonel Rajnai beside me in civilian dress. On the way he showed me Greater Budapest, which was then being built, and Stalin City in the vicinity of Dunapentele. Stalin City was a new major project on some 1,375 acres of land. It was not an ordinary city, he said, but a "socialist city, including a steel plant"; its production of iron and steel exceeded by a third all the other plants in the counrty. Stalin City, he told me, contained department stores, schools, canteens, hotels, movie houses, doctors' offices, a hospital, a cultural center, a museum, an office building, a stadium, parks, an open air theater; 400 acres of woods separated the foundry from the residential and commercial areas.

The city had 35,000 inhabitants but no church; none was permitted to be built there, and no religious services were held. Stalin City was one of Rákosi's creations. Perhaps that was what he had in mind when he came to Hungary in 1944 and declared: "We shall go all the way to the stars."

But only half a decade was to pass before this ungrateful city rejected the name of Stalin! In 1956 this Bolshevistic modern Babylon waged the fiercest struggle in all Hungary against the Stalinist spirit to which it presumably should have been so attached.

God is everywhere. God also enters those places from which the rulers of this world would like to ban Him. Thus I had the pleasure of reading in the communist county newspaper on December 30, 1956, that with permission of the Bureau for Church Affairs and with the consent of the local party organs, Holy Mass was celebrated for the first time in the lobby of the public school of Stalin City.

Püspökszentlászló, where I was taken, is situated about eight miles from Pécs at the foot of wooded Mount Zengő. It is a small community, really a suburb of Hetény, and at the time had only 108 inhabitants. At the beginning of the eighteenth century the bishop of Pécs had a summer residence built there, and this castle was now assigned to me. The government issued a statement to the effect that the episcopate had picked this building belonging to the Church and had designated it as my place of residence. But that was untrue, for the government had long since confiscated the castle.

We got out in Hetény and had to shift to a Jeep because an ordinary car could not travel the road.

So far this village had remained untouched by the "progress" of the past decade. We drove some two-and-a-half miles through a wooded, mountainous area threaded by many brooks. In my honor the castle had been provided with a new high-board fence, signifying that some kind of imprisonment awaited me here too.

As I started to climb the stairs, I suffered a heart attack. The young doctor who accompanied me, Dr. Sugár, examined me, then had me sit down and ordered a half-hour rest on the ground floor. The steward of the building, a well-meaning man, came around and introduced himself. His name was Angyal, which means "angel," so that I addressed him as "My angel!" The two men helped me up to the first floor, where two rooms had been placed at my disposal. Both were in a decent condition, which could not be said of the washbowl, however, or of the plumbing and electricity.

Meanwhile my escorts from Budapest went through my suitcases and packages. I protested because I had been promised at the penitentiary that whatever I wrote would remain my property. My protest did little good.

The colonel then informed me that I was free to use the balcony and walk in the garden if the secret police, members of the AVO, who were also quartered here, permitted me. However, I would have to ask permission each time. I replied that if this were the case I could get along without the balcony and the garden. He left, and returned half an hour later to say that I could use the balcony and garden as I pleased. My mother, too, would be permitted to visit me here. A special room would be kept available for her; she herself could decide how long she wished to stay. In parting he commented that they were being generous jailers, were they not? Not so generous as the Habsburgs whom they were always denouncing, I replied, and I reminded him of Bishop Telekesi of Eger, who after the defeat in the war of liberation was thrown into prison. King Joseph I gave him a priest as a secretary; and this condition remained unchanged under his successor, Charles III. The colonel said nothing and left; but on July 20 he reappeared bringing me a cassock.

Afterwards a priest, János Tóth, came too, bringing credentials from the apostolic administrator of Esztergom. He had been a parish priest in Budapest, but had been displaced from his parish. The Rákosi regime had torn down his parish church, "Regnum Marianum," to make room for a monument to Stalin. At last a consecrated priest was beside me at the altar again, was with me at table and on my walks.

The only times I was forbidden to go out was Sundays and holidays. The people who came to services in the church of the castle were not supposed to see me.

On a slope at the side of the church lay the cemetery, to which I felt particularly drawn. There had also been cemeteries alongside the reception prison and the penitentiary. A cemetery instructs; it conduces to serious thought. I often asked myself whether I should have to end my life as a prisoner.

At this time I was not badly off as far as food and drink, air and exercise were concerned. The police often wore sullen looks, but that was understandable. Here in this isolated place they could scarcely maintain their own connections with their families and the world. They, the doctor, and the rest of the staff constantly complained in their reports to the ministry about the unhealthy conditions in which we lived.

In my baggage I found my watch, my forty-nine forints, and my underclothing. A small packet labeled "strictly confidential" was also with the rest. I wondered how it could possibly have got there. Opening it, I found it contained various papers, with a photograph of my mother on top. She had sent the picture to me in 1950, signed with loving words; but it had never been turned over to me. Then there was a letter from the International Red Cross inquiring about my health. There were letters from abroad which I had been supposed to sign as proof that I was still alive. I also found reports from the doctors, reports from the warden's office, regulations regarding my mother's visits in Vác and so on. Later, in Petény, this "strictly confidential" packet in my belongings was to produce grave difficulties for me.

My priest now informed me in detail about what had been happening during the seven years I had been cut off from the world. He told me about other priests, other prisoners: who had died, who had remained loyal, who had wavered. He spoke of the dwindling of religious life in the capital, of the decline of religious education. Of the great novelties he brought me was the proclamation of the dogma of Mary's bodily ascension into heaven and the canonization of Pius X. The priest regularly received two newspapers. He also had a radio, from which he received the latest news and passed that news on to me, although he was forbidden to.

On October 10, 1955, Archbishop Grősz of Kalocsa was brought to the castle with the greatest secrecy. He was assigned the priest's apartment, and the priest was given my mother's room. Thus my mother, in spite of the earlier arrangement, was unable to stay longer than a day when she came for her second visit. In compensation I was permitted to talk to my mother without the presence of a supervising police officer.

Next day, when I looked out of my window, I saw Archbishop Grősz just returning from his walk, accompanied by his guards. They were looking at the fish and frogs in the pond outside the building. I went out on the balcony, and we two prisoners looked at one another—for the first time in six years. As old experienced convicts we knew we were not permitted to greet each other.

Nevertheless, in the course of the next few weeks I visited Archbishop Grősz three times. We also exchanged letters. I was especially interested in what he could tell me about the years 1948 to 1951, during which the Church had suffered its severest tribulations.

When I first knocked on his door and entered his room, he was greatly surprised. He knew quite well we were not supposed to see each other, still less to meet, and he asked me how I had managed it. I commented that life imprisonment could not be extended, so I did not mind the risk. In any case, it was very easy:

"If somebody starts up the creaking stairs from the ground floor, we'll hear it up here and have plenty of time to separate. I've learned these little things in the four months I've been here. Besides, I've sent the priest down to fetch newspapers for me. The newspapers are lying around everywhere downstairs; the policeman on duty is busy gathering them up, and the priest is undoubtedly alone in the vestibule. But I won't be able to come frequently. I'll tuck letters under your door and ask for answers by knocking."

Soon we were exchanging three or four letters a day.

The castle was by no means the sanatorium the authorities were loudly proclaiming it to be in their propaganda throughout the country. It is true that they had spent a good deal on equipment; the building was supposed to make a good impression from outside. It had been painted; furniture, rugs, and curtains had been provided and flower beds laid out. But the efforts of the "interior decorators" and the gardeners could not cover up the fact that we were confined to a rainy region with a notoriously unhealthy climate. Our whole "court," consequently, was often in an irritable mood. There were many depressing days, nights, and weeks. The building also had "tenants" who had sublet it. It was swarming with mice.

On October 8, 1955, on orders from above, Steward Angyal had my things packed. But then we waited another three weeks. At last, late at night on October 31, trucks drove up. The entire building was cleared out. Only the two rooms occupied by Archbishop Grősz and myself were left untouched. On the evening of November 1, 1955, two men I did not know arrived to drive me to the hospital in Pécs for a thorough physical examination. The doctor who examined me indicated that he was content with my condition.

In Püspökszentlászló we were given no supper, for my escorts had already ordered theirs in Pécs. While I was being examined, they had eaten. However, without having eaten, I set out with them around ten o'clock at night. On the way we met the truck which was moving the furniture from my rooms.

Toward four o'clock in the morning on November 2, we arrived in Felsöpetény, our new home. Several smartly dressed young men asked where they were to serve my meal—it seems I was to have two rooms; hence the question.

"Thank you, I don't want anything now."

"Why not?"

"I want to say Mass, since today is All Souls Day."

In the corridor these men and the irate cooks discussed the situation. The latter reported anew that supper was ready.

"Thank you, I don't want anything. I am going to say Mass."

"Have you already had supper?"

"No."

"Then aren't you hungry?"

"When a priest wishes to offer the Holy Sacrifice it does not matter whether or not he is hungry."

The cooks and the young men took their leave.

☿ "Guest" of the Secret Police

MY NEW RESIDENCE was the nationalized Almássy Castle, set in the midst of a vast park on the fringe of the village. The building appeared decent enough, although a good many parts of it had suffered under communist management. Before we arrived the building had sheltered Young Pioneers. After their departure a squad of more than a hundred workers was unable to repair all the damage. I was given a room that also served us as a dining room; there was also a bedroom and half a chapel. The archbishop of Kalocsa received exactly the same amount of space. The warden held the rank of a major in the secret police but wore civilian dress. He had been a worker in a textile factory and was now a university student and a loyal party-line Communist. Fifteen guards were under his command; they were equipped with machine guns, submachine guns, and three wolfhounds. These dogs were supposed to be kept away from us, but they nevertheless visited us, wagged their tails furiously when they came near us, and jumped to lick our faces.

The park had a rich stand of ancient evergreen trees and many fruit trees as well. But we were not allowed to use all of the orchard. A hedge, reinforced by barbed wire, marked off the restricted zone. Our walking area was changed almost every day. Several times the warden offered to accompany me on my walks, whenever Father Tóth was not available. But in such cases I preferred to do without the walk. Several days before Christmas the steward whispered to my priest that my mother would be allowed to spend the holidays with me if I asked. I would certainly have been glad to be with her on Christmas Eve. But to ask would have compromised my whole stand. And so the holidays passed without my mother's visit.

The representatives of the rulers, as well as the guards, had already begun spreading the word in Püspökszentlászló that I was no longer a prisoner, merely a guest. This sort of hospitality reminded me of all those placards telling the worker in the socialist state and the farmer in the production cooperative: "The factory is yours, the land belongs to you, the cooperative belongs to you." But the factory and the collective farm remain more alien to them than ever, and they would sooner see the present "Peasants and Workers Government" in hell. That was how I felt about the hospitality so generously extended to me. The first time I heard the phrase, that I was a guest, I started to my feet: "So I'm not a prisoner. Then why am I enclosed by two fences, one of them of barbed wire? Why are there fifteen secret policemen and three wolfhounds and an arsenal of weapons in my immediate vicinity? You know, I wouldn't treat any of my guests that way." No one answered that sally.

Later I decided to put their hospitality to a practical test. I let my beard grow. By this time I had been given razor blades, and for a while I used them regularly to shave myself. But then I heard by chance that there was a barber among the secret police who shaved both officers and men. I stopped shaving. When I was starting to look quite shaggy, the steward asked me why I did not take care of myself, saying: "It really isn't proper for a person so high in the Church to run around unshaven."

"Is it proper for the host to have a barber but the guest none?" I replied.

Next day he returned and asked whether I was doing anything at the moment, for if not he could send the barber.

"What I am doing is time, so I certainly have time for the barber."

My mother was able to visit me at Almássy Castle twice. She came at Whitsunday, and again for twenty-four hours at the beginning of August. But she was not permitted to talk privately to the priest assigned to me, let alone to me. Even when she was in chapel with me, the warden's deputy wanted to enter. But I ordered him out, and he left, probably fearing that my mother might spread the story of his rudeness.

On the whole the treatment was growing more and more unfriendly. We were met with a cold politeness. Before the transfer I had been told that Dr. Sugár would come over occasionally from Budapest to check my health. But he did so only once. On the other hand, there was no lack of medicines. However, I was supposed to take them only in the presence of witnesses, which I refused to do.

Naturally I asked what had happened to the owner of the castle, Count Almássy, and learned that he was living somewhere in the countryside, in a single room with an earthen floor. His castle was called an "ecclesiastical building," for the sake of public relations. But it was nothing of the kind even though ecclesiastical prisoners were held there. The Church itself was among the robbed, not among the robbers.

Arrangements in the building were distinctly military. Consequently, during the three months I was held there I did not have another opportunity to visit my fellow prisoner, Archbishop Grősz, as had been possible in Pükspökszentlászló. There was an anteroom between his and my room which served as guardroom for the secret policemen. The time for my daily walk had been set for twelve o'clock. From my window I saw that Archbishop Grősz took his solitary walk in the garden at eleven every day. I heard him going out and returning. Once I observed that he left the garden early, at fifteen minutes to twelve, and lingered a little in the anteroom watching the guards at their card game and making remarks. Hearing him, I hoped for the chance of a meeting. I therefore went into the anteroom, greeted everybody, and said: "Well now, is my brother here also?" The policemen leaped to their feet, throwing down their cards.

When I returned from the walk, the warden's deputy came to see me, very angry about my "lack of discipline." "What time was it when I came out of my room?" I asked. "No one has told me there is not to be a walk when the police play cards and even have kibitzers watching."

The man subsided into silence and left my room.

Petény is a historic site; four centuries ago it was owned by the famous legal scholar Werbőczy, and our country's first systematic lawbook, the *Ius Tripartitum*, was written there. While I was at the castle, from November 1955 on, a whole array of newspapers was placed on my table for me to read. Every day I received *Szabad Nép* (Free People) and *Magyar Nemzet* (Hungarian Nation); every week *Uj Ember* (The New Man) and *Kereszt* (The Cross), and every month copies of the "Statistical Survey." Obviously some reaction from me was expected. At the beginning the steward called my attention to articles here and there. He would drop in on me and try to find out what effect the reading had had upon me. The regime certainly could have used some sign of praise, approval, or approbation from me, in order to distract the public from the country's economic and political miseries.

One day a high dignitary and a companion came to see me. He didn't give his name or position, but his status was obvious. He declared that György Parragi, a deputy in Parliament and a member of the Patriotic People's Front as well as editor in chief of the newspaper *Magyar Nemzet*, had asked the government for permission to visit me in Petény and interview me for his newspaper. The regime itself must have cooked up this plan, I thought. I therefore answered in writing to the minister of justice, pointing out that I could not possibly, after two weeks of reading newspapers, form a picture of the past seven years, during which I had been entirely without information. Therefore I was not adequately equipped to answer an interviewer's questions, I said.

Some time later, on January 19, 1956, we experienced a kind of invasion; a veritable caravan of investigating commissioners descended on us. On the pretext that my conduct had insulted the government, a thorough search of the premises was conducted. Afterwards it was announced that I had obtained possession of confidential documents, which in fact had been in that packet given to me at my previous abode. Since these articles had not been confiscated in Püspökszentlászló, I protested and refused to sign a warrant for the search. The documents, which had lain in plain sight, were now confiscated, along with all my manuscripts. That afternoon I was interrogated sharply by two men. Although I asked their names, they refused to tell me, but tried to make an impression on me by their haughty, arrogant manner.

They charged me with the theft of "confidential" documents while I was in the prison hospital and with having kept these documents and taken them with me to Püspökszentlászló. It was absurd—as if I had been in charge of the files at the hospital, or had had access to their police files. There was no doubt that a new tactic was being tried out. The packet in question had been put together by the police themselves. The various documents could scarcely hold any great interest for me—at most the medical records which indicated that the condition of my lungs was worrisome and that a cavity had formed. But perhaps this did not even record the findings of my own X rays; it might have been a trick, the purpose of which was to prompt me to ask to be transferred to a sanatorium, or even to be released, with the idea that the government could then attach conditions to whatever "favor" it granted.

The priest who had been assigned to me was sent away at the beginning of the search on the pretext that his vacation was long overdue. Thus all he saw of the entire operation was the procession of automobiles. My patience was wearing thin, and this time I decided that instead of taking the disturbance calmly I would protest by going on a hunger strike. At noon, and then again in the evening, I ate nothing. One of the investigators appeared and asked me whether I had enjoyed my meal.

"Just as much as at noon," I replied.

"Why aren't you eating?"

"I was fed up long before lunch."

I continued my hunger strike through the next day and the next. At this point everyone in the place began to worry. The little girl who brought the food could scarcely restrain her tears. On the morning of the fourth day my priest appeared and pleaded with me to take some nourishment. At this point the thought went through my mind: "You're sixty-four years old, have seven years of prison behind you, are emaciated, and your lung is probably affected. If you don't want to die, this had better be enough." And so, after seventy-five hours, I ended my fast at noon. Everyone uses what tools he owns: the government, force; the prisoner, at his own expense, fasting.

☩ *My Guardian Angel in Prison*

A DECADE before my long imprisonment I wrote the following words about mother love:

You will be forgotten by your superiors after you have served them, by your subordinates when they no longer feel your power, by your friends when you run into difficulties. . . . At the prison gate only your mother will be waiting for you. In the depths of the prison, you have only your loving mother. She alone descends with you. If you are thrust even deeper into dungeons, into the chasm of the penitentiary or the death house, she alone does not shrink from accompanying you. . . .

At the time I wrote my book it did not occur to me that my aged mother would be the sole star in the dark skies of my imprisonment and that she alone would visit and embrace me during my eight years of solitary confinement.

Who is my mother? A woman who has had six children, who in her eighty-fifth year lived in her home in Mindszent surrounded with respect and love by her fourteen grandchildren and as many great-grandchildren. At the time of my arrest, and while my name was being dragged through the dust, she was seventy-four years old and had been widowed for two years. From her simple village environment she hastened to my aid; with intelligence and adroitness she stood by me until her death. She knew how to trace me through that cruel world of the communist prison system. Never before had she set foot in a government ministry. But now she went straight to the heads of the party, men who had come to power unjustly and illegally. To make these calls was a hard cross for her to bear. But wherever she went, in the ministry, in prison, in the penitentiary, her bearing testified to her spiritual strength.

When I was appointed primate, many people said to her: "What a happy mother!" Everywhere, in Hungary and abroad, there were those who begged her to accept them as spiritual sons and daughters. When bishops Badalik and Rogács visited this modest old woman in her rustic home, I regarded their act as a special honor. On December 16, 1948, during the last episcopal conference held under my chairmanship in Esztergom, she dined with the bishops and archbishops, sitting at my right side, again making a striking impression on all by her quiet, modest demeanor. From December 26, 1948, on, the day of my arrest, a darkness as of night frowned over the radiant goodness, sweetness, and kindness of this woman.

As I have mentioned earlier, she had been staying with me since November 19 and therefore had witnessed my arrest. She had wanted to go with me, but of course that was forbidden. Next day she nevertheless came to the capital to find a defense counsel for me. She was back home when she heard, with deep sorrow, of the events at 60 Andrássy Street, and was horrified to hear of my conviction and sentencing. The torrent of slander washed over her also. She would have been ready to sacrifice her life to save her imprisoned son, but there was no one would have accepted such an offer.

She had to undergo the painful experience of having many of her former friends gradually withdraw from her. Letters and visits ceased. Acquaintances and even relatives took to meeting her only outside of her house.

She was able to visit me in the reception prison, and once again after nine months before I was transferred from there. But she was not permitted to see "my room" and could talk with me in Vác only in the presence of a guard. The packages of baked goods, grapes, and meat she brought with her for me were opened and examined. As I have related, we were allowed to talk only about family affairs; but she nevertheless repeatedly managed to tell me at least in general outline about what was happening in the country and the world. She reported on the "bearded bishops," that is, the civilian officials of the Bureau of Church Affairs. She told me about heroes and weaklings, about atrocities toward nuns and monks, about persecuted and incarcerated priests from Zalaegerszeg and Szombathely, about the fate of other bishops. Along with all that she would make remarks and keep me informed of family matters—reporting on deaths, marriages, the arrival of new great-grandchildren. She spoke of my nephew, county executive Jozsef Légrády and his family, and of the suffering these relations had been forced to endure for my sake. From my mother I also learned of Stalin's death and of the tensions and disputes that had erupted over his legacy. Whenever she left me, her last words were always sustained by faith. Each time we asked ourselves wordlessly, but so that both of us sensed the question, whether we would see each other again in this earthly life.

Her mother's eye immediately saw through the deception when I was always brought before her in the black suit instead of in the convict's uniform I ordinarily wore. She perceived my weakness and the breakdown of my health. When she saw me so emaciated, the time I weighed 97 pounds and looked like a skeleton, she cried out and berated the colonel so furiously that he was at a loss for an answer. When she was warned that she would not be permitted to engage in politics, she replied unruffledly that an eighty-year-old ignorant village woman could know nothing about politics anyhow, and so they had nothing to fear from her.

It was her greatest joy during those years of imprisonment that one time in Pükspökszentlászló she was again able to receive Holy Communion from the hand of her son.

My book *The Mother* was strongly influenced by my mother's own character. Possibly not a single page of this book is left in Hungary, for the government may have ordered it destroyed to the very last copy. But what I wrote from the bottom of my heart was preserved for me by my mother, by her life. For me, she was the most wonderful gift of Providence. I cannot thank God sufficiently for having given her to me and for having preserved her life so that she was with me in the most difficult of times for me. In 1948 she asked me not to stay in Hungary, to go abroad. But when she saw that I could not do that, she resigned herself to my decision. If, later, I had taken the easier course, she would certainly have felt such a betrayal keenly. Our task is to fulfill God's will, however it may confront us. But at the same time on all our ways we are always in God's hand. She knew that just as clearly as I did.

The places that formed the backdrop of her life were the Church; the family home with her two daughters, her grandchildren, and great-grandchildren; the graveyard; the vineyard; and her daughters' house; also my episcopal seat of Esztergom; and after Christmas 1948 the various prisons.

Often she looked down from the vineyard to the cemetery where my father, my parents' parents, our relatives, the parish priests, and the teachers rested, and where she too was awaited. After my arrest Dr. Gyula Géfin and Professor Jósef Vecsey devoted themselves lovingly to her; the latter accompanied her on her visit to me in Budapest. The dean and assistant priest of the village, and the precentor helped her with the vintage and the field work. The expenses of so much traveling used up her small savings; her property was overburdened with taxes. Nevertheless, she gladly helped young seminarians, the future laborers in the Lord's vineyard, and repeatedly had Masses said for her son.

For more than eight years we were not permitted to exchange letters. Even while I was in the American Embassy, letters could not be exchanged. It was not until 1959 that the third volume of the Mindszenty Documents came to my hand, and in the appendix I found nineteen letters which my mother had written during my imprisonment to Éva Treffner, her spiritual daughter and benefactor in New York. From these letters I learned a great deal that I had not known. My mother had come to Budapest while I was still a prisoner in Andrássy Street. She had made many efforts to find defense counsel for me. It was certainly not her fault that she was unable to visit me; likewise that she was unable to be present at the trial. I learned that on February 23, 1949, she had gone from pillar to post trying to arrange a meeting between us. She came to the capital thirteen times without success. The refrain of all her letters was: "I am grief-stricken; I am treated like dirt; I no longer find any comfort on this earth."

She also appealed to Archbishop Grősz and the other bishops for aid. In response to their inquiry the authorities replied that "the mother always has the right to visit her son." But this right existed only on paper.

In May 1950 she had a picture taken of herself for me, wrote a dedication on it, and sent it to the minister of justice with a request that it be turned over to her imprisoned son. Even this natural human request was not granted. I did not receive the picture until five years later, on July 17, 1955, along with my other belongings. Aside from a photograph of Pope Pius XII, it was my only picture from the world outside. I put it on my table and kissed it every night. During my imprisonment I daily prayed a part of the rosary for my mother.

✝ *Attempts at an Agreement*

ON APRIL 25, 1956, Dr. Gyula Czapik, archbishop of Eger, died after a long illness. Since my imprisonment he had been temporary head of the Hungarian conference of bishops. He certainly did not want to go to prison. (He made this remark to Archbishop Grösz.) It is for God, not for us, to judge such an attitude. Even an iron constitution can scarcely endure prison, and his feeble, sickly frame was certainly not made for it.

At the funeral in Eger the rulers put on a remarkable display of piety. Even the communist press took notice of his death. But the political situation within Hungary and with regard to the Church remained very complicated. Two archbishops, one of them the rightful head of the episcopate, were in prison. I learned that Lajos Shvoy, the senior bishop of Székesfehérvár, appeared disinclined to take over the presidency of the conference of bishops during my absence. The regime would not have liked that anyhow, since he was regarded as an "adherent of Mindszenty." I therefore had the impression that the release of one of the archbishops would now follow. It wouldn't do for critics abroad to be able to say that of three Hungarian archbishops, one was dead and the other two in prison. Although Tóth, the priest who had been assigned to me, imagined that the choice would fall on me, I could hardly think so.

The other bishops also doubted that I would be released from confinement without imposition of unacceptable conditions. I knew that Archbishop Grösz had negotiated with the Communists while he was in Pükspökszentlászló. For that reason he was separated from me in the middle of February 1956 and taken to a rectory in Tószeg, in the diocese of Vác. There he was permitted to make contacts with others; he was allowed to travel and to move about unhindered. Later he remarked to foreign journalists that he intended to follow the example of the late Archbishop Czapik. Something of the sort, of course, was precisely what had been demanded of him. He also made remarks about me, denying rumors being spread in the world press that I had again been incarcerated. Archbishop Grösz, a man ever kind and loyal, tried in his own way to guide the ship of the Hungarian Church through the reefs. The "peace priests," who since Grösz's sentencing in 1951 had joined his adversaries and slanderers, soon became his admirers.

Evidently he held his tongue about a good many injustices, but he also tried to preserve the Church from further troubles and more attacks in the courts. But under the existing circumstances such an effort could not succeed in the long run. His vacillations weakened rather than secured his own situation. Soon the "peace priests" found themselves in a position to circumvent the entire episcopate, including the loyal priests, and to foment more harm within the Church.

For seven months after the departure of Archbishop Grősz nobody from Budapest visited me. That didn't trouble me, although the reason alleged for my transfer to Petény had been that the place was close to the capital and therefore would make it easier for people to come to see me. The steward had frequently remarked to Father Tóth that if I wished to hold a conference, I could receive whomever I liked at any time; I need only make the request by telephone. I denied myself and my adversaries any such request.

In the summer I received reports on political meetings. In Csepel the premier, András Hegedűs, had said: "Every honorable Hungarian can regain his freedom if he is willing to work for the Hungarian people and stand loyally by the government." On August 20, 1956, a highly placed personage unexpectedly came to see me.

"How are you?"

"Jailish, thank you. Like an old tree in a small space: I don't spread myself and I don't weep either."

"You are no longer a prisoner."

"Then what is the barbed wire for, and the secret police and the dogs?"

"Even in Esztergom there is a fence."

"That is true, but it had to be paid for only once and is meant to keep out those who are outside, not to keep in those who are inside. Besides, it isn't made of barbed wire."

"The nine months of newspaper reading has surely given you enough of an opportunity to become more thoroughly acquainted with our situation."

"Well, the nine months were longer than the preceding two weeks. But now the difficulty is a different one. The two newspapers I am given to read admit that they previously disseminated falsehoods. Am I to believe that they are now telling the truth? The newspaper *Kereszt* put out by the "peace priests" ceased publication after it had been put on the Index by the Holy Office. I gather that in a public discussion a speaker said, and was applauded, that not even the statistical data correspond to reality. How, then, can anyone become better acquainted with the situation?"

"But there are also successes that have benefited the people."

"Which ones? The rehabilitations? The economic emergency?"

"Our international situation has improved."

"Yes, you have had to pay the Titos dearly. Never before in the hundred-year's history of Hungarian parliamentarism has a premier apologized in such obsequious language as Premier András Hegedűs has done in regard to Tito when he spoke in Nagykanizsa. If you had respected the nat-

ural law and the rights of man that I referred to so often in my pastoral letters, the acts of violence that are now regretted would never have been committed. The illegal deportations of the Germans would not have taken
place, nor the shameful forced resettlement and exchange of populations in
Upper Hungary. We also would not have to hear of an economic and moral
collapse, nor of humiliation before Tito. We would not have to lament mass
murders and listen to the confession of lies. Now there is talk of legality.
But where is it and what is it? Neither in 1945 nor in 1948 did the government stand on a legal basis. I don't know how many violations of the law
were committed and permitted then. If legality is proclaimed and pledged
today, that can logically mean only that up to now the Hungarian people
have not lived under conditions of legality. So what innovations can we
now expect? So far all of your 'laws' remain valid. The invididuals who
control the government have remained the same, with few exceptions. Such
men hardly offer any promise of changes. They have even violated the law
again by letting the principal miscreant, Rákosi, go free."

"We have broken with him," the visitor said. Only my attitude was
unchanged, he added, and that was where the trouble lay. And he left.

September 2, 1956, was approaching, the hundredth anniversary of the
consecration of the cathedral in Esztergom. That consecration had been a
great event at the time and a token of the compromise reached between the
king and the nation in 1867. Ever since I had been presiding in Esztergom I
had in mind to commemorate the anniversary as a festival in honor of the
religious and national awakening of the entire country. The people knew
this and wanted their primate to be present at the ceremonies. "The primate can conduct the festival service and deliver the festival sermon if he
asks," the steward informed my priest. "It is not we who are holding him
captive. It is he who does not want to get out."

But my resolve was firm that the cathedral would not see me on its festival day, not under existing conditions.

I thought back to the consecration ceremonies of 1856. At that time the
monarch, Franz Josef, came accompanied by the archdukes, by cardinal-
archbishops Rauscher from Vienna and Haulik from Zagreb. There were
also six more archbishops from home and abroad, nineteen bishops, many
priests, aristocrats, military and civilian notables, including Ferenc Liszt,
who took an active part in the celebration, and ten thousand of the faithful.
A representative cross section of the population of the entire country was
present, praying and hoping that the cross of national oppression would not
have to be borne much longer. The primate, Archbishop Scitovszky, presented a petition signed by 124 representatives of the nobility, requesting
the restoration of a constitutional national government in Hungary. The petition was addressed to Franz Josef who had not yet been crowned king.
The consecration of the cathedral was like the bursting of the buds of our
national liberty, a festival of rejoicing.

But now, in 1956, there were no foreign guests. The episcopate was not fully represented; at most an archbishop and two bishops came. Only small members of the laity were present. One pilgrimage after another had been canceled by the government. But the deputy chief of the Bureau for Church Affairs turned up in the cathedral, which is the heart of the Hungarian Church.

Ought I to return there "pardoned" and resume my work fettered by the "mercy" that had been shown to me? In 1856 Primate Scitovszky had employed other means to break the chains of national bondage. Should this centennial produce a night of inconsolability, a conclusive acceptance of the cruelest of all shackles? Was I to issue declarations extracted by force, or even to rise in the pulpit after eight years of slander and suffering to sing anthems of gratitude to the regime? Should I become the witness not of Christ but of the Antichrist? *Verbum Dei est alligatum*—"Is God's word bound and tied?" I had no right to sit down at the same table and drink with the representatives of the Bureau for Church Affairs, when a hundred years ago Ferenc Deák would not even sit with the as yet uncrowned Franz Josef and kept strictly away from him. Pious clerics and laymen alike would inevitably cast doubtful looks at their shepherd, and the Communists would regard me as already more or less one of their own. Was I to go and to find out amid the "joy" of the centennial what had happened to Esztergom in the meantime? And was I to approve of everything? The cathedral has four mottos in its coat of arms: *coepit, continuavit, consummavit, conservavit* ("It began, it continued, it perfected, it preserved"). Was I to be responsible for adding a fifth, such as: *Jubilavit in abominatione desolationis* ("It rejoiced amid the horrors of devastation")? No, I would not be able to stand beside the cathedral without heartbreak, nor to look at the vast seminary and the teacher training school, all of them now stripped of their former functions.

St. Lawrence Street in Esztergom now no longer belongs to the actual old martyr, but merely to "the martyrs." But who are these? One of them is Tibor Szamuelly, and Otto Korvin-Klein is the other. In the meantime streets and squares in Esztergom had been named after Lenin, Voroshilov, Makarenko, László Rudas, Tolbukhin, among others. Was I to rejoice on the streets of such people? Was I to go to Esztergom to see for myself the city's humiliation? The city had been the capital of the county; it had been deprived of its rank. No longer permitted to be the chief city of its district, it had been subordinated to Dorog. The former capital of Hungary was losing all the importance it had possessed in the course of its long history.

It seemed to me far better to stay in the wilderness of the Börzsöny Mountains and to hold fast to thoughts Ferenc Deák had formulated a hundred years ago: "I will not surrender any of those things that we cannot surrender and have no right to surrender."

A week later Father Tóth heard from the warden that I was expected to ask for a pardon. But I wrote no such petition; I wanted not mercy but justice. If I asked for amnesty, I thought, I would have to be ready to meet my adversaries' conditions, which would very likely amount to confirmation of the following points:

1. An agreement officially recognizing the government bureau for church affairs and the peace priest movement.
2. A declaration of support for so-called world peace and for collectivization of the factories and peasant homesteads.
3. An oath of allegiance to the government.
4. A ceremonial visit to President Dobi, to Premier Hegedűs, and to First Secretary Gerő.
5. A total assent to everything that had hitherto been done in Hungary and to me.
6. Accepting my salary from the government.

Had I still been in the penitentiary, I might have inclined to think over and perhaps accept some of these conditions as paths to freedom. But in the meantime I had regained my spiritual and intellectual energies, and in consequence my resolve was unshakable. Faced with the alternative of death in prison or liberty at the price of ignoble compromise, I would sooner choose the former.

The one priest who was at my side during this period repeatedly tried to win me over to acceptance of "freedom." His failure may have proved rather uncomfortable for him.

As a result of his urging, I finally wrote a petition to the minister of justice. But I pleaded for nothing; instead I made proposals, and none of them in my own behalf. I summed up conditions for a general amnesty as follows:

1. All prisoners over seventy years of age to be released.
2. Sick prisoners over sixty-five to be released.
3. All nuns to be immediately and unconditionally set free.
4. The promised rebuilding of the demolished parish church "Regnum Marianum," which had been repeatedly postponed, to be begun and speedily accomplished, thus removing a situation that had scandalized the country and the world.
5. All sentences to be reviewed as quickly as possible.

I dispatched this letter in the first half of September. During the two following months I received neither a written nor an oral reply. Along with many others among the Catholic faithful, the few pilgrims in Esztergom must have been wondering why the primate did not leave his prison, since the newspapers had stated that the government was granting him his freedom. There was no way I could let them know my reasons.

VII. THE 1956 REVOLUTION
☦ *Sudden Freedom*

EARLY IN THE MORNING on October 24, 1956, Father Tóth came rushing breathlessly into my room. "There's a revolution in Budapest!" he cried. The only thing we could do to deal with our inner turbulence was to say Mass. In the two Mementos I remembered all the sons of Hungary, living and dead. After the Mass my young priest vanished, leaving me in uncertainty about events in the capital. I was filled with foreboding. But I did not want to ask any questions. There was no radio or newspaper to tell me what was going on. From the village I could hear the shouting and chanting of young men. They were singing:

> Hurray, spring has come at last!
> We hope to see Rákosi dead!
> What our people want is bread!

Inside the building there were anxious faces. Everyone could feel that events of world-historical importance were happening all around us. But for the present nothing at all happened. Four days later the warden came to my room in the evening and said nervously: "Get ready to leave at once. Dress warmly. We're leaving because you're not safe from the mob here. The rabble has repeatedly shouted "Mindszenty" in the course of the past few days. We must protect you from this scum."

"Where are we bound for?"

"Budapest. But don't ask any questions; we're starting in half an hour." He bustled off.

I sat down and reflected. The rabble who are shouting for Mindszenty are not likely to be dangerous to me, I thought.

Half an hour later the steward came rushing into my room. Startled, he asked: "Why aren't you preparing to leave?"

"I want to see Father Tóth. I must talk to him privately first; then I may tell you what I'll do."

"Really! Well, Father Tóth's down below in the car and has been waiting for you for some time. Besides, I have to be present when you talk to him."

"I will speak to him only in private."

"Get dressed!"

"No! I have no reason to fear the Hungarian people. I am not a mass murderer, nor a liar, nor a robber or an exploiter. I would walk alone through Budapest and anywhere in the country at any time."

"So you're not coming?"

"No."

"Then I'll use force."

"Do so."

He rushed out of the room. But instead of force, Father Tóth appeared, all alone and dressed for traveling.

"Have you been here all along?"

"Yes, but they didn't let me see you."

"What is going on in Budapest?"

He told me what he had been able to gather from a series of completely contradictory radio broadcasts.

"They pretend they want to take me to a place of safety," I said. "But I won't go."

Father Tóth was called out again, and once more the steward appeared. This time he shouted:

"This is about enough—now get ready!"

"I will not," I replied.

"We'll see about that."

Three policemen appeared. Another brisk exchange followed.

"Where is your winter coat?"

"I don't need it because I am not leaving."

"Then we'll take you without your coat."

"I call your attention to the fact that every Catholic who lays violent hands on a bishop is subject to ecclesiastical penalties."

They hesitated for a moment, but then they showed themselves to be the AVO policemen they were. Two of them lifted me from my armchair. I made myself stiff. My cassock tore. The men cursed and panted, but they were unable to drag me out of the room. And so they left to fetch reinforcements.

I sat down again and began to read, although I must admit that I absorbed little of a book that really interested me. Ten, twenty, thirty minutes passed, and I was still alone. Suddenly the commandant reappeared. He informed me that a transfer would not be possible today. Amazingly enough, he also brought my archbishop's robe, which had been stripped from me eight years before and which I had not seen since.

I said to him: "I shall be celebrating tomorrow morning. I want Father Tóth to be with me constantly."

"Yes, of course; I kept him away only to make sure you would not be disturbed."

"Did you now?"

"We are endeavoring to protect your life at the cost of our own. But if we can't because of your opposition, we disclaim all responsibility for your safety."

Next day, the morning of October 29, the steward, who was a party-line

Communist, sent me a book which, amazingly, was bound in the Hungarian national colors. At three o'clock in the afternoon he came in person and informed me that János Horváth, the chairman of the Bureau for Church Affairs, wished to see me.

"Send him in."

A small, stocky man entered, looking weary and broken. He said he had been asked by the new national government to take me, during this dangerous period, to a place where I could enjoy protection and security. Moreover, this would give us a chance to discuss our future cooperation.

If he really were the emissary of the national government, it was rather strange of that supposedly new government to send the chairman of the notorious bureau to me. I therefore told him:

"By now you must know that I am not leaving here. During the past years the government has held me in seven different places. I no longer have any desire to exchange this present place for still another. Besides, I am not in the slightest danger. If I leave here, it will be only to go to Budapest or Esztergom. In addition, a prisoner cannot enter into any binding discussions. If you had come here to tell me I was free, we would be able to begin negotiating.

He excused himself briefly, saying he wanted to report to the government by telephone what I had said. In the course of the day he three times sent word to me that he could not continue the conversation because he had been unable to put through his call; perhaps he would manage during the night.

On the morning of October 30 I said Mass as usual and then waited for news of the results of the telephone call. None came. Toward noon I went out into the yard. Outside our building stood an armored car bearing a red flag. Next to the driver's seat lay a large piece of bread. I have seen many kinds of bread: poor people's bread, convict's bread, army bread, wartime bread, but I had never seen a bread like that.

"Whom does this bread belong to?" I asked three policemen who immediately came toward me.

"A Russian armored brigadier."

"So that's the kind of bread they have in Paradise?" I said with a touch of sarcasm.

The connection with Budapest still did not go through. While I was walking in the garden, Father Tóth at last was able to rejoin me. Both of us wondered why Chairman Horváth was still waiting around but doing nothing. At last Horváth himself reappeared and said he had talked with Budapest yesterday, and again this morning. The government was about to hold an important meeting; he himself would now be going to the capital to bring my reply. Then he made the surprising proposal that I should visit my mother now; they would take me to her at once. The offer sounded suspect to me; I did not like it at all. I therefore replied:

"At a time like this I cannot go to Mindszent. Other obligations await me."

Horváth left. We heard his car roaring away and thought: they won't be coming back.

For the time being we were left in uncertainty.

An hour later a delegation of the inhabitants of Petény appeared. Naturally the people knew of my imprisonment in their village. In the autumn and winter, when the hedge around the garden was leafless, a woman would every so often take her heavy basket from her back, stand still, and peer through the twigs at the walker in the cassock. I could only guess at what went on in the souls of these people who thus stared at me. They had never had the opportunity to express their feelings in words because the distance between us was too great.

Now, they thronged excitedly to the gate and the fence. But they were not allowed to come in, for of course they were the "rabble" from whom the police were supposedly protecting me. Nevertheless, the demands of the populace became louder and more imperative, and finally the guards had to allow a delegation to enter. The delegation insisted on seeing me first of all, to determine whether I was still here and had not been carried off somewhere, for they had seen the armored car, the armed Russians, and the AVO police.

My dear, my marvelously faithful Hungarians! Your warm hearts, your emotion, your attachment, your millennium of painful history cut me to the quick! For six years I had not wept; now I let my tears flow freely. How could I repay the kindness of these villagers and of the land of Hungary? I took the two pictures so precious to me from the wall, the picture of the Holy Father and of my mother. Those good people wept with me. They wept with a cardinal, although they were almost all Lutherans or Baptists.

At six o'clock a delegation of five guards under the leadership of the commandant appeared. He declared that the guards and the entire staff had formed a revolutionary council of their own, which had determined that the primate's imprisonment was illegal. They would no longer consider themselves my guards; I was free.

"The Lord had loosened my bonds; broken my fetters; he led me out into the broad fields."

I decided to go to Buda at once, but there was no available vehicle. Horváth and his comrades had roared off in the only car stationed here. Waiting for their return seemed a poor prospect. For that matter, waiting for supper was likewise a poor prospect. The provisions in the building had been used up, and no new supplies from Budapest could be expected. Late in the day somebody brought a chicken from the village.

Suddenly the tramp of heavy boots sounded in the corridor. The door was wrenched open. A detachment of officers of the Honvédség of Rétság entered. Major Pallavicini said in clipped tones: "You are free. We can set out for Budapest at once. Transportation, suitcases, trunks, everything necessary is at your disposal."

Those loyal Honvédek! I don't know who was the more moved, they or I, when I gave them my blessing.

Dante has inscribed over the portals of Hell the words: "*Lasciate ogni speranza* . . ."—"Abandon all hope . . ." Above Purgatory, however, there hovers the glow of a joyful confidence. Imprisonment, too, is not different from waiting in Purgatory. The prisoner is always waiting. As long as he continues to wait, he has hope. The captive St. Paul stresses hope against all hope: "I am well assured that this will make for my soul's health, with you to pray for me, and Jesus Christ to supply my needs with his Spirit. . . . I am certain of that, and I do not doubt that I shall wait, and wait upon you all, to the happy furtherance of your faith" (Philippians 1:19, 25).

My mother's prayers and those of all the faithful certainly helped bring about my liberation from a predicament that only a few months earlier had seemed hopeless. And the force of those prayers was joined by the heroism of the workers, of the youth in countryside and towns, and of many other groups in the population.

Who could properly describe the blessed calm of the first free day? "I am leaving hell behind," the poet sings. Every prisoner feels something of the sort, although a religious person does not refer to these matters lightly. The sense of freedom after long years is ineffably sweet.

☩   Return to Buda

NOW THE GATE of the castle stood open. The people hastened to the spot in large numbers to see the primate of the country. They could scarcely believe that he had not been carried off by Russian armored units. Many actually felt me and kissed my clothes; they constantly asked my blessing.

The Protestants came, with sincere joy, led by their pastor; they were followed by the Catholic minorities and the Baptists: young men, girls, old men. It was a long time since I had seen such great rejoicing in the faces of Hungarians. So this was the "mob" that Kádár, Münnich, and my guards were supposed to protect me from. The people surrounded me; they did not want to let me go. More and more came; soon the crowd was far greater than the number of inhabitants in the village. Darkness fell. I blessed them all; then we set out. All Soul's night the year before, I had been taken the same way along which I was now returning. In Bánk and in the neighboring villages I had to get out of the car. I visited the ministers and priests. The joyousness of the people was boundless; I wondered how I could possibly get to Buda in a reasonable time at this rate. And in fact, that day I got only as far as Rétság, chiefly because my liberators had been the Hungarian "Red Soldiers" of Rétság. They and their commander now asked me to stay with them overnight because many other people wanted to greet me here. Sure enough, soon students who had joined the freedom fighters appeared, and then sailors and workers who had set out intending to free me. They came too late, but they decided to accompany me to Buda. I asked them: "Won't the Russians claim that I didn't dare return to Buda except with an armed escort?"

All burst into laughter.

Toward midnight my suffragan, Bishop Vince Kovács, came from Vác with his secretary. They greeted me warmly and invited me to spend the night in Vác. However, I preferred to stay with my liberators, the Honvédek. But it was impossible to get to bed. Officers came and went, and with them many members of their families. I had to give people my autograph until four o'clock in the morning. Then I finally lay down, exhausted, but could not fall asleep. I prayed: "There is none like thee, O God, none like thee. Ah, how often thou hast made me see times of bitter trouble! And still thou wouldst relent, and give me back life, and bring me up again from the very depths of the earth" (Psalms 70, 20).

That is what happened. The sacrifices of the freedom fighters in the capital and the tank unit of the Honvédeg of Rétság opened the gates of the underworld for me. God's hand played upon the organ of the world history— although He employed human hands for his purposes. I was like the apostles whose fetters were struck from their wrists by the aid of angels. What in prison I had not dared to hope for had happened: I was free again, and felt healthy and joyfully eager to work. Again and again the plea rose to my lips, that my suffering and the distress of these past years might prepare the way of the Gospel.

On October 31 we set out from Rétság. I had risen out of the deepest pit and now rode between lines of cheering crowds. Our procession was overwhelming; there were even tanks and motorized artillery taking part in it. Major Pálinkás (Pallavicini) and Lieutenants Spitz and Tóth took seats in my car. The driver's name was Rahoczki.

Imre Nagy is supposed to have denied later on that the ceremony of my entry into Budapest was organized at the government's orders. According to the Communists, the instructions for it came from Tildy, the premier's deputy. Certainly I was not the one to issue any orders; I knew nothing about the reception, nor did I want one. My intention had been to arrive in Esztergom or in Buda at night, and I had stayed in Rétság only out of respect for the soldiers' wishes.

We drove slowly through the villages. The bells peeled; flowers were tossed to us. Deeply moved, I blessed the waiting crowds. Everyone was looking happily and hopefully to the future. Amid ruins, destroyed Russian monuments, and struck factories, a new age seemed to be dawning for Hungary. What hard battles had been fought all along this way!

In the capital an enormous crowd poured toward the primate's palace. Soldiers, students, workers, mothers with children cheered and wept. All of us shed tears for the joy of this reunion and the sorrows of a whole decade. I blessed the kneeling crowd and then entered the building I had not seen for years.

Gradually, I learned the story of the past week. On October 23 a demonstration had taken place. At first the demonstrators had been unarmed. When Minister Gerö ordered the AVO police to fire into the crowd, the demonstrators tried to arm themselves, and the consequence was a battle between the people and the police in which the Russians intervened. The rebels resisted bitterly and for the time being were the victors.

Hungarians had never been a herd people; for them the individual, the family, the clan were always what counted. These Hungarians were subjugated by Moscow and its henchman, Rákosi, only by violence and deception. But the character of Hungary, her Christianity, her urge for freedom, and her pride were not broken by oppression. Hungary was compelled, it is true, to accept the rule of Moscow; but nothing like attachment, respect, let alone affection, could ever grow from such a situation. The Hungarians merely could not allow their dislike to show, because open resistance was impossible.

Let me here give a very abbreviated chronicle of the events of the Hungarian uprising:

On February 24, 1956, Stalinism was condemned at the Twentieth Communist Party Congress in Moscow. Stalin was dead; but the Hungarian people were more concerned about their still living Stalin, Rákosi. In May, criticism of Rákosi began to appear even in the Communist party press.

On July 18 came Rákosi's fall.

On October 6 the executed László Rajk was rehabilitated and accorded a state funeral. Some 200,000 persons attended this ceremony and plainly expressed their dissatisfaction and anger with the regime.

On October 13, Imre Nagy, who had been expelled from the Communist party in January of the previous year, was readmitted. That was a first flash of lightning in the realm of Moscow's satellites. Nevertheless, anyone who might have ventured to predict that revolution would break out in ten days would have been laughed at. It is not impossible that Moscow itself secretly promoted the uprising in order to have a pretext for intervening with overt force and quenching all opposition with blood. No one in Hungary was sufficiently alert to see this trap.

☦ *Hungarian Catholicism's Way of the Cross*

IN PRISON I could not form a correct picture of the Catholic Church's sufferings, which had continually mounted in the period since my arrest. Only my mother's cautious remarks, and the answers she gave to my covert questions, enabled me to deduce, with painful concern, to what extent the Communists had been suppressing religious life in Hungary. I obtained my first solid information on the situation that had arisen after my arrest from Dr. Béla Ispánki in the prison hospital, and later in my solitude at Püspökszentlászló from Father János Tóth. I did not know of the tribulations of the other bishops until Archbishop József Grősz was brought to Püspökszentlászló as a prisoner. Not until after the uprising began did I become aware of the real plight of Hungarian Catholicism. During the additional fifteen years of my compulsory confinement in the American Embassy I was better able to follow the destiny of the Church and could also collect data on the preceding period of persecution. It is not possible, within the framework of these memoirs, to go into the many dramatic details. I shall have to content myself with sketching in the bare outlines of the persecution that prevailed during the eight years of my imprisonment.

The most severe blow, which had struck the Church even before my arrest, was the secularization of the Catholic schools. The aim of it all was to more efficiently alienate the youth from religion. In awareness of this danger we tried to send our most forceful priests into the state schools, in order to maintain the moral and religious education of the young people on as high a level as possible despite the new situation. But the regime very soon began driving the priests we had chosen out of the schools, although to placate the parents the government repeatedly promised that obligatory religious instruction in the nationalized schools would be continued and that there would be no interference with it. Only a year after the closing of the parochial schools, however, there were new regulations ushering in optional religious instruction.

Anyone who thinks of freedom of religion as it is understood in Western countries will regard this change as unimportant and will not give it a second thought. Why should it be an abuse or an evil if the will of parents is respected? But in the communist system what happens, precisely, is that the will of religious parents is not observed, although such parental rights are solemnly guaranteed by the constitution. Section 54 of the constitution of the Hungarian people's democracy assures every citizen the right to the free exercise of his religion and upholds the independence of the Church in the following words: "The Hungarian people's democracy guarantees the citizens freedom of conscience and the right to free exercise of their religion. In the interests of freedom of conscience the Hungarian People's Republic has separated Church and state." At the beginning of the new school year, 1949–1950, religious instruction suddenly became optional, once again in "the interests of freedom of conscience," and parents were now required to demand religious instruction for their school-age children either in person or in writing. The object was to make things difficult for the parents.

The bishops acted quickly. In a joint pastoral letter they reminded the parents of their duty to their children. The regime was both surprised and embittered when 95 percent of the parents requested obligatory religious instruction for their school-age children. The ideologues of the Communist party attributed this development to the "threatening" tone of the pastoral letter, which they declared to be "offensive to freedom of conscience," and they promptly launched a counterattack against this church propaganda. The school authorities and the teachers as well were told to use every method they could to reduce the number of children registered for religious instruction. Pressure was exerted upon the pupils by withdrawing stipends, by preventing them from entering secondary schools, and thus blocking their path to technical schools or universities. In addition, the parents were constantly pressured and intimidated. But above all the teachers of religion were given to understand that their presence in the new democratic society was undesirable. In many schools demonstrations against these teachers were organized; the newspapers demanded that such teachers be fired since they were influencing young people to be "reactionary" and "antidemocratic."

In this artificially engendered atmosphere of tension many parents, at the beginning of the next school year, feared to register their children for religious instruction. Others, affected by the continual harassment during the school year, took their children out of the religion classes. Thus, during the first year of optional religious instruction the number of pupils participating was reduced by between 25 and 30 percent. During the following years religious instruction practically ceased. The introduction of optional religious instruction proved to be simply a step to the complete abolition of moral and religious education for young people.

I should like to remind the reader that as early as 1947 we had clearly recognized this danger and for that reason alone had so fiercely resisted the moves by the government to introduce optional religious instruction at that time. I had already pointed out this danger in my pastoral letter of April 12, 1947." *

The Communists employed similar techniques for repressing the religious education of the youth in the churches and even inside families. If need be, an intact family can still provide for the religious education of a child. But now the young were systematically drawn out of the family circle. Inexperienced boys and girls were taught in school that their parents were backward, were prisoners of old superstitions, and were altogether reactionary. A deep gulf was artificially produced between parents and children, and fatal wounds were inflicted upon parental authority. All the youth organizations worked in this same direction; so did the Communist party press and books for young people. On Sundays the time of the young people was completely taken up, so that parents could not take their children with them to Mass, either in the mornings or the evenings. Moreover, informers kept watch on those who attended church, those who went to confession and communion, and in general all those who practiced their faith, especially teachers and educators. Citizens who professed their religion could count on losing their jobs, and thus their livelihoods; frequently arrest, forced labor, and prison awaited them.

The next severe wound inflicted upon the Church during my imprisonment was the dissolution of the religious orders. During the protracted negotiations with the bishops the party ideologists justified this measure on the grounds that in a socialist state the tasks formerly carried out by the religious orders would naturally be assumed by the organs of the state. However—and this fact was never properly discussed—at the time of the dissolution all members of religious orders were in any case engaged solely in the area of the cure of souls. For when the Communists expelled them from the schools and from social institutions, the bishops had promptly fitted them into the service posts in the dioceses and the parishes. Thanks to this activity, religious life once more flowered. But wherever it could, the regime employed the police to obstruct their work. Harsh regulations were systematically introduced to harass members of religious orders. That was the reason the superiors of the orders on April 15, 1950, jointly petitioned the government for relief.**

This petition was never answered, but the harassment increased and the weight of oppression grew heavier. Finally, on the night of June 9–10, 1950, all members of religious orders were driven from their monasteries and convents along the southern and western borders. The report Archbishop Grősz of Kalocsa received from the superiors of the orders about the initial forcible removal makes painful reading.†

During the second nocturnal removal on June 18, 1950, the number of monks and nuns forcibly expelled or deported was even greater than during

* See Document No. 53.   † See Document No. 80.
** See Document No. 79.

the first, and their treatment even crueler. The situation grew even tenser because of the widespread rumor that the religious would be transported to Siberia if the bishops proved unwilling to enter into negotiations with the Communists. The bishops naturally did not want to negotiate under such duress, since they knew that an "agreement" on the Soviet pattern would be demanded of them. But finally the bishops, concerned for the fate of several thousand religious, nevertheless sat down at the negotiating table with the Communists in this atmosphere of deliberately provoked emergency.

On the basis of information from Archbishop Grősz I know that they intended to negotiate solely about the situation of the monks and nuns and the injustice that had been inflicted upon them. But Rákosi, who personally conducted the negotiations, affected to regard the question of the religious as an incidental item, and agreed to include it in the agenda only on condition that after settlement of that problem negotiations be continued looking toward an agreement between Church and state. These negotiations lasted a full two months, during which the problem of the members of religious orders was discussed for between five and six weeks. The discussions led to the following results:

1. The bishops recognize the dissolution of the religious orders, although they protest against any such plan, and after the decree to that end takes effect will assist in carrying it out. (In return Rákosi withdrew from the agenda his demand that the government exercise the previous royal rights of patronage within the Church.)

2. The Communists will allow 400 of the 2,500 monks to enter the service of the diocese.

3. The regime will return to the Church, or rather to four of the teaching orders, eight nationalized schools; each school may maintain a staff of twenty-five to be drawn from the ranks of the order.

4. After dissolution the regime will permit two or three former members of an order to live together and keep a common household.

5. The regime is prepared to build and maintain old age and invalid homes for aged and unemployed members of orders.

The dissolution affected 187 monasteries and 456 convents containing in total about 11,000 members. With the exception of the 200 authorized teachers, all members of orders had to leave their monasteries or convents by December 31, 1950. The buildings, with everything in them, including libraries and archives, passed into the possession of the state.

The monks and nuns themselves were scattered among the population. Most of them took up the humblest sort of labor. Of course there were some who did not stand up to the test of this difficult situation, but the majority of them carried on fruitful spiritual missions in barracks and poorhouses, in factories and elsewhere in the country where misery had forced people to the outer fringes of society. At a time when the "peace priests" controlled all the higher posts in the Church and by their scandalous lives were shaking the trust of the faithful, the Hungarian people still were able to turn to these quietly praying religious, who continued their work "illegally," and to consult them on spiritual questions.

The secularization of the schools, the cessation of religious instruction, and the dissolution of the orders virtually killed the ample, flourishing organism of the Hungarian Church, leaving only the skeleton of the dioceses. The diocesan offices and the parishes working under the supervision and guidance of the bishops could not simply be abolished on the grounds that they were inessential components of the Church. So they were permitted to survive; but measures were taken so that their activities could be supervised by the Communist party. That was accomplished by the agreement for which the Communists had previously strived in vain. Under my leadership the conference of bishops had firmly rejected this agreement on the Soviet pattern. My resistance to it had been the principal reason for my arrest. As late as 1950 the bishops continued to reject the idea of an agreement. Nevertheless the regime forced the issue by interning monks and nuns at the same time that it called for negotiations. This pressure continued until the majority of the bishops was prepared to accept the idea of an agreement. Still there were some who offered hard resistance, like Bishop József Pétéry of Vác. The government tried to frighten such recalcitrants by ordering their homes searched.

With such threats hanging over the 11,000 religious, the episcopate finally accepted the concordat. The document was signed on August 30, 1950, by Josef Grősz, archbishop of Kalocsa.*

For the church this agreement was a profound humiliation, to which the bishops had acceded only to save the monks and nuns. Of course, the humiliation was part of the Communists' plan; it was the one way they could undermine the enormous prestige of the Church, especially among those who at considerable cost to themselves had offered vigorous resistance to atheism and the encroachment of foreign colonial powers. But the most outrageous thing of all was that priests were now forced to take a line directly contrary to their own inclinations. For there were any number of patriotic citizens whose national pride was offended, who were being maliciously persecuted and condemned to silence in their own native land. The priests now had to ask these citizens to collaborate with the atheists. The regime, which had objected to my pastoral letters as improper interference in political affairs, now demanded that the clergy throw its weight behind all those political and economic measures that it hated—collectivization, forced deliveries to the state, and so on. (The pastoral letters and sermons the priests were forced, on the basis of the agreement, to read aloud from their pulpits could only be called caricatures of religion.)

The Communists also broke the resistance of the pastors by recruiting through coercion and fraud a dissident group of priests whom they could

* For the text see Document No. 81.

use for their own purposes. These were the "peace priests" I have mentioned; the people called them that because they chiefly appeared in public at peace meetings. Their role consisted largely in undermining the unity and strength of the Church from within by following the directives of the Communists. The baneful effects of this fifth column will be easier to understand, I think, if I sketch briefly and in order the events that took place after the signing of the concordat.

Hitherto the efforts of the Hungarian Communists to muster up a progressive Catholic group to support their aims had always foundered upon the energetic opposition of the bishops. Even after my arrest there were, for a considerable time, only a few priests whom the regime could present at peace meetings as representatives of the Church or the clergy. The press hailed these priests loyal to the government, and a plan was conceived to publish a newspaper called *Kereszt* as the organ of these peace priests. This plan was at first set back when the priest chosen to be editor shrank from his role as Judas, attempted to escape abroad, and died with a border guard's bullet in his head. Then the regime negotiated with Dr. Miklós Beresztóczy, a canon from Esztergom who had spent several months under arrest at 60 Andrássy Street. The frightful tortures he endured there had so broken him that when offered release he declared his readiness to take over the organization and leadership of the peace priests.

The recruiting that began with great impetus throughout the country had small success. Even after a whole year had passed the situation was such that there were only thirty-five names to sponsor the invitations to the constituent general assembly. The meeting was held on August 1, 1950, and was sparsely attended. Out of the 7,500 allegedly registered priests a total of 150 actually turned up, and some of these had been brought to the capital by trickery or force.

But after the concordat the situation changed. The police functionaries whom the Communists had put in charge of recruiting peace priests henceforth considered absence from the movement as an act of hostility toward the government. They referred to the clause in the agreement requiring the bishops to "support the peace movement." The bishops, however, refused to accept this cunning interpretation of the text and forbade their priests to enter the movement, as they had done earlier. On that account the newspaper, *Kereszt*, which began publication on November 1, 1950, savagely attacked them. Meanwhile various clever methods were used to enhance the prestige of the peace priest movement. The government managed to plant peace priests in several important parishes in the diocese of Esztergom and Eger. In the spring of 1951 the ministry of religion and education negotiated with these peace priests on the question of ecclesiastical salaries and the credit was presumably theirs when these negotiations resulted in higher salaries for all priests.

Nevertheless all these tactics proved to be fairly unsuccessful because the majority of the priests obeyed the bishops' ban and held aloof from the peace priest movement. Faced with this resistance, the Communists decided they had to break it by force.

Their next crushing blow against the obstinate bishops and priests was the arrest, on May 15, 1951, of Archbishop József Grősz of Kalocsa, who was then put through a show trial similar to mine and sentenced to fifteen years imprisonment. Simultaneously with the archbishop's arrest the regime forced a vote on Article I of the Legal Code for 1951, setting up a state bureau for church affairs which was to handle all concerns between government and the denominations, chiefly with regard to execution of the agreements and arrangements concluded with each of the denominations. On the second day of the Grősz trial, June 23, 1951, bishops Endre Hamvas of Csanád, Bertalan Badalik of Veszprém, József Petéry of Vác, and Lajos Shvoy of Székesfehérvár were placed under house arrest. The police and the functionaries of the bureau for church affairs compelled these bishops to fill the posts of their vicars-general and chancery chiefs with peace priests recommended by the police. This was how Bishop Hamvas, then administrator of my diocese, came to appoint Dr. Miklós Beresztóczy as vicar-general of the Esztergom diocese.

On July 3, 1951, the bishops met for a conference under the chairmanship of Archbishop Gyula Czapik of Eger. The four bishops placed under house arrest were, of course, missing. The new vicars-general, the peace priests, came in their place. This weighted conference of bishops issued a declaration of unqualified loyalty to the regime in the name of all Hungarian Catholics, and pledged itself to support the peace movement "in the spirit of the agreement." In practice, of course, this meant recognition and approbation of the peace priests. Thus the Communists had achieved their goal; they could now proceed to undermine church discipline and religion. The Church was being brought to heel.

On the same day that the last barriers to the peace priests movement were removed, the regime issued the new regulations for the filling of ecclesiastical offices. Under these new regulations appointments to leading posts in the Church would require confirmation by the government; the measure, moreover, applied retroactively back to January 1, 1946. The Communists deigned to recognize those appointments which had been made without their consent on condition that all bishops, superiors of orders, and vicars-general solemnly swear allegiance to the state. This mass pledge took place on July 21, 1951; it caused general indignation among the Christian populace.

All this happened under the chairmanship of Archbishop Gyula Czapik, who by yielding was trying to save whatever could be saved. The Church even abandoned passive resistance, and itself dissolved the various institutions already destined to go, such as the seminary for boys and most of the theological academies. Without opposition, the peace priests took control of the bishops' chanceries in all dioceses; they were supervised closely by the liaison men of the bureau for church affairs. The latter moved into the episcopal palaces, and as signs of their power they took into their hands the seals of office, the keys to the treasuries, and the archives. They checked on incoming and outgoing mail. Neither priests nor laymen could call on the bishops without their approval. They determined which students in the few remaining seminaries would be allowed to prepare for the priesthood and permitted consecration, and what assignments a new priest would receive. The people called these supervisors "the bearded bishops." Who received a salary, who was authorized to give religious instruction, which priests would be transferred to more important or more lucrative posts, depended on them. Hard-working pastors loved by the people were shifted from their flourishing parishes so that a peace priest could take over and trample the sprouting seed. Well-trained and gifted priests were sent to minor posts; and it was quite common for the bishop to send them right out of the diocese—at best with a pension. Only peace priests received church medals and distinctions "for their efforts in building socialism." The merits of those thus distinguished were in general in direct proportion to the damage they had done to the Church and the religious life of the faithful. (When Bishop Petéry showed himself disinclined to honor such dubious services, he was interned in Hejce; only after the 1956 revolution was he able to return briefly to his see.)

All episcopal offices became mere executive arms of the bureau for church affairs. That notorious government bureau was officially subordinate to the ministry of religion and education, but in fact received its instructions from the minister of the interior, while its officials were drawn from the ranks of the state security police (AVO). Thus the secret police were keeping close watch on every act of the Church, and skillfully perverting anything that was done into a means of persecuting the Church. No one who does not know the situation intimately can form an accurate picture of this perverse and humiliating situation; the servility, wickedness and irresponsibility of the peace priests naturally made it all the more debasing. Initially some of these might not have been activated by evil motives. But in the course of time, working intimately with the antireligious employees of the bureau for church affairs, participating in entertainments that were utterly unsuitable for priests, above all neglecting regular prayer, they lost faith itself. In this ambiguous role they tried to stifle the voice of conscience, and at best they governed themselves by an individual conception of their religion. But among them were even party members and higher-ranking party functionaries who had been graduated from a party school or academy. Some were also AVO officers. Of course all such matters were kept stringently secret, but they came to light during the revolution. The training of these men for special tasks was also conducted in secret. As apostate priests they were sent to a distant diocese and there took over the posts of vicar-general or chancery chief.

These infiltrators also served the interests of communism by their travels abroad and their attendance at congresses. On such occasions their task was to furnish Christians of the free world with false information about the relations between the Church and communism. Usually they took with them bishops or priests who already had connections abroad and who then—in presence of these emissaries, of course—assured their acquaintances of the "normal" state of affairs in the ecclesiastical life of Hungary. But it also happened sometimes that persons in high positions in the Church unaccompanied by such escorts would go abroad and deliver the required reports about the "normal" situation in the Hungarian Church.

☦ My Own Measures and My Radio Address

FROM THE MORNING of October 31, 1956, on, I received, in Buda, a whole series of visitors both from the country and abroad. All came joyously of their own accord, to see me and greet me. The only exceptions I made initially were the peace priests; I did not want to receive them right away. I made use of these conferences to inform myself as best I could on the political and religious situation arising from the struggle for freedom. The first imperative seemed to be to issue a ban putting an end to the activities of the peace priests. But I waited a while with this because I had invited Archbishop Grősz and the bishops of Szekesfehérvár and Vác to a private discussion. After we had conferred I called upon the ordinaries of the dioceses to command the peace priests within their districts to return to their own dioceses, and to dismiss all peace priests from higher positions. Since the situation was worse in Budapest, I decided to expel all peace priests who hailed from elsewhere. They would no longer be permitted to remain in my principal diocese.

The new national government that had been formed during the revolution kept me informed of the political situation. Thus I heard directly from the premier's deputy, Zoltán Tildy, about discussions being conducted with the Russians. He came to visit me at my house three times, if I recall correctly. The first time he called on me was on November 1, accompanied by Colonel Pál Maléter and two field officers. Maléter, the hero of the struggle for freedom, made a good impression on me. On the other hand I was unable to talk with the officers, since Tildy quickly sent them away. He wanted to be alone with me so that we could discuss quietly all that needed doing in the country. He was not very optimistic, and I said bluntly that it was impossible to trust the Bolshevists and so it was of the utmost importance to request and obtain the intervention of the United Nations as soon as possible.

Tildy began talking about the fact that his mother was Catholic. Probably he realized, while imprisoned by the Communists, to what extent he himself had injured the Church and the people by his misguided political conduct. Perhaps that was the reason he ordered the military parade for my entry into the capital. Possibly he regarded it as making up for his sins of the past. Suddenly, while sitting with me, he keeled over, whimpering "I feel ill." I ran out to the corridor and returned with a glass of water, gave him a drink and wiped the sweat from his face and brow. He thanked me and took his leave.

In connection with my radio address Tildy had two requests to make: that I not touch on the question of landownership, and that I talk circumspectly about the Russians. We had already, even without his recommendation, given special attention to these two matters. Thus, without any coaching on the part of Tildy and the government, the text already contained the statement that we would "do everything in our power to promote the sound development of the country" and would not oppose "the state of affairs which has already been proven right by the course of history."

When I read this address to the nation over the radio on November 3, 1956, Zoltán Tildy, the premier's deputy, sat beside me. He had tears in his eyes, and at the end he thanked me in the name of Imre Nagy and his ministers for the "great help" I had rendered to the new national government by my speech. He particularly thanked me for my calling on the people to go back to work, for my approval and support of neutrality, for censure of all acts of personal revenge, for my emphasis on the need for impartial judges, and for my condemnation of all partisanship.

After my radio address I returned Tildy's visit, calling on him at his apartment in the parliament building. He was delighted. If his wife and my escort, Dr. Egon Turchányi, had not been with us, he might again have been overpowered by emotion as he had been previously when visiting me in the primate's palace. After the visit I hurried back to my apartment on Úri Street, while the radio was already broadcasting parts of my address in all the major languages of the world.

In this address I only touched on the relationship between Church and state. But even from my brief remarks it was evident that the bishops were eager to settle all open questions by negotiation. What we did carry out on our own, since it fell within our own sphere of action, was liquidation of the peace priest movement. We regarded checking the damage it had already caused as an internal matter for the Church and therefore felt fully entitled to take action. The Communists had forced the machinations of the peace priests upon the Church without the slightest authorization, simply with destructive intent. That was why I called the peace priest movement "the coercion and deception of the toppled regime." Even after the collapse of the struggle for freedom Bishop Imre Szabó, vicar-general of my archiepiscopal diocese, continued to carry out orders I had issued for the Church, and removed the peace priests from their positions.* All obeyed with the exception of one member of the regular clergy, who however had been excommunicated on orders from Pope Pius XII. In a further decree the Holy See declared all peace priests unsuitable (*inhabiles*) to hold any leading positions in the Church. When this decree from Rome had been implemented in every diocese, the leadership of the Church was free again, and the peace priest movement had been dissolved de facto.

The Kádár government installed in power by Moscow was forced to accept this situation. In fact, in order to ingratiate itself with the bishops and public opinion it went so far as to formally dissolve the Bureau for Church Affairs. This was done on December 29, 1956.

VIII. ASYLUM

✝ *Escape to the American Embassy*

ON NOVEMBER 3, I delivered my radio address in Parliament. I returned home totally exhausted toward midnight and promptly went to bed; but I had barely lain down when the telephone rang. Tildy asked me to return to Parliament; the Soviet troops had opened fire, he said. Hundreds of big guns were bombarding the city. The sky was lit by the ghostly glare of explosions and fires. For a while I had to go down into the cellar; but then I drove to Parliament, accompanied only by my chauffeur.

In Parliament I learned that Minister of War Maléter, Minister Ferenc Erdei, Chief of Staff István Kovács, and Colonel Miklós Szücs, all of whom had been at the Russian military headquarters in Tököl negotiating the technical aspects of a withdrawal by the Russian army of occupation, had been treacherously placed under arrest shortly before midnight. No less a personage than General Serov, chief of the Soviet secret police, had come from Moscow to see to these arrests.

I met with ministers Zoltán Tildy, B. Szabó, and István Bibó. Zoltán Vas also appeared and declared he would remain on the side of the Hungar-

* My address, often attacked and often deliberately falsified, is printed in Document No. 82.

ian people. Tildy wanted to see Imre Nagy but could not find him. Every-where people were asking for instructions. The army wanted orders—for there were no longer a minister of defense and a chief of staff. Tildy there-fore decided to take measures on his own initiative. In the general confusion he dismissed the army men without giving them any orders, and raised the white flag on Parliament building. I could no longer bear to see everybody losing his head, and went out into the corridor. There I encountered Dr. Egon Turchányi, who in the course of the past several days had offered to assist me. I wanted to return home to celebrate Mass. But Turchányi in-formed me that in the interval my car had vanished. We considered walk-ing, but heard that this was no longer possible because the bridges had been blocked and were being used only by troops. The entrances to the parlia-ment building had likewise been sealed off by the Russians. I therefore quickly inquired which embassy was nearest. Somebody said it was the American embassy. We therefore decided to go there as quickly as possible. We concealed our cassocks under our coats and made our way between rows of Russian tanks safely to the embassy of the United States of America.

Minister Edward Thompson Wailes welcomed me cordially as a "symbol of liberty." After eight years of imprisonment and now shipwrecked after three and a half days of freedom, I clambered aboard the saving deck of the American Embassy to escape being carried off to the Soviet Union and to wait for the day that would once more permit me to work in behalf of my native land. A friendly and likable officer, a major or colonel in the uniform of our national army who unexpectedly joined us before we reached the em-bassy, said something in much the same vein about my holding myself in readiness.

Barely half an hour passed before cabled permission to take me in arrived from President Eisenhower. After another four hours Dr. Turchányi was also granted asylum. President Eisenhower had just been elected to his sec-ond term, and I promptly sent him a cable of congratulations and thanks. At the time it rather surprised me that my case was handled so promptly.

A few days later, however, I read in foreign newspapers that Imre Nagy had already asked the Americans to grant me asylum on the preceding day. If that were so, the officer had accompanied us in an official capacity, but he certainly had not mentioned Imre Nagy. If it is true that Imre Nagy ap-pealed to Washington in my behalf, it would have been a noble action and evidence that although he may once have been a Communist he was no longer one at this time.

While we were lingering on the ground floor waiting for word that Tur-chányi might remain, cannons were drawn up in the vicinity. Their barrels pointed menacingly at the embassy. Suddenly someone called out: "There may be an air raid; hurry down to the shelter!" In the shelter I met Béla

Kovács, the former secretary-general of the Smallholders party. He had returned ill and broken from imprisonment in Siberia. He too had fled to the embassy together with four other politicians. We fell into conversation, but he did not say a word about his having also asked for asylum. When I looked for him the next day I was told that he had not received asylum and had left to return to his native village of Baranya. Naturally I felt anxious about his fate; Kádár, however, did not have him arrested. Later on when Béla Kovács lay sick in the Pécs hospital the government used his name, without authorization, in connection with a recruiting campaign for *kolkhozes* (centrally managed large estates).

The National Catholic Welfare Conference offered to contribute a thousand dollars annually towards my keep. Probably Cardinal Spellman initiated this step in order to forstall complaints in America about a priest being provided for indefinitely. So far as I know, however, there never were any protests on this score in the United States.

The ambassador generously offered me his own office to work in. I was particularly moved because I knew that he himself needed it, all the more so because he could not really feel at home here yet. He had just arrived and his wife was not yet in Budapest.

During the night all the Hungarian employees remained in the embassy. They were afraid of being arrested. Confidential documents were burned because nobody knew what might happen in the next few hours. I celebrated Mass on the ambassador's desk at one o'clock in the afternoon, in his presence and that of all the employees. We had no cross, but we had ordinary bread and wine, and a champagne glass served as a chalice. Later an American of Hungarian descent showed us to our bedrooms on the upper floor.

During the period that Dr. Turchányi remained in the embassy, he assisted me at Mass. Through the kindness of an American army chaplain I received the vessels, robes, and books needed for celebrating the Holy Sacrifice. Thereafter, while I remained in the embassy, I celebrated in my room. At first the members of the embassy officials, their families, and the Hungarian employees took part. Later however, they were not permitted to come to the services because to do so would have violated the rules of asylum.

On the evening of my second day in the embassy my secretary appeared, to my astonishment, to ask me to come downstairs; reporters were waiting there. I did not show my surprise, nor did I ask the question that sprang to mind, whether so much freedom and contact with the world was still being permitted in the embassy. I met a veritable drumfire of reporters' questions. Dr. Turchányi served as interpreter for the American reporters. This former politician and militant deputy handled the task adroitly.

The first question was: "What do you say to the Russian aggression?"

"I condemn it, unqualifiedly."

"Which is the legal government of Hungary, the Kádár or the Nagy government?"

"Although Kádár was also a member of the Nagy government, I consider the government of Imre Nagy to be the sole legal government of Hungary. Kádár was installed by foreigners; I reject him and his illegal government."

There were many other questions but I regard those two as the most important. The Kádár government did not permit a word about this press conference to be printed or broadcast by the media in Hungary. They no doubt know why. We know also.

A List of my American Hosts from 1956–1971

Edward T. Wailes, Minister	1956–1957
A. Spencer Barnes, Chargé d'Affaires	1957
Garret G. Ackerson, Jr., Chargé d'Affaires	1957–1961
Horace G. Torbert, Chargé d'Affaires	1961–1962
Owen T. Jones, Chargé d'Affaires	1962–1964
Turner B. Shelton, Chargé d'Affaires	1964
Elim O'Shaughessy, Chargé d'Affaires	1964–66
Richard W. Tims, Chargé d'Affaires	1966–1967
Martin J. Hillenbrand, Ambassador	1967–1969
Alfred Puhan, Ambassador	1969–1971

☿ A Glimpse of the World

THE UNEQUAL STRUGGLE of the country and the capital against the power of the East had been going on for a full week. The Hungarian armed forces offered resistance, but had no leadership. Gradually, the silence of a graveyard descended upon Budapest. Hundreds of dead and wounded lay in the streets. According to unverified reports the number of dead in eight days of fighting amounted to 5,000; the number of wounded approached 20,000. Deportation trains moved in the direction of Siberia; many of the unfortunates on these trains were youths between the ages of ten and eighteen, girls and boys who threw scribbled messages out of the moving trains in the hope that word of their fate would be transmitted to their parents. Violent struggles were also waged in the provinces. But the regime's newspapers published false reports on the fighting, although members of the government had so recently sworn at Rajk's funeral: "No more lies!"

During the years between 1944 and October 23, 1956, Hungary had been a dungeon. For eleven days (I myself for only four) we had been able to breathe freely. After November 4 the country became a prison once more.

The moral force, the solidarity, the tenacity of the Hungarian people were sublime, and the sympathy of the outside world was a great solace to us. But what became of the seed that had been sown? The nations of this unhappy globe were promised freedom, equality, prosperity. What came instead was terror imposed by a minority, misery and massacre. Three times in succession the working people of Europe experienced the fire of machine guns and tanks; in Berlin, in Poznan, in Budapest, and in the Hungarian industrial districts. In Poznan fifty-three dead and hundreds of wounded were carried out of the crowd that was calling for bread. And in Hungary the number of victims could no longer be counted. The solidarity of the Western World with my fighting nation was beyond all doubt and was expressed in magnificent words; but we were bitterly conscious that our cries for help met with no response in deeds.

The great powers of the world quailed before the Soviet army while schoolchildren fought that army for an entire week in the streets of Budapest and in the mutilated torso of Hungary.

The Belgian statesman Paul Henry Spaak declared: "Although the West would like to help Hungary, it is basically powerless." In the French Chamber of Deputies, Bidault denounced the West's weakness on the Hungarian question. Foreign Minister Pineau commented on the "great helplessness" of the United Nations. At the session of the Council of Europe of January 11, 1957, the French foreign minister said: "Only the Western Powers take the decisions of the United Nations seriously; the Soviets laugh in their sleeves." The two losers in the Hungarian struggle for freedom were on the one hand world communism, whose moral standing sank to a new low, and on the other hand the West and the United Nations, whose impotence was exposed. But the West was blind as well as impotent. By promising a change of policy the Bolsheviks had made themselves acceptable even at royal courts. They were permitted to lay wreaths at the tombs of famous men in venerable cathedrals. Western premiers and foreign ministers scrambled to get to Moscow sooner than their rivals. The nations of the world marched on Moscow's leading-strings. The great lesson of 1955–1956 was that as the nations behind the Iron Curtain came increasingly to detest the Soviet world and its whole mentality, Russian influence in Western countries steadily grew. It took a sea of Hungarian blood to make the West aware to some degree of the nature of the Soviet system. But all efforts to elicit action from the West failed.

How different was the attitude of Pope Pius XII. He utilized all the means at his disposal; on a single day he made three successive appeals to the entire world in behalf of Hungary. His rejoicing on November 2 was as great as his grief when tyranny once more suppressed the Hungarian freedom fighters. Like a father protecting his threatened children, in his radio address of November 10 he upheld the civilization, the humanity, and the justice of our nation against "brutal and illegal oppression." With a glance at the Great Powers he even declared, speaking in the name of religion, that in this case a defensive war would be justified. He posed the question: "May the world remain indifferent when the blood of so many innocents has been shed? When once more so much sorrow and so much killing has been inflicted?"

The pope's attitude was also that of the Church. His then secretary of state, later Archbishop and Cardinal Montini who ultimately succeeded to the papacy after the death of John XXIII, carried a cross on his shoulders during a torchlight procession in Milan, as a symbol of the newly subjugated Hungarians. By this symbolic action he wanted to demonstrate his sympathy with our nation, which had collapsed under the weight of the cross. Cardinal Spellman in New York and Cardinal Cushing in Boston showed the same solidarity and sympathy.

As the pope speaks, so speak his legates. During the Eucharistic Congress in Manila (1956) the papal legate referred to the recent sad events in Hungary and sharply condemned Soviet intervention and the repression of the struggle for freedom. The press in Manila at the time was filled with vehement criticism of the Russians.

I learned after several days that Dr. Egon Turchányi had also been arrested. The Hungarians in the embassy voiced suspicions of his Hungarian traveling companion, but I did not share their views. The Kádár press now began publishing vicious attacks on Dr. Turchányi as well as on me. He too was put through a show trial and sentenced to life imprisonment. It was 1960 before I learned, from a book written by his traveling companion, that Turchányi had been arrested at an intersection at Tatabánya. Plainclothes policemen on the main street had stopped the car and dragged him out of it. He fell to the ground; his heart nearly stopped, and he collapsed unconscious. The AVO policemen dragged him away by his feet and threw his limp body into a truck. During the night his traveling companion was brought to the building where Turchányi was being held, though not to the same room. At one o'clock in the morning he heard screams of pain.

I kept thinking of the fallen heroes, of the wounded, the deported, the starving, and the homeless, and above all of the flood of refugees. I kept asking myself: What will those fine Honvédsek of Rétság have to pay for freeing me? Their "sin" was certainly a grave one, and the more so that among the many groups that were hurrying to liberate me, they had been the first, and they had also provided me with an honor guard.

I requested the U.S. Embassy in Belgrade to help the refugees by giving them leave to go to the United States by way of Yugoslavia. Fortunately this appeal of mine was granted.

The execution of Major György Palinkás (Pallavicini) profoundly shocked me. It seemed that he had given up his life for mine. But it is also possible that vengeance would have been exacted even if he had not been connected with me.

The members of the Újpest Committee of Revolutionaries were arrested by the Kádár government. They were accused of "attitudes hostile to the people": it was alleged that they had sentenced to death János Horváth, chairman of the Bureau for Church Affairs.

The fate of my nation preyed on my mind. To be sure, the retaliations were terrible, yet I could not comprehend the mass flight that now began. Flight of the armed freedom fighters surely should have sufficed.

When the American ambassador did not pay a courtesy call on the Kádár government, his credentials were not accepted. By and by the embasssy was told that its staff had to be reduced by one third, allegedly so that there would be fewer "spies" in the country. That meant, of course, that chiefly the Hungarian employees had to be dismissed.

I also had the opportunity of receiving Congressman Michael Feighan, that great friend of Hungarians. When Richard Nixon, then vice-president, visited Hungary, he came to the embassy. He conducted negotiations in a room adjacent to my office, but did not come in to see me. During Kennedy's presidency two of his sisters stayed at the embassy. They attended Mass and the sermon; it was diplomatically more appropriate for them to attend Mass than to pay me a direct visit.

In general the American authorities were rather strict concerning the matter of visits to me. Missionaries, American rabbis, Catholic priests, and tourists were astonished when their requests to see me were refused. There were some who tried repeatedly to gain admittance, but always to no avail. Relatives of embassy personnel, however, or members of their families, could visit me without any difficulty. Their visits did not violate the law of asylum; but my cousins, on the occasion of my golden anniversary as a priest, found closed doors. I did not understand why many of my letters were never answered, and brought this matter up in the embassy, but my hosts were unable to give me an explanation.

After 1963 Cardinal-archbishop König of Vienna visited me several times at the behest of popes John XXIII and Paul VI. Without attempting to apply any pressure, Pope John XXIII inquired whether I did not wish to come to Rome to take over a post in the Curia. In that case, he indicated, he might be able to fill the vacancies that had occurred in the episcopal sees. I replied that I would accede to his plans if they meant furthering the liberty of the Church. Henceforth the state department of the United States permitted correspondence between the Vatican and myself to go by diplomatic pouch. That was the only way I could resume written contact with the outside world.

On July 12, 1965, Cardinal König came to attend my golden anniversary as a priest. He brought me a cordial letter and a gold chalice from the Holy

Father. I am also grateful to my neighbor cardinal for having brought to me on this occasion his own guest, Cardinal Valarian Gracias, archbishop of Bombay, for a quarter of an hour.

My golden jubilee nevertheless was not celebrated with any gaiety. Only my two sisters, three nephews, and my confessor were permitted to participate. The embassy had not known that this anniversary was approaching, and I myself had made no preparations. In consideration of the majority of the participants, I preached in English.*

Inside the building I was permitted to have contacts with the Hungarian employees of the embassy after office hours. One of them always accompanied me on my evening walks in the yard. Now and then the heads and officials of other embassies came to visit with their wives. There were no objections to that. As long as I was in fashion, so to speak—that is, during the period of the Cold War—they came more frequently. I am especially grateful to the ambassadors of France, Italy, and Argentina, and their families. Later the moves toward political and ideological coexistence changed my situation in this respect also.

The number of those present at the Sunday and holy day Masses always depended on how many Catholics happened to be working in the embassy at the time. The number tended to increase. The devoutness of the American Catholics was exemplary. Almost all those who came to Mass took Communion. But other Christians, and even Jews and nonbelievers, attended my services.

The officials of the embassy were changed approximately every two years. In the course of ten years I thus made the acquaintance of quite a few of them. I was able to keep in touch with a good many; they stopped by occasionally, and we exchanged letters.

The ambassador and his deputy called on me once a week. My table and my altar were always kept well supplied with flowers. In spring—because I could scarcely experience the seasons and enjoyed the sun almost exclusively in the form of fruit juice—one couple brought me a big flowering branch from their cherry tree and set it up in the middle of my room. I was frequently the recipient of similar kindnesses.

I remember the heads, the officials, and the staff of the embassy with deep gratitude. I also want to thank publicly the attachés, who along with their rather considerable official duties also obligingly took care of my affairs (going shopping for me, making repairs, and so on). My semi-imprisonment was made more bearable by Messrs. Géza Katona, Lajos Toplovszky, Tivadar Papendorf, Gheshinka, David Beltz, Robert Jackson, Mr. Flood, and Titus Ross. I was never confined to my bed during my time at the embassy, but I suffered bouts of minor illness every so often as a consequence of my years in prison. Whenever that happened, I was given the

* See Document 83.

most solicitous care. The American Embassy physician came first from Bucharest, later from Belgrade, to attend me. During the early period this was a Dr. Linsky, who was extremely conscientious and concerned about me. Then, equipped with a whole medical laboratory, came the chief physician of the U.S. military hospital in Landshut, Bavaria, Lieutenant Colonel Forrest W. Pitts, who spent a day with me. Later Colonel Seiberth became my regular doctor.

I was particularly happy about the embassy library, with its wealth of books, newspapers, and magazines. Although private study had been very important to me ever since my schooldays, I had intensive knowledge only of the Germanic sphere in Europe. Now I was able to familiarize myself with the Anglo-American world through its press, its publications, its ecclesiastical and secular literature. Although this opportunity came to me only toward the end of my life, I am nevertheless extremely grateful for it. I had formerly thought that Latin and German were sufficient to enable a person to acquire a general higher education. Now I discovered that ecclesiastical literature alone would forfeit great wealth if deprived of works in the English language.

I was also in a better position to appreciate the nature of Catholicism in the United States, and thought much better of it than I had formerly done. Wherever human beings live there are lacks and inadequacies. But it was astonishing to me that the Catholics in the United States had no daily newspaper of their own, although they published excellent weekly and monthly periodicals in editions of millions. They devote great care, however, to their Catholic school system. Their labors are well rewarded, for the school is and remains, particularly in an age of diminishing faith, the foundation of Catholic life.

On the fields of organized charity and of religious associations the American church had made notable progress. In twenty-two years Cardinal Cushing collected $1.4 billion and founded thirty-five parishes and many orphanages and hospitals. Cardinal Spellman established 373 new parishes. The figures are tremendous: 45 million Catholics in the United States have some 11,000 elementary schools, 2400 secondary schools, and more than 300 universities.

I also studied the historical documentation issued by the U.S. state department, and sent for the records of hearings. I wanted to obtain a clear idea of what lay behind American attitudes in World Wars I and II, and to understand the positions of Woodrow Wilson and Franklin Roosevelt. My study of documents was supplemented by the readings of memoirs from all over the world. I also assembled a private library; although relatively small, it contained the books that were important to me.

Even when I was tired I daily went through the Hungarian communist newspapers, and looked into the latest books, although usually with some pain and a great deal of boredom.

The window, too, made for a bond with the outside world. I saw parades
that passed by the embassy with a great deal of fanfare. April 4, the "day of
liberation" by the Soviets was celebrated annually; this "celebration" awakened bitter memories.

Across the street, in the garden of the Partisan Club, "Hungarian"
women and men on Saturdays and Sundays danced vulgar dances to jazz
music. Usually they kept up their hubbub until eleven o'clock at night.
How often I wished for colder weather to put an end to this entertainment.
Mornings and afternoons children from the kindergartens and schools in the
vicinity played outside the embassy, in Freedom Square. In earlier times
children used to sing serious songs in praise of their mothers; but such
songs had not been heard for years. The phrase the children repeated most
frequently was: "You idiot." The bigger children played soccer toward evening, often shouting obscenities to each other. They were the same obscenities that the head physician of the reception prison had used during my stay
there.

When I looked down into the street, I saw few baby carriages and even
fewer second or third children beside the carriages. Unfortunate Budapest!

But I also witnessed two significant mass demonstrations: the parade of
women in front of the embassy, and the international colored and red demonstration against the embassy. There was a yawning abyss between these
two acts.

After November 4, 1956, the workers demonstrated for some eight to ten
days to protest the deportation of the youth to the Soviet Union. The AVO
smashed the men's demonstration. It was then decided that only the women
and girls were to demonstrate. They did so with aching hearts, although
deportation, arrest, and even death menaced them. On November 23 they
came pouring out of the surrounding streets from many directions and as-
sembling in great numbers in front of the embassy on Freedom Square.
There they unfurled the flag and sang the national anthem. They then per-
sistently cried out their appeal to the impotent arbiter: "The United Nations must help us!" A delegation of them also appealed to the American
ambassador for help. Behind drawn blinds, I suffered in my room. As they
again and again chanted their slogans, the police intervened, took away
their flags, and dispersed the crowd of demonstrators. Scattered cries could
be heard for a long time coming from different directions. But the United
Nations did not help us. The United Nations rested content with rhetoric.
Poor Hungarian women! Poor Hungary!

On February 13, 1965, the embassy received from the foreign ministry a
report on preparations for a demonstration of African and Asiatic students.
That might have been a courtesy warning, but it might also have been the
sign of an officially organized demonstration.

Prompted by Moscow and using the slogan "Vietnam" as a pretext, two
hundred African students appeared carrying slanderous posters and pressed

toward the embassy. They did not get far at the guarded main entrance. Consequently they went around to the rear, where they broke into the ground floor and were able to wreck the cafeteria and the film archives. In the kitchen they destroyed food supplies and smashed crockery. Finally they fell upon the cars that were standing outside the embassy and wrecked them.

Naturally the chargé d'affaires protested to the foreign ministry. Next day the deputy minister paid a call and expressed his regrets.

On February 6, 1957, the Communist party organ stated that I had interrupted my imprisonment of my own accord (in plainer words, I was regarded as an escaped convict). From that day on the embassy that had granted me asylum, and I myself, were the daily objects of attacks in the press. There was also mention of plans for an escape. These were pure inventions of the press.

The year 1970 brought the twenty-fifth anniversary of my appointment as primate and of my installation. My compatriots made no comment. A cordial recollection of the event appeared only in the newspaper *Életünk* (*Our Life*)—the organ of the Hungarian exiles—which was sent to me regularly. There my former chaplain and the present editor of the newspaper, Dr. József Vecsey, pointed out that in spite of a difficult destiny I had been rewarded with a long life. Of the seventy-two Hungarian primates, he wrote, only János Kanizsay had administered this office longer, for he had been primate of Hungary for thirty-one years. The title of the editorial sounded a note of bitterness: "A forgotten anniversary."

☦ *Return of the Peace Priests*

IN THE SPRING of 1957, half a year after the Russians had stifled in blood the fight for freedom, the Kádár regime felt secure enough to respond to the regulations against the peace priests issued by the bishops. It revived the earlier decrees that had governed religious instruction and the staffing of positions in the Church, and sent the "bearded bishops" back to the dioceses. For a while, however, these old decrees could not be applied either in the schools or in ecclesiastical appointments. There was too much resistance. Eighty to eighty-five percent of the school children had registered for religious instruction, and the religious teachers were able to provide it without hindrance. The bishops, too, were able to continue filling posts in the church with suitable priests in complete freedom.

But then it turned out that the regime had reinvoked the decrees only in order to blackmail the Church. The idea was to soften up the bishops for the pending negotiations and force the church to support the dishonest peace movement. There was just as much hypocrisy on the regime's part as there had been in the harassment initiated in 1950 by the perfidious interpretation of the text in the agreement aimed at the parish priests. The bishops now declared their willingness to support the "struggle for world peace" if three conditions were fulfilled:

1. That they themselves led the peace work.
2. That the regime officially as well as unofficially liquidate the old peace priest movement.
3. That the weekly *Kereszt*, which Rome had placed on the Index and which had shamelessly slandered bishops and priests, be no longer permitted to publish.

In the meantime, however, the bishops had published a statement to the effect that they were "watching the efforts of the government with confidence as it sought to eliminate the errors of the past and correct earlier injustices. They support the government in its efforts to increase the well-being of the Hungarian people and to promote world peace."

In this way the Catholic National Peace Commission, the *Opus Pacis*, was founded. Representatives of the former peace priest movement were given places in the leadership. One of them, a provincial deputy, explained this turn of affairs as indicating that the bishops recognized the Kádár government and approved and supported its work. The Holy See thereupon once more issued a decree forbidding priests in Hungary, under threat of excommunication, to accept mandates as deputies. In the summer of 1957 the reports of the U.N. committee for the investigation of Hungarian affairs, consisting of five members, likewise reached the public. The Communists denounced these reports as an assault against world peace, and the Kádár government ordered the National Peace Commission to protest against the "Committee of Five," alleging that its activities constituted a threat to peace. On August 29, 1957, the bishops issued the required statement. After declaring that "Mutual trust, the prerequisite for peaceful cooperation between Church and State, has been restored in recent months," the bishops deplored the report of the U.N.'s Committee of Five "since by its onesidedness it is calculated to increase international tension and imperil the true interests of our country. The bishops therefore cannot approve the United Nations' intention to treat the Hungarian question on the basis of such a report."

At that time the conference of bishops was headed by József Grősz, the archbishop of Kalocsa, who had been through the mill of Communist show trial and Communist prisons. He was only too familiar with the regime's ruthless methods. Nevertheless, fear was not the motive for his compliance, but rather the hope that in this way he might be able to preserve imperiled religious instruction in the schools and avert the even greater peril that would result if the peace priests returned to their posts.

But Archbishop Grősz's hopes were disappointed. For soon after the bishops issued their statement, the Communists revived the old regulations concerning religious instruction, issuing a new executive order which afforded the Kádár regime ample opportunities for crude abuses. A single specific day was appointed when parents had to register their children for religious instruction; there would be no second opportunity. It was made illegal to give the children private religious instruction. The principals of the schools were to supervise closely the work of the religious teachers. The bishop could appoint a religious teacher only with the consent of the government, but the government was authorized to rescind the teacher's certification at any time. Even the religious books had to be approved by the government. The teacher of religion was permitted to remain in the school building only during the religion lesson; outside school he was forbidden to have any contact with his pupils.

The bishops' declaration had done a great deal of harm to their prestige, and still had not saved religious instruction in the schools. But Archbishop Grősz continued to hope that he would at least be able to prevent the return of the peace priests, for he assumed that given the "good relations" that now prevailed between Church and state the Kádár regime would refrain from applying the ruling on appointment to posts in the Church.*

Thus the bishops had reason to fear that they would again have to dismiss the priests who had returned to their posts in the course of the struggle for freedom, so that peace priests could once again be installed in these positions. They regarded that as so grave a threat that they issued the desired statement. In mentioning these threats I should not fail to point out that József Pétery, bishop of Vác, who at the time of the uprising took command in his diocese once again, had been interned in Hejce even before the issuance of the statement. Bertalan Badalik, the bishop of Veszprém, suffered the same fate. The peace priests also played a part in determining the conduct of the bishops, not only by persuasion but by continually reminding the bishops of the Communists' threats. Moreover, a very prominent leader of the peace priest movement, Pál Brezanóczy, was already a member of the conference of bishops. He had been elected vicar-general by the cathedral chapter of Eger after the death of Archbishop Czapik in 1956, the bureau for church affairs having taken an active part in this election. After the arrest of Bishop Badalik a second vicar-general who was also a peace priest—Sándor Klempa—became a regular member of the conference of bishops.

Under the chairmanship of Archbishop Grősz, on whom the Kádár regime had meanwhile conferred the Banner Order of the People's Repub-

* See Document 84.

lic, the bishops were much concerned not to spoil the "good relations" that had formed between state and Church. They kept a sharp eye on the priests, so that the regime would have no cause for complaints about their behavior. Aside from the bishops' work in the *Opus Pacis*, they also showed themselves cooperative by agreeing to make no appointments to newly vacant posts in the Church without the approval of the liaison man in the county cultural department. In return for this concession the regime permitted the bishops to obey the orders of the Holy See and pass over former peace priests when making appointments to leading positions in the Church. But this situation lasted only until the summer of 1958. On April 18, 1958, Premier Gyula Kàllai issued the following official statement:

We support the *Opus Pacis* movement initiated by the bishops. We believe, however, that *Opus Pacis* can be a strong and successful peace movement only if it is not limited to the narrow circle of the higher clergy. It must be founded on the broadest possible mass base of the democratically minded clergy. *Opus Pacis* cannot be set in opposition to the mass movement of the democratic priests, which is rooted in the life of the Hungarian people. If the bishops sincerely desire cooperation with the state they must base their activities upon those friends who through the years have demonstrated by their work that they are fighting alongside the masses of the people for peace and the building of socialism. This is the basis on which they ought now to develop good cooperation between Church and state. . . . The relationship between Church and state must be placed upon the firm ground of principles, so that it does not become a mere matter of peaceful but passive coexistence. Rather, it must be an active, positive collaboration aiming solely and firmly at the building of socialism.

In their terms, of course, the building of socialism meant consolidation of the atheistic atmosphere.

Kàllai's declaration signified no more nor less than that the bishops would once more have to place the peace priests in leading positions in the Church, not for the sake of "peace and the building of socialism" but in order for the Kádár regime—like its Stalinist predecessor—to bring the life of the Church firmly under its control and guidance. That summer the Russian national church council invited a Hungarian church delegation to the Soviet Union. Inevitably the delegation consisted almost mainly of peace priests under the leadership of Bishop Hamvas, later archbishop of Kalocsa and administrator of Esztergom, who had appointed the highest-ranking peace priest to be vicar-general of the archdiocese.

After the delegation returned home, its members were taken from diocese to diocese so that they could report on their experiences in the Soviet Union. The National Peace Commission nonchalantly organized the lectures, and also used the opportunity to establish branches of the *Opus Pacis* in various towns. Both propaganda and police pressures were applied to make sure that all priests attended the lectures and offered no opposition to the installing of peace priests in the leadership of the local Catholic commit-

Troops parading in front of the Stalin monument in Budapest.

One of the first acts of the revolutionaries was to topple the statue from its pediment. (*Deutsche Presse Agentur, Frankfurt/M.—Berlin.*)

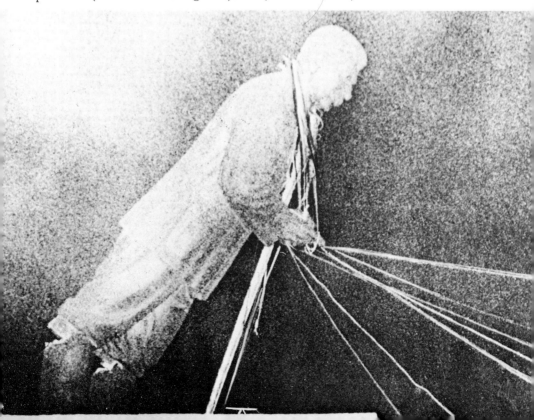

Revolutionaries ready to fight to the death.
(*Associated Press, Frankfurt/ M.*)

The revolutionaries celebrate their victory.
(*Associated Press, Frankfurt/M.*)

Cardinal Mindszenty reading a statement to foreign journalists in the courtyard of his Budapest residence on November 1, 1956. He is standing in front of his episcopal residence, which had been heavily damaged during the fighting. (*Katholische Nachrichtenagentur Pressebild, Nürnberg.*)

Pál Maltéter, the military leader of the revolution. (*Süddeutscher Verlag, Bilderdienst, München.*)

(Süddeutscher Verlag, Bilderdienst, München.)

The Russian troops counterattack.

(Deutsche Presse Agentur, Frankfurt/M.—Berlin.)

The American Embassy in Budapest. (*Süddeutscher Verlag, Bilderdienst, München.*)

Cardinal Mindszenty celebrating Mass in his quarters in the embassy; in attendance are members of the embassy staff.

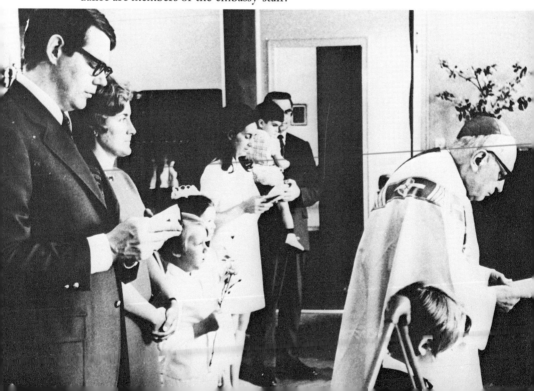

On his arrival from Budapest, where he spent 15 years' asylum in the American Embassy, Cardinal Mindszenty is greeted warmly by Pope Paul VI in the Vatican gardens. (*Katholische Nachrichtenagentur Pressebild, Frankfurt/M.*)

Pope Paul VI showing the cardinal the Roman skyline from a window in the Vatican. (*Religious News Service Photo.*)

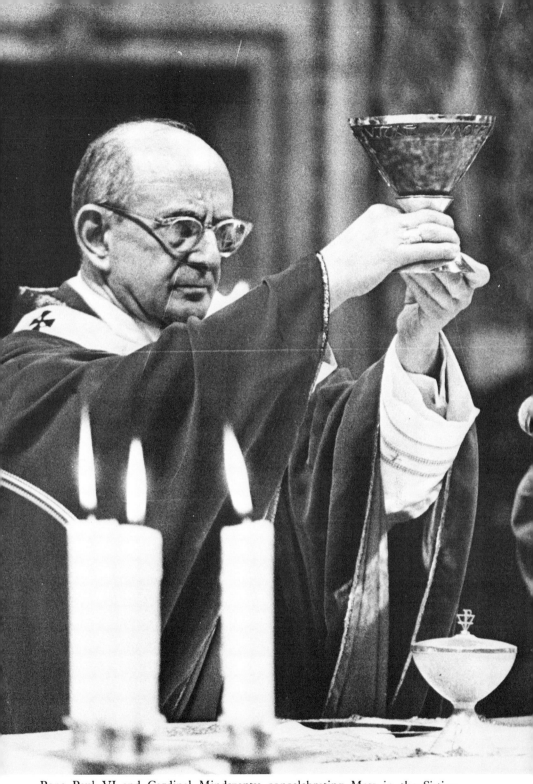

Pope Paul VI and Cardinal Mindszenty concelebrating Mass in the Sistine Chapel at the 1971 synod of bishops. (*Süddeutscher Verlag, Bilderdienst, München.*)

With Joseph Cardinal Frings in Cologne. (*Katholische Nachrichtenagentur Pressebild, Frankfurt/M.*)

With John Cardinal Heenan in London. (*Thomson Newspapers, London.*)

With Julius Cardinal
Döpfner of Münich.

With Francis Cardinal
König of Vienna.
(*Ernst Hausknost,
Wien.*)

In his study at the Pázmáneum, the cardinal works on the manuscript of his *Memoirs*. (*Deutsche Presse Agentur, Frankfurt/M.— Berlin.*)

Cardinal Mindszenty celebrating Mass in the Pázmáneum, the seminary in Vienna where he now resides. At his left is Msgr. József Vescey, his assistant.

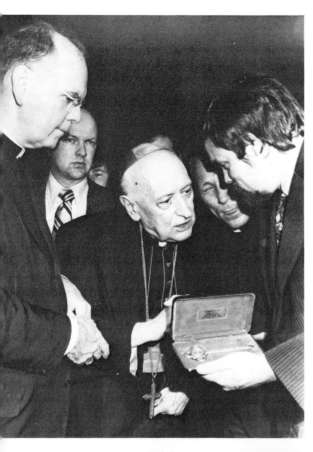

At Kennedy Airport, Cardinal Mindszenty accepts a key to New York City. At the cardinal's right is Terence Cardinal Cooke, archbishop of New York. (1973) (*Wide World Photos*.)

Cardinal Mindszenty being welcomed to Washington, D.C. by Patrick Cardinal O'Boyle and Archbishop William Baum. (1974) (*Leslie A. Toth*.)

Cardinal Mindszenty being met at the St. Louis airport by John Cardinal Carberry and Miss Eleanor Schlafly, executive director of the Cardinal Mindszenty Foundation. (1974) (*Paul Ockrassa*, St. Louis Globe-Democrat.)

Cardinal Mindszenty with Carl Albert, Speaker of the House of Representatives. In the background, from left to right: Msgr. Tibor Mészaros, the cardinal's traveling secretary; Senator Vance Hartke of Indiana; and István Gereben, vice president of the World Federation of Hungarian Freedom Fighters. (1974). (*Leslie A. Toth.*)

Cardinal Mindszenty being greeted in Washington, D.C. by András Pogony, president of the World Federation of Hungarian Freedom Fighters. (*Leslie A. Toth.*)

Since 1971, when he left the asylum of the American Embassy in Budapest, Cardinal Mindszenty has been traveling the world, ministering to Hungarians wherever they are found—Europe, United States, Canada, South Africa, Australia, South America.

Above, a moment's reflection in the monastery chapel at Mariápócs, Matawan, New Jersey. (*J. B. Eory.*)

tees. Thus the leadership of so-called "peace work" was taken from the bishops and given into the hands of the peace priests. The peace priest movement of evil memory absorbed the *Opus Pacis;* and in contrast to the situation before the uprising, all priests were now enrolled in the movement, led by the bishops themselves. From August 24, 1958, on, the movement's weekly, *A Katolikus Világ* ("The Catholic Word), began appearing; it exhibited the same harmful tendencies that had led the Holy See three years earlier to place its predecessor, *Kereszt,* on the Index.

The Communists forced my archiepiscopal vicar, auxiliary Bishop Imre Szabo, to abdicate. Archbishop Grősz then obtained permission from Rome to entrust auxiliary Bishop Mihaly Endrey of Eger with my archdiocese. In the summer of 1958 the Kádár regime demanded that Endrey place peace priests at the head of three parishes in the capital. He did so, but refused to make additional transfers in favor of the peace priests. For this he was interned in the remote village of Vàmosmikola. By the usual Bolshevistic methods resistance was then smashed in the other dioceses, and after the passage of barely three years the regime had reinstalled peace priests in leading positions, in spite of the ban from Rome. In many respects the situation of the Church was worse than it had been in the years before the uprising.

Meanwhile "coexistence" and "détente" had become magic words in international politics. Even the blatantly communist dictatorships wanted to appear in a good light, chiefly so that public opinion in the West would not oppose the forthcoming disarmament, economic and trade conferences with the Soviet bloc. The prestige of the Kádár regime had reached a particular low. Around this time it had been repeatedly condemned by the United Nations (twenty times altogether).

But who could better assist a communist, antireligious dictatorship to win international recognition than the Vatican itself? If you want visible triumphs, seek to associate yourself with the Roman Church, which is still regarded as the foremost moral authority in the world. Such was the advice that world communism's brain trust apparently offered the Kádár government. And so János Kádár appeared wearing a mask of peace and took the first steps toward Rome. The regulation concerning appointments to ecclesiastical posts had all along been suspended like a sword of Damocles over the Church's head. On April 6, 1959, Kádár ordered it to come into force. Its final clause read:

When a church office falls vacant and the ecclesiastical authorities do not fill the vacancy, the appropriate government agency will take the necessary steps to ensure the ministry of the priesthood, the proper administration of the Church, and the training of priests. The government will take such action 90 days after a vacancy occurs in posts listed under Article 1, and 60 days after a vacancy in posts listed under Article 2, of the regulation concerning appointments to ecclesiastical offices.

Two months later, on June 2, 1959, resumption of work by the "appro-
priate government agency," the Bureau for Church Affairs, was ordered.
When, two and a half years later, Msgr. Agostino Casaroli undertook negotiations with the Kádár regime on the part of the Vatican, the regime had
already succeeded, by bringing in its peace priests and the Bureau for
Church Affairs, in completely silencing the true voice of the Hungarian
Church. Consequently the Vatican diplomat scarcely heard the demands of
Hungarian Catholicism, and it was for that reason, in my opinion, that diplomatic agencies of the Vatican entered into negotiations without a precise
knowledge of the situation—negotiations that could bring only advantages
to the Communists and grave disadvantages to Hungarian Catholicism.

☿ My Mother During My Asylum in the Embassy

DURING THE PERIOD of asylum in the American Embassy my mother came
to visit me, with the permission of the Communists, every three months—
at Christmas, at Easter, on the feast day of Saints Peter and Paul (June 29)
in the summer, and in the autumn at the time of the vintage. At Christmas
she was present at midnight Mass and communicated. That was a joy for
her but also a loss, for in the embassy no Hungarian Christmas carols could
be sung. At least I read for her and my sister, who accompanied her, the
Gospel and Scriptures in Hungarian. They stayed three days and were
allowed to stay overnight in the embassy.

Here, too, in my semi-imprisonment, my mother was the light of the sun
for me. In the deep wisdom of her heart she would tell me a great deal
about the religious life in our village, about religious instruction and attendance at church. Usually she was accompanied by one of her daughters,
and one Christmas one of her grandsons came with her. This incident cost
him his job; he was told that he was being dismissed because he had accompanied someone to the door of the American Embassy. On that occasion the
embassy car drove her back to her village. At Easter 1959 the car made the
trip both ways, so that she was able to come alone. We spent forty-eight
hours together that time, as we used to do in my homes in Zalaegerszeg or
Veszprém or Esztergom. Mother admitted to me that she was becoming
steadily weaker. In the time that still remained to her she had only one

wish, she said: to have me with her once more in Esztergom and at home in the village. I think she wished this more for my sake than hers. This world needs such faithful, deeply religious mothers on both sides of the Iron Curtain.

Some parts of my memoirs were already written and finished by Christmas 1956. I gave her several chapters to read. She went through them very carefully, reading with bated breath, for she found mention of facts that she had not known or had only guessed at. I could see by her expression how deeply moved she was by each chapter.

But my mother also had her happy days, as was apparent from her own stories. In church the cardinal-primate's mother occupied her old place, the third pew—the place where all her predecessors had sat. During my imprisonment the village had a special pew in the choir set up for her.

From her I found out what form the uprising had taken in our home village, and what effect it had had on the family. On November 4, 1956, the village's church day, the inhabitants of Mindszent and of neighboring Mikos-széplak paraded to our house. They saluted my mother and sang Magyar songs. My mother received the congratulation of individuals and groups. The warmth of feeling made her forget all her sorrows. One day later mother led the village in the direction I had propounded over the radio on the eve of all Saints' Day: "forgiveness." She admonished all our relations: "Do not forget that you are the primate's kin, and what you owe to the primate and to yourselves. Everything is to be forgiven and forgotten."

The entire village joined the rebels. Even the Communists were converted. Aside from a minor brawl, nothing ugly took place. And even the brawl, which involved a hated official, was instigated by a stranger to the village. The official had been brutal, ruthless, and a strict party-liner. The former chatelaine, a widow and the daughter of a colonel of the hussars, whose castle and estates had been confiscated and who was subsequently evicted even from the servant's cottage where she had been living, had applied for the post of church organist. It would have been given to her, but the communist official, who had no authority whatsoever in the matter, forbade her employment and spat upon the applicant in front of the whole village.

But even this official came through the days of the struggle for freedom unharmed. The collective farms were broken up again. In several villages they were heavily in debt, so that the burden of the debts now passed to the new individual owners. The statue of Stalin, which had stood in the new house of culture, was thrown into the roadside ditch. This was the act of former hired hands who had been given land in 1945 only to have it taken from them again when they were forced into *Kolkhozes*. Thus in the villages it was the farm workers, while in the capital it was the factory workers, who were most eager to smash the symbol of the Stalinist era.

Those who had put their signature to statements denouncing me were now trembling. It was rumored that they were to be marched through the village in a parade of shame. But this plan was dropped in response to my mother's persuasions.

How horrified my mother and sister had been when I told them that during the Slansky trial in 1952 the child of one of the defendants, still a minor, had written a letter to the court asking that his father be given the death sentence because he had so gravely sinned against the great Stalin. When Khrushchev made his famous speech concerning Stalin's crimes, this young person committed suicide.

My mother visited me twenty-two times during my imprisonment. Of the seven places where I was held prisoner, she saw three: the prison hospital, Püspökszentlászló, and Felsöpetény. She had not been allowed to come to the other four places: Andrássy Street, Markó Street, the penitentiary, and the second hospital. To make her journeys she had covered a distance of some 7,500 miles. But her captive son, when God called her from this life, could not even attend her funeral, could not even make this small gesture to repay so much toil and sacrifice.

She came to see me the last time at Christmas 1959, accompanied by my younger sister. This time the American Embassy was unable to send a car to Mindszent for her. Count Franco, the Italian ambassador, therefore sent his car to fetch her. She spent three days with me then. After my Mass the participants and the officials of the embassy showered solicitous attentions on her throughout her stay.

At that time she was very downcast about the impending recollectivization of our family's vineyards, fields, meadows, and woods. It was not the idea of the material losses that primarily grieved her, but the loss of the spiritual values associated with lifelong attachment to one's own piece of land. The independence of families was being destroyed; the education of children would inevitably suffer, and it would become more difficult to observe the Sundays and holy days. I offered the comfort that collectivization was, after all, a blow that would strike the entire country. But this thought did not cheer her.

I hoped that I would have another visit from her at Easter. But she said: "This Christmas visit will be the last." That winter her health was worse than it had been in the past several years.

Two weeks after her return home she sent me pillows and pillowcases because she had heard that I'd asked my sister to buy these for me.

On February 5, 1960, my eyeglasses broke, and could not be immediately replaced. As a result I was able to say only the rosary. I had to read the text of the Mass with a magnifying glass. As always, I named my mother in the *memento* for the living; but I should already have included her in the prayers for the dead. At eleven o'clock that same day the embassy secretary came in with a telegram for me. He had not even placed it on the table when I knew: My mother is dead.

That was in fact the news that the telegram brought, as well as the time of the funeral.

I was even poorer now. Now the one dearest to me could no longer come for the holidays. Bishop Prohászka wrote on the death of his mother: "The precious chalice shattered into which God had given your soul in this world." When Bishop Virág of Pécs was still head parish priest of Szekszárd, his church burned down, and at the same time his mother died. He said: "Two temples have turned to ashes." My mother was a gleaming star in hard and confused times. God had now summoned her from life to eternity.

On that black day I had no need for food or any book; death had violently shaken me. I prayed her favorite prayer, the rosary. I wept over the loss of her; then I grew calmer. My gratitude for having had her in life had to be greater than my sorrow at her passing.

Mr. Garret Ackerson, chargé d'affairs of the embassy, came in and comforted me with the greatest kindness. I was not troubled about my mother's soul. I trusted in the immeasurable divine mercy. Her earthly life had always been a preparation for the eternal life. She had always made a point of visiting the dying and praying with them. Fundamentally her mood had always been hopeful, without spiritual unrest.

During those hours I reflected upon the days in Ostia and the tears of St. Augustine, then already converted to Christianity, for his mother.

On January 24 she was present at Mass for the last time. January 28 was her sixty-ninth wedding anniversary.

From that day on she was more on the other side than here on earth.

On January 31, in a storm that raged like a hurricane, she set out for church. The family wanted to keep her from going. They called the doctor. He came and reassured the family, saying that her heart was still sound. In God's judgment it was surely better.

At Candlemas she received the last sacraments. With the greatest calm she joined in, praying aloud. She was not afraid of death. For her, eternity held no terrors.

At the beginning of the following week she made her will, appointing her grandchildren her heirs. She was still not yet about to die. As late as February 4 she held one of her great-grandchildren on her lap and opened the gate for the wagon returning home, husked corn, and prayed the rosary, as was her daily habit. Since she had not seen the vineyard for some time, she set out for it next day. The family begged her not to, because the paths were bad at this time of year; she could wait until spring, they urged. That night my sister noticed a change in her. The priest was quickly called. My mother knew that she was going to die. The candle for the dying burned in her hand.

It afforded her a final joy that I had asked Pope John XXIII to send a blessing to her in her illness. The message was sent to the address of the parish priest of Mindszent and arrived there on January 2, 1960. It was signed by Cardinal Tardini.

During the last quarter hours my mother prayed reverently with the members of the family and then, without a death agony, sank into slumber and passed into eternity in her sleep.

She who had so deeply venerated the heart of Jesus and as a young woman had repeatedly undertaken the pilgrimage to Egyházashetye on the festival of the Sacred Heart of Jesus, died on a First Friday three hours after midnight.

At my mother's coffin a woman of eighty, at whose wedding my mother had been bridesmaid, cried out loudly to please take her along with her because the world had grown so cold and mean. A week later she herself was buried.

A river of humanity passed by my mother's coffin to bid good-bye to her. They did not come out of curiosity or convention, but out of authentic sympathy. All stood by her bier with tears in their eyes and murmured prayers. A businessman, himself already sixty-eight years old, thanked her especially for having taught him the *Confiteor* so that he would be able to serve Mass. The district health officer, who had treated her for years, came and fell to his knees beside her coffin, praying with tears in his eyes. Finally all her grandchildren and great-grandchildren came. The portrait of her son was placed beside the bier. It had been a faithfully guarded treasure of her room.

She was buried on February 7. If ever anyone should have been at her funeral, I should have. But I could not surrender to the hands of my persecutors; it would have been a foolish risk, tempting God.

Mr. Ackerson, the embassy chargé d'affaires, wanted to drive to Mindszent with his two secretaries, but was not granted permission to do so. The trip was flatly forbidden. The Italian ambassador and his wife and the French ambassador and his wife did go to my mother's funeral. They took my wreath with them. It bore the inscription: With thankfulness and deep grief, in the hope of a reunion!

The family, meanwhile, was suffering constant anxiety that I might decide to come after all. Thus it was a great relief to my relatives when only the wreath and my greetings arrived at the graveside. For secret police had already filled the village the previous Saturday. Word went around that I would be arrested the moment I stepped out of the embassy car. The massive deployment of police scarcely redounded to the credit of the regime.

The episcopal requiem had to be omitted because the diocesan bishop who had escorted my father to the grave was ill. Aside from the two village priests, five other clergymen took part in the funeral. The school-children attended, but the teacher was missing. One of the priests had arranged the funeral in so dignified a manner that the diplomats were profoundly impressed, as I could tell from the accounts they gave me.

The members of the rosary society walked praying beside the coffin, burning candles in their hands. There were a great many flowers and wreaths. After the ceremony the dean prayed for all mothers who had borne a priest for the Church. Pope John XXIII's message expressed his sympathy to the family.

At Christmas 1960 my sister came bringing photographs of mother's grave and told me about the observations of villagers who lived near the cemetery. Wagons and automobiles from other parts of the country would stop, people would get out, go to the grave, and pray silently. In 1971 the picture of a seminarian from Esztergom was found on my mother's grave. The young man had written a vow of loyalty to the captive primate on it. Fortunately for him, my sisters found the picture before it fell into the hands of the police.

My mother had made a habit of annually spending the Easter vigil together with her friends, other women of the village, praying at the cemetery, amid the graves. She would not return until dawn, when she would go home to prepare the Easter provisions for the blessing. Faith in the resurrection of the dead was deeply rooted in her heart. For her the resurrection of Christ and the resurrection of all flesh were articles of faith that belonged together, in keeping with the doctrine of the Apostle Paul. She knew in whom she believed, and therefore she will not be confounded; that is my firm conviction.

In Hungary the newspapers were silent. But in the foreign press my mother was mourned—among them the *Katolikus Szemle* ("Catholic Review"), published in Rome, and the Swiss church newspapers, in which an article about her by József Vecsey appeared.

While I was still parish priest in Zalaegerszeg a beautiful church had been built in Fairfield, Connecticut, for Hungarians who had left their native land behind them. For the silver anniversary of this church the Franciscans from Transylvania, who supplied the priests for this church, set up in it a statue of Our Lady of Hungary. The figure of my mother had supplied the model for Our Lady: she was portrayed as a simple village woman holding the child Jesus. May God bless the sculptor, Bertha Hellebrandt, and also the kind priests and those from whom the idea had come. A nun from Hungary had taken a photograph of my mother with her to the United States, and the statue was modeled on that.

How often I had thought: "When the time comes that she is dead and buried I will truly perceive her worth, the immeasurable grace that has been conferred upon me in her."

Today I feel not only the poorer; I also feel a profound sense of gratitude toward that grave which I was never allowed to visit and which I shall probably never see in this life.

My mother was like a saint. I never saw, in her or around her, anything that was bad; only goodness and beauty. I firmly believe that she is happy in eternity, and here in this vale of tears I long for a glad reunion with her.

IX. EXILE

✝ *Complete and Total Exile*

ON JUNE 23, 1971, Cardinal König informed me that Msgr. József Zágon would be visiting me from Rome. He came as the personal envoy of the Holy Father, accompanied by Msgr. Giovanni Cheli, and called on me at ten o'clock in the morning on June 25. As a gift from the pope, Cheli gave me the first volume of the new breviary, and after transmitting to me the greetings of the cardinal-secretary of state, he left my apartment.

When we were alone, Monsignor Zágon informed me of the Holy Father's concern about the fate of my person. He explained the reasons that had prompted the Holy Father to advise my leaving the embassy.

I received the impression that the United States government, in view of the changed situation and in consideration of my age, regarded my leaving the embassy as desirable. Monsignor Zágon also mentioned my illness and the complications that would ensue if I were to die in the embassy. He continued: "Therefore the Holy Father has arrived at a solution that will place Your Eminence's sacrifice in a new light, so that your moral importance will be seen by the entire world public to have increased. You will have lost none of your well-earned credit and will be able to serve as an exemplar for the whole Church. The Holy Father wishes to do everything in his power to bring this about."

Monsignor Zágon stressed that there was little chance of my memoirs being published in my lifetime unless I were able to take my manuscripts abroad and personally see to publication. I could also be of eminent assistance to the Hungarian Church and nation. As primate of Hungary I would be able to participate in the exiles' celebrations of a thousand years of Hungarian Catholicism and thus contribute a great deal to the renewal of the moral and religious life of Hungarians abroad.

I made my objections, the chief one being that I did not want to abandon my flock and the Church in their difficult situation. I also wanted to end my life in my native land, in the midst of my flock. My departure would serve only the interests of the regime, would be harmful to the Church. The Bolsheviks could be trusted, I said, to exploit any change in my situation for the ends of the propaganda. I therefore wanted the Holy See to use my departure as a bargaining point and in return, before I made my final decision, to insist that the regime make some amends for the damage it had inflicted on the Church. Monsignor Zágon then assured me that the Holy See itself would insure that the Communists would not be able to exploit my leaving the country for propagandistic proposes. As for making up for the wrongs the Church had endured, the Vatican would fight tenaciously during the negotiations, and in many respects there already appeared to be some hope of a détente.

I myself placed primary emphasis on guarantees of freedom for religious instruction and on the elimination of the peace priest movement. But the pope's envoy saw no prospect for détente in these two important areas.

After lunch we continued our discussions. I thanked the Holy Father for his benevolence toward the Hungarian Catholic Church and toward me personally, but I asked for time to consider it, so that I could make my decision after conscientiously weighing all the circumstances. In a matter of such importance I owed it to the Hungarian Church and to my country not to decide until after mature reflection. Moreover, I would have to arrange for the transportation of my belongings and also to attend to family affairs in connection with my sister, who at the moment was hospitalized. There were things which could not be settled from one day to the next. A certain amount of time would be needed. But I promised that I would not put off my decision for anything like a year. I said I was ready to subordinate my personal interests to the welfare of the Church, now as always; but I wanted to know under what conditions I would have to leave the embassy and possibly my country as well. Zágon then summed up the conditions as follows:

1. My titles of archbishop and primate would not be affected, but the rights and duties associated with the exercise of that office in my native land would be abrogated. In my stead an apostolic administrator appointed by Rome would administer my diocese. I expressed the desire to stay permanently at the Pázmáneum and asked that this Hungarian seminary in Vienna be returned to my jurisdiction. I also asked that in the Papal Year-book the notation *impeditus* (hindered) should continue to be placed beside my name, as had been customary ever since 1949.

2. The second stipulation was that I would not be permitted to publish statements or pastoral letters, but would be required to leave the country "altogether quietly." I accepted this condition in the expectation that the Holy See itself would inform the public concerning the true causes and circumstances of my departure from Hungary. Zágon proposed that I sum up my reasons for leaving in a letter. The Vatican press agency could then, using my letter as a basis, inform all the major world press agencies and thus forestall misinterpretations.

3. The third condition gave me cause for serious concern. What was asked of me was nothing less than that once abroad I should make no statements that "might disturb the relations between the Holy See and the Hungarian government or might be offensive to the Hungarian government or

the People's Republic." I declared unequivocally—and my statement was placed in the record of the discussion—that I could not let the communist regime of Hungary, which was causing the destruction of the Hungarian Church and of the nation, be the judge of what I could or could not say. I forthrightly rejected any conditions of that sort. What I myself demanded from the regime was that I be completely rehabilitated after the "judicial murder" that had been inflicted upon me. I added that it was only for the Holy See to decide whether remarks I might make were harmful to the relationship between itself and the Hungarian government. Some Vatican circles later interpreted this remark as acceptance of the third condition.

4. The fourth condition concerned this present book. I was requested to commit myself to keeping my memoirs secret and to withholding them from publication. I was supposed to will my manuscripts to the Holy See, which would then see to their publication at an appropriate time. I indicated that I was greatly surprised by this request. After all, among the inducements for leaving, Zágon had mentioned the possibility of my publishing my memoirs in my lifetime. After looking over my manuscripts he declared—and this too was included the record—that he saw no obstacles to having my memoirs published during my lifetime, "at least the essential parts." Adding that I could keep the manuscripts with me and in case of my death have them turned over to a priest who enjoyed both my confidence and that of the Holy See, he even promised that the Vatican would pay for necessary typing expanses.

Our discussions lasted for three days. In the meantime I discussed with Zágon the draft of the letter to be sent to the Holy Father in which I briefly mentioned the suffering to which I had been subjected and offered my own opinion of the charge that I was the "greatest obstacle to a normal relationship between Church and State." * I sent this letter to the Holy Father by courier.

Monsignor Zágon wrote out a minute of the discussions and asked for my signature. I refused to sign. Above all, I objected to the concluding sentence which indicated that we had arrived at the agreement that I would be able to go abroad as a free man under no restrictions "except for the conditions noted in Points 1–4."

Zágon urged me to decide, but I went on maintaining that I needed time for reflection.

After Zágon departed I wrote a letter to President Nixon informing him of my situation and asking whether it would not be possible for me to remain in the American Embassy. His reply arrived with unexpected speediness. He recommended that I bow to my fate. Despite the courtesy of the tone I realized from the president's reply that from now on I would actually be an unwanted guest in the embassy. I therefore had only the alternatives

* See Document 86.

of leaving the embassy, and by that act surrendering to the political police, or leaving the country for the West, as the pope desired.

If I could have been certain that I would be put into prison, or kept in house arrest as I had been in Felsőpstény, I would gladly have stayed in Hungary. But I was fearful that the regime might impose on me a fate like that of Cardinal Stepinac, whom Tito had "mercifully" ordered interned in his home village. An American journalist had once brought me an account of the cardinal's plight. The journalist had attended one of my Sunday Masses in the embassy. Afterward he stayed on in the room, introduced himself, and gave me a direct message from Cardinal Stepinac. My brother cardinal, who already had one foot in the grave, urged me absolutely not to accept house arrest in my home village, lest I fall into his predicament. For, according to the journalist, sixteen policemen had come with the cardinal to his native village near Zagreb. His widowed sister had turned her single room over to her brother, the cardinal, while she and her children moved into the kitchen. The prisoner's guards had settled down in the storeroom. Whenever the cardinal went to church to celebrate Mass, he was escorted by the police. But that would not have been the worst of it. . . . A group of policemen took the sister's eldest son, who had not yet reached the age for military service, to a remote barracks. He was returned to his mother two months later, but his mind had become deranged in the interval. At home now he shirked work, and day and night he roamed the woods, fields, and roads. The people of the village and the vicinity looked on with pity, reflecting on the miseries brought down upon this poor family by their relationship with a cardinal. (Such was the journalist's account. In exile, however, I learned that the foreign correspondent's description was not wholly accurate. For example, the cardinal was not staying in his sister's house but in the rectory of his native village.)

Horrified, I thought that Kádár might very well have organized such a scenario, for I too had a widowed sister, the mother of several children, in my native village. They were already suffering sufficiently over my fate. Had I the right to impose more of the weight of my own cross upon them? In the families of my two younger sisters in Mindszent lived fourteen children and several grandchildren. Had I the right to expose them to the fate of the Croatian cardinal's nephew? I believed the account and cherished my brother cardinal's "warning" as a sacred legacy, and in the end it was *the* factor that caused me to decide not merely to leave the embassy and take the consequences, but to accept exile.

I knew quite well that I had become an undesirable guest in the embassy not only because of my illness but also because I stood in the way of the policy of détente. It is, however, also true that my earlier illnesses were once again reaching an acute stage. Since 1960 my exopthalmic goiter had reappeared, accompanied by high blood pressure and cardiac insufficiency. In 1964 gastric complaints appeared, and a year later there was a resurgence of the pulmonary tuberculosis which the doctors in the Pécs hospital had pronounced cured. Naturally reports were sent to the White House on my health. These were probably transmitted to the Vatican. An Irish Catholic named O'Shaughnessy, himself something of an invalid, became chargé d'affaires at the embassy at this time. One evening in 1965 he called on me, bringing with him a report on my medical condition, and tried to persuade me to enter a hospital in the capital to undergo treatment there. In a calm voice I told him that I would not set foot inside a Bolshevistic hospital in the capital to undergo treatment there and that I had ample reason for taking this stand. If, however, there was concern about my possibly infecting the staff, my meals should simply be put outside the door. I would take the tray in and return it to the same place after I had eaten. We could continue to manage like that, I told the chargé, until I recovered or if God willed, until my death. He gave orders accordingly; that same evening my meal was brought to me as I proposed, and that continued for another four or five weeks.

The embassy physician, Dr. Linsky, very tactfully asked me not to dispense Holy Communion during my illness. Since those who attended Mass the following Sunday expected me to, he allowed it this last time, but only after I had washed my hands. During Mass that Sunday I mentioned that because of my illness I would not be able to dispense Holy Communion. After a few weeks the illness disappeared, thank God. In 1966 O'Shaughnessy fell severely ill, was taken to a hospital in Budapest, and to my intense regret died there a few days later.

My health during the period between 1960 and 1965 provided the advocates of the so-called détente policy with a pretext to keep my case continually on the agenda. It did not matter to them that in the meantime I had completely recovered.* The vascular constriction in my legs, from which I suffered in 1971, was not dangerous, although my feet were always swollen. This trouble also disappeared completely once I was abroad, where I had more exercise and more intensive medical treatment. In 1971 reports of my severe illness were assiduously sent out in order to divert notice from the true causes of my departure from the embassy. Such reports also implied that it was my illness which was making me a burden on the staff of the embassy.

The Holy Father's letter of July 10, 1971, reached me very soon after President Nixon's. He had taken note of the fact that I was prepared to leave the embassy; his personal emissary would be spending four days in Budapest once again, from July 14 on; and he asked me to arrive in Rome at

---

* For that recovery I should like to express my warmest gratitude to the solicitous and successful embassy doctors. The physicians who treated me from 1965 to 1971 were Lieutenant Colonel Forrest W. Pitts, Colonel William Dunnington, Dr. James E. Linsky, Dr. Richard Rushmore, Lieutenant Colonel James J. Lane, Lieutenant Colonel Jay Seibert, Dr. Charles E. Klontz, and Dr. Donald McIntyre.

least in time for the opening of the synod of bishops in September. Monsignor Zágon prepared my departure. It was settled that I could receive a Vatican diplomatic passport and that he himself and Monsignor Cheli, together with the papal nuncio, would come from Vienna in two automobiles to fetch me and would accompany me from Budapest to Vienna. We would take with us the most essential of my belongings; everything else, including the manuscripts of my memoirs, would then be sent by diplomatic courier to the American Embassy in Vienna. Departure was finally fixed for September 29, 1971.

At 8:30 A.M. I descended the stairs, which were lined by employees of the embassy, to the ground floor. Together with Ambassador Puhan I stepped out through the gate into Freedom Square. I shook hands with the ambassador; then I spread my arms and blessed the capital and the entire country. I got into the car in which Monsignor Zágon and the nuncio, Monsignor Rossi, were riding; in the other car sat a doctor and Monsignor Cheli. Both cars were accompanied by secret police, and we left Budapest without a word. We drove toward Győr and reached the border. At Hegyeshalom I beheld with a shock—though only through the window of the car—the "Iron Curtain." In the century of freedom and democracy the sight of such a frontier is truly saddening.

The nuncio directed the car straight to the Vienna airport. At 12:55 we boarded the regularly scheduled plane for Rome. Here Archbishop Casaroli joined us. In Rome I was received by Secretary of State Cardinal Villot and conducted from the airport to the Vatican. There Pope Paul VI awaited me at the entrance to the Torre di S. Giovanni, where I was given princely quarters. He embraced me, took his pectoral cross and hung it around my neck, offered me his arm, and led me into the building. He rode up in the elevator with me and showed me through the whole of the splendid apartment that had been placed at my disposal. Patriarch Athanagoras had stayed there before me. Later, too, the pope gave me almost daily signs of his paternal benevolence. The most impressive of these was the invitation to me to celebrate on the Pontiff's right the Holy Mass with which the episcopal synod opened. In his address the pope dealt with Hungarian Catholicism and spoke of me. He said:

Among Us today is Our venerable brother, Cardinal József Mindszenty, archbishop of Esztergom, who has just recently come to Rome after many years of enforced absence. He is a guest whom We have awaited with longing, who is concelebrating with Us as a glorious symbol of the living unity between the Hungarian Church and the Apostolic See, a unity that has existed for a thousand years. But he is also a symbol for the spiritual bond with those brothers who are prevented from maintaining normal relations with Us. He is a symbol of unshakable strength rooted in faith and in selfless devotion to the Church. He has proved this first of all by his tireless activity and alert love, then by prayer and long suffering. Let us praise the Lord and together say a reverent, cordial *Ave* to this exiled and highly honored archbishop!

After the Mass the pope took my hand and conducted me, to the applause of the archbishops and bishops, out of the Sistine Chapel.

During my brief stay in Rome I received many visitors. Among them were cardinals, archbishops, high officials of the curia, priests, and laymen. The Holy Father invited me to his table and frequently sent his secretaries to me with messages or gifts. I too paid visits to several cardinals, some of the Roman congregations, and the secretariat of state. At the Congregation of Rites I looked into the pending Hungarian canonization proceedings. I also visited my titular church, S. Stefano Rotondo, as well as the Hungarian pilgrims' home and the four great cathedrals. In St. Paul's a priest joined me, seized my hand, kissed it, and thanked me for my sufferings for the Church. Finally he introduced himself: "I am Cardinal Siri." Meetings with many persons made deep impressions upon me, among them Cardinals Tisserant, Ottaviani, Wyszynski, Cicognani, Seper, Wright, Döpfner, Höffner, Cooke, and many others. In grateful remembrance I celebrated Mass in St. Peter's at the tomb of Pope Pius XII.

The mail daily brought me a flood of letters and telegrams from all over the world. I was surprised to find in the letters of many non-Catholics great veneration for the Catholic Church. The letters from my fellow countrymen revealed especially gratifying attitudes. It was reassuring to me to see that the historic Magyar spirit—faith and loyalty to Church and country—had remained a vital force. For me this has always been a great consolation, at once light and hope in my exile.

The world press also paid close attention to the situation of the Catholic Church in Hungary, and to my own case. Most newspapers took a well-disposed and objective tone, but of course there were some dissonant voices. On September 28 the *Osservatore Romano* actually portrayed my departure from Hungary as though this had removed an obstacle hampering good relationships between Church and state. For me that was my first bitter experience, for I realized that the Vatican was not paying any attention to the specific terms I had formulated in Budapest. I experienced my second disappointment when I learned that the Holy See had lifted the ban on the excommunicated peace priests two weeks after my departure. I also encountered general indifference to my affairs. In June I had specified that while abroad I wished to live in the Pázmáneum, and I assumed that Vatican representatives would inform the Austrian government of this. But that probably was not done. Even the Austrian chancellor is supposed to have learned of my intention from the newspapers. In a memorandum to the Vatican secretary of state I made the grievances of the Hungarian Church known.

After three weeks in Rome I made known my plans to go to the Pázmáneum in Vienna, the seminary that was to be my permanent residence henceforth. Many friends objected to this, pointing out that Rome offered me more security. But I held to my original choice. At my request Monsignor Zágon initiated the preparations for my moving. The Austrian ambassador to the Holy See then called on me and tried to persuade me to postpone my departure. Nevertheless, I fixed October 23 as the date for my leaving for Vienna. On that day I celebrated Mass with the Holy Father. The Hungarian priests and the members of religious orders in Rome took part in the Mass, singing Hungarian hymns. When after Mass we went into the sacristy, the pope sent away everyone else who was there. He then turned to me and said in Latin: "You are and remain archbishop of Esztergom and primate of Hungary. Continue working, and if you have difficulties, always turn trustfully to us!" Then he summoned Monsignor Zágon and speaking in Italian in my presence declared, *inter alia:* "I am giving His Eminence my cardinal's mantle so that it will protect him from the cold in that cool country and will serve as a symbol of the love and respect I have for him."

Monsignor Zágon was requested to assure me in the Holy Father's name that my destiny would in no way be subordinated to other aims. "The cardinal will always remain archbishop of Esztergom and primate of Hungary."

Late that evening I left Rome for Vienna, accompanied by Monsignor Zágon. Archbishop Casaroli, as representative of the Vatican, was present at the airport to bid me good-bye. I arrived at the Pázmáneum in Vienna before midnight, and moved into the rector's quarters.

When I went into exile, I found some feeble consolation in the thought that if God gave me life and strength I would, even abroad, be able to serve three important Hungarian goals. They were: as primate of Hungary to take the many hundreds of thousands of homeless Catholics under my episcopal care; to warn the world public of the peril of Bolshevism by publishing my memoirs; and perhaps now and then to concern myself with the tragic fate of my nation.

Even while I lingered in Rome I had obtained some facts about the religious and intellectual life of exiled Hungarians. In Vienna I systematically collected accounts of the religious and cultural circumstances of my fellow countrymen all over the world. I obtained many details from letters and from conversations with my visitors. Beyond doubt there were gladdening facts and comforting aspects to the situation; but the lacks and disabilities resulting from exile far outweighed them. Above all there was a lack of priests to minister directly to the spiritual needs of the exiles, since the majority of our priests entered the service of foreign institutions and dioceses. Churches that had been built from the saved pennies of our own flock would be lost, as in America, for instance; and yet large groups of Hungarians had no parishes, no parish priests, no schools, no convents or monasteries or old-age homes. Even now after the Second Vatican Council, parish work in the language of the people is greatly impeded in many places.

The defects in Hungarian parish work undoubtedly derived from the fact that Rome—quite rightly—had withheld from the Hungarian episcopate, which as a body was completely subject to the communist regime, the faculty of sending priests to Hungarian Catholics living abroad. In view of this extraordinary situation I asked the Holy See at the end of 1971 to make it possible for me, as the rightful head of the hierarchy and as primate of Hungary, to leap into the breach in place of the excluded hierarchy of Hungary. I wanted to establish an organization which would take over the cure of souls for Hungarians abroad, assuming the task of representing Hungarian Catholics in all foreign countries. At the same time I asked to be allowed to appoint suffragan bishops for the 1.5 million Hungarian Catholics living abroad.

My requests were not granted. Obviously the Vatican was well aware that my pastoral work might vex the regime in Budapest, which could well assume that under my guidance such ministrations might have an undesirable effect upon the exiles and would affect their social, political, and cultural lives. That is probably the principal reason that the regime has not changed its tactics even now that I am in exile. It wants to persuade people—and now the Vatican—that I am "playing politics" in the guise of religion. For that reason, in 1971 the regime attacked my pastoral letter for Advent, in which I alluded to my prison experience and to the Iron Curtain surrounding our country. The Hungarian government succeeded in influencing a few officials in Austria and in whipping up the emotions of several "progressive" Catholics. The artificially incited press campaign did not end until the Austrian chancellor assured his Parliament, in response to interpellation, that what I had written was in no way a reference to the Austro-Hungarian frontier, but only to the Iron Curtain. The sentence in question had read: "With faith and hope in God, we crossed the threshold of prison and the temporary, death-dealing frontier." At the very outset of the attacks my office had issued a statement explaining that by "temporary and death-dealing frontier," at which so many human lives were snuffed out, I meant not the Austro-Hungarian frontier but the Iron Curtain. Every Hungarian who is loyal to his country regards this boundary as merely "temporary." But during this press campaign, which was obviously without the slightest basis, not a single official ecclesiastical organ came to my aid. On the contrary, I was informed from Rome that henceforth I must submit every one of my statements, even my sermons, to a Roman adviser, who would be assigned to me, for his approval. I could not accept such a reprimand. After negotiations and several letters I declared myself willing to submit my statements to the Holy Father in person, but only to him alone when he explicitly requested me to do so.

Lacking a suffragan bishop, I set out in person to conduct pastoral tours of Hungarians in exile. First I visited the Hungarian Catholics in Europe, then I went to Canada, to the United States, and to South Africa. In the course of these travels I naturally sought meetings with the diocesan bishops of each place in order to discuss with them the problems of the Hungarian Catholics and their priests. My first such visit took me on May 20, 1972, to the Federal Republic of Germany. In Munich I was the guest of Cardinal Döpfner, to whom I expressed my gratitude, in the name of the Hungarian people, for the generous campaigns of assistance with which German Catholics had responded during the postwar years to the distress of Hungarians at home and abroad. On May 21, Pentecost Sunday, I went to Bamberg to take part in the ceremonies in honor of St. Stephen, which had been organized by Hungarian Catholics in Germany. Thirty-five hundred pilgrims participated in this Hungarian celebration abroad. In my address I enjoined them to continue to cherish in their foreign surroundings the ethical and cultural tradition of Catholic Hungary. I protested the Hungarian abortion law, pointing out its sad and tragic consequences. There was an associated meeting of boy scouts, which I greatly enjoyed, and I was delighted to take part in the festivities in honor of St. Stephen that afternoon. Next day I celebrated Mass in Frankfurt cathedral and also delivered a sermon. In the afternoon I visited the bishop of Würzburg. The following day I visited an old-age home in Munich run by Hungarian nuns.

During my second tour in the Federal Republic I visited the Hungarian secondary school in Kastl. I arrived there on June 14, 1972, for the celebration of the institution's fifteenth anniversary. The occasion gave me an opportunity to thank the bishop of Eichstätt and several representatives of the West German government for the precious support they have given our young people year after year.

On August 26, 1972, I flew to Brussels, where I spent four days. I enjoyed the unforgettably cordial hospitality of Msgr. Iginio Cardinale, apostolic nuncio. On the first day of my visit I met with representatives of the social and charitable institutions of the three Benelux countries. On the second day I concelebrated in the enormous Sacred Heart of Jesus Cathedral with several bishops, Hungarian, Dutch, and Belgian priests, and with parish priests who had come from Scandinavia and England. It was generally estimated that some 7,000 of the faithful attended this Mass; Hungarians filled the entire huge nave of the cathedral. There was a festive meeting that afternoon, and although the great hall assigned for it could hold 3,000, it was scarcely large enough for all who wished to attend. On the third day I went to Liège, Tongerlo, Banneux, and Aachen. On the fourth day I took part in a conference of the deans of the Hungarian parish priests in Europe.

On September 17, 1972, we celebrated the millennium of St. Stephen in Mariazell, accompanied by Bishop István László, fifty Hungarian curates, and about 1,500 Hungarian pilgrims.

In all my speeches, and in radio and television broadcasts, I dealt with the grave predicament of the Hungarian church and with the fate of our much-tried people. It therefore did not surprise me when I learned that the Hungarian communist regime took a very dim view of the ceremonies, protested to the Vatican against my remarks, and demanded that measures be taken to silence me. Subsequently bishops from Hungary quite often appeared at the Holy See, in obedience to instructions from the Bureau for Church Affairs, to complain about the "harmful" nature of my activites. Because of me, they said, the regime was taking vengeance on the entire Catholic Church. They demanded that I be reduced to total silence.

These protests were received in the Vatican, and on October 10, 1972—in the thirteenth month of my exile—I was informed by the papal nuncio in Vienna that the Holy See in the summer of 1971 had given the Hungarian Communist government a pledge that while I was abroad I would not do or say anything that could possibly displease that government. I replied that in the negotiations conducted from June 25 to June 28, 1971, between the Holy Father's personal emissary and myself there had been no mention of any such pledge. Had I known about any guarantee of this sort, I declared, I would have been so shocked that I would have asked the Holy Father to rescind all the arrangements that had been made in conjunction with my departure from Hungary. After all, the fact was widely known that I had wanted to remain in the midst of my suffering people and to die in my native land. I asked the nuncio to inform the appropriate Vatican authorities that a sinister silence already prevailed within Hungary and that I shrank from the thought of having to keep silent in the free world as well.

This admonition came to me on the eve of my journey to Fatima. In spite of everything the Holy Father did not ask me to show him the address I had prepared for Fatima; but the nuncio's office in Lisbon censored it behind my back when it was already in the printshop. A whole paragraph was deleted, including such sentences as the following: "The East proclaims that there even the worst athiests have become gentle lambs. Do not believe it! You shall know the tree by its fruits. It is possible that in the East there are more churchgoers than in many a Western country, but that is not to the credit of the regimes there, but of those Christians who manage to walk bowed down by the weight of the cross."

I arrived in Portugal on October 11, 1972. At the airport I was received by the patriarch, several bishops, and many leaders in secular and church life. On the evening of the twelfth I took part in the torchlight procession in Fatima and in the rosary procession the next morning. I concelebrated Mass with Cardinal Bibeiro, with the members of the Portuguese episcopate, and with many European, American, and African priests. On October 14 I visited one of the visionaries of Fatima, Sister Lucia, in Coimbra. On the morning of the fifteenth we made the stations of the cross at the Hungarian Calvary and I celebrated Mass in St. Stephen's Chapel. That afternoon we flew to Madeira. In Funchal, at the tomb of King Charles IV, whose body was being exhumed for the initiation of the canonization proceedings, I celebrated Mass for Hungarians. The theme of my address was that the sorrowful destiny of the last Hungarian king and the partition of our country have called attention to the almost unbearable sufferings of the

Hungarian people. The following day I prayed at the graves in Lisbon of Regent Miklós Horthy and his wife.

In 1973 I undertook more pastoral tours. From March 15 to 19 I was in Innsbruck, from April 28 to May 1 in Cologne. On June 30 I met several thousand Hungarian Catholics in Augsburg. Everywhere the bishops received me with great cordiality and responded with great friendliness to my suggestions concerning pastoral work among the Hungarians. I shall always remember the brotherly love and kindness of Cardinals Frings and Höffner in behalf of our Hungarian Catholics. I can say the same for Msgr. Paul Rusch, the bishop of Tyrol. Approximately 1,500 Hungarian pilgrims assembled to celebrate the 1,000 anniversary of St. Ulrich; all of them attended my Mass on June 30. In my sermon, in which I gave considerable space to local and historical matters, I pointed out the many sacrifices that Hungarians had made in defense of Christendom for the past thousand years. After Mass I visited the diocesan bishops and the papal legate, Cardinal Suenens. Then I hurried on to the millennial celebration in honor of St. Stephen of Hungary. After the end of the ceremonies I received delegations from Hungarian associations in Europe.

During 1973 I undertook three more extended pastoral tours. The first led me to England, from July 13 to 17; the second to Canada and the United States, from September 18 to October 4, the third to the Union of South Africa, from November 22 to December 5. In the course of two years I covered some 36,000 miles by car, train, and plane. I gladly assumed the burdens of this traveling in order to bring comfort and encouragement to Hungarians in foreign lands.

I do not wish to prolong this account of my travels unduly, for I need the space for other important events. I shall therefore be brief about my July trip to visit Hungarians in England. In London, Cardinal Heenan received me with brotherly love and hospitality. Twice he turned his cathedral over to me and my companions. On the first day it was filled with Hungarian Catholics, on the second day by English. My host's sermon was not calculated to win applause from the Communists. Among other things he said:

> While Cardinal Mindszenty remains an exile the world will not be allowed to forget that communism is inflexibly hostile to religion. To regard dialogue with Marxists as if it were a purely academic exercise is ingenuous and dangerous. We who live in liberty must not rest while men and women of any religion are persecuted. If world communism is in earnest about spreading peace let it cease from persecution. Let Hungary invite its Cardinal Primate to return home to the people for whom he is father and hero.

I also visited the Hungarians in Manchester and Bedford. In Manchester I celebrated Mass with the bishop of Salford, with two suffragan bishops, the members of the cathedral chapter, and 120 priests in the presence of some 2,000 persons who filled the cathedral.

On the last day of my stay in England I accepted the invitation of a number of prominent individuals to take part in a banquet in Parliament. One hundred and thirty MPs published a statement declaring that Great Britain cordially welcomes Cardinal Mindszenty as the most prominent freedom-fighter in Europe, who fearlessly opposed Nazi and communist repression and for that opposition suffered prison and persecution. Undoubtedly the Hungarian communist regime was even more irritated by the English cardinal's remarks and the above statement. The result was that after my trip to England, Budapest pressed the Vatican even harder to depose me and reprimand me. The question of my memoirs also became involved in these events.

My memoirs were already prepared for the press in Hungarian and German in the summer of 1973. In July I sent the manuscipt to the Holy Father. He wrote me on August 30 that he had read the manuscript with great interest and emotion. He was grateful to me for having sent it, because he was thus able to acquaint himself with my "valuable" and painful biography. The manuscript was truly valuable, fascinating, overwhelming, he said. The reader was afforded insight into my fate; admiration and sympathy were aroused and the conviction established that in God's eyes so much trial and suffering could not be in vain.

The pope did not object to anything in the text. However, he called my attention to the fact that the Hungarian Communist regime could retaliate in two ways. It might revive the slanders of me, and it might punish the entire church of Hungary.

In my reply to the Holy Father I made the following points, among others:

1. I am already accustomed to incessant slanders from the enemies of the Church and am already resigned to the idea that the so-called progressive and leftist Catholics will join these enemies in systematically attacking me. But it is my human right, and as a bishop it is actually my duty, to rebuff the slanders if I can do so in full freedom. Aside from the fact that I have forgiven my enemies, in my memoirs I describe only facts. As the Holy Father was able to see, I have avoided any provocative or polemical tone which might prompt base vengeance on me personally or on the Church.

2. The history of Bolshevism, which already goes back more than half a century, shows that the Church simply cannot make any conciliatory gesture in the expectation that the regime will in return abandon its persecution of religion. That persecution follows from the essential nature and internal organization of its ideology. Not even the Russian Orthodox Church managed to escape persecution. It was persecuted during the period of coexistence and the period of subjugation. The experiences with negotiations between Budapest and the Vatican prove the same point. For although ever since 1964 the Vatican's diplomats have been negotiating about peace priests, religious instruction, and unhampered pastoral work, the

peace priest movement has been revived and has flourished during these very years, and religious instruction has been completely suppressed in the towns and many villages also. Almost without exception the capable and devout parish priests are separated from their flocks by force or fraud. The sole result of the spectacular negotiations, which the Communists have exploited for propaganda purposes, has been to bring into the Church those bishops who have been selected by the bureau for church affairs mostly from the ranks of the peace priests. The activities of these bishops have been profoundly detrimental to ecclesiastical discipline.

I then informed the Holy Father that in the autumn we would be giving rights of publication of my memoirs to a large European or American publishing house. I pointed out that for some time Catholics and non-Catholics alike in all parts of the world had been urging the publication of these memoirs. After my arrival abroad I set up, with the aid of several benefactors, the Cardinal Mindszenty Foundation. The bylaws of this foundation provide that its funds are to be used for charitable purposes. I now turned over to this foundation all the rights to my memoirs. The directors of the foundation then entered into a contract with the West Berlin publisher Propyläen Verlag.

From everything that happened afterward I can deduce, with a high degree of probability, that the pope could no longer resist the bombardment of the Budapest regime, which demanded fulfillment of the Vatican guarantee. On November 1, I was asked to resign my archiepiscopal office. The pope asked this of me with "bitter reluctance" since, he said, he knew very well that this represented still another sacrifice to add to the sufferings I had already experienced. But he said that he had to consider "the pastoral necessities" of the archdiocese of Esztergom, now orphaned for twenty-five years. Otherwise it would continue to be "without the direct and personal leadership of a bishop," and that would "inflict great harm on souls and on the Hungarian Church." The letter concluded with the remark that after my abdication I would be "freer" to arrange the publication of my memoirs.

After my tour of South Africa, which lasted from November 22 to December 5, I answered the pope's letter. My reply, after mature consideration, was dated December 8, 1973. In all reverence I informed the Holy Father that because of the present condition of the Catholic Church in Hungary I could not abdicate my archiepiscopal office. I sent him a long treatise on the pernicious activities of the peace priests, on the State-Church system that had been organized by force, and I noted all the negative consequences of the Vatican negotiations which had been going on with the Communists for the past ten years.

I said that I feared my abdication, and the subsequent occupation of the post of primate of Hungary by a churchman who would be chosen with the consent of the Bureau of Church Affairs, would contribute to legitimizing the present catastrophic ecclesiastical conditions in Hungary. I listed all the disadvantages and damage to Hungarians abroad that might be the outcome of my abdication, since I had taken over the task of ministering to them for lack of an auxiliary bishop abroad. Finally I pointed out to the Holy Father the possibility that if I were relieved of my office there might well follow attacks upon him personally.

After all this, exactly on the twenty-fifth anniversary of my arrest, I was pained to receive a letter from the Holy Father dated December 18, 1973, in which His Holiness informed me with expressions of great appreciation and gratitude that he was declaring the archiepiscopal See of Esztergom vacant. In a letter of January 7, 1974, I expressed my profound grief. But I also informed the pope that neither personal sorrow nor clinging to office were the reason for my being unable to accept the decision. I cannot accept the responsibility, I wrote, for the consequences of this decision because such measures only add to the already difficult predicament of the Hungarian Church. They are harmful to religious life and sow confusion in the souls of Catholics devoted to their faith and priests devoted to their church. I asked him to rescind this decision. But nothing of the sort was done. Instead, on the twenty-fifth anniversary of my show trial, on February 5, 1974, the announcement of my removal from the see of Esztergom was published. Next day, to my profound sorrow, I found myself forced to issue a correction through my office:

A number of news agencies have transmitted the Vatican decision in such a way as to imply that József Cardinal Mindszenty has voluntarily retired. The news agencies furthermore stressed that before the papal decision there was an intense exchange of letters between the Vatican and the cardinal-archbishop, who is living in Vienna. Some persons have therefore drawn the conclusion that an agreement concerning this decision had been reached between the Vatican and the Hungarian primate. In the interests of truth Cardinal Mindszenty has authorized his office to issue the following statement:

Cardinal Mindszenty has not abdicated his office as archbishop nor his dignity as primate of Hungary. The decision was taken by the Holy See alone.

After long and conscientious consideration the cardinal justified his attitude on this question as follows:

1. Hungary and the Catholic Church of Hungary are not free.

2. The leadership of the Hungarian dioceses is in the hands of a church administration built and controlled by the communist regime.

3. Not a single archbishop or apostolic administrator is in a position to alter the composition or the functioning of the above-mentioned church administration.

4. The regime decides who is to occupy ecclesiastical positions and for how long. Furthermore, the regime also decides what persons the bishops will be allowed to consecrate as priests.

5. The freedom of conscience and religion guaranteed by the Constitution is in practice suppressed. "Optional" religious instruction has been banned from the schools in the cities and the larger towns. At present the struggle for optional

religious instruction in the schools is continuing in the smaller communities. Young people, contrary to the will of their parents, are being educated exclusively in an atheistic spirit. Believers are discriminated against in many areas of daily life. Religious teachers have only recently been confronted with the alternative of choosing between their professions and their religion.

6. The appointment of bishops or apostolic administrators without the elimination of the above-mentioned abuses does not solve the problems of the Hungarian Church. The installation of "peace priests" in important ecclesiastical posts has shaken the confidence of loyal priests and lay Catholics in the highest administration of the Church. In these grave circumstances Cardinal Mindszenty cannot abdicate.

This is the path I traveled to the end, and this is how I arrived at complete and total exile.

DOCUMENTS

☿ 1. My Farewell Sermon in My Parish Church of Zalaegerszeg, 1944*

Dearly beloved in Christ,

A piece of paper is lying on a table in the rectory, waiting to be signed. I postponed signing it until today, for first I wanted to celebrate the Mass with you once more. I wanted to have the chance to speak to you this one last time and to address you as "my dearly beloved in Christ." The paper I must sign has called me away from this parish and this church, called me away to my new vocation. It grieves me deeply that I must leave you now, my faithful people. Twenty-seven years ago, in February 1917, a young priest arrived in Zalaegerszeg to teach secondary school here. As I got off the train, I was worrying about whether I would be able to fulfill all my duties as a priest. Now twenty-seven long years have gone by, years in which I faithfully performed all the duties the Church requires of her shepherds. I proclaimed the Word of God, celebrated the Mass, and administered the sacraments.

Yes, I proclaimed the Word of God. I must thank Him Whose divine grace enabled me to carry out the duties of my vocation. I no longer have all the records of my ministry; but I know that over one ten-year span, I preached 537 times to the Marian Congregation alone.

For my parishioners I used to celebrate Mass seventy-two times each year; and every day I prayed for our city and for all the faithful, both living and dead. People thronged into this church at every Mass. Seeing them all, I besought our

---

* Most of the documents in this book can be found in *Mindszenty Okmánytár (Compendium of Mindszenty Documents)*, three volumes, edited by József Vecsey, D.Th., Munich, 1957. Some of the documents that follow are given in a condensed or paraphrased form.

Lord Jesus Christ to bless the faithful, guide the unbelievers to our church, and protect the children from harm. After the consecration, in the memento, I always meditated on the dead to whom I had administered the last rites, along with all those who had died in the faith; and I besought Our Lord Jesus to ease the sufferings of the souls in Purgatory.

I also faithfully administered the sacraments. No spider ever spun cobwebs in *my* confessional! If there are some among you who never came to confess to me, at least it was not because I was absent from my post. Some of you may not have received the sacraments from me. I pray that you will receive them at the hands of the new priest who comes to take my place.

[At this point in my sermon, I spoke about some of the congratulatory letters which had begun to pour in immediately after my appointment as bishop of Veszprém. Then I continued.]

The letters I have received from local parishioners have been lavish in their expressions of affection and of grief at my departure. These letters lead me to believe that my parishioners must have felt as close to me as I have felt to them. Nothing can truly divide one Catholic from another. There is hardly a person here who has not knelt in my confessional, asking absolution; there is hardly a family I do not know, or a child whose face is not familiar to me; and few of you have known pain or sorrow which I was unaware of and did not try to ease.

I ask you all to do one thing for me: whatever happens, always remember that a priest can never be the enemy of his flock. A priest is a member of every family in his parish; and all of you in turn belong to his family, to the single great family of the Church. I have tried to imitate Our Lord Jesus Christ in serving people of all classes and stations in life. If I have failed any of you, I ask you to forgive me in His name. If I have unwittingly harmed any of you, I did so only because I was trying too hard to do what I thought was best for you. I may sometimes have been overzealous; but I always tried to make amends for it later. When a man is sincerely seeking God, even his faults may serve some useful purpose.

I wish to thank the municipal authorities of Zalaegerszeg and the county of Zala, as well as various government officials, for the help they gave me in carrying out my work. And finally I must thank all the faithful people of this region for the generosity with which they supported my efforts. The workmen, merchants, and farmers have earned my special thanks for their devoted service.

2. Memorandum to Premier Ferenc Szálasi, October 31, 1944

Mr. Premier:

Fully aware of their responsibilities as members of the Hungarian hierarchy, the undersigned bishops of Western Hungary hereby address an appeal through the premier to those who hold the fate of the country in their hands. We request that the still undevastated sections of Western Hungary be not turned into a battle-ground. Should this happen, it would mean that all the encounters of the retreating armies would take place on this last remaining bit of undespoiled Hungarian terri-tory. If Western Hungary is destroyed by war, the last section of the Hungarian fa-therland and the last hope of Hungary's recovery in the future will be lost.

This part of the country will become a moving theater of battle for two gigantic armies. The lives of 3,441,853 inhabitants of Western Hungary, constituting the main element of the nation's population, will be endangered as well as those of countless refugees from other parts of the country. Beautiful cities, villages, immea-surable wealth, historical treasures and the last remaining food reserves will be de-stroyed. We say this because it is foreseeable that the retreat of one army and the advance of another will be accompanied by constant fighting; as its fury grows the thirst for blood and destruction by fire will increase. Whatever population remains will face death through famine, and because of lack of housing, there will be suffer-ing from cold, and epidemics will remain unchecked since there are no physicians left in many districts.

The destruction will be even more terrifying and the responsibility more dreadful if, as a consequence of the evacuation of Budapest, its population of 1,160,000 souls (if we count Greater Budapest, more than 1,500,000), together with the refugees from Upper Hungary, the regions between the Danube and the Tisza and the Southern regions, are crowded into this area.

Has the hope that the recent change of regime would alter the course of battle been fulfilled? Has Hungary's non-occupied territory increased in the slightest in these past two weeks? It would be heartening if we could even write that our country had the same frontiers as on October 15th.

After the last two weeks' experience, can you still, with due regard to your moral responsibility, maintain the attitude that either we must destroy or we will be de-stroyed? How is it possible to administer a decisive blow when not one line of defense has been constructed, while the frontiers remain unprotected, and when we have only an unequipped army which, with its exhausted and retreating supporters, faces a steadily advancing force? It is wishful thinking to presume that we are capa-ble of destroying great world powers when we ourselves are so close to another pos-sibility—complete annihilation. After Muhi, Mohács, Majteny, Világos and Trianon, Hungary was able to rise again; but from utter annihilation there is no resurrection.

An individual may sacrifice himself for the nation. Tens of thousands of our na-tion even in this World War died for their fatherland; but to push a whole nation to suicide just for your ideas is impossible. A sense of responsibility and conscience will not allow this.

If one asks by what right do we lift our voices, we answer: We are Hungarians; we live and wish to continue to live in indissoluble union with our nation. Our role in the secular and moral leadership of our country was commanded by God and St. Stephen, established by laws a thousand years old. The question of life and death that now faces us is no longer primarily a political matter but a moral consideration. Therefore, we not only must and can speak, but it is our duty in conscience, before history and before the judgment of God to do so. And we exercise this responsi-bility on behalf of three and a half million souls of Western Hungary.

Hoping that our serious warning will meet with serious consideration (etc.).

Signed by all the Catholic Bishops of Western Hungary

☊ 3. *Pastoral Letter, May 1945*

Beloved in Christ:

Since the last time we addressed you, a fearful war has raged through our country, leaving desolation in its wake. We have suffered one of the most dreadful catastrophes in the history of this land. Now we sit desolate among the nations, covered with shame and sorrow, with bitterness in our hearts.

And yet we humbly thank God for His mercy in allowing us to speak to you once more; and we thank Him that the sounds of battle have ceased throughout all Europe. Now we pray without ceasing that all trace of madness and murder may soon vanish from our land, leaving behind the spirit of peace and the opportunity to build again.

We are all laboring to rebuild the ruins. But let us never forget that the ruin of our souls is far more tragic than the ruined cities we see all around us. Our people have lost respect for the laws of God. They have also lost that respect for authority which is a cornerstone of all civilized society.

Our sufferings resulted from the failure of our leaders to observe our traditions and our ancient faith. There are many who believe that human beings, and in particular the government, have the right to violate divine laws whenever it seems expedient to do so. This kind of thinking caused innocent people to be interned in concentration camps, robbed of all their possessions, exiled, or murdered outright. Those who issued and carried out such orders, or merely approved of them, all forgot one thing: Whenever a conflict arises between human and divine law, we must obey God rather than men. Those who governed this land chose to place themselves above the laws of God. They failed to realize that in doing so, they were undermining the foundations of their own authority.

Even in wartime we must still obey the sixth commandment. Under any and all circumstances, it is our duty to defend the purity of marriage. But women who were raped by violence may rest assured that they are without sin. We feel deeply the anguish suffered by the women and girls of this land. But we are also proud of our people for producing women capable of heroically defending their honor.

Dear faithful Catholic people, we know that the present government is described as merely "provisional." Nevertheless, this government is our sole representative abroad. It is responsible for maintaining order throughout our land. Thus as long as it does not compel us to violate the laws of God, it deserves our respect and obedience. But in order to merit our obedience, those who govern us must keep in mind their responsibility for our welfare.

The present government has enacted many new laws. The laws which most profoundly affect the structure of our society are those relating to land reform. The problem of land reform is very complex. We have already expressed to the government our views regarding the moral and constitutional aspects of the problem. Therefore in this letter we will speak only of its effects on the Church. Up to now, our seminaries and churches have been supported by the income from various Church properties. But who will support them in the future? And what of the expense of maintaining the administrative apparatus of the Church? What of our schools and other institutions? To be sure, we rely on the love and generosity of you all, our faithful Catholic people. But the Catholics of a war-torn and poverty-stricken land cannot bear the expense of maintaining all our institutions. Hence we are filled with anxiety about the future.

We are faced with many material cares. But we have not forgotten something far more important—the cares and sufferings of our people. Many Hungarians are still prisoners of war. They have known nothing in this war but misery and defeat. When they return home, let us not greet them with reproaches and contempt, but only with love and respect. We offer daily prayers for those heroes who sacrificed their lives for their country. For there are more than ten commandments. There is also the commandment of love, the commandment to love even our enemies. If we cannot love others, we will cease to be Christians.

We who were appointed to guard the laws of God ask you to respect and honor those laws, and to recognize their eternal validity. We are deeply concerned about the future of our nation. That is why we must do all we can to ensure that not only individuals, but our whole society, should live in accordance with the laws of God. Let us hold fast to our faith, which has sustained this nation for a thousand years. Only our faith can guarantee our survival as a people. Long ago our nation was conquered by the sword; but it was preserved and nourished by the Cross. Those are more than empty words. No nation has ever survived in this world unless it was founded on justice and morality. And the foundation of all justice is the Church. . . .

Democracy and freedom are the watchwords of the hour. And what good words they are! Democracy implies that every citizen and every social class is equally entitled to participate in shaping the common fate of us all. Democracy should come naturally to all Catholics, for the Gospel teaches us the meaning of true democracy. We who know the Gospel know that we must never use our democratic freedoms to promote our own selfish ends.

In a country where the citizens fear God, they will respect the law. Where they respect the law, they will live in peace. A nation filled with peace is a strong nation. Religion has more power over men than any social force or institution. For religion does not rule by intimidation or terrorize men into obedience. Its power comes from inside the human heart. Religion maintains order by teaching men to govern their instincts and passions. You must all struggle to guard those rights which enable you to love as good Catholics should. Guard your rights in the schools which teach your children. Guard your rights in the communities where you live out your lives.

☿ 4. *Article in* Uj Ember, *September 23, 1945*

Times of trouble and storm are often the gravediggers of past ideas and institutions; on the other hand, new vitality and new approaches seem to emerge out of the chaos. And so, the tasks of the Church are multiplied at such a time. Her most urgent problems are: Catholic self-assurance, consolidation of all Catholic forces, increased Catholic social welfare activities, intensified educational work, intensified propaganda, extension of the Catholic press. . . .

We have long had our parish communities, our convents and monasteries and sodalities in Hungary. But in 1919, after the Great War, these institutions were animated by a new vitality and a new movement spread throughout Hungary.

The year 1945 is likewise a year marked by a rallying and unifying spirit. The reason is the same as it was in 1919. We must establish new Church communities, new parishes, since the recent resettling of the population requires it. Barely necessary in 1919, today it has become an urgent duty in certain communities. We must also deepen and reanimate the life in communities which already exist. This is one of the chief demands of this stormy year.

The modern watchword is democracy—the will of the people. We do not care whether it is Western democracy or the Eastern version; what we desire above all is the integration and consolidation of the people of God. The various classes of the faithful are united in the Church. We do not exclude or reject any soul. There is no predominance of any particular class in the Church.

The political parties dismember society into different classes—peasants, workers, etc. The Church, however, unites all in Christ and in His Mystical Body. In opposition to the claims of the totalitarian State, the Church proclaims the rights of the individual, human rights and the rights of the family. In this shattered age the Church seeks to realize the prayer of Our Lord that "All may be One!" State and society, as well as each individual, should be grateful to the Church for her work of unification and integration. She is the point of crystallization amidst this chaos: And this focal place, where we find the *Catholicum*, the worldwide universal unity, is in the parish community itself.

The number on the party membership card looms large today in our political life, but quality seems only of minor importance. The Church, however, has always looked for quality and personal character. Representation in the parish community is the best manifestation of this appreciation of quality. There is no higher distinction for the Catholic layman than to represent his fellow Catholics in the cooperative activities of the parishes. It is not his social standing that matters—only his Catholic qualities.

It is here that the great problems of Catholic life are settled: Church, Catholic schools, Catholic films and theater, cemeteries, family, education of the children, care for the poor and the sick. It is here that the injuries and losses of our day are most deeply felt—damaged or destroyed churches, ransacked or neglected schools, desecrated cemeteries. It is here that the struggle for that priceless treasure, the souls of the children, is most ardently fought. The purpose of all this work is to continue our traditions of nine centuries. From here arises the renewal of faith to go forth and battle against all the spiritual and material devastations of the war.

It is consequently the duty of the faithful to activate the life of the Church. Now is the time to put our hand to the plough. Let us arise and labor for our most sacred values, for Church, homeland, family and the individual! Leaders, investigate carefully what needs most urgently to be done in your parish! It must not be an ailing, moribund one like that of Corinth, but a helpful, serving one, ready to sacrifice all. . . .

☦ 5. Extract from Cardinal Serédi's Radio Message, 1942

"The primate of Hungary combines two offices. He holds the highest rank in the Hungarian Church, and at the same time is chief guardian and interpreter of the law. Thus he symbolizes the dual nature—both spiritual and secular—of the Christian kingdom of Hungary.

"This remarkable and privileged post in Hungarian society was created by our first king, the holy St. Stephen. With the consent of the Holy See, Stephen named the primate as archbishop of Esztergom, which was then the capital and metropolitan of all the Catholic dioceses of Hungary. Shortly thereafter, the pope combined the office of primate with that of papal legate, so that the primate's ecclesiastical jurisdiction was extended throughout the country. Thus, ever since the days of King Stephen, the primate has been the highest constitutional authority in the land after the king himself, second only to the head of the state.

"The primate must fulfill a twofold obligation. His dual burden makes constant demands on his time and strength. He must indeed die himself in order to live and work for the Hungarian Catholic Church and for the Hungarian nation."

♱ 6. Installation Sermon, October 7, 1945

Dearly beloved in Christ,

By the grace of God I have become your new shepherd. In my thoughts I am traveling to Rome to pay homage to the head of our universal Church, Pope Pius XII, who rules over us all in the suffering and splendor of his great office. At his feet lies the faithful but struggling soul of Hungary.

Today all mankind is raising its eyes from the ruins of war to behold the Rock of Peter. We look up filled with repentance and with trust. As we travel our road to Jericho, we can find healing for our wounds in the eternal truths founded on the rock of St. Peter. What a consolation it is to know that this power exists on earth, the power of which it is written that the gates of Hell shall not prevail against it (Mt 16: 18)!

In my thoughts I also come to stand before the coffin of my predecessor, Archbishop Serédi. Throughout his life he never ceased to point us toward the right path. He defended the sacraments and the rights of man and always counseled us to be vigilant in our faith. But the insane delusions of our leaders and the devastating violence of their followers prevented many of us from obeying the admonitions of our good archbishop. His was the voice of one crying in the wilderness (Jn 1:23). As the fruits of evil grew ripe and we were all overwhelmed by the universal ruin, Archbishop Serédi was taken from us.

Over his coffin I drape the flag of all true Christian soldiers; and beside it I place the flag of our nation. He was truly a patriot as well as a man of God.

Leaving behind me the eternal Rock and the freshly dug grave, I turn now to you, my faithful Catholic people. In this grim year of turmoil I bring you the Easter message of our eternal High Priest, "Peace be with you."

Now I ask myself a question—the same question which St. Bernard asked himself as he stood on the threshold of the monastery: "Why have you come to this place?" And this is my answer:

There are many gaps in our knowledge of the former primates of Hungary. But according to historical tradition, I am the ninth of these shepherds to have come from the Queen's city, Veszprém. The first of the nine was a Martyrius. He was followed by Archbishop Robert, who saw the country being run by faithless and renegade men and punished them with excommunication. Then there was Ferenc Forgách, leader of the Catholic reform movement. In my mind's eye I can see the wealthy, ninety-three-year-old György Szécsenyi, an archbishop renowned for his works of charity. I see, too, Count Imre Esterházy, whose skill at politics helped guide Hungarian affairs at the time of the Pragmatic Sanction, which brought our people two hundred years of peace. And finally I look back with reverence at Archbishop József Kopácsy, who built on the ruins of the past a national sanctuary where we can pray for the welfare of our country.

The primate of Hungary now stands guard where his predecessors stood before him. His highest constitutional authority is derived from nine hundred years of Hungarian tradition. Your archbishop is a *pontifex* indeed—that is, literally a "bridge builder." He will join with his people in building a bridge across the abyss of the past.

The year 1945 is indeed a year of abysses. Even if your new archbishop had the wisdom and strength of all the former bishops of Veszprém put together—which alas he does not—he could scarcely solve all the problems we face. Hungary is bleeding from many wounds. Our country is suffering the greatest moral, legal, and economic crisis of its entire history. Now our psalm must be "De profundis," our prayer the *Miserere*, our prophet the lamenting Jeremiah, our world that of the Apocalypse. We are sitting beside the waters of Babylon, and with our broken harps we must learn to sing the songs of a strange land.

The greatest evil of all was not the war itself, but the aftermath of war. Dysentery is rife among us. Physicians report that, because of widespread malnutrition, more than half the children and old people with dysentery will die. Tuberculosis now afflicts twice as many people as before, and venereal disease has increased by five times. And instead of the lamenting flute, we hear the sounds of the gypsy violin. For the young people of Hungary seek after frivolous pleasures. They are very sad young people indeed, to want to strike up dance music in such a tragic hour. Perhaps their names, their language, and their blood are still Hungarian; but vast oceans separate the Hungary of bleeding wounds from this Hungary that thinks only of dancing. In the midst of the blood and the ruins, the poverty and the tears, these children are making merry. Indeed they know not what they do.

Our nation is filled with sin and impiety. We who are the shepherds of souls must respond to the increasing need we see around us. The people of this land no longer honor natural law and the revealed law of God. There is only one way to stem the chaos of worldliness and immorality: by deepening the life of faith. I myself have been a shepherd of souls for more than a quarter of a century. I want to be a good shepherd—one who, if need be, will lay down his life for his sheep (Jn 10:15), his Church, and his country.

Dear Catholic people, let us become a people of prayer. Once we learn to pray again, we will possess an inexhaustible source of strength and faith.

With the help of God our Father and of the Virgin Mother Mary, I will strive to become the conscience of our people. I will be a divinely appointed watchman knocking at the doors of your souls. Errors and false teachings are being noised abroad. But I will proclaim the old eternal truths and breathe new life into the sacred traditions of our people.

When Daniel O'Connell felt that his end was near, he set out to travel to the Eternal City. But he only got as far as Genoa. There he wrote the following instructions in his will: "When I am dead, carry my heart to Rome, but bring my body back to my own beloved country"; Rome and my own country: those are my guiding stars. I would truly rejoice if we would all follow those stars, bringing new life to our Hungarian homeland and new life to our own souls. For only our inner renewal will bring us into the bliss of eternal life. Amen.

☿ 7. *Address in Budapest, October 1945*

My dearly beloved Faithful of Budapest,

By the grace of God I was chosen to be your shepherd. I have just been installed in my new office. At once I hastened to visit you, the people of the Hungarian capital. I have come here because 750,000 Catholics belonging to my diocese live in this great city. But above all I have come because I see that a Cup of Sorrows is being poured out on all the people who live here. More buildings were destroyed in Budapest than anywhere else in our land; and more hearts were destroyed too. The people of the capital endured their fate like heroes. They showed us all how to resist the temptations of evil. I have come here now so that we two, the shepherd and his flock, may look into one another's eyes and read each other's hearts. And I have come so that we may pray to God together to give us strength. The storms of war passed away from this land more than half a year ago. We rejoice that the storm is past. The Danube Valley is no longer a Vale of Blood. But it is still a Vale of Sorrow, a Vale of Tears. Winter is approaching, a winter like a mighty and deadly bird of prey descending on our country. This may turn out to be the hardest winter in all the one thousand years of Hungarian history.

I dread the thought of this winter. I dread it as a Christian, a Hungarian, and a man. The summer visited us with pestilence. Half the people stricken with dysentery died of the disease. What will become of us when we must endure cold, starvation, inflation, and the collapse of all our public institutions? We may well shudder at the future. For even the historian Josephus Flavius, who described so many calamities, never protrayed a scene as bleak as this.

Our Hungarian people are proud and self-reliant. They do not like to beg, and they do not like to betray the fact that they are suffering. Therefore the primate of this land will carry the sack of the beggar in their place. He will turn to the rest of the world, to all the peoples and nations, and shout his appeal for help in every direction: "Save my Hungarian people from destruction!"

☿ 8. Radio Appeal to Hungarian Catholics in America, November 18, 1945

Our Hungarian brothers in America!

I was no sooner installed as archbishop when I saw our country confronted with disaster. For this coming winter may prove to be the most difficult winter in all the thousand years of Hungarian history. On October 14, speaking from St. Stephen's Basilica, I appealed for help to all the nations of the world. I asked them to show their generosity by saving the Hungarian people from annihilation.

Our country faces all the horrors of starvation. We have no meat, no butter, no lard. It has been estimated that 400,000 infants are now suffering from rickets. My prayers to the world have been answered. But we have repeatedly been asked whether this generous aid will ever reach those who are in need. I want to reassure everyone that we have carefully organized our emergency program. Let me tell every institution and every individual donor that the Church will be responsible for distributing all gifts. Donations can be transferred to us through the Red Cross or some other reliable organization. Never has it been more truly said that "He who gives swiftly gives twice as much." All those who generously give in this hour of need will be rewarded by the grateful tears of parents and children alike, and by the blessing of Our Heavenly Father.

☿ 9. Thanks for Donations, 1946

Catholics from Recsk and Prónayfalva have given a signal example of devotion to the needy. Catholics from the other dioceses have also risen to the challenge, doing all they can to show their love for their fellow Hungarians. The young "soldiers" of the Most Sacred Heart of Jesus, members of the Marian Congregation and of the Catholic girls' clubs, and many others have given generously to the poor. They have shown a true spirit of self-sacrifice, sharing the little they had with their fellow countrymen and fellow Christians. Their food packages have saved lives, dried the tears of the suffering, and brought them new hope.

☿ 10. Appeal to the Central Committee of the Parish Communities

We have met together to discuss the fundamental questions of our lives as priests. Throughout the thousand years of Hungarian history, close ties have always existed between priest and laity. Pázmány says that the Hungarian priest has never reacted passively to the events of the day, but has always read the signs of the future and helped to shape it. After the great battles of Muhi and Mohács, the Hungarian priests withdrew into the swamp land along with the remnants of their people. They all prayed together in the wilderness, and together they survived on roots and berries.

A year ago, when the war was almost over, we were all confronted with the question: Should the three million people of Budapest and Western Hungary evacuate their homes and migrate to the west, or should they remain on Hungarian soil? The Church made the decision: "We will stay where we are." So the Hungarian priest and the Hungarian people remained together on Hungarian soil.

[I admonished the lay leaders of the various parish communities, saying:]

We must gather all our strength for what lies ahead. Our first duty is to care for the poor. Our faith and love will be tested by how valiantly we struggle to save the poor and starving. The supplies we have received from abroad will not meet the needs of our people. We ourselves must give away all we have. If any of you has two coats, then give one to someone who has no coat at all. If you have a slice of bread, give half of it to someone who has none.

☿ 11. Address to the Leaders of Hungarian Caritas, 1946

We cannot rely solely on help from abroad. However great our own poverty, we must not shut our doors to the needs of others. To be sure, flour, wood, and clothing will be in short supply; yet there will always be some way in which we can help one another. True charity never depends on the size of our purse, or on what we have in our pantries and our wardrobes. The best offering we can make to one another is a loving, compassionate heart. For if we love each other, we will find a way to give each other the material goods we all need. Hungary has lost a great deal in this war. But thank God, we still have our Hungarian hearts, and would give the shirt off our backs in exchange for a word of thanks.

☦ *12. Statement of October 23, 1946*

Hungarian Catholics are impatiently waiting to hear their government's decision regarding the transport of American food supplies now on hand in Vienna. On August 8, the Catholic Action group set up its first canteen, preparing meals for starving Hungarians from American food. Since that day, canteens all over this land have been active, preparing hot tasty meals for 14,000 human beings. But starving people will wait in vain to be fed unless we find some way to transport 827 tons of food in time. It now appears that these desperately needed supplies may be diverted to other uses. It is absolutely essential that these donations from American Catholics be brought into Hungary without delay.

☦ *13. Address to Young People, October 14, 1946*

Only one man on earth has ever had the right to say, "I am the way, the truth, and the life. Whoever follows me shall not abide in darkness." Christ is the way that you all must walk. He is the truth that you must believe. He is the life you must live, even in the darkness and confusion of these times. St. Paul says that no man is permitted to lay down another foundation than the foundation laid by Our Lord Jesus Christ; and even if an angel from heaven should descend and preach to us a different gospel from the Gospel of Jesus, we should not listen to him. Of course I am not saying that winged angels are going to come down from heaven to tempt the young people of Hungary. But many people today are confused and full of hatred; for a volcano has erupted in our midst. Nevertheless, I believe that love will triumph in the end. That is why I am full of trust in the future. In order to bring about this future, we must all strive to build a Hungary based on faith and morality, a Hungary of boys and girls who love their country and are dedicated to their Christian faith. Each of you young people must become a cornerstone, a pillar supporting your country. Then all together you will be what you just sang about in your song— "a pure, heroic, holy youth."

☦ *14. Sermon to Budapest Physicians, October 21, 1946*

The true physician views his service to the suffering as a priestly labor, a way of worshipping God. . . . Holy Scripture tells us concerning St. Luke, the patron saint of physicians, that he served St. Paul as his "beloved physician," his faithful companion and helper. Every physician must possess three virtues—kindness, devotion to duty, and the desire to serve others. Every Christian physician should strive to develop these qualities. All doctors have received scientific training; but a good doctor must possess a compassionate heart which feels the sufferings of patients he may never have met before. How many physicians have died in the faithful pursuit of their calling! A physician's role resembles that of a mother. He must question the sick person, listen patiently to the answers, and then do whatever he can to help. A Christian physician may even assume the role of a priest, reconciling cold hearts and broken souls to God in their last hours on earth.

☦ *15. Reply to the Communist Party on the Question of Salary, 1946*

You have not been told the truth about this matter. . . . The land reform laws demanded the confiscation of Church property. The government promised to compensate the Church for the loss of its property, but has never done so. The minister of religion and education has in fact allotted the Church a certain sum in the form of "personal stipends"; but these fees are infinitesimal compared to the income formerly derived from Church properties. . . . The government contributes something to the support of Church institutions, but not enough to guarantee their continued existence. A government stipend was in fact offered to József Mindszenty, formerly bishop of Veszprém and now archbishop of Esztergom; but he has never accepted a single penny. Moreover, it is untrue that the archbishop is a "declared enemy of democracy." On the contrary, he is a devoted adherent of true democracy. But he is not the friend of a democracy which is nothing more than the dressed-up remains of a bankrupt totalitarian regime that has not yet had the honesty to declare that it is bankrupt.

☩ 16. Catholic Parents' Support for their Schools, 1946

On June 29, 1946, I attended a session of the Catholic Parents' League at the Convent of the Sacred Heart. I was deeply moved by the efforts of the people to overcome their desperate financial situation. The convent and the school had both been severely damaged during the war; but workers belonging to the Parents' League had rebuilt them, refusing to accept any payment for their work. Men and women of all social classes had joined together in cleaning the new school and getting it ready for use. I was also shown the supplies which had been contributed to the school for the following year. Although it was only June 29, the parishioners had already laid in a supply of wood sufficient to heat the school throughout the coming winter. In a corner of the garden stood a stove that had been used every day for the past year to prepare hot meals for fifty-one of the poor girls of the parish. Forty-seven pairs of shoes had been collected for needy children. I remember saying to myself: "No matter what trials we must undergo, we Hungarians will somehow survive. For the cruel blows of fate have awakened the courage and devotion of our people. We must all thank God for that. . . ."

✝
17. *Pastoral Letter on the Elections, November 1, 1946*

Beloved in Christ,

World War II has come to an end. All the guns have fallen silent. Now that the fearful devastation is over, mankind faces a staggering task. We must lay aside the horrors and hatred of the past and prepare to build a new world. We must all be prepared to make many sacrifices. And we Hungarian Catholics must accept our share of the responsibility for building the new world.

In our last pastoral letter, we spoke of the need we all have to overcome the bitter past. Now our nation has entered into more peaceful times, and we must consider the question of how to shape the future. Soon elections will be held in our land. We wish to address you concerning these elections, for they will determine the shape of the future. We do not wish to participate in pre-election campaigns; we are not supporting any particular party. We simply wish to speak about certain basic principles of truth and duty, so that every faithful Catholic will be well equipped to make his own choice.

The coming elections will reorganize our entire government. This great change must be carried out according to democratic principles. In our last pastoral letter, we spoke of our faith in the ideals of democracy. For the world has suffered long enough under the various forms of tyranny.

It was a tyrannical government that caused this insane and murderous war and forced it to drag on and on. For years this government trod underfoot the most sacred rights of mankind. It stifled freedom of conscience, despised family ties, and refused to recognize the rights of parents to educate their children as they chose.

The democratic nations sought to end this contempt for basic human rights. But they did not wish to exchange the totalitarian rule of a Führer for the equally totalitarian rule of some other dictator. They did not want to create nations which would use the violence of one group to counteract the egotism of another. True democracy is based on the recognition that every human being possesses certain inalienable rights—rights which no power on earth may wrest from him.

To understand the true nature of democracy, we can do no better than to keep in mind the wisdom of Pope Pius XII, who in his Christmas message of 1942 set down the basic principles which should guide us all in building our postwar society. If men desire to become truly human, they must learn to obey these basic principles, which reflect the divine will of almighty God. In our last pastoral letter, we were full of hope for the future. We expressed our joyful assent to the creation of a new, democratic state of Hungary. Secretly we feared that certain forces in our society might prevent the creation of this democratic state. But we suppressed our doubts, hoping for the best. The representatives of democracy in this country made many promises; they even expressed in concrete terms their favor toward the Church. We trusted those who had taken over the reins of government. We overlooked their abuses of authority, believing that such abuses were the inevitable accompaniment of change and hoping that they would cease with the passage of time. We waited long and patiently. Often we wished to intervene; but we chose to give our new government the benefit of the doubt.

Now the time has come for national elections, and we can no longer keep silent. We must publicly declare that no Christian voter can support a party that rules by violence and oppression and that tramples underfoot all natural laws and human rights. Regretfully, we must agree with the British foreign minister who said that Hungary seems to have simply exchanged one totalitarian regime for another. It is tragic that we must make this statement; for Hungary already suffered enough disgrace a year ago, when our weak government turned this land over to the occupation forces of Hitler's Germany. Today we must learn to avoid the errors of the past.

From the very beginning of its history, the Church has defended the sanctity and indissolubility of marriage. Later the Church regarded this sacrament as a means to perpetuate and renew the Hungarian nation. It grieves us deeply that the provisional government has chosen to attack the sacrament of marriage. In doing so, the government has overstepped the bounds of its authority and violated the deepest feelings of all Christian people in this land.

We must also point out that the land reform laws betray a secret desire to completely eradicate certain classes of this society. We do not wish to oppose land reform itself. But the land reform movement is being exploited to satisfy the lust for revenge. Even more disturbing is the fact that the new government has displayed a tendency to violence. Everywhere in this land there have been instances of violence and oppression. Suddenly people are being indiscriminately thrown into prison. They are arrested on the basis of some vague accusation. Often they are denounced to the police by someone who has a grudge against them or simply wants them out of the way. Priests have been imprisoned because of sermons they preached on the feast of St. Stephen. The leader of the secret police stated that these priests would be sent to Siberia if they ever again, either explicitly or indirectly, protested against the present government. Unfortunately, these are not just isolated cases; the number of such cases is growing at an alarming rate. These incidents could not occur if the parties which govern this land had any real respect for the law.

Dear Catholic people, we call on you to vote only for those candidates who represent law, morality, order, and justice. Vote only for men strong enough to hold to their beliefs no matter what the cost. Do not yield to threats. The less people resist violence, the stronger it grows. Every tyrant begins by asking his fellow citizens to vote for him. But he ends by throwing them into forced labor camps, leading them to war, and dragging them all down to death and destruction.

All Hungarian fathers and Catholic mothers concerned for the earthly and eternal welfare of their children must take a stand. There is only one way to vote in this election.

In the name of the bishops of Hungary,

> József Mindszenty
> Primate and Archbishop of Esztergom

18. Letter to Zoltán Tildy, December 31, 1945

Dear Premier:

I have heard a persistent rumor which causes me deep concern. To be sure, this rumor has not been officially substantiated. But in case what I have heard should prove true, I feel obliged to take some stand at this time. I understand that the government plans to undertake a massive reform of our nation, abolishing the 1,000-year-old kingdom of Hungary and proclaiming it a republic. I repeat, I have not been officially informed as to the truth of this rumor. However, 900 years of Hungarian history entitle the primate to speak his mind regarding Hungarian law and other affairs of state. I wish to protest strongly against the projected reform of the state of Hungary.

József Mindszenty,

Esztergom, December 31, 1945   Primate and Archbishop of Esztergom

19. Radio Address, December 31, 1945

This is the last evening of the year. Today we must all examine our consciences, think about our past mistakes, and remember those good deeds that we have left undone. I ask all Hungarian people to think hard about this past year. Last year we Hungarians were frequently reminded of the sins of the past. Sometimes it seemed that other peoples considered us the dregs of European society, the scum of the earth, an accursed race living among a choir of angels. Other nations have openly reviled us. They have forgotten that, during the war, we often tried to help countries enslaved by the Germans—Belgium, France, Denmark, Holland, and Greece. They have forgotten that we braved the rage of the National Socialists to ensure decent treatment for French and Polish prisoners of war. They have forgotten that the only Polish secondary school that was not closed down during the war was located in Hungary, in Balatonboglár. In fact, there is no end to the sins others lay at our door. Moreover, Hungarians themselves are denouncing their own people. The whole world has acquired a distorted view of Hungary's role in the war. Our country is filled with dissension—dissension which certain political groups are exploiting for their own ends. I have the conscience of a Christian as well as of a Hungarian. My conscience will not allow me to believe that Hungary is truly responsible for all the crimes she is accused of.

☦ 20. Sermon, January 20, 1946

Our nation is suffering great affliction. In a short time, peace will be concluded throughout Europe, and Hungary will face great trials. For now we must learn to take our place among the democratic nations of the world. Our people must turn their eyes to our "pearl of great price," St. Margaret. (The Latin word *margarita* means "pearl.") Her works of penance and atonement are a fountain of living waters that can purify all Hungary, a blessed river that can wash the blood and tears from Hungarian soil. Much of our country has been destroyed. But Christ still lives, rules, and triumphs over all. And we still have the power of faith and of prayer. We pray for the penitential and purified Hungary, the Hungary of atonement. *Pannonia sacra!* O come and redeem the Hungary that is full of sin.

☦ 21. Pastoral Letter for Lent, 1946

Whenever we sin, we must do penance. Sin is always punished by the wrath of God. But we ourselves must voluntarily make reparation, turning to God in prayer, and expressing through good works our compassion for our mocked, scorned, and suffering Lord Jesus Christ. Veronica once wiped the sweat from His brow with her cloth. We too must seek to lend Him comfort by participating in His sorrow. Let us therefore obey the justice of God, and restore order and morality to our sinful land!

Repentance begins when we turn to Jesus Christ, asking forgiveness of our sins. The second step is to suffer along with Him. Third, we must offer ourselves up in service to others. After their defeat at Sedan, the repentant French built a great basilica, Sacré Coeur, on the Hills of Martyrs in Paris; they consecrated the church to the Most Sacred Heart of Jesus. We Hungarians are poor. We cannot afford to build a splendid cathedral to make up for the wrongs we have committed. We can only struggle to rebuild the churches destroyed during the war. Then we can pray in our churches, do penance, and renew our service to others. Every church and chapel left in this land must become a place of penance. So must every family and every Christian soul. Instead of the thorns and nettles of sin, our land must grow the fir trees and myrtles of repentance described by the prophet Isaiah (Is 55:13).

✝ 22. Extract from Article in Uj Ember, February 10, 1946

The priests and faithful of the Hungarian Catholic Church expect journalists to give accurate accounts of Church affairs in the national and foreign press. We demand accuracy not only for the sake of the Church, but for the sake of the nation as a whole. Recently, the reporting of Church affairs has been greatly distorted. We are forced to believe that this distortion was intentional. The primate has no desire to quarrel with the secular authorities of this land. He devotes all his energy to fulfilling his apostolic duties and his duties as a Hungarian citizen. Night and day he labors and struggles to be worthy of his post. But he is the friend of truth, not of falsehood. The press has been conjuring up fearful specters, suggesting that the primate is the enemy of the democracy. This is not the case. As long as the secular powers of this land respect democratic principles and honor the freedom and rights of the Church, there is no reason for any conflict between the government and the primate of Hungary.

✝ 23. Pastoral Letter of October 17, 1945

In the past, we obeyed our Christian duty and spoke out to protect both baptized and unbaptized Jews who were threatened with persecution. Nor can we keep silent now; for once again, people are being persecuted in this country. The new wave of persecution is not a direct result of the war. But ever since the war ended, some people in this country have been inflamed with hatred and a desire for revenge.

We must all come forward and defend loyal Hungarians of German extraction who are being unjustly accused. We do not wish to absolve of war crimes those Germans who lived outside our borders. Nor will we defend war criminals who lived in Hungary itself. We condemned war criminals in the past and we condemn them now. But it is our duty to protest against the indiscriminate persecution of any racial or religious group.

All Hungarians of German extraction are being indiscriminately driven from their homes. Such persecution violates Christian principles and fundamental human rights. Among the accused, there may be some who are actually guilty of some crime. We are not speaking of the guilty. We are speaking of fellow Hungarians who have been condemned without a trial. It has not been proved that these people have committed any crime whatsoever. It is now regarded as a crime against the Hungarian nation for Hungarians of German extraction to speak the German tongue. Let us remember those Hungarians living in Czechoslovakia who were persecuted for speaking their own Hungarian language. When we heard about this persecution, all of us here in Hungary raised a hue and cry against the Czechoslovakian authorities, accusing them of a terrible injustice. Now Hungarians of German extraction are suffering the same persecution in our own country. It is time to remember the lesson we learned in Czechoslovakia.

☩ 24. Sermon, December 23, 1945

Dearly beloved faithful, my brethren,

Peace be with you. How glad I was to respond to your invitation. I came to Csepel, to the diocese of the bishop of Székesfehérvár. Even though this is not my own diocese, I feel quite at home here. During the thousand years of our nation's history, seventy-eight men have held the office of primate. I am the seventy-ninth. The primates converted the people, led them into battle, and enacted laws; they called attention to abuses in the government and in the religious community itself. All these great bishops felt at home on every acre of Hungarian soil. Like every Catholic priest, my primary mission in visiting you here is to act as the ambassador of Christ. I have come to you to preach Christ crucified (I Cor 1:23); and so I will speak to you not of hatred but of love. During the last decade, the boiling lava of hatred has flooded the whole world; and even now it threatens to engulf us all. But we did not come to preach hatred; we came to preach the gospel of love, the message of Christ and His Church. The source and foundation of this love is God himself. For according the Apostle John (I Jn 4:8), God *is* Love. Let us look at ourselves in the mirror of the Our Father. Then we will see that we are all children of the same Father, all brothers, all members of the same Mystical Body of Jesus Christ, the Church (I Cor 6:15). Any one who is full of hate does not belong to Christ; nor can he be a complete human being. Both Jesus and the holy deacon St. Stephen taught us to love our enemies. Only through love can a human being reveal his true worth; only through love can he overcome himself.

☿ 25. Pastoral Letter on Schools, May 4, 1946

You may rest assured of this: Catholic schools and the religious instruction they offer will never conflict with democratic ideals. The Church has granted stipends to many underprivileged children enabling them to get a good education and to improve their lot in society. Many non-Catholics owe their present position and success to education supplied by Catholic institutions. This fact should prove that Catholic schools do not rigidly indoctrinate children. The hallmark of democracy is freedom. But will Hungary be free when Catholics are no longer permitted to have their own schools? Will Hungary be free when all the schools are run by the government, so that minority views can be imposed on the majority of our people? New political parties come into power every day. No doubt each of these parties would like to have control of the educational system in order to ensure the preservation of its own power. But it would violate the principles of freedom and democracy if education were subject to the changing whims of politics. . . .

☿ 26. Statement of May 11, 1946 by Central Administration of Catholic Schools

Catholic secondary schools are coming under increasing attack. Many schools are now undergoing official investigation. In most cases, the investigations have proceeded so swiftly that the newspapers have not even had time to report them. In five cases, the inquiries have already been concluded. The cases involved five schools:

the Benedictine school in Esztergom, and those of the Premonstratensians in Keszthely, the Piarists in Nagykanizsa, the Cistercians in Pécs, and the Piarists in Vác. All the accusations against these schools proved to be completely unfounded. Two other schools are still undergoing investigation—the Piarist school in Budapest and that of the Franciscans in Esztergom. But it is already clear that the charges against these two schools were, at the very least, highly exaggerated. Nevertheless, we instruct all directors of Catholic schools to maintain among their students that discipline and order for which our schools have always been justly famed. For we must not give outsiders any excuse for further interference in our school system.

☩ 27. Address at St. Stephen's Academy, May 21, 1946

The Creator Himself endowed families with the duty and the right to educate their children. No earthly power or social institution, including the government, may deprive parents of the right to educate their children. The ancient right of families to rear children as they choose derives from the biological fact of parenthood itself; it is founded in both natural and divine law. The Church has always defended this basic right; and not even the Church would dare to violate it.

It is indeed an inalienable right of families to educate their own children. However, certain institutions outside the family may assist parents to fulfill their obligation. In a sense, a baptized child does not belong to his parents alone, but also to the Church. For through baptism an infant becomes the child of the Church. From that time on, the Church—which is the Bride of Christ—plays a maternal role in the child's life. Every child has a natural mother; the Church is a supernatural mother. It is the Church's right and duty as a mother to help educate her child. She must protest against any interference with her parental rights.

The proper role of government is to provide for the secular welfare of citizens. Ultimately, the welfare of citizens depends on the educational system of their country. Thus the government has the right and duty to assist parents in the education of their children. Both Church and state are deeply concerned with the problems of education. However, they approach these problems from different vantage points; thus sometimes a conflict may arise between them. Modern societies are characterized by ideological and religious pluralism. In a pluralistic society, secular and religious authorities may often disagree. Nevertheless, they must struggle to maintain an attitude of mutual respect and cooperation.

How then can we best approach the problem of Hungarian education? We in the Church are satisfied with the traditional approach to education in this country. We oppose any attempt to alter the respective educational roles of Church and state. The Christians of Hungary stand united in their ancient traditions.

☿ 28. Address on Interdenominational Cooperation, 1946

When our nation suffered the terrible defeat at Mohács, many Hungarian men, women, and children were carried away into slavery. Those who remained fled the open country; they hid in the swampland or the wild mountain gorges. Most of them had no clothing, shoes, livestock, or bread. They lived on roots and whatever fruits they could find in the forest. In the misery of the present they recalled a happier past and dreamed of a better future. They began to sing a new song that was destined to survive many centuries and many generations, a song that will never cease to echo through this land:

> O Mother, refuge of sinners,
> Hear the anguish of your children!
> Lady, we fold our hands before you,
> Asking you to save our country from affliction.
> We pray for the mercy of Heaven.
> Do not forget your poor Hungarian people.

Some of you may be thinking that songs are all very well and good; but doesn't the devotion to Mary cause a rift in the unity of our nation? I don't believe that is the case. For the mothers of Hungarian families and the Mother of God do not represent two separate principles. All mothers reflect the image of Mary; thus she forms a bond between all our people. In the past, Protestants and Catholics engaged in bloody wars. I bitterly regret the fact. For these two groups of Christians should compete in only one thing: their love for their country. A true Christian, Catholic or Protestant, will see that the devotion to Mary is not a source of division. It is a source of piety and morality in this land.

☿ 29. *Address to Parents Association in Kalocsa, May 30, 1946*

I left Budapest with these charges still ringing in my ears. As soon as I arrived here, I asked the heads of all the Catholic schools to supply me with data concerning the relative distribution of wealth among Catholic students. This is the information I received:

1. In the Jesuit high school, 40 percent of the students come from well-to-do families, including the families of civil servants. Sixty percent come from families in very modest circumstances; they are the children of working-class people, small farmers, and so on.

2. In the Roman Catholic secondary school, the ratio is 35:65.

3. In the Roman Catholic teachers' college, it is 17.5:82.5.

4. During the past five years, the school for kindergarten teachers was attended by 233 students from well-to-do families, and by 366 children from poorer families.

5. In the teachers' college for women and the girls' secondary school there have been 104 students from wealthy, 488 from poorer families.

These statistics reveal the falsity of the charges made against Catholic schools in Kalocsa. In the past, we Catholics defended the basic civil liberties of other Hungarians; during the war we gave shelter to persecuted Jews. Now the rights of our own Catholic children are being threatened. We must all rise to their defense; for our children have the same natural rights as other people do. We believe that non-Catholics will support us in our struggle for our basic civil rights. The Calvinists and Lutherans have already assured me of their support.

☿ 30. *Protest Sent to Premier Nagy, June 1946*

Premier Ferenc Nagy,
Budapest.
Following upon the General Convocation of 12,000 Catholic Parents in Kalocsa,

the league and local members of Catholic parents' organizations held a conference on May 30, 1946. In the course of this conference, they decided to submit to you the following memorandum:

1. We solemnly swear to devote all our strength to the economic and moral development of our nation.

2. We will work to keep our nation from repeating the sins and errors we committed during the war years.

3. We will urge all Hungarians to honor those ethical precepts which were the salvation of Hungary in all the crises of the past.

4. We are deeply concerned with the moral fiber of our nation. Hence we have been greatly troubled by recent attacks made on parochial schools. These attacks have been principally directed against our own Catholic school system. Hungarian law guarantees every Hungarian citizen certain basic rights, including freedom of worship. The Allied Forces guaranteed all citizens of European nations the same fundamental rights. Yet despite these guarantees, parochial schools and religious instruction in Hungary have been subject to increasingly virulent attack.

5. We protest against any attempt to secularize our Catholic schools, or to abolish compulsory religious instruction.

6. The charges recently made against Catholic schools are completely unfounded. The majority of Hungarians are Roman Catholics who love and revere their Church. We ask you, Mr. Premier, to defend our Catholic schools against these misguided attacks.

7. We hope to see Hungary develop peacefully into a democratic nation. Without the Catholic school system, we can hardly achieve this goal.

☦ 31. Memorandum to Minister Keresztúry, 1946

Mr. Minister of Religion and Education:

We the directors and members of the Catholic organization in Budapest, and the Catholic parents of this city protest:

1. We protest against the persistent, unfounded attacks against Catholic schools. We are not attempting to defend the guilty.

The investigations of Catholic schools have now been concluded. All these schools were proved innocent of the charges against them. We had hoped that you, as minister of public worship and education, would present the results of these inquiries to the minister of the interior and to the press. We had hoped that you would defend Catholic schools against false accusations and flagrant violations of their rights. But we were disappointed in our hopes. We are living in a nation where no one seems willing to defend parochial schools against persecutions. We ask you, what will become of education and morality in such a land?

2. The majority of Hungarians are Roman Catholic. Both Catholics and other Hungarian Christians believe that parochial schools should continue to teach the children of this land. For these schools will teach future generations the basic values of religious faith, morality, and respect for their fellow man.

3. We expect compulsory religious instruction to be maintained in public schools. Moreover, the education offered in public schools should not be permitted to conflict with Christian teaching.

4. We demand that schoolchildren in public schools not be exposed to teachers or textbooks expounding anti-Christian views. Moreover, children should not be taught contempt for Hungarian history.

5. Our children have been forced to attend rallies, meetings, and lectures designed to alienate them from their Christian faith. As parents we protest against the compulsory attendance of such functions by our children.

6. We demand that foreign aid offered to Hungarian youth should not be withheld from Catholic youth because of their faith.

7. Catholic citizens pay taxes which help to support the Budapest theater. This theater is now being used to spread political propaganda; it is performing plays which distort the true facts of Hungarian history. This sort of propaganda has no place in our theaters; it should be confined to political conventions.

☿ 32. Letter to Premier Ferenc Nagy, July 21, 1946

Mr. Premier:

The Hungarian bishops feel compelled to raise their voices in protest against another grave violation of the freedom of religion which was guaranteed by the law of this country and by international agreement in the spirit of democracy. In particular we want to protest against those arbitrary measures which have been and are still threatening religious communities and organizations.

With decree No. 7,330/1946, issued by the prime minister, the Hungarian government put all associations under the supervision of the ministry of the interior. Bill 1938/XVIII, which deals with the abolition of abuses said to have been caused by the freedom of associations, authorizes the minister of the interior alone, to the exclusion of other ministers, to execute the above bill. This minister has already taken steps against some associations and dissolved them, in particular certain Catholic ones.

The new regulation cited above contains only one modification applying to the minister in charge of its execution. Otherwise the former bill remains in force. Among all associations whose affairs are regulated according to definite statutes, those are to be dissolved which "continue clandestinely an activity which deviates from the statutes."

The fundamental requirement is, of course, that "any activity which deviates from the statutes" must be thoroughly investigated and incontestable proofs furnished in each case. If the authorities proceed in this manner and severe steps are taken against an association on the basis of full evidence, everyone will understand and fully agree.

The manner in which the dissolution of associations is handled at present, however, gives no assurance whether a given case has been investigated at all and whether there is any evidence to justify so severe a punishment. It is most alarming, moreover, that considerations of an entirely different kind play a role in this matter.

Thus, for instance, our Catholic institutions and schools are publicly denounced from certain quarters and subsequently put on trial for matters hardly worthy of mention. Public opinion in Catholic circles was highly alarmed. We, the bishops of Hungary, would like to give expression to this opinion and to define our position with regard to the case of Catholic associations.

The alarmed state of public opinion, for which we cannot take any responsibility, can only be allayed by thorough and unbiased investigation into the activities of any suspected association and by giving the public full information regarding the case. Should the authorities fail to do this, their proceedings must be regarded as arbitrary measures in contradiction to the ideals of freedom. It has always been a very dangerous and pernicious method for the authorities to take severe measures on the ground of general denunciations and suspicions without searching for concrete facts.

Catholics have always protested against abuses of such a nature. We, too, feel ourselves compelled to raise solemn protests against the practice of taking far-reaching measures against Catholic associations on the bare ground of unproved denunciations. In the face of world opinion, we cannot remain silent.

We wish, above all, to define our position to you, Mr. Premier, and to request you to see to it that the proceedings of the authorities are determined by law and justice.

Accept, Mr. Premier the expression of my deep esteem.

József Mindszenty
Cardinal, Prince-Primate of Hungary
Archbishop of Esztergom
In the name of the Hungarian Bishops

☦ *33. Letter to Premier Nagy, August 1, 1946*

The fighting lasted much longer in other countries and yet it seems that these countries are finding their way back to peace sooner than we. The detestable ideologies of the last decade took much deeper root in Germany and Italy than among our people, yet clashes are not as violent there, nor are subhuman impulses unleashed so that men assault one another as they do in this country.

If it was possible to find a path of reconciliation and appeasement in the homeland of the worst war criminals and in France with its burning hatred of the Germans, it should be possible in this country, too, for Hungarians to enter upon the path of reconciliation and forgiveness.

Perhaps there are certain camps which still cherish their suppressed feelings of hatred; however, leaders and all farsighted men have different views, because of their experience and their knowledge. They know full well that neither a house nor a government can be built upon a crackling and crumbling ground of lava. . . .

May the government, disregarding the opposition of a small minority, enter upon the path of unity and peace. Those err sadly who hold that public order can be maintained only by crowding the jails and concentration camps. Such a view is contrary to the commonsense and natural discipline of our people. Fully aware of our responsibility, we assure the government that public order is much more safely maintained in a general atmosphere of forgiveness than it has been heretofore.

In such an atmosphere the strong revival of anti-semitic tendencies appearing at present could easily be stopped. Prisons should house only murderers, thieves and robbers. Those persons, however, should be released who have now been in jail for months and will never come to trial. Those, too, should be released whose guilt consists only in their social or professional status and not in any offence committed by them personally. The release of the sick, the aged, of doctors and of mothers who have several children at home would have a most beneficial effect.

☦ 34. *Letter to Premier Nagy, August 10, 1946*

In our pastoral letter of May 24, 1945, we the bishops of Hungary expressed our feelings toward the Soviet army of occupation. In that letter, we stated the following: our initial fear that the Russian troops would destroy the Church in Hungary had proved to be unfounded. Indeed, the occupation forces showed the Church many signs of favor. Our Catholic churches remained open; we were still permitted to celebrate Mass in this land. Thus the clergy did not speak out against the occupation forces.

Even the government admits that the occupation troops committed many crimes against Hungarian citizens. Yet for some time the Church continued to overlook these crimes. Now we can do so no longer. We have repeatedly asked the government to intervene and halt these flagrant abuses of Hungarian rights.

We bishops have refrained from making any statements which might offend the occupation forces or interfere with the development of Hungary into a democratic state. To our knowledge, no one has made any concrete charges against us. Recently the government publicly denounced the clergy; but this denunciation does not clearly state wherein we have erred. The government demands that we acknowledge our debt to the occupation forces. Is this really a just demand? Our Church has continually suffered grievous insults even during the time of the provisional government. We have reported our grievances to the prime minister, and through him to the other government ministers. We have pointed out that this country has suspended diplomatic relations with the Holy See. We have mentioned the attacks on our schools. Catholic religious organizations have not been proved guilty of any crime; and yet they have all been dissolved. Catholics have been forbidden to engage in religious processions. Our priests have been thrown into prison. Our repeated demands for official inquiries into these matters have been ignored. We have been forbidden to publish a daily newspaper or to found our own political party. We have repeatedly been attacked in the press, particularly in Red Army publications. The occupation forces are attacking us on all sides. How can we be expected to express our gratitude to them? We ask for the restoration of our civil liberties; and we ask to be allowed to carry on our work in peace. Once our rights have been restored, we are willing to cooperate fully with the present government.

I ask that you communicate our grievances to the proper authorities. The government's denunciation of the Church has been widely publicized. We ask that our reply be broadcast as widely. We Catholics have two weekly newspapers, and we are still permitted to write pastoral letters. But at present we have no other means of making our statements public.

☩ 35. *Address of November 7, 1946*

In most modern nations, the Church enjoys unrestricted freedom. But in some countries, people only talk about freedom; they do not translate their words into deeds. When people lose their religious freedom, they invariably lose all their other rights as well. The first three centuries of the Christian era, the French Revolution, and the Hitler regime all teach us one lesson: those who restrict religious liberty will soon deprive citizens of all their other human rights.

Throughout her history, the Church has preached the Gospel; but she has also defended her legal rights. Above all, she has insisted on maintaining her independence from secular authority. The popes have repeatedly condemned all doctrines which regard the Church as the mere handmaiden of the state. They have denounced Caesaropapism, Gallicanism, Febronianism, Josephinism, state control of the law and courts, and all forms of totalitarian rule. Moreover, the Church has always opposed government interference in matters of faith or Church administration.

In modern times, governments still wage war against the Church; but now they are waging a new kind of war. In the past, Christians were deprived of their churches. Now the churches are being emptied of believers.

Cardinal Faulhaber described National Socialism as a Satanic movement. During its twelve-year reign, the Hitler regime attempted to destroy the Church's influence over the people. Hitler's Germany began its war against the Church by concluding a false peace, a deceptive concordat. Shortly thereafter, the lines of communication were cut between the German bishops and Rome. The outside world knew little of what was really going on inside the Third Reich. The noose around the Church's neck grew tighter. The government attempted to totally secularize German national life. The press, theater and films, radio, exhibits and advertising posters, public lecturers and political parties all disseminated anti-Christian propaganda. Meanwhile, the Church was forbidden to publish its own periodicals or to hold public addresses or assemblies. Private letters were opened and read, telephones were tapped. The authorities did not even respect the privacy of the mail. Renegade religious sects and apostate priests joined forces with political agitators to combat the Church. The faithful were encouraged to leave the Church. The country was saturated with propaganda, with the swaggering and odious vocabulary of tyranny. The words "blood," "race," "folk," "state," "Führer," and "black front" were on everyone's lips. The propagandists denounced Rome, the German bishops, the German clergy, and the Catholic laity. The law no longer afforded any security to the embattled Church and her people.

At first the persecution remained subtle and discreet. Later it became brutal, treacherous, and bloody. The bishops were denounced at political rallies; they were accused of being liars, swindlers, and traitors. The clergy were vilified and physically assaulted on the streets; many priests were deported. The secret police repeatedly raided and searched the archbishop's palace in Munich. Members of the clergy were tried on morals charges. The Church was deprived of its property and hence of all means of subsistence. The government accused bishops and priests of engaging in subversive political activity and of aiding the communist powers. The ministry of justice, the ministry of the interior, the police, the Gestapo, and the National Socialist party attempted to suppress the teaching of Christian doctrine. They interfered with religious services and persecuted priests. They tried to halt charitable activities and to destroy Catholic schools and seminaries. Christian teachers were forced to abandon their faith. Crosses were destroyed and prayer was abolished in the schools. The authorities banned religious instruction and prevented the clergy from writing pastoral letters. Meanwhile, they invented flimsy excuses to reassure the public and concealed the fact that they were trying to destroy the Church altogether. In 1937, Kerrl, the federal minister of church affairs, stated that the government had done nothing to persecute priests, prevent the celebration of Mass, or suppress the teaching of Catholic doctrine. Various organizations were declared to be subversive; their members were accused of being "conspirators in the service of Moscow." The authorities banned all organizations which did not support the government. People who wanted to meet to sing religious music or read Scripture together had to publicly advertize their meeting at least one month before it was to be held.

In 1941, sixty convents and church schools were closed down in the archdiocese of Breslau alone. Sixteen hundred Bavarian nuns were left homeless after their orders had been stripped of their property.

Finally the authorities resorted to open violence. They closed down innumerable churches, sending the priests to Dachau and other concentration camps. On March 15, 1945, 1,943 German and foreign Catholic clergy were found in these camps. The clergy included one archbishop, two bishops, two abbots, four prelates, 482 parish priests, and 342 chaplains.

The German government tried to alienate young people from their Christian faith. The Hitler Youth were forbidden to participate in Corpus Christi Day processions. Later, young people were forced to assemble for gymnastic drills during Sunday church services. Bormann claimed that the clergy were all involved in subversive activity and secretly ordered the Gestapo to destroy the Church. The Church has had many enemies, but none more violent and destructive than the National Socialists.

We must all admire the heroic spirit of the German bishops, priests, and Catholic laity. Many young Germans remained faithful to the Church. The tenacity and faith of the German clergy and laity sustained them in their trials. German Catholics indeed have the right to claim that "the swastika has fallen in Germany; the Cross is still upright."

Let us therefore keep in mind the following things:

1. Many political movements loudly proclaim the word "freedom." But once they have gained power and unfurled their flags over the land, they reveal their true intentions. Those who claimed to be liberators soon dig a grave to bury all our freedoms. Religious persecution has two faces, just like Janus. One of its faces may shine brightly and promise us liberty; but its other face glares at us with the grim gaze of a tyrant.

2. Various laws and charters guarantee the nations of the world the right to

religious freedom. On January 30, 1946, our parliament guaranteed all Hungarian citizens certain inalienable civil and human rights. The new laws expressly stated that the following rights belong to every citizen: personal liberty, freedom of assembly, freedom of worship, the right to vote, the right to work, the right to police protection, the right to receive a living wage, and the right to education. Our parliament declared that "No one can be deprived of these basic rights except by due process of law." A Marxist representative of the provisional government emphasized the following point: "We strongly favor the passage of this bill guaranteeing Hungarian civil rights. We consider this document a solemn and binding declaration of fundamental human liberties."

In this world the Church must suffer and bear her Cross. She will never celebrate her true and perfect Easter on earth. Her true Easter will come at the end of time, when the whole world stands before the judgment seat of God. On that day, the enemies of the Church will all be judged. The Cross will shine over the world and the gates of Heaven will open (Ps 23:7). The suffering Church Militant will become the Church Glorious. Until that great day, let us take comfort in the promise of Scripture, "Be of good cheer: I have overcome the world" (Jn 16:33, for the gates of Hell shall not prevail against the Church.

☩ 36. *Pastoral Letter, October 15, 1945*

Dearly beloved in Christ:

The hand of God rests heavy on us all (1 K:5). If our sufferings could cry out, their cry would reach to Heaven itself. For everyone in this land—every person, family, city, and town—has a grievous cross to bear. But much as we are suffering, others are suffering even more. Their cross is heavier than ours, their wounds more burning.

For over 900 years we have shared our Catholic faith with Hungarians living in the northern part of this diocese. [This diocese is now in Czechoslovakia.] Now we are hearing grim news about our fellow Catholics. We are hearing of unspeakable sufferings, of terrible reprisals. Catholics in the north are suffering the same persecution Jews suffered during the war. Throughout the summer we have received reports of torture and imprisonment. Many Catholics have been sent to concentration camps. These unfortunate people have not been tried in a court of law; they have not been accused of any crime.

Armed police are arresting nuns and priests in all the towns and cities of the north. Many religious are being driven across our newly established borders into exile. For months now, thousands of Hungarian people have spent their nights cowering in their homes, fearing the worst. Families are being driven from their homes; they are not even allowed to take along the most basic necessities. Many of these families include old people and small children.

Even those who may be allowed to remain, because of the outrage of the outside world, fear that they will not have access to a Hungarian priest or a Hungarian school. In this, the twentieth century, they will lose their basic human rights, including the freedom specified in the Atlantic Charter. The aim is to smite the shepherd through the persecution of priests, so the flock will be scattered. (Mt. 26:31). And the flock is the unfortunate Hungarian people.

Dearly beloved people, I am not reporting this painful situation to inflame your hearts with hatred. I wish rather to awaken your compassion and love for your fellow man, for the victims of inhumanity who are not only your brothers but also your brothers in the faith.

When your pastors have put all this before you, pray for your suffering brothers. Pray for the conversion of those sinners who torture their fellow man redeemed by the blood of Christ. Pray for truth and life, for the world of peace and love that is to come.

Esztergom, October 15, 1945

József Mindszenty,
Primate, Archbishop of Esztergom

 # 37. Statement on Deportations, December 21, 1946

We do not wish to interfere in the internal affairs of other nations. However, we have been forced to become involved in the internal affairs of Czechoslovakia. The Czechoslovakian government maintains that Hungarians living in that nation are compelled by law to labor in the service of the state. We bishops and all other Hungarian Catholics appeal to the world for justice. We demand that a nonpartisan international committee be sent to Czechoslovakia to investigate the problems of Hungarians living there. Furthermore we ask that the United Nations intervene to protect the basic rights of Hungarians in Czechoslovakia and to maintain peace. S.O.S.! May God grant that the nations of the world hear our appeal. For all nations are responsible to the Almighty to use their power in the service of good.

Esztergom, December 21, 1946

        In the name of all Hungarian Catholics and the bishops of Hungary,
        József Mindszenty,
        Cardinal and Primate, Archbishop of Esztergom

38. Cable to King George VI and President Truman, February 5, 1947

I respectfully call your attention to the cruel persecution of 650,000 Hungarians who for the past two years have been living inside the borders of Czechoslovakia. These people have not been charged with any crime. Nevertheless, they are being systematically deprived of all their civil and human rights, their property, their native language, and their religious freedom. The United Nations and the Allied Powers solemnly guaranteed all citizens of European nations certain basic and inalienable rights. Since November 16 of this year, in the name of some sort of labor service, Hungarians in Czechoslovakia have been uprooted from their homes. The deportations have included children, old people, expectant mothers, and invalids. Independent merchants, small farmers, and priests have been wrenched from their communities and shipped off in cattle cars. They have been transported 300 or 400 miles from their homes and put to forced labor. The deportation took place in bitter cold weather of only 36°F. Many sick people and infants died along the way. Two years ago, the Church intervened to prevent the deportation of Hungarian Jews. Now I appeal to you to end the deportation of Hungarian Catholics. The persecution taking place in Czechoslovakia violates the eternal laws of God and all fundamental human decency. The sufferings of our people cry out to Heaven for relief. I appeal to you to protest against this infamy.

József Mindszenty,
Cardinal, Primate of Hungary

39. Telegram to Premier Lajos Dinnyés

Near Bátaszék and in other regions of Hungary, Germans are being driven from their homes. Since former members of the German Reich and the German secret police are now so poverty-stricken that they own no property, they will not suffer from its confiscation. But most of the Germans whose land is being seized remained loyal to Hungary during the war. For the sake of justice and for the honor of the Hungarian people, I appeal to you to halt these deportations. I also ask that you permit nonpartisan observers to thoroughly investigate the matter. In making this appeal I am following in the footsteps of St. Stephen, who united concern for religion with concern for his nation. I pray for your aid. If you do not grant it, I will be forced to turn to foreign nations to ask help for my oppressed homeland.

Cardinal Mindszenty, Primate

☩ 40. Declaration on the Deportations from Slovakia, Summer 1947

I have no choice now but to resort to desperate measures. I have appealed to various authorities to halt the deportation of Hungarians and the confiscation of their land; but my appeals accomplished nothing. Now I ask the press to publish one last appeal. I want to alert all Hungarians, the Hungarian government, and the governments of foreign nations to the fact that Hungarians are being deported from their homes. Some people have decided that the best way to ensure peace in a country is to deport all people of foreign extraction and ship them off somewhere else. Thus, thousands of people are being dragged from homes where their ancestors have been living for centuries. They are being punished for speaking their mother tongue and for the fact that their forebears came from a foreign country. Their property is being seized; they themselves are condemned to a life of poverty and homeless wandering. In Czechoslovakia, the government is trying to deport 600,000 Hungarians whose ancestors settled north of the Danube River some 1,000 years ago. The authorities are driving them from land they owned long before the Second World War. The deportation of these hapless Hungarians has been conducted with great secrecy; hence we know little about their sufferings. Nor do we know the anguish of those thousands of Hungarians of German extraction who are being torn from their native Hungary and transported back to Germany. For a time it seemed that these brutal practices had ceased; but now they have begun again. All around us we hear voices loudly proclaiming the blessings of democracy and the dignity of man, the freedom of the individual and the right of all citizens to live and work without fear. But the hearts of those who truly love their fellow men are bleeding in this hour.

My own conscience and the laments of my fellow Hungarians have forced me to speak out. I turn to all the nations of the world and appeal to them for aid.

41. Protest in the Name of the Hungarian Bishops, August 1948

To the Foreign Minister, Budapest:

In August the Hungarian and Czechoslovakian Communist parties agreed to suspend the civil rights of 15,000 Hungarians, drive them from their ancestral homeland in Czechoslovakia, and confiscate their property. The two parties are vainly attempting to lend a semblance of legality to this atrocious persecution.

Before God and our posterity I protest against the persecution of our innocent Hungarian people. The agreement between the Czechoslovakian and Hungarian Communist parties reveals a profound ignorance of the sufferings undergone by the deportees. Moreover, both parties are clearly determined to ignore the dictates of conscience. This persecution of Hungarians does not serve the interests of the Hungarian people but only the interests of Czechoslovakia. The renewed sufferings of our people cry aloud to Heaven. I call those responsible to stand before the judgment seat of God.

József Mindszenty,
Primate

42. Reply to Cabinet Statement

The Primate wishes to convey the following information to the Cabinet:

The primate of Hungary was duty bound to do what he could to help the suffering people of Hungary. He will gladly reveal what he has done to the nation and the world. He asks the government to publish various letters in which he has stated his views concerning the deportation of Hungarians in Czechoslovakia. Then the public and the world will be free to judge the primate's actions and the truth of his claims. These letters show that the primate has no desire to prevent the governments of Hungary and Czechoslovakia from reaching a satisfactory agreement regarding the fate of Hungarians living in Czechoslovakia. On the contrary, the primate urges that these governments should conclude an agreement satisfactory to all parties, including the suffering Hungarians. The publication of the primate's letters would reveal that the accusations made against him are unfounded; his letters do not reflect a chauvinistic point of view. The primate has not been guilty of chauvinism, but of defending human rights. The only chauvinism in this affair has been exhibited by the Czechoslovakian government. This government has deported the Hungarian population of Czechoslovakia, deprived them of all their rights, and confiscated their property. Even the Hungarian government has been moved to protest at this flagrant violation of Hungarian rights.

The primate has also been accused of overstepping the limits of his priestly authority. Let us recall that all the independent political parties of Hungary acknowledge the Church's right to take a stand on public issues.

☦ 43. *Address of April 28, 1946*

In times of crisis, the Church always comes under attack. Many people disapprove of the positions she takes on public issues. But we may rest secure in the knowledge that she will always be true to herself and to her people. We should always keep in mind the following facts: Throughout her 2,000-year history, the Church has always maintained her internal unity. She has always struggled to defend the fundamental dignity of every human being. She has never abandoned the truth and never ceased to minister to her people. She has defended the weak, the oppressed, and women and children.

In the past the Church ministered to those Hungarians who were carried off into bondage by the invading Turks. Two new religious monastic orders came into being—the Trinitarians and the Mercedarians. Both orders labored to free the hapless prisoners of war. Over the span of three hundred years, the Trinitarians paid a total of 5.5 billion francs to buy back one million prisoners from the Turks. Often the monks also paid with their own blood. At the hands of the Turks, 7,115 monks suffered martyrdom. Many monks voluntarily entered into slavery in order to redeem their brothers from a life of misery, imprisonment, and pain.

☦ 44. *Address of June 16, 1946*

St. Ambrose lived in an age of class struggles and party rivalries; but he never served the interests of any one class or party. He himself was descended from an aristocratic family. Yet he often attacked the wealthy people who prided themselves on the pedigrees of their horses and dogs and completely ignored the sufferings of the poor. St. Ambrose reproved the poor as well as the rich. He scolded people who did not have a single stitch of clothing or a single morsel of bread to eat the next day and yet would spend their time lounging about in inns and taverns, keeping an eye out for anything they could beg, borrow, or steal. St. Ambrose was all things to all men; yet he himself belonged to no one and nothing but the truth. During his lifetime, a great war was being waged between Christianity and paganism. But St. Ambrose never wavered in his convictions. He did not try to please the government by becoming a "practical politician."

☿ 45. *Address of October 20, 1946*

Some of us wear our hair cut short, while others prefer to part theirs down the side; some of us eat meat, others are vegetarians. These are matters of personal taste; they affect no one but ourselves. But what if I start raising tobacco in my back garden or my neighbor decides to distill a bit of liquor without bothering to tell the revenue office about it? Now our behavior is no longer "a matter of personal taste"; for it also affects the society around us.

Many "personal matters" are far more important to society than the production of tobacco or alcohol. For example: Is there a God and do we have immortal souls? Is there any relationship between God and the soul? What is our relationship to our fellow men? Or are we no more than a pack of howling wolves? People who separate religion from the rest of life are trying to get rid of religion altogether; for they do not want it to interfere with the way they live. The Church teaches that we must not kill, we must not fornicate, we must not lie or bear false witness. There is a good reason why some people want to silence the voice of the Church. It is written that we know people by their fruits. Societies which regard religion as a personal matter, unrelated to the conduct of public life, will soon be swallowed up in corruption, violence, and sin. I have long been a student of history. I have studied with particular interest those eras when religion was regarded as a purely "personal" matter.

Hitler and his followers regarded religion as a private matter which should be kept in the home. We have seen the results of this attitude: Dachau, Auschwitz, a nation of prisons and gas chambers, ruled by the Gestapo. The precursor of this terrible kingdom was Nietzsche, who proclaimed that "God is dead" and that we must all pass beyond the antiquated concepts of good and evil. What a splendid life they led, these human beings who had dispensed with God! Old, sick, and crippled people were killed by doctors acting under government orders. The Jews were driven into gas chambers. Sixty million soldiers waged war on all fronts, ten million more fell on the battlefield, and twenty million homeless refugees wandered across the face of Europe. The whole world went mad inside this Vale of Tears. Then a tiny revolver changed the world again: Hitler shot himself. For the "private matter" of religion had caused the world to rise up against him. Now all the prophets of his kingdom have disappeared; they no longer tell us that religion should be kept in the home. Hitler's world went bankrupt. But now other people have come to seize his bankrupt estate. All humanity waits with bated breath to see who will take over his kingdom and what they will do with it.

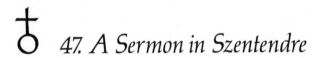

46. Address to the Youth in Budapest

I asked these young people the question, "What is the proper goal of Hungarian youth today?" And I answered them: "Some people want to sweep away all traces of the past. But do not be too hasty in using your nice clean broom! For why should we sweep away the past when we can find some way to use it? Many things in the past are still worth saving. The most beautiful image in our past is the image of our mother. We would never be willing to sweep it away with a broom. Nor would we ever sweep away the image of our teachers, who taught us all we know and whose wisdom and good character showed us the way into the future. And what of the two stone tablets on which the Ten Commandments were written? No broom will ever be able to sweep them away! And we must take care that no one sweeps away our 2,000-year-old mother, the Church, or our 1,000-year-old mother, our Hungarian homeland.

47. A Sermon in Szentendre

Praise to Our Lord Jesus Christ!

My dear faithful of Szentendre!

You belong to one of the largest parish communities in my diocese. I had a deep desire to visit you here. I wanted to bring the Holy Spirit to your young people, so that He could give them the strength to hold fast to their faith and to combat the forces of evil all around them. I also wanted to see you all, both young and old, face to face.

In the venerable language of the Church, I am paying you a canonical visit. I have never before been in Szentendre. His Holiness Pope Pius XII has just made me your new primate. Before coming to visit you, I wanted to know something about the religious history of Szentendre. So I looked over the records of canonical visits former primates made to your town. I was especially interested in the period 1732–1781. The words written on that yellowed parchment will surely interest you as much as they did me, for, after all, Szentendre is your home. You will want to know all you can about your ancestors, your relatives, and the religious life they led in past centuries.

Your ancestors are first mentioned in 1741, when they personally renovated their own church. The church stands in the middle of the cemetery. In the Middle Ages, people built churches inside cemeteries in order to express the unity of all the faithful. As the people entered the church, they could glance around them at the kingdom of all those who had died in the faith; at the same time they could reflect on the eternal joy of Heaven and the suffering souls in Purgatory. Nowadays, for hygienic reasons, churches are no longer built next to cemeteries. But we must never forget the fundamental unity of the church and the graveyard.

Your ancestors willingly labored to build their own church. Now, two hundred years later, I can still vividly picture them drawing up plans and devotedly working to complete their difficult task. Let us all place a reverent palm branch on the graves of your ancestors, as a sign that we still remember them. And then let us strive to model our lives on theirs.

I discovered another interesting fact about how your forefathers lived two hundred years ago. They not only felt close to their dead but they also cared for their sick and dying. During the reign of King Charles III, a canonical visit was made to your town. The records of this visit state that after Mass was celebrated in your church, the people prayed for the sick and dying, calling them all by name. The moment of death is a crucial moment for us all. The state of a soul in the moment of death determines its fate for all eternity. You must always encourage the dying to think about their eternal fate, and make sure that they receive the last rites. Even if someone dies very suddenly, you should still summon the priest to the dead person's side. For sometimes the moment of physical death does not coincide with the moment of actual death, and the priest may still be able to reach the person's soul.

I also discovered in the records that your ancestors were deeply concerned about the sick. The lesson of today's Mass tells us to care for widows and orphans and for all those suffering some need, whether that need is of the body or the soul. We can tell a great deal about a family by observing how well they treat their sick members. In the same way, I judge a religious community by the concern they show for sick members of their flock.

I also learned that the Catholics of Szentendre were zealous in their faith. They loved their church, walked in religious processions, and often went on pilgrimage. Never forget that you are walking in footsteps two hundred years old. Do not neglect to attend Mass on Sundays and feast days. For your ancestors left you more than the land you live on: they also left you a spiritual inheritance. In the past, your people attended early Mass; they walked in processions on Easter and on Corpus Christi Day; they came to midnight matins. They used to come and kneel at the communion rail, waiting to receive the Body of Our Lord. You should not ever give up these sacred practices; you should make them a part of all your lives.

I found out something else about your ancestors. Some of the people living in

Szentendre two hundred years ago were people of very lukewarm faith. Don't worry, I wasn't at all surprised, or offended either. In Hungary we have a saying that "Our fingers are not all the same length." Not all people are equally devoted to their faith. But that is no reason for us to let our faith grow weak. The Holy Spirit declares, "I know of thy doings, and find thee neither cold nor hot; cold or hot, I would that thou wert one or the other. Being what thou art, lukewarm, neither cold nor hot, thou wilt make me vomit thee out of my mouth." (Apocalypse 3:15–16). Many souls are destroyed by their tepid faith, their indifference to spiritual matters. Spiritual torpor causes great harm in the world.

While reading over the records of canonical visits here, I learned that two hundred years ago a Catholic schoolteacher taught your children writing and arithmetic and assisted your priest in giving religious instruction. Thus centuries ago you had your own Catholic school. Nowadays we often hear it said that parochial schools make people narrow and inbred and prevent them from getting along with their fellow citizens. But our ancestors were very wise people. This whole region was filled with parochial schools of various denominations. Children were not allowed to grow up indifferent to their faith. Because the children in each school were of the same faith, there was no dissension among them. Once they had learned to love their faith, they expressed that love in their own lives and preached the Kingdom of God. We who belong to the Church have never hated or harmed those of other faiths. We regard all people as our neighbors, deserving of our love. The only thing we condemn is sin and evil. Your wise ancestors established parochial schools in this region. You too should be faithful to your Catholic schools so that your children may learn about their faith. They will apply the truths of religion to everything they study. You good people are not filled with hatred toward others. Give your children a chance to learn the spirit of love by coming to know the revealed Word of God.

The number of Catholics in this parish has been steadily increasing. In 1781, there were 2,351. In 1941 there were 7,500. I must hope that the worm of sin has not begun to gnaw at the lives of the Catholic families of our nation. Some Hungarian families are suffering from various "modern ailments" like abortion and divorce. Do not let your own families suffer from such ailments. Remember the example of your forefathers, who would not permit anything to undermine the structure of the family.

The modern family is exposed to many temptations. All Catholic young people must struggle to remain pure in body and soul. Also keep this in mind: the life conceived in the womb already constitutes a living individual, a person like ourselves. An unborn child has just as much right to live as a child lying in the cradle or in its mother's arms; it has as much right to live as you or I. It is also sinful to "be careful"—to deliberately attempt to avoid pregnancy—for all rights involve responsibilities. Those who attempt to avoid the responsibility of conceiving a child turn the sanctuary of marriage into a den of iniquity. The marriage partners become companions in sin. Their marriage will never be blessed by God.

My dear Catholic people, we have spent some time thinking about the past. Your ancestors loved their church, their schools, their dead. They honored the sacred institution of the family. These four things are always closely related. The thresholds of the church, the school, the cemetery, and the home all lie side by side. Even today, in the twentieth century, we all pass back and forth over these thresholds.

Faithful Catholics must love all four of them. Your ancestors sleep in the cemetery; but they are still speaking to you, trying to teach you. Do not let theirs be voices crying in the wilderness. Follow the example of your forebears, your parents, and grandparents. If you keep your faith, then two hundred years from now, other people will be standing in this church. A new primate will come to speak comforting words about the past. He will tell the people about us and how we lived.

Above all we must remember one thing: The way we live will determine whether or not we receive the gift of eternal joy in Heaven. I have been speaking about past centuries. One day the passage of time will sweep us all away. Each one of you here will enter the kingdom of the dead. Both you and I will take leave of this life and be carried out to the cemetery. For this earth is nothing but a huge waiting room. We human beings come and go; none of us can remain here forever. But our souls live forever. We must save our immortal souls from this transitory world; we must rescue them by keeping our faith, leading good lives, and turning to the sacraments for strength.

On the day your children are confirmed, try to renew the faith you had at your own confirmation; ask again for the grace you received then. When you were confirmed, you promised to be the faithful soldiers of the Holy Spirit. On the day you renew your faith, remember that you must continue in His service until the coffin lid closes above you and you enter into God's presence to see Him face to face. Amen.

☩ 48. A Sermon in Szentgotthárd

Once great castles stood guard over the Hungarian marches. This region was defended by Némétújvár, Szalónak, Körmend, and Csáktornya. These castles are now a thing of the past. Only fables tell us of their former glory; only the ivy that entwines the ruined stones still bears witness to the great events that took place beside them long ago. But modern Hungarians need their fortresses too. And thank God, our fortresses are still standing. They are our parish churches, our Catholic schools, our family homes, and our consecrated churchyards.

What his heart is to a man, the church is to a town. The church is "the house of God and the gate of Heaven" (Gn 28:17). The church is a place where we offer the Holy Sacrifice of the Mass. It is the fortress of souls and the visible expression of a community's faith. Our Mother the Church dedicates all new churches with special prayers and with the Body and Blood of Christ. Over the centuries, our churches were consecrated over and over by many pious devotions, by the sacraments of Baptism, Penance, and the Eucharist, and by the living communion of all our ancestors. Whenever we enter a church, God's presence reaches out to touch us. The worn stones under our feet should remind us of the prayerful spirit of our forefathers.

The twin sister of the Catholic parish church is the Catholic school. At the very foot of the altar, our Mother the Church began to rock the cradle of the Catholic school. For when our holy King Stephen ordered a church to be built for every ten villages in Hungary, he also commanded the building of schools.

Long ago, no one in Hungary had even thought of building separate schools. In those days, the Church taught the people as they stood or knelt beside the altar, the chancel, and the baptismal font. She taught them religion, reading, writing, arithmetic, agriculture, and various trades. The numbers of the faithful grew, and finally the people were taught in buildings separate from the churches. But the schools and the churches never stood far apart. The schools kept the sacred inheritance of their forefathers, the Gospel, and the two stone tablets on which the Commandments were written. Like our churches, our schools must always minister to the souls of the faithful. If they do not, they fall into decay and become the workshops of evil. History shows us that when schools grow away from the Church, they grow closer to the prisons. They become houses of sin and damnation. The school must be the house of virtue and knowledge. When schools cease to teach virtue, then we all need protection from their knowledge!

The third fortress in our midst is the sanctuary of the family. In our homes, we raise a new generation to take the place of our own. All fathers reflect the divine prototype of our Father in Heaven; all mothers are made in the image of the Most Blessed Virgin Mary; and all children resemble the Child Jesus. Each time a faithful Catholic looks at the faces of his family, he should see in them the blessed faces of their prototypes in Heaven. Each time a Catholic family sits down to pray together, they are imitating the holiest of all families. All fathers and mothers are holy, for they can all see their own image in the mirror made in Nazareth. Their child gives their life its meaning; he is the apple of his parents' eye and the glory of our nation.

The threshold of the family home should lead straight into the threshold of the church and the Catholic school; for only then will the family serve as a strong fortress. These three institutions form a protective circle all around us. We must all live and struggle inside this charmed circle, until the day we leave to enter into the churchyard.

The consecrated churchyard is our place of rest. It is the place where all the generations of God's people must lie until the trumpets of the Last Judgment sound over the earth. On that day our true Easter will begin, for the Resurrection will become reality for us all.

The churchyards may be filled with the marble monuments of world-famous men and with crosses made of oak and precious woods. But more important, above the dust of our beloved dead rise the three great sanctuaries of our faith: the cemetery, the chancel of the church, the rostrum of the school. From the world of the dead we hear the voices of generations of Catholic families calling out to us, the living: "You who are our descendants, do not forget the message of earlier generations: Hold fast your fortresses!"

Whatever new plague may come to destroy the world, remember that the church, the Catholic school, and the family will always be sacred. Guard your fortresses bravely!

☿ 49. Extracts from the Note of General Weems to General Sviridov, March 5, 1947*

The government of the United States . . . is impelled at this time to express its feeling of concern at the political crisis which has now been precipitated in Hungary. The pattern of recent political developments in Hungary appears to threaten the right of the people to live under a government of their own free choosing, for it involves foreign interference in the domestic affairs of Hungary in support of repeated aggressive attempts by Hungarian minority elements to coerce the popularly elected majority.

Unable to achieve their political ends through normal constitutional processes, the Hungarian Communists together with other members of the leftist bloc have endeavored to implicate a number of representatives of the majority Smallholders party in a recently revealed plot against the Republic and, by demanding the withdrawal of parliamentary immunity from Smallholders deputies, to weaken the parliamentary position to which that party was duly elected by the Hungarian people. Simultaneously police and administrative authorities responsive to the dictates of these minority elements have utilized their powers of investigation of the conspiracy, not toward the expeditious judicial resolution of a threat against the state, but to conduct a general campaign against their political opponents.

The Soviet High Command in Hungary has now, by direct intervention, brought the situation to a crisis. Following the refusal of the Smallholders party to abrogate, in connection with the investigation of the conspiracy, the parliamentary immunity of Deputy Béla Kovács, until recently Secretary General of the Smallholders party, Soviet occupation forces have arrested Mr. Kovács. . . . On the basis of its present information the United States government believes these grounds and the charges are unwarranted.

These developments, in the opinion of the United States government, constitute an unjustified interference in Hungarian internal affairs. . . .

* *Foreign Relations*, 1947, vol. IV, pp. 273–5.

☿ 50. General Sviridov's Reply to General Weems, March 9, 1947*

General:

In reply to your letter of March 5, 1947, in which you express the views of your government regarding recent political events in Hungary, I have the honor to inform you of the following facts:

The democratic government of Hungary was threatened by conspiracies which attempted to overthrow the republic and its constitution. These conspiracies were not led by the parties of the left bloc. The parties of the left bloc are devoted to the constitution of Hungary. They did not attempt to deprive the independent Smallholders party of their legal rights or to impose a minority dictatorship on the land.

The Smallholders party has admitted the existence of a conspiracy directed against the constitution and the new democratic state of Hungary. The party and its leader, Ferenc Nagy, have repeatedly discussed this matter in the press. Several leaders of the independent Smallholders party are known to have taken part in the conspiracy. Neither the police nor the left bloc are responsible for the participation of the Smallholders party in subversive activities. The independent Smallholders party has publicly acknowledged the guilt of certain of its members and has voluntarily agreed to the suspension of their parliamentary immunity and to their trial by the proper authorities. Thus your statement that the minority parties attempted to force leaders of the independent Smallholders party into participation in a conspiracy, is totally unfounded.

You must be aware that the investigation of the conspiracy has now been concluded. The independent, democratic court of the Republic of Hungary is now conducting legal proceedings against the conspirators. Thus I must reject your proposal that the Soviet authorities and the government of the United States undertake a joint investigation of these matters. Such an investigation would constitute an unjustified intervention in the internal affairs of Hungary and a violation of the legal rights of the Hungarian people's court.

I can only regard your intervention in the case of Béla Kovács as an attempt to interfere with the rights of the Soviet army of occupation. The Soviet authorities are empowered to protect Soviet military forces in Hungary. Therefore, I cannot permit the intervention of the government of the United States.

Béla Kovács was arrested for a crime committed against the Soviet army of occupation. Therefore his arrest does not constitute an unjustified intervention by Soviet authorities in the internal affairs of Hungary.

With my sincere compliments,

V. P. Sviridov,
Lieutenant General

* *Foreign Relations*, 1947, vol. IV, p. 281.

☿ 51. The American Note of March 17, 1947

The United States government cannot, in the light of all the information available, agree with the interpretation of Hungarian political developments contained in your communication under acknowledgment. It seems clear to the United States government that minority groups under the leadership of the Hungarian Communist party are attempting to seize power through resort to extra-constitutional tactics. In the opinion of the United States this clearly threatens the continuance of democracy in Hungary. In such a situation, the United States government considers that the powers signatory to the agreement concluded at Yalta in regard to liberated Europe are obligated to undertake concerted action to investigate political conditions in Hungary. The need for such consultation and investigation becomes all the more imperative because of the fact that there is disagreement between the Soviet and the United States governments on a matter of so basic importance to Hungary. In my government's view it cannot be contended that such an investigation would, as you suggest, improperly impair the legal rights of the Hungarian courts nor that my government's concern with regard to the case of Béla Kovács constitutes an infringement of the right of the Soviet occupation authorities to take reasonable measures for the maintenance of the security of the occupation forces.

✝ 52. Address in Győr, Spring 1947

Cruel hands are reaching out to seize hold of our children. They are not the hands of Jesus or the arms of the Church; they are claws belonging to people who have nothing but evil to teach our children. . . . A large part of Hungarian inheritance has been taken from us. We Hungarians know that we will leave less land and fewer possessions to our children than our parents left to us. But it is our sacred duty to guard for all future generations the spiritual inheritance of our Hungarian past. . . . Those who wish to discard our Hungarian traditions do not have our children's best interests at heart. Full of evil intentions, they are slinking around our cradles and our school desks. The hand which closes the door to religious instruction flings wide the gates of the prisons and penitentiaries. Hungary today is filled with people who promise religious freedom and then offer us institutions which teach nothing but atheism. They are the worst kind of hypocrites.

☦ 53. *Pastoral Letter, April 12, 1947*

We are deeply troubled by the government's attempts to halt compulsory religious instruction in the schools. Our nation faces many pressing problems. Yet the government has chosen this moment to bring up the relatively incidental matter of religious education. We fear that this government is waging a secret war against the Catholic Church. Everywhere we hear the slogan, "First democracy, then socialism!" We believe that the government is following a systematic plan to abolish the Christian religion in Hungary. First it will eliminate religion from the curriculum altogether; and finally it will introduce courses teaching a materialistic ideology!

We have been called to our office by God Himself; hence it is our duty to speak out on this matter. We must all be prepared for further attacks upon Christian education in Hungary; and we must refuse to be driven into forsaking our faith.

The government demands that compulsory religious instruction be abolished in our schools. We are told that religious instruction deprives our children of their freedom of choice. But religion is the source of all freedom. Are we to defend freedom against the source of freedom? A year ago we wrote a pastoral letter concerning Catholic education. In that letter we pointed out that compulsory religious instruction offers no more threat to freedom than compulsory instruction in history, geography, natural history, civics, or ethics. Indeed, religious instruction teaches us freedom of choice. It teaches us that every individual has a free will and may choose the truths of religion. Often students avail themselves of this freedom and reject the Christian faith.

Catholic parents will not be swayed by the argument that compulsory religious instruction deprives children of their freedom of choice. When parents take their children to be baptized, they voluntarily accept the responsibility to give them a proper religious education. Once they have accepted this obligation, they cannot refuse to fulfill it. What would happen if everyone suddenly decided that they wanted to be free to choose, and stopped doing all the things they were supposed to do? Our entire nation would be destroyed.

The teachings of the Church are not threatening our freedom of choice. Why doesn't the government concern itself with a far more serious threat—the violence and force terrorizing the people of this land? Many Catholics have complained to us that they have been forced to join a political party whose views they do not support. They have been threatened with political persecution, with blacklisting, and with the loss of their jobs. The young people of this land have never considered religious education a limitation of their rights. The true threat to our freedom is not religious instruction, but political tyranny.

We confront another threat to our freedom. The government has assumed complete control of the publication of textbooks to be used in our schools. Thus the ruling political party in this land will now have the power to indoctrinate our youth.

Those opposed to compulsory religious instruction tell us that we must imitate the Western nations. No doubt foreign nations have many valuable things to offer us. But not everything that comes from abroad is automatically superior to what we have at home. Our Hungarian people have been educated in parochial schools, and they did not turn out so badly. Where foreign nations are concerned, let us always remember the words of the Apostle Paul: "Scrutinize it all carefully, retaining only what is good, and rejecting all that has a look of evil about it" (1 Thessalonians 5:21). We have already suffered enough from our blind adulation of foreign lands. Let us rely on our own resources for a change! Besides, even many progressive Western nations support schools offering compulsory religious instruction. [At this point I named thirteen countries permitting compulsory religious instruction in the schools. I also mentioned that in various countries, educators were founding institutions designed to guarantee the religious and moral education of the young.]

Some schools have never offered religious instruction. No doubt it would be a fine idea to introduce optional religious instruction in such schools. However, in schools which have always offered compulsory religious instruction, it would be very harmful to make religion an optional class. For the students would feel that they no longer needed to take religion seriously. The teachers and school officials would probably allow their religion courses to deteriorate. On report cards, religion would be treated as a matter of secondary importance.

Some people believe that the abolition of compulsory religious instruction is essential to the progress of our nation. No doubt these people would eventually demand that religious training be eliminated from our schools altogether. We have just mentioned a number of countries where compulsory religious education still obtains. For example, in England—definitely a "progressive" country—educators are attempting to expand religious instruction rather than suppress it. Besides, what does "progress" really mean? Would it be progress if our young people no longer knew anything about the Ten Commandments or had never read the most significant book ever written, the Bible? Would it be progress if our children knew nothing about the most important figure in history, Jesus Christ? They would see religious paintings in world-famous museums; but they would not know what the pictures meant. They would not have a chance to hear some of the most famous stories in the world, like the tales of the Prodigal Son and the Good Samaritan.

The most important faculty our young people possess is their sense of right and wrong. But conscience is something that must be developed. In order to be moral people, we must first be taught the rudiments of ethics. What will happen to our children if they are never exposed to biblical precepts, and never permitted to take part in the feast days of the Church? They will no longer receive answers to the greatest questions of life, questions like: Where did the world come from? Where did people come from? What is the purpose of our lives? If our young people are not taught religion in the schools, they will not grow up to be ethically responsible human beings—for religion and morality go hand in hand. A man without religion is rarely an ethical man.

We would like to offer a single example of the beneficent influence of moral teachings on the nature of man. During the war, an obviously distraught enemy soldier forced his way into a Hungarian home. He shoved the frightened family out of the way, threw himself down on a bed, loosened his coat, and promptly fell asleep. A medal consecrated to the Blessed Virgin shone out from beneath his open coat. Seeing the medal, the family returned to their work greatly reassured, saying "We needn't be afraid. He seems to be a Christian man. Let's just let him sleep." Of course, we are not saying that all non-Christians are immoral people. The sense of right and wrong can never be completely rooted out of human nature. No matter how depraved their environment may be, some people are instinctively attracted to goodness. They are gifted with a sense of right and wrong much as some people are gifted with artistic talent. But unless we receive proper moral training, most of us are unable to withstand the influence of an evil environment. Those who carried out the barbarous deeds of the Hitler regime first had to renounce their faith. Atheisim always goes hand in hand with evil. It promotes the decay of the family and the rise of juvenile delinquency, including juvenile prostitution. In view of these facts, how can we venture to abolish compulsory religious instruction in our schools?

The children who most readily lose their faith are those who receive little religious education in the home. There is only one hope for these children: They must receive their religious instruction in school. Moreover, the poorest children in our society will suffer most from the loss of religious instruction. For the poor have the deepest need of faith. Hungarian social structures are falling into ruin. We do not need *less* religious instruction, but *more*.

The same interparty conference which debated the question of compulsory religious instruction also devised a three-year plan for our economy. The delegates at the conference discussed our material resources and our industrial productivity; they estimated our future national income and expenditures. But they neglected to discuss one thing: the ethical resources of our nation. We fear that any plan for the economic renovation of our land is bound to fail unless our people retain their sense of duty. If Hungarians cease to be God-fearing, hard-working people who respect the law and are willing to work together toward a common goal, how can they possibly contribute to the rebuilding of this nation? Dishonest, treacherous, self-seeking people who yield to all their urges and brutally defend the interests of their own party will never save our country from economic ruin.

We of the Church want to preserve our nation; we want to ensure its economic and moral advancement. Therefore we support compulsory religious instruction in the schools. We support religious education for the same reason that a physician supports the practice of inoculating people against smallpox: we do not wish to see the plague of moral infection spread through this land. The only way to prevent its spread is to strengthen people with the knowledge of God and Christ and with the hope of eternal life.

Sometimes people point out that, despite the religious education of our people, crime and immorality are on the increase. This is not a convincing argument for abolishing religious education. After all, despite all the efforts of physicians, people continue to get sick and sometimes there are even epidemics. But the fact that they cannot completely abolish disease does not make physicians give up; they simply try all the harder to fortify the weak bodies of their fellow men. In a corrupt society, we must improve the religious education of souls to strengthen their resistance against the temptations of the world.

We are convinced that Catholic parents would not voluntarily withdraw their children from religious instruction. The parents who have spoken with us on this matter have been unanimous in their support of compulsory religious instruction.

You all want your children to learn the Ten Commandments, including the commandment to honor their fathers and mothers. But what will happen if compulsory religious instruction is abolished in our schools? We fear that the poor classes of Catholics may be pressured into withdrawing their children from the optional classes in religion. Yet it is precisely the poor who have the deepest need of religion, which teaches the basic dignity of all human beings. Religion is a source of comfort to the poor. It would be tragic indeed if poor people were forced to pay for their bread with the faith of their children.

Dear Catholic people, the Church is often accused of promising her children happiness only in the next life. "Whereas we," the materialists say, "want to make people happy on this earth. But in order to make them happy, we have to distract their attention from the next world and show them that only the goods of this world really matter. Religion teaches them to raise their eyes to Heaven. We must do away with religion so that people can enjoy this life." These are the people who are opposed to religious instruction. But in reality, the happiest people are not those who revel in sensual pleasures. For the goods of this world are transitory and unstable; they always disappoint us in the end. When our passions and instincts are freed from the control of religion, they cause great misery to everyone. We Catholics are perfectly free to enjoy the pleasures of life. But if these pleasures disappoint us, we still have the hope of eternal joy in Heaven. Thus we need never lose our sense of peace. Unbelievers can look for happiness only in this world; when this world disappoints them, they have nowhere else to turn. They are happy neither in this world nor the next. We Christians love best those signs which are eternal; but the Lord promises us that He will give us the goods of this world as well (Mt 6:33). We want our children to be happy in this world and in the next. Why then should we deprive them of their eternal happiness by abolishing religious instruction in our schools?

☿ 54. *Program of the Government Coalition, July 30, 1947*

The parties of the Hungarian Independence Front swear to uphold freedom of religion in this land and to safeguard the right of the Hungarian people to practice their Christian faith.

The party pledges to defend the independence of the Hungarian nation.

The party will not tolerate foreign intervention in the internal affairs of Hungary.

It upholds the right of private enterprise and the right to own private property gained by honest labor.

It will defend the rights of the small property holder.

It will guarantee the right of the Hungarian people to vote as they choose.

☉ *55. Bishops' Statement of July 25, 1947*

After careful consideration of the present political situation in Hungary, we the Catholic bishops regretfully declare that we cannot support any particular party in the coming elections. Voting regulations have been altered so that many Hungarians have been disfranchised. However, we ask all faithful Catholics who have retained the right to vote to dutifully exercise that right. The Hungarian bishops pray God to help the Hungarian people in this crucial hour.

☉ *56. Bishops' Letter to the Premier, August 14, 1947*

The bishops of Hungary do not wish to take part in political or party conflicts, or to express any opinion in political matters. However, we whom God has appointed to guard the morality and laws of this nation must protest against the fact that many Hungarian citizens have been disfranchised.

In a democratic society, all citizens possess certain basic rights. Moreover, the Hungarian constitution guarantees Hungarian citizens their civil rights. These rights are now being violated. Citizens are being falsely accused of crimes and deprived of their right to vote. The Hungarian government must halt these violations of the law and ensure the complete legality of the coming national elections. With my sincere compliments.

Esztergom, August 14, 1947

> In the name of the Bishops of Hungary
> József Mindszenty

☩ 57. Brief Survey of Hungarian History

We Hungarians are of Finno-Ugrian extraction. Our ancestors came from the Caucasus and the land around the Don and Kuban rivers. Around the year 890, they entered our present homeland. In a few short years they managed to conquer the whole Carpathian basin. They pressed on toward the west and finally reached the banks of the Enns. For half a century they lived side by side with Christian races; but they did not give up their own customs and beliefs. Now and then Christian missionaries entered their land, but the missionaries made very few converts.

Our forefathers were a warlike people. They attacked towns and villages, settlements and cloisters. Their raids led them deeper and deeper into Western Europe. In one respect, their attempt to invade the West proved to be a blessing in disguise. On August 10, 955, the Hungarian army suffered a terrible defeat near the banks of the Lech River. But as a result of this defeat, the Hungarian people received the Christian faith. The first Hungarian to be baptized was Prince Géza (970–997). Of course, he became a Christian for rather political reasons. But he did summon priests into Hungary. Prince Géza remained a pagan at heart. So did his warlike wife, who was as ready as he to turn their conversion to political ends. But the son of these two pagans was King Stephen—the father, apostle, and saint of our people. Under his leadership, the Hungarian nation became a part of the culture of Western Europe. King Stephen also led his people to drink the living waters of the Christian faith. He lived in the spirit of Cluny and brought this spirit into the land of Hungary.

The Christian faith thrived in Hungary. In the year 1000, King Stephen (997–1038) received from Pope Silvester the Crown of Stephen which later became so famous in our land. Stephen also received the right to found bishoprics and cloisters. Churches and basilicas were built all over the country, and priests and religious orders began to establish schools. On August 15, 1038, shortly before his death King Stephen dedicated our land and people to the Mother of Our Lord, Hungary's "Great Lady." Nine hundred years before the shrine was established at Fatima, Hungary was consecrated to the Mother of God. Ours was the first country in the world to pledge itself to the Virgin. Since that time Hungary has been officially known as "Mary's land."

In the year 1046, dark times once more descended on our land. The people sought to throw off their Christian faith. The country was torn apart by civil war. Then Divine Providence appointed the saintly Ladislaus to guide our land. Under his rule, law, virtue, and the Church began to thrive once more. The people practiced pious devotions, striving to imitate the holy confessors and martyrs of their faith: they reverenced the Blessed Virgin and Our Lord and Saviour. Ladislas was an able general, a wise lawgiver, and a far-seeing ruler.

After Ladislas, our country was ruled by its first royal dynasty, the house of Árpád. Thirteen members of the house of Árpád were pronounced blessed or canonized as saints. I will mention only Stephen, Emmerich, Elizabeth, and Margaret. St. Margaret played a major role in our nation during the period of Tartar rule. In the year 1241, Hungary was conquered by the Tartars. The faith of our people had weakened; perhaps that is why they were defeated. The battle of Muhi was the first great military defeat of the Hungarian nation. As their end drew near our people rioted and laughed; they were filled with worldliness and depravity. During Lent, they did not meditate on the bitter sufferings of Christ. By the end of Lent, 50,000 Hungarians were standing at the River Sajó, face to face with 100,000 Tartars.

The Eastern barbarians walked into Europe over mountains of Hungarian dead. The battlefield became our cemetery; our kingdom became the prey of the Tartar hordes.

Seeing the desperate plight of their country, the royal family offered their daughter to God as an act of atonement. Margaret willingly complied with her parents' wishes and entered a Dominican convent. In three years' time she had completely forgotten her royal blood. She walked the Way of the Cross with her Savior, serving in the kitchen, tending the sick, however contagious their diseases, fasting and praying the whole night through. I believe that her life brought God's blessing to the entire land of Hungary. After a single year of oppression, the Tartars withdrew from our land. Their Great Khan had died. Thus the Lord had ordained both life and death in our land, granting Hungary the opportunity to redeem its past sins. Once again order, law, and peace ruled our nation. When King Béla IV lay dying in his palace close by his daughter's convent, his kingdom was secure. Hungary was more respected and powerful than ever before. For the life of St. Margaret had won the favor of Heaven itself.

After the Árpád dynasty, our land was ruled by the house of Anjou. Hungary became a leading power in Europe during the reigns of Charles Robert (1308–1342) and Louis the Great (1342–1382). Our nation retained its power under Sigismund of Luxemburg. Sigismund's general was János Hunyadi, who later became regent of Hungary. Pope Calixtus III called Hunyadi the "Warrior of Christ." This great general won decisive victories against the invading Turks. Bonfini wrote this about Hunyadi: "If Hunyadi had not been born in those dark times, then Hungary, Austria, Germany, and all Christendom would have been destroyed."

Hungary continued to flourish during the glorious reign of Matthias Corvinus (1452–1490). But she lost her power under the Jagiellos (1490–1526). In 1526 the Turks won the battle of Mohács. Our capital, Buda, fell to the invaders in 1541. For the next 150 years, large areas of western and northern Hungary, as well as the Hungarian lowlands, remained in the hands of the Turks.

Whenever I traveled from Esztergom to Budapest, I used to pass the fortress of Visegrád. I always thought painfully about those days when five European rulers met here with the king of Hungary to discuss the future of Europe.

I think I understand why Hungary sometimes suffered such bitter defeats. In the beginning, our country was a blooming garden, tended and protected by the Most Blessed Virgin. But whenever Pannonia forsook the protection of Our Lady, an abyss opened wide to swallow us, and the battlefield became our common grave.

I believe that modern times confirm my thesis. Whenever Hungarians have been unfaithful to Mary and forgotten the lessons of battlefields like Mohács, our nation has been defeated. Hungary was finally freed from Turkish rule by men devoted to Mary. Most of the army officers who drove the invaders from our land were members of the Marian Congregation. On September 2, 1686, the war trumpets sounded beneath the walls of Buda. Soldiers devoted to Mary stormed the walls, calling out to Hungary's Great Lady for aid. Immediately after their victory, the Hungarian soldiers raised the flag of Mary over the fortress. It was then that Count Esterházy composed his wonderful prayer beginning with the words, "Remember us to God, Glorious Mother, Hungary's Great Lady."

I was thinking about Hungary and Our Lady on the day when I spoke these words to our Hungarian youth: "Ten days ago I was standing, deeply moved, in the Franciscan chapel at Szécsény. In the year 1705 Rákóczi, who was devoted to Mary, used to come to this chapel every day to attend Mass and pray the rosary. Accompanied by his pages, he prayed to Hungary's Great Lady, asking her to protect this land. Remember his devotion to Mary and imitate his example."

After the 1848–1849 war of liberation, it was another devotee of Mary, Ferenc Deák, who brought peace to our land, reuniting Hungary with the Hapsburg dynasty. Deák refused to participate in a conspiracy against the dynasty. As he put it, "Why should we take poison when there is a far more effective remedy at hand?" His "remedy," his unfailing counselor and friend, was his own conscience. His conscience had been formed by our Great Lady herself. To the end of his days he wore the scapular. He commended our land and people to the care of the Blessed Virgin, and before sessions of parliament he often prayed the rosary.

In recent times, anticlerical and liberal ideas have sown the seeds of atheism in our land. The morals of our people have decayed. Hungarians have lost respect for the sacrament of marriage. Our whole nation is diseased. Yet the grace and prayers of the Virgin have enabled our country to survive its many afflictions.

During the twentieth century, the dreadful night of world war has twice descended on Hungary. The peace treaties of Trianon and Paris left a shattered nation in their wake. The war dealt Hungary many cruel blows. The nations at the Paris Peace Conference were indifferent to conditions in Hungary and refused to acknowledge any of her claims. Even the great powers recognized the injustice of the Treaty of Trianon; but they made no attempt to revise it. Instead, the new treaty signed on February 10, 1947, robbed Hungary of even more land. It demanded that she pay war debts at devastating cost to her own economy.

Before the 1920 Treaty of Trianon, Hungary comprised about 109,000 square miles of land. When the treaty was signed, only 35,000 square miles remained. The original population had been 18,264,533; afterwards, it was only 7,980,143. Beneš and Masaryk showed fraudulent maps and statistics to the other delegates at the conference. Thus the great powers believed Hungary to be a weak country composed of many rival nationalities; they proceeded to hack it to pieces. The British prime minister, Lloyd George, once confessed that the victorious Allies were prejudiced in favor of those nations that fought on their side, and hence appropriated Danzig, the Corridor, and certain regions of Hungary. These seizures of land led to many subsequent injustices. The prime minister went on to say that supposedly accurate statistics had led the Allied powers to seize land from Hungary and assign it to the new state of Czechoslovakia.

Hungary had for centuries been a united nation whose people shared a common geography, history, and economy. According to the 1910 census, 54.5 percent of the population were Hungarians, and 64.7 percent spoke the Hungarian language. The peace treaty of Trianon carved up the country on the grounds that its people belonged to several nationalities. President Wilson had proclaimed the right of self-determination; but this principle was completely ignored when the Allies lopped off two-thirds of Hungary. No one bothered to consult the people about their wishes. No less than 10,283,390 inhabitants were torn from their native soil. Of these 10 million people, 30.2 percent were Hungarians, only 27.4 percent were Rumanians, 16 percent Slovaks, and 4.1 percent Serbs. A united country had been cut into pieces. What were the consequences? The people of Rumania had all been of the same extraction, as were those of Serbia. When they acquired Hungarian land and people, Rumania and Serbia became countries composed of several nationalities—precisely what the Allies had been trying to avoid! A third nation was also created: The new country of Czechoslovakia also contained peoples of various nationalities.

The Paris Peace Conference did nothing to revise the unjust terms of the Treaty of Trianon. On the contrary, the new treaty stole even more of Hungary's land, apportioning the right bank of the Danube to Czechoslovakia. The Treaty of Paris placed 3.5 million Hungarians under foreign rule. It did nothing to ensure that the rights of this minority would be observed in their new lands. The treaty also called for the payment of huge reparations which our poverty-stricken nation could not possibly pay. Under the pretext that they were administering the payment of these reparations, the Russians destroyed almost completely the Hungarian economy.

Moreover, the new treaty did nothing to alter the agreements made at Yalta and Potsdam, which left Hungary the helpless prey of the forces of bolshevism. This was done to Hungary in spite of the often cited second article of the Atlantic Charter, in which the United States and the United Kingdom declared: "They desire to see no territorial changes that do not accord with the freely expressed wishes of the peoples concerned."

On February 10, 1947, the peace treaty was signed. At the time we held a worship hour in St. Stephen's Cathedral in Budapest. I concluded our prayers with the plea: "It is Thy divine decree that human arrangements are transitory. Since this is so, from this nadir of our destiny we cry out in humble and continual prayer to Thee, our just God, and to Hungary's Great Lady, the mirror of righteousness."

The Soviet Union was responsible for administering the payment of the enormous sums Hungary owed under the terms of the Paris treaty. Thus the Soviet government had complete control of the Hungarian economy. The first Hungarians hoped that the Red Army would leave our country as soon as Hungary regained its national sovereignty. The Treaty of Paris stipulated that all occupation troops were to leave Hungary within ninety days after the treaty came into effect. But an additional clause permitted the Soviet Union to station sufficient troops in Hungary to maintain communications between the Soviet army and the Soviet occupation forces in Austria. Thus the original Soviet divisions remained, disregarding international agreements limiting the number of troops in occupied countries. The Soviet supreme command also ignored international regulations restricting its legal authority. The supreme commander of the Red Army did not hesitate to intervene in the internal affairs of our nation. He and his forces were the real power behind the throne of the Hungarian Communist party. Without the support of the Soviet Army of occupation, the Communists would never have gained control of our government.

☦ 58. *Announcement of the Marian Year, August 14, 1947*

Throughout our history, we Hungarians have felt a close bond with the Virgin Mother of God. . . . All Hungarians have felt that Hungary was Mary's Kingdom. Even the Protestant rulers of Transylvania had the image of Mary stamped on all their coins. . . . It was St. Stephen who first dedicated our land to the Virgin, and his covenant with her has never been broken. . . . The events of Hungarian history reflect the providential hand of God. Hence, we Hungarians need never lose hope, no matter what storms rage through our nation. We call out to you, dear Hungarian people, to imitate your ancestors: Place yourselves in the hands of the Virgin and through her in the hands of God. For the year 1947–1948 will be the Year of Mary.

☦ 59. *Sermon, August 15, 1947, in Esztergom*

In the years 1038, 1317, 1697, and 1896, our ancestors swore an oath of fidelity to Hungary's Great Lady. Let us, who live in the anguish of 1947–1948, imitate their example. For we Hungarians know that no nation can survive unless it respects its own traditions. Let us then confront the future armed with the experience of the past. The lessons of the past will point the way into the future.

[Homily in Csongrád!] We Catholics must draw strength from these Lady Days. Remain true Catholics and Hungarians! Beware false prophets! They sow hatred and reap the fruits of their selfish desires. Be Hungarians, be the people of St. Stephen and of the holy Mother of God.

✝
Ö   *60. Speech to*
    Catholic Men's Group,
    Szombathely, September 2, 1947

What will help our nation most today is the vision and determination of loyal Catholic men. Hungary is filled with warring ideologies; many people have forgotten Hungarian traditions. This makes it all the more essential that loyal Catholics stand up for their faith, which was sealed by the Blood of Christ and confirmed by His Resurrection. Throughout two thousand years of human history and one thousand years of Hungarian history, we have reaped the fruits of our Catholic faith.

✝
Ö   *61. Speech of September 3, 1947*

Our country today is filled with pagan views. Godlessness lays siege to the souls of our young people, trying to destroy their faith, their love of country, the purity of their souls and bodies, and their spirit of unselfish love. Hungarian young people, beware! For our land is full of swamps into which you may sink. In this year dedicated to Mary, I call out to young people all over this land. I call out to parents, teachers, and all others responsible for our children's future: Be mindful of my warnings!

✝ *62. Speech of September 14, 1947, Mariaremete*

Satan has played a terrible role in world history. For Satan is not just a bogey man invented to frighten little children. He is a living reality. He is the Evil One, the Father of Lies, the seducer and destroyer of all mankind. . . . A human being who kneels before the majesty of God is a man who stands tall. The claims of God do not diminish the dignity of man. No, only man destroys the dignity of man.

✝ *63. My 1948 New Year's Message*

Throughout the second half of 1947, unceasing praises of Mary were heard on the banks of the Tisza, in Szombathely, in Eger, and in the capital. . . . This fact brings us joy at a time when there is little joy to be found anywhere in this land. It comforts our soul to recall these pious devotions. . . . We can never be truly poor and wretched as long as the glorious light of Mary shines at the foot of the Cross. . . . Will we take this light along with us into the new year that is just beginning? . . . How terrible it would be if, through our own indifference, we broke St. Stephen's covenant with Our Lady. For if we dissolved our covenant with Mary, Hungary would perish. An inescapable abyss would open at our feet.

☿ 64. Pastoral Letter of May 23, 1948

This same minister told the parliament on February 23d that, "the Catholic Church had played an enormous role in the educational development of our country; and that fully aware of the historic and social situation of this country, the Hungarian democracy does not want to deprive the denominations of their schools" (Parliamentary Report, February 23, 1948/586).

Since this "enormous role of the Church in educational development" has been forgotten after three short months, the minister's pledge of free optional religious instruction cannot allay the anxieties of the bishops and the parents. We are wondering rightly whether this declaration is also a matter of mere tactics like those employed on February 23d. The temporary alleviation of anxiety regarding the schools in February was only a political maneuver. . . .

The minister has openly acknowledged that "religion is deeply rooted in our people" (Parliamentary Report, February 23, 1948/No. 571); these people have made it unmistakably clear that the right to educate their children in the faith is a part of their religion. They cannot be satisfied by two weekly lessons devoted to religious instruction. Religion must permeate all instruction. What purpose would these two weekly lessons serve if in history, literature and geography, teachers, trained in a spirit of materialism, destroy the fruits of religious instruction?

The Church vigorously and entirely repudiates the unfounded accusations of "circulating irresponsible superstitions and of waging a campaign of intimidation and spiritual terror". . . .

Moreover it was officially stated that in more than one district, children have a three-hour walk to reach their school (Parliamentary Report, March 13, 1947/739). And speaking of negligence, there is one sphere in which the state alone is responsible—namely, university education. The minister should turn his attention to this. In the universities, negligence has reached a shocking point and has resulted in a disastrous lowering of the standard of academic education. The degrees of our doctors and engineers are no longer acknowledged abroad. A university professor who could hardly be labeled "reactionary" declared recently in parliament that, "university education has been lowered to the level of a frivolous joke and undergraduates are in a state of despair" (Parliamentary Report, February 6, 1947/146 and 147).

☿ 65. Letter of the Bishops' Conference of May 29, 1948

We know nothing of these "many disobedient priests." There are thousands of loyal priests in this land for every one that is disloyal. And after all, one among the twelve apostles was disloyal, too. . . . We have received hundreds of letters from our Catholic people expressing their gratitude for our clear statement of Catholic views regarding the issues of the day. A number of the teachers in our Catholic schools have been led astray or deliberately forced into disavowals of the Church. On the other hand, many government employees have given heroic testimony of their faith. In one government-run factory, the workers unanimously expressed their support of parochial schools. But the telegram reporting this expression of faith was deliberately distorted; the authorities made it appear that the workers had actually spoken out *against* the Catholic schools. . . . Lies and deception have triumphed in this land as never before.

☿ 66. Extract from Mindszenty's Second Letter of May 29, 1948, to Minister Ortutay

Permit me to call your attention to various violations of Hungarian law. The government's attack on our Catholic teachers and school system is now more virulent than ever before. . . . Supervisors have gone to all our schools, and with threats and lies have tried to force our teachers to revolt against Church authorities. Hatred of the Church is fomented in all sectors of this nation—in the parliament, in the radio and press, and in all the government bureaus. The provisions of the peace treaty of Paris are being ignored. Officials are being dismissed from their posts for exercising their right to religious freedom. Catholic students are being barred from the university. Religious celebrations in honor of the Virgin provoked a wave of persecution reminiscent of persecutions during the Hitler regime. . . . The press is attacking the Church with ever-increasing venom. It appears that the Church will be afforded no legal protection against this onslaught of lies and calumny. . . .

☦ 67. Mindszenty's Reply of June 4, 1948, to the Minister of Religion and Education

In your letter dated June 4, you ask the Church to take appropriate steps in response to recent events in the community of Pócspetri.

Before receiving your letter, I knew nothing of what had occurred in Pócspetri. I have no other information on the subject. Therefore I am unable to take a position at this time. I know that the projected secularization of the parochial schools has aroused a storm of protest in this land. Only one thing would reassure our Catholic people: The government must strike from the agenda all debate on the subject of the secularization of parochial schools. On May 29, the college of bishops wrote to you a letter making this same proposal.

You imply that your government is under attack by an organized subversive movement. There is no foundation to this charge.

☦ 68. Communism and the Russian Orthodox Church

I will briefly describe the struggle which has continued for a quarter of a century between the powers of communism and the Church. From my account the reader will be better able to understand the position of the Hungarian bishops.

According to the communist view, religion can survive only if it is supported by the state. Its strength depends upon religious instruction in the schools, on extensive contact between clergy and laity, and on the cultural and charitable activities conducted under its aegis. The Communists were convinced that religion as such would die as soon as it was no longer bolstered by the state and was driven from the cultural and charitable areas. Thus in 1917 the Soviet Peoples commissars quickly proclaimed the separation of Church and state, the expropriation of church property, the secularization of the schools, and the banning of the religious press, all of which were designed to deprive the Church of all social influence. Naturally the powerful Russian Orthodox Church bore the brunt of all these measures. An Orthodox synod dealt with this crisis, and Patriarch Tikhon vigorously protested this assault. He issued a pastoral letter calling upon the faithful to resist these arbitrary measures.

The struggle between the Church and the new rulers continued for another year. The Church tenaciously defended itself and in many places was able to prevent pillaging on the part of the rabble. Moreover, as the forces of the counterrevolutionaries seemed to be gaining strength, the Soviet government had its hands full and could not pursue its campaign against religion.

During the civil war, Patriarch Tikhon endeavored to maintain the neutrality of the Church. In the great famine that followed the war, the patriarch spared no effort to ease the suffering of the people. Sizable donations came from Rome and the Anglican Church in response to his appeals for help. He also authorized the sale of church valuables for the alleviation of the general distress. However, when the Soviets were sure of their victory over the counterrevolutionary forces, they resumed their assault against the Church. In line with Marxist doctrines, the authorities, after stripping the Church of her possessions and means of subsistence, set out to destroy her internal organization.

On May 10, 1922, Patriarch Tikhon was placed under house arrest. Legal proceedings were instituted against him. He was charged with refusal to sell Church treasures to alleviate the famine. In reality, the Patriarch had only given instructions for the churches to retain those sacred vessels which were absolutely essential for the dispensing of the holy sacraments. Even before Tikhon's arrest, at the instigation of the Communists and with the collaboration of certain liberal-minded priests bent on reforming the Church, a national Soviet of Priests was formed. Heading the soviet was the infamous Vedensky of St. Petersburg. Vedensky, leading a delegation, betook himself to see the imprisoned Patriarch and proposed that he assume the vacant office. At first Tikhon refused to authorize anything of the sort, but was finally persuaded to entrust Vedensky, for a stipulated period only, with the conduct of church affairs. The Soviet of Priests was thereby given the appearance of legitimacy. The new reform movement began to call itself the "Living Church" and gradually infiltrated the church organization. This would not have been possible without the support of the Soviet authorities, and it was precisely this support which opened wide the gates to terror and blackmail.

Most of the bishops opposed the "Living Church." The metropolitan of St. Petersburg excommunicated Vedensky. For this the metropolitan was arrested, sentenced to death, and duly executed. Other members of the hierarchy, as well as countless parish priests and faithful members of their flocks, were similarly executed or thrown into prison.

On April 29, 1923, the leaders of the "Living Church" held a synod at which they reached the following decisions: (1) The Church would pledge its unqualified support to the Soviet government. (2) The hierarchy was to surrender many of its rights. (3) The rights of the parish priests were to be extended. (4) The laity would play a greater role in the life of the Church. (5) Liberal trends in theology would be encouraged. (6) Married priests would be permitted to become bishops. (7) Widowed priests would be permitted to remarry. The synod also abolished the patriarchate and expelled Tikhon from the priesthood.

Had all these propositions been carried out, the Orthodox Church would have been totally destroyed. But a severe economic crisis prevented the regime from pushing on with these plans. In order to mollify the general discontent, the government had to adopt a conciliatory attitude toward the Church. Tikhon was restored to the patriarchate, but had to reciprocate by a show of Bolshevik "self-criticism," confessing his "sins" against the Soviet power. He acknowledged the legality of his trial but asked to be spared the decreed prison term. He promised that the Orthodox Church would henceforth no longer offer resistance to Soviet rule and would break its ties with emigré and monarchistic elements identified with the West.

While the patriarch clearly hoped that his public act of submission would preserve the Church from the very worst, the confession in fact did great harm to his prestige. For the time being the government seemed to be content with this attitude on the part of the Church. Harassment of church authorities ceased, but the secret terror continued. The faith of many people had been shaken. Others were strengthened by adversity and became firm pillars of the Church in the darker days which followed. Patriarch Tikhon had been deceived in his hopes of saving the freedom of the Church. He was removed from office once more and taken to a hospital, where he died on April 7, 1924. There was a persistent rumor that he had been poisoned.

After Tikhon's death, the election of a new patriarch was prevented. Finally Sergei, the metropolitan of Novgorod, was permitted to take over the conduct of the office, but was not allowed to transfer his seat from Novgorod to Moscow. Following in the footsteps of his predecessor, Sergei attempted to defend the freedom of the Church. His efforts were rewarded by three months of imprisonment. The price of his release was a new declaration of loyalty to the government.

The wording of this declaration makes it clear that the text was dictated by the Soviet authorities. It includes a denunciation of the actions of Sergei's predecessor. The church leaders themselves are reprimanded for standing in the way of peaceful church-state relations. They are accused of failing to suppress counterrevolutionary currents within their ranks. Sergei called upon the clergy and the people to offer trustful cooperation with the government. He hoped that such an attitude would ensure for the faithful the freedom to practice their religion. Two ordinances in 1929 brought disappointment to Metropolitan Sergei. All the Orthodox parishes were completely subordinated to Soviet control. The propagation of the faith was made a punishable offense. Henceforth it became a crime to defend the Christian faith in any manner whatever.

The Soviet economy had by now become a socialist economy. The road to socialism had been paved with ten million dead. All farmland had been collectivized. Village parishes had been eradicated. Parish priests were deprived of their means of livelihood. Churches were closed down and their interiors stripped. Ikons, books, and sacred vessels were sold or destroyed. The third wave of anticlerical vandalism continued until 1932. When protests came from the Western nations against the persecution of the Church in the Soviet Union, the hapless Sergei was forced to issue the following statement:

1. According to the Constitution of the Soviet Union, every citizen is guaranteed freedom of conscience.

2. The state punishes people only for counterrevolutionary activities.

3. No penalty has ever been attached to the practice of religious faith within the Soviet Union.

4. Any report concerning the existence of religious persecution in the Soviet Union is an outright slander.

The persecution of the Church continued until 1934, when the government began to foster a rebirth of Russian historical and cultural traditions. It was now official policy to acknowledge the role the Church had played in the past and to grant it some part in national life in the present. But the League of the Godless continued its drive against Christianity. With an arrogance worthy of Voltaire, it predicted that by 1937 there would not be a single priest left in the country, nor a single believer to fill up the empty churches. The forecast failed to come true. Statistics of 1937 show that 30 percent of the city dwellers of that time and 70 percent of the rural population identified themselves as believers.

In 1937 the government launched its fourth major campaign against the Orthodox Church, stripping it of its last means of support, destroying the last remnants of its organization, and robbing it of its internal freedom so that even the single religious service which was still permitted was subject to state supervision. Here was final proof that all the Church's efforts at peaceful coexistence and humiliating cooperation were in vain. For communism is an atheistic doctrine which is by nature the enemy of religious faith. A kind of inner compulsion, something akin to fear of the spirit and the soul, drives it to struggle against religion. It merely conceals its fundamental hostility to religion only when concern for the preservation of its power forces it to do so.

When Hitler attacked the Soviet Union on June 21, 1941, Metropolitan Sergei issued a pastoral letter calling on believers to join the struggle for the salvation of the motherland. In a solemn religious service he prayed for the victory of the Red Army. This attitude surprised even the Communists, and it is alleged that Stalin scented deception. But by the fall of that same year Stalin rewarded the Church for its aid by dissolving the League of the Godless and banning all antireligious propaganda. The Soviet authorities even displayed forbearance when priests and believers violated government regulations that interfered with the views and canons of the Church. Sergei also ordered a collection for the benefit of the Red Army. A sizable sum was turned over to the government as a donation from the Church. This was the beginning of that dialogue between Church and state which led to a meeting between Sergei and Stalin on September 4, 1943. Thereafter permission was given for Sergei's election to the patriarchate, and on September 12, 1943, he was installed in his office in Moscow.

The news of this reconciliation between the regime and the Church was spread throughout the country and the world. This was a matter of the greatest importance to the Soviet Union, engaged as she was in a life-or-death conflict and therefore dependent on the internal unity of the entire population. The Communist party readily shook the proffered hand of the Orthodox Church. Abroad, this concord aroused hopes that the Communists were beginning to accept democratic principles and were on the road to "bourgeois" respectability. In reality, nothing of the sort was taking place. The Church did not have its internal freedom restored, but was subordinated to a governmental bureau. In other words, it was straitjacketed into the system of the atheistic state. The relationship, with all its restrictions and obstacles, could not even be compared with the Caesaropapism of the Czars. For the Czars themselves were frequently believers and therefore guarded the interests of religion, whereas the Communists were fundamentally bent upon liquidating religion. Nevertheless, the new reciprocal relationship was approved by the Church.

After Sergei's death a synod was convoked which elected Alexei, the metropolitan of Leningrad, as his successor. The synod approved the new constitution for the administration of the Orthodox Church. It elected the patriarch on the basis of a prearranged agreement with the government bureau for church affairs. It is true that the appointment and deposition of bishops lay within the patriarch's jurisdiction, but he could act only after consultations with the government bureau.

Thus the government had obtained in full measure the influence it sought over the Church. What is more, this arrangement secured the government a significant advantage: henceforth, as far as the public could see, the Church itself bore the responsibility for the appointment of unworthy men or the removal of worthy churchmen. The people's anger was no longer directed against the government.

A cloak of silence was now spread over the period of persecution and the martyrs it had produced. A yearbook of the Orthodox Church, published during the war in handsome format, contained an unsigned article denouncing the Church's martyrs as political criminals. In the foreword Sergei himself wrote: "What our enemies call persecution of the Church, the congregation of the Orthodox faithful regards as a return to the spirit of the Apostolic Age."

☦ 69. Mindszenty's Reply to Ortutay, June 15, 1948

Sir:

With regard to your letter of the 14th of this month, I wish to express my regret that this letter makes impossible further fruitful development in the matters which are pending. You wish to free yourself and the government from responsibility for the repeated delay in the matter and to burden the Hungarian episcopate and me personally with this responsibility. We cannot, however, accept this.

In order to provide a safe basis for our negotiations, we proposed three points to be settled before entering into negotiation. We failed to receive any reply to our proposition.

With regard to the first point in our conditions, in which we demanded that the nationalization of the schools be taken off the agenda, we are now faced with the fact that this matter is already being taken in hand. Our schools and their premises are being closed down by the authorities and occupied by the police, even before the question has been brought before parliament. Such a procedure is customary in cases where property has been acquired in an illegal manner. In the present case, however, the lawful owners are treated like thieves or at least like men who are suspected of crimes. This is most offensive and deeply humiliating.

Such is the treatment of that Church which has exercised so beneficial an influence upon the nation for many centuries. Such proceedings mean that not only have our conditions for entering into negotiation not been fulfilled but they imply a blunt refusal of our proposals. After all this, it is senseless to continue to talk of further discussons. This question of nationalization would have been one of the most essential items of these negotiations. The manner in which this question is being solved renders further negotiations impossible in spite of our willingness to enter upon them. The only fair procedure would have been for both parties to refrain from taking any action in controversial matters until negotiations had been completed.

Not only have our conditions not been fulfilled, but we are asked to show good will when we are not the parties who have taken prejudicial action. Our willingness to continue negotiations found clear expression in the fact that we put our conditions confidentially before you, and trusted that our point of view would find understanding and consideration. Events have shown, however, that our views are disregarded by the government.

In your own name and in the name of the government, you hold out the prospect of further endeavors to reach an understanding so that, through further negotiations, the rightful claims of the Church could be fulfilled. We acknowledge this promise. In the interest, however, of a general pacification, we ask you once more urgently to issue a public declaration stating that the question of nationalization of the schools is taken off the agenda. We must firmly insist on this point.

Having duly advised you of the decision of the Bishops' Conference of today, I am,

With salutations,

Joseph Mindszenty
Cardinal, Prince-Primate
Archbishop of Esztergom

☦ 70. Bishops' Statement of November 3, 1948

The bishops of Hungary are deeply disturbed and grieved by the recent disgraceful attacks made against Cardinal Mindszenty. Our primate has been frequently attacked in the press, in radio broadcasts, and in public addresses. The college of bishops, speaking in the name of religious freedom, protests against this campaign. We assure His Eminence the Cardinal of our sympathy and trust. We support all his efforts to serve the Church and the Hungarian people.

☧ 71. Mindszenty's Statement of November 18, 1948

Beloved in Christ:

For many weeks attempts have been made to stage "resolutions" directed against me in all the townships and village communities of Hungary. I am blamed for counter-revolutionary plots and activities hostile to the people, because of the Marian celebrations in 1947–1948. It is complained that, as a result, adjustment of relations between the Church and the state was frustrated, and demand is made that these "activities detrimental to the welfare of the people" should cease.

The goal of those celebrations in honor of Our Lady was the deepening of the traditional Hungarian devotion to the Blessed Virgin and the strengthening of faith. Never were purely political matters made the subject of speeches on those occasions. We preached only the virtues of the Mother of God, the ten commandments, the dignity of man, love and truth.

The purpose of the Marian Days was achieved. The bishops of Hungary, who are the competent judges, testified to this in their letter of November 3rd. They identified themselves with me against the attacks which were launched against the Marian Days. This same testimony has been given by the millions who represent the majority of public opinion in this country. Against their heroic patience measures had to be adopted which degrade those who employ them—measures that stand in opposition to the principle of religious freedom, guaranteed by democratic laws. But all to no purpose!

As to the legal aspect of these "resolutions," it should be noted: In spite of many official promises, no elections of local autonomous administrations have been held since the Second World War, except in Budapest. Consequently all these decisions or "resolutions" staged in counties, townships and villages lack any legal basis. The signatures to them have been wrung from the people under threats of loss of bread and liberty. The country is condemned to silence and public opinion is made a mere frivolous jest. Democratic "freedom of speech" in this country means that any opinion that differs from the official one is silenced. If any man dares to raise his voice in contradiction, he is dismissed from his position for criticism of democracy, or he is punished in other ways. Many instances bear proof of this procedure. I feel the deepest sympathy for those who have been forced into such a position. I have been greatly impressed and deeply moved by many wonderful examples of unflinching courage and loyalty.

As to the offensive statements [contained in the "resolutions"], we must repudiate them now as we have done before. We asked the government to publish those letters of mine to which such strong exception has been taken, and to submit them to the judgment of world opinion. But this has not been done. They continue to indulge in defamatory generalizations.

As to the fact that between Church and state—or perhaps we should say "parties"—no agreement has yet been reached, everyone knows that the Church was invited to negotiate an agreement only after a delay of three months, although she had repeatedly and publicly declared her willingness to enter into negotiations. At first it was announced that the questions pending between Church and state must be settled by mutual agreement. When, however, the Church was at last invited to negotiate, the main point—the problem of the schools—had been already settled by the state. The Church, of course, was forced to play the role of scapegoat.

And yet, let us bear one thing in mind: the complaints resulting from the incidents of Péliföldszentkereszt, Mariagyüd, Baja, and Celldömölk were not raised by the Church, but came from the side of the leaders in temporal power. If walls could speak, those of the prison of Köhida, in which twenty-six priests and myself were held prisoners, could give loud testimony. It would be heartening if this could be acknowledged by those who were never in that or any other prison.

I look on calmly at this artificial whipping up of the waves. In the place where I stand, not by the grace of any party, but by the grace and confidence of the Holy See, seething waters are not an extraordinary phenomenon. History lives in change.

Of my predecessors, two were killed in action, two were robbed of all their possessions, one was taken prisoner and deported, one was assassinated, our greatest one was exiled. Károly Ambrus visited and nursed the plague-stricken and himself died of the epidemic.

Of all my predecessors, however, not one stood so bare of all means as I do. Such a systematic and purposeful net of propaganda lies—a hundred times disproved and yet a hundred times spread anew—has never been organized against the seventy-eight predecessors in my office. I stand for God, for the Church and for Hungary. This responsibility has been imposed upon me by the fate of my nation which stands alone, an orphan in the whole world. Compared with the sufferings of my people, my own fate is of no importance.

I do not accuse my accusers. If I am compelled to speak out from time to time and to state the facts as they are, it is only the misery of my people and the urge of truth which force me to do so.

I pray for a world of truth and love. I pray for those who, in the words of Our Lord "know not what they do." I forgive them from the bottom of my heart.

Joseph Mindszenty
Cardinal, Prince-Primate of Hungary
Archbishop of Esztergom

☿ 72. Mindszenty's Reply to the Open Letters, December 8, 1948

The letters claim that the Church has suffered because of public positions I have taken. They state that I am responsible for the heavy cross now being borne by the Hungarian Church. Furthermore, they demand that I alter my stand on various public issues. . . . The authors of these letters deplore the fact that the Hungarian Church does not enjoy the same friendly relations with the government as the Church enjoys in other Eastern European nations. Journalists and politicians who have traveled abroad accuse the Hungarian Church of being reactionary and outmoded compared with the Church in Czechoslovakia, Yugoslavia, Rumania, Bulgaria, and Poland. We are told that church leaders in these other lands—men like archbishops Beran, Sapieha, and Cisar—conduct church affairs more "democratically" than their Hungarian counterparts. One of these archbishops is praised for taking part in the resistance; another greeted the establishment of the People's Republic with a fervent Te Deum; the third led a procession of bishops to swear an oath of loyalty to the state. If we are to judge by these letters, then the Church must indeed be thriving in other Eastern European nations. And yet Archbishop Beran and Cardinal Sepieha have already been branded traitors. In Rumania, four bishops have been thrown into prison. . . . The authors of these letters are ignoring an important fact. Neither I nor the Church provoked the enmity of the Hungarian government. Communism is an atheistic idealogy; hence by its very nature it is opposed to the spirit of the Church.

☿ 73. Fabricated Letter to the Minister of Justice, January 29, 1949

Dear Minister of Justice:

I respectfully petition the Minister of Justice to review my case. I have repeatedly been charged with attempting to prevent the establishment of peaceful relations between the Church and the Hungarian government. I have also been charged with maintaining a hostile attitude toward the duly established government of this land. It is true that I have contributed to the discord between the Church and the government. But now my desire is to help to establish peace. Acting in accordance with the penal code, the government has charged me with certain offenses. I voluntarily confess that I did in fact commit the offenses with which I am charged. In the future I promise to exercise greater restraint in commenting on the internal and foreign affairs of this nation. I promise to respect the sovereignty of the Republic of Hungary.

Now that I have presented this confession of my crimes against the state, it appears to me no longer necessary that I undergo a formal trial. I ask that you show consideration not for me personally, but for my high office. I believe that it would greatly simplify matters if my hearing on February 3 were adjourned. I believe that a dismissal of the charges against me would more effectively reconcile Church and state than would a formal trial and sentence.

After thirty-five days of sober reflection, I also wish to state that my aforementioned hostile attitude toward the government may in fact have prolonged the state of discord between Church and state. I consider it essential to the welfare of our nation that peaceful relations be established between the Church and the Hungarian government. I who revere the teachings of a peace-loving Church would gladly contribute to the establishment of harmonious Church-state relations. Unfortunately, in the past I attempted to sow discord; hence no one can be blamed for doubting my good intentions now. I would not wish my presence at the negotiations to act as a stumbling block in the path of peace. All parties concerned should be free to devote their attention to eliminating sources of dissension. Therefore I willingly absent myself from the negotiations. I will voluntarily renounce the exercise of my office until these negotiations are concluded.

If the college of bishops wishes to establish harmonious relations with the government, I will not stand in their way. Nor will I attempt to influence the Holy See, which has the final decision. I present this petition in the belief that genuine peace between Church and state is to the interests of both. Furthermore I believe that our country will suffer discord and disunity until peace is established between Church and state.

With my sincere compliments
January 29, 1949
József Mindszenty

☿ 74. Letters to the American Ambassador, Arthur Schoenfeld, December, 1946

Your Excellency:

The Hungarian government has conducted a purge of servants and public employees. Official reports state that 120,000 government employees have been dismissed from their posts. Most of these men were heads of families, thus we can estimate that some 600,000 people have been affected by this step.

The jobless civil servants cannot find new positions. They are dependent on the trade unions for new jobs, and the unions have closed the doors to the nation's factories against them.

The authorities would have us believe that this massive dismissal of personnel was undertaken as a retrenchment measure. This hardly seems likely; for vacated posts are being quickly filled. The new employees are put through accelerated courses to train them in the necessary skills. On the one hand the newspapers tell us that the government can no longer afford to maintain its large body of personnel; on the other hand, they assure us that the benevolent state has provided work for many new public employees.

Although the government promises universal employment, civil servants who were fired from their posts have been prevented from finding new positions. This penalization of former public employees has all the earmarks of political persecution. Moreover, other civil servants who have not been dismissed from their posts have undergone various forms of persecution and coercion. As public employees, they once were required to swear that they did not belong to any particular party. Now they are being penalized for observing the terms of their oath. Other civil servants may belong to another political party than that which has imposed a reign of terror upon this land. In order to keep their jobs, both groups of civil servants have been forced to join one of the parties favored by the government.

The leaders of the government are terrorizing the entire nation. No one any longer has the power to resist them. All over this country, patriotic, nonpartisan, devout Hungarians are becoming victims of tyranny. This includes the various government bureaus, county officials, private businessmen, and simple villagers. Many of these victims do not even hold positions in the government bureaucracy.

I am a shepherd of the Hungarian people; hence I am responsible for their souls. In all conscience I must protest against the injustice being done them. Thus I presume to call your attention to what is going on in this country. Crimes are being committed against the people in the name of the Republic. The various political parties lend their endorsement to the terrorist methods of the government. I appeal to you for aid.

> With my warmest regards,
> Esztergom, December 12, 1946
> József Cardinal Mindszenty
> Primate of Hungary

[The second letter I sent to Ambassador Schoenfeld read as follows:]
Your Excellency:

At the Yalta Conference, the Allied Powers assumed certain responsibilities toward the nations of Europe. In an attempt to fulfill these obligations, the state department of the United States has repeatedly conferred with the Rumanian government, encouraging Rumania to establish a system based on the principle of free elections and dedicated to the welfare of the people. The American secretary of state has emphasized that his government is committed to uphold the basic principles of democracy, among which are freedom and justice.

I am certain that the governments of the United States and of His Majesty the King of England would wish to see democracy prevail in Hungary as well as in Rumania. I may be the only man left in Hungary who has remained independent of political influence and whose office entitles him to intervene in national affairs. Thus I appeal to you to take action to ensure the welfare of Hungary and the triumph of democratic principles in this land.

Hungary may appear to be a democratic nation. Our government and Parliament often remind us that they were chosen by the people in the free elections of 1945. These elections were not entirely as democratic as they seemed, for only six political parties were permitted to take part. Most Hungarians wanted a democratic government; but their views were not adequately represented by any of the authorized candidates. People were forced to vote for one of the six parties. The majority rallied around the Smallholders party, as the nearest approximation of their views.

The present government does not reflect the true distribution of power among the various political parties of Hungary. During the election, the Smallholders party received 57 percent of the votes, the Communist party 17 percent, the Social Democratic party 17.4 percent, the Peasant party 6.9 percent, the Radical party .1 percent, and the Bourgeois party 1.6 percent.

The Hungarian Parliament consists of only one house. In addition to its regular members, it selected twelve delegates to supervise the intellectual and cultural affairs of the nation. After the elections, seats were assigned to the various political parties. The parties received the following percentages of seats:

Parties	Delegates	Percentage
Smallholders party	245	58.2
Communist party	70	16.6
Social Democratic party	69	16.4
Peasant party	23	5.5
Radical party	—	—
Bourgeois party	2	0.5
Independents	12	2.8
	421	100.0

Only the first four parties are actually represented in the government. Hence the Smallholders party should have been given 60.1 percent of the cabinet posts. But apart from the post of prime minister, it was given only 50 percent. The principal cabinet posts—the ministry of the interior, the ministries of trade, justice, and finance, the ministry of religion and education—were all assigned to members of other parties. In the economic council, the Smallholders party has almost no power, it is treated like a poor relation. The minister of the interior, a Communist, holds full authority over public assemblies and organizations. He also controls the police. Only 15 percent of the town and county councils are controlled by the Smallholders party. Moreover the persons who actually run the various ministries are almost all Marxists, and these have purged the civil service and taken over all key positions.

This then is the situation in Hungary: A party which at the time of the elections was a minority party has abrogated the rights of a majority; it has occupied all the positions of power. The Communist party behaves as if it had actually won 57 percent of the votes rather than only 17 percent. Such an anomaly has never occurred in the history of parliamentary government. On May 5, 1946, the *Sunday Times* suggested that the strange political situation in Hungary results from the fact that 37 percent of our parliamentary representatives have no more than an elementary school education.

Hungary is not a true democracy. There is no room in the country for anything but a Marxist police force, a Marxist press, and innumerable prisons and concentration camps. The country is ruled by Soviet adherents, Rákosi (foreign minister), Rajk (minister of the interior), Gerő (minister of trade), and Révai, the party ideologue, in league with party-controlled courts. The government is totally unrelated to the needs of the Hungarian people. The people live the life of pariahs in their own country and have been reduced to misery and despair.

These are the consequences of the deplorable political situation in Hungary:

1. A treaty has been concluded between the Russian and Hungarian governments; Hungary's economy is now completely dominated by Moscow. A board of skilled politicians loyal to Moscow is in control. Their fellow politicians are either so naive that they do not understand the true state of affairs or are so corrupt that they are willing to fall in with all the wishes of the Soviet Union.

2. The country is being systematically ruined. People whose politics are displeasing to the Communist party are ruthlessly eliminated from government bureaus. Communications with America and England have been severed. Free enterprise has been abolished; as a result the economy is stagnating and famine threatens. The currency has remained stable for only one reason: there is hardly any money left in the country. Péter Veres, an important government aide and leader of the Peasants party, summarized the situation in his party newspaper *Szabad Szo* ("Free World"). In an article dated November 24, 1946, Veres said: "There is no progress in this country; what movement there is, is all in the wrong direction."

Nepotism and corruption are everywhere. We all know of the scandal involving the east-west trading firm. The ruling party coalition is riddled with rivalry and dissension. Péter Veres had described the government as shot through with "internal corruption" and "the stench of decay." In the past, the despotic rulers of a feudal society lived parasitically on the toil of the working classes. Today we have a new parasitic element among us: the rulers of the "People's Democracy" of Hungary. The government triumphantly proclaims that 100,000 bureaucrats have been installed to superintend the economic development of the nation. Are conditions so desperate that we need 100,000 overseers to watch over the country?

4. We have no freedom of religion. Religious processions and Catholic organizations have been banned. We have been denied the right to publish a Catholic newspaper. Church buildings and property have been confiscated. Spies have been planted in the church hierarchy. Many of our most devoted priests have been thrown into prisons and concentration camps, where they are left to languish without trial. During their imprisonment, they are tortured and starved. That is the kind of religious freedom we have in Hungary! The government has twice intervened to prevent Catholic bishops from issuing pastoral letters, and Russian troops dispersed the faithful who had gathered at the churches to hear the letters read. A group of Catholics who prayed before the statue of the Virgin at St. Rochus Church in Budapest were arrested by the police.

5. Hungarian citizens can no longer count on the most elementary kind of security. Cab drivers in Budapest do not dare venture into the outskirts of the city after dark, for murder and theft have become a normal part of life in Budapest and even in rural districts.

6. We are living in a world of sham, a Potemkin world where starvation is masked by rhetoric and lies. Mr. Curtis, representing the United Nations Relief and Rehabilitation Administration, reports that the many deaths in Hungary ascribed to illness are in fact the result of hunger. The world has responded with contributions of food, but the supplies seldom reach those in need because means of transportation is lacking. While our people are starving, trucks which should be assigned to transport food supplies go traveling around the country decked out with red flags and party posters. The rolling stock with which we might transport food is denied to us. Yet Marxist party members can easily hire railroad cars to bring their people to political rallies. Péter Veres, the leader of the Peasant party, has written: "Our people are filled with rage and despair. We are all wondering what kind of a 'democracy' we are living in. After the war, we all expected many changes. But we never expected anything like this." (*Szabad Szo,* November 24, 1946.)

As long as the Soviet army of occupation remains in Hungary, the power of the Communists will go unchallenged. Armed squads go about the country terrorizing government employees who have already been fired from their jobs and forcing them to join the Communist party. The party continues to enlarge the lists of the disfranchised. It is gradually robbing the Catholic Church of all its rights.

In view of these facts, I appeal to the United States and England, the defenders of freedom and justice the world over, to come to our aid. I ask them to rescue us from the oppression and corruption overwhelming our land. I ask them to reach out to our poor Hungarian people who will be otherwise cut off from the great family of Christian European nations.

With the help of the democratic nations, we Hungarians will find a way to master our problems. I myself can recommend various courses of action. I am also ready to support all the statements I have made in this letter with concrete evidence.
With my sincere regards.

> Budapest, December 16, 1946
> József Cardinal Mindszenty,
> Primate of Hungary,
> Archbishop of Esztergom

☩ 75. Selection from the Prosecutor's Summation

By Mindszenty's own confession at his trial, he and his fellow-conspirators wanted to bring about World War III. He and his accomplices conspired with imperialist politicians, both private individuals and representatives of the United States government, which is the sworn enemy of all the People's Democracies. Mindszenty and his cohorts led foreign nations to believe that there was a widespread desire in Hungary to abolish the Republic and restore the monarchy. They also led other nations to believe that the Hungarian people would welcome another world war. The conspirators tried to incite the American imperialists to declare war on our country (*Black Book*, p. 143).

☩ 76. Selection from the Prosecutor's Summation

At his trial, the accused József Mindszenty expressed his regret for his past crimes. Furthermore he stated that he would not attempt to prevent the establishment of cordial relations between the Hungarian government and the Roman Catholic Church. He expressed his willingness to withdraw for a time from the performance of his ecclesiastical duties.

These statements on the part of József Mindszenty would seem to indicate that he felt genuine remorse for his crimes. But in the judgment of the prosecution, the accused only pretended to feel guilt. During his imprisonment, he attempted to send to American Ambassador Chapin the letter which we have just produced in evidence. József Mindszenty acknowledges the authenticity of this letter. The letter clearly reveals that the accused had every intention of continuing his intrigues against the People's Republic of Hungary. During his interrogation, József Mindszenty attempted to save himself from legal prosecution by sending a letter of appeal to the aforementioned ambassador (*Black Book*, p. 150).

☥ 77. A Sample of Government Rhetoric

The traitors now stand before their judges. Their leader is Cardinal Mindszenty, who has betrayed his Christian faith and attempted to plunge his whole nation into ruin. He joined in a secret political conspiracy to snatch their newly won democratic freedoms from the Hungarian people. The vigilant Hungarian police succeeded in unmasking this criminal league composed of spies, conspirators, and currency smugglers. . . . The People's Court should issue the sentence these conspirators deserve, the most severe sentence prescribed by law. . . .

☥ 78. Pronouncement of Pius XII, February 14, 1949

We have summoned you to this special holy consistory in order to inform you of Our deep affliction. You all know the cause of this affliction: a grievous crime has been committed against your illustrious college, The Roman Catholic Church, and all defenders of the freedom and dignity of man. We have learned that Our dear son, cardinal of the Holy Roman Church, József Mindszenty, archbishop of Esztergom, has been wantonly thrown into prison. He has been shown none of the respect due him by virtue of his high office. As soon as We learned of this event, We sent a letter of commiseration to Our worthy brethren, the archbishops and bishops of Hungary. In this letter We fulfilled the duties of Our Office by solemnly protesting against the injustice done to our Church.

This worthy prince of the church has been subjected to the worst humiliation. He has been sentenced to prison like a common criminal. We feel we must repeat Our solemn protest in the presence of you all. We utter this protest in defense of the holy rights of religion, which for so long were fearlessly and vigorously defended by this brave guardian of the Church. We join the universal outcry of all free nations and peoples, who have expressed their outrage in both the spoken and the written word. Even those who are not members of the Catholic Church have joined in the universal cry of protest.

You all know that somewhere behind closed doors his captors determined the fate of this prince of the church, who struggled so nobly to restore the Christian faith and Christian morals to the land of Hungary. We are deeply troubled by various reports we have heard. Visitors from many nations have attempted to enter Hungary in order to observe the trial of Cardinal Mindszenty. As soon as it became clear that they would give an accurate and unbiased account of the proceedings, these persons were forbidden to enter Hungary. All thinking persons now believe that the authorities conducting the trial in Budapest are attempting to conceal all knowledge of the case from the public. Any court of justice worthy of the name refrains from reaching a verdict until it has heard all the evidence. It encourages further investigation and guarantees every accused person the freedom to think and to speak in his own defense.

Cardinal Mindszenty has not been openly denied these rights. However, objective observers of the trial have noted many suspicious signs; what they have been witnessing, they believe, is a mock trial. The proceedings are being conducted with great haste, and the arguments of the prosecution appear specious and sophistical. Both these factors point to duplicity on the part of the authorities. Moreover, the health of the accused archbishop has greatly deteriorated. His physical state can only be explained as the result of deliberately concealed procedures. Cardinal Mindszenty had an iron constitution and was in the prime of life. Yet suddenly he appears so weak that he can hardly stand. His weakness during the trial does not result from a sense of guilt, but rather constitutes an accusation against his accusers.

Clearly the authorities are conducting this trial in order to confuse and disarm Hungarian Catholics. They are pursuing the policy described in Holy Scripture, "I will smite the shepherd, and the sheep of the flock shall be scattered abroad" (Mt 26:31).

☦ 79. Petition of the Religious Orders

. . . Monastic property is being seized, including the cloistered areas, the surrounding farmland, orchards, gardens, furniture, and utensils. We are losing our chapels, our retreat houses, our printing presses, our libraries, and cultural artifacts. We are not allowed to run our missions for the poor, to hold devotions, or to receive pilgrims. We are even forbidden to minister to the sick and to Catholic families. Seminaries and novice houses have been expropriated. Persons collecting funds for the Church have had misdemeanors imputed to them and their movements restricted. Members of religious orders no longer have the right of other Hungarian citizens to practice their chosen profession. Over the protests of patients and physicians, many nursing sisters have been dismissed from their hospital posts. Often a sister has been told that she may keep her job provided she leaves her order; some sisters have even been offered bribes.

☦ 80. Report to Archbishop Grösz, June 1950

The superiors of the various religious orders sent Archbishop Grösz of Kalocsa the following account of the first deportations: "In the southern provinces . . . religious orders have virtually been abolished. Under the pretext that their presence was a "threat to public safety," all male and female religious have been forcibly evicted from their establishments and transported to bishops' palaces farther north. About one thousand of those affected were sick and physically disabled people, some eighty to eighty-five years old, and strictly cloistered nuns. Religious were forbidden to leave the premises where they had been interned. Existing establishments were suddenly filled far beyond their capacity so that they took on the aspect of ghettos. No consideration was given to the problem of sheltering and feeding the evacuees; many lacked the most basic necessities of life. The evacuation and deportation were always conducted at night, without previous warning. Hence the monks and sisters were caught unprepared; they had only moments to gather a few belongings. Many were not given time to finish dressing. Even if they went without resistance, they were rudely and cruelly treated; no effort was made to respect the modesty of women. The following day, people learned of what had taken place during the night. Some tried to rally in protest. The Communist party functionaries responded by circulating unspeakable lies and anticlerical propaganda among the people. . . ."

☦ 81. Text of the Agreement of August 30, 1950

The government of the People's Republic of Hungary and the Hungarian bishops, desirous of the peaceful coexistence of the government and the Catholic Church and wishing to unite the Hungarian people and contribute to the peaceful progress of our nation, have conducted negotiations and reached the following agreements:

I.

1. In accordance with their duties as Hungarian citizens, the bishops of Hungary recognize and support the government and the Constitution of the Hungarian People's Republic. In obedience to Church law, the bishops promise to discipline members of the clergy who break the laws and obstruct the peaceful development of the Hungarian People's Republic.

2. The bishops sternly condemn any sort of political activity designed to overthrow the present social order of the Hungarian People's Republic. Furthermore, they will not tolerate the debasement of the Catholic Church and the Catholic laity into instruments of treason and revolution.

3. The bishops appeal to the Catholic laity to fulfill their duties as citizens and patriots by doing all in their power to implement the Five Year Plan instituted by the government of the People's Republic. This plan is designed to raise our standard of living and to ensure social justice. The bishops particularly ask parish priests not to oppose the movement for the establishment of cooperative farming communities. The collective farm is a voluntary union of farm workers based on the moral principle of human solidarity.

The bishops support the peace movement. They support the efforts of the Hungarian people and their government to ensure peace, and they strongly condemn efforts to incite our nation to war. The bishops wish to register their condemnation of the atomic bomb. The first government which chooses to make use of the atomic bomb will be denounced by the bishops for crimes against humanity.

II.

1. In accordance with the Constitution of the Hungarian People's Republic, the government of the People's Republic guarantees the Catholic Church and laity full religious freedom.

2. The government of the Hungarian People's Republic agrees to restore to the Catholic Church six boys' schools and two girls' schools, a total of eight in all. Furthermore, the Church may continue to support an appropriate number of monks and nuns to teach in these schools.

3. The government of the Hungarian People's Republic will make the same provision for the Catholic clergy as it has made for members of other denominations. The government agrees to subsidize the Catholic Church for a period of eighteen years, until the Church develops its own means of support. The amount of the subsidies will be reduced every three to five years. The government of the Hungarian People's Republic will thereby underwrite the ministry of the Catholic clergy.

This treaty will be administered by a commission composed half of representatives of the government and half of representatives of the episcopate of the People's Republic of Hungary.

Budapest, August 30, 1950
In the name of the Hungarian bishops,
József Grősz, Archbishop of Kalocsa.
In the name of the cabinet of the Hungarian People's Republic,
József Darvas, Minister of Religion and Education

☿ 82. *Mindszenty's Radio Address, November 3, 1956*

Nowadays it is often emphasized that the speaker breaking away from the practice of the past is speaking sincerely. I cannot say this in such a way. I need not break with my past; by the grace of God I am the same as I was before my imprisonment. I stand by my conviction physically and spiritually intact, just as I was eight years ago, although imprisonment has left its mark on me.

Nor can I say that now I will speak more sincerely, for I have always spoken sincerely. That is, I have always said without many words what I thought to be just, and I will continue to do so now when I am speaking to you directly—that is, my voice is not recorded and I am addressing the whole world and the Hungarian nation. Our extremely severe situation must be viewed from a foreign and from our own perspective. I wish to make statements from a distant viewpoint, from where there is a broad view, but at the same time so near to our own fate that what I have to say will have a practical value for all of us. Addressing foreign countries, it is my first chance to thank for what has been given us. In the first place I address my personal thanks to His Holiness Pope Pius XII for having so often remembered the head of the Hungarian Roman Catholic Church. Beside him, I want to express my deep gratitude to those heads of states, leaders of the Roman Catholic Church, of the various governments and parliaments, to the public and private men who while I was in prison have shown concern for my country and my fate. May God bless them for this. I feel the same gratitude toward the the world press and radio whose electrical wave network is the only true power in the air. I am happy that at last I am able to say this freely. Then again I want to say that the entire cultural world has stood by us as one man and helped us. For us this is a far greater help than we ourselves possess. We are a small nation. A small nation of this earth. Yet there is one thing in which we are foremost. There is not a single nation which in the course of its thousands of years of history has suffered more than we have.

After the reign of our first king, St. Stephen, we became a great nation. At the time of the Nandorfe-hervar victory, of which we are celebrating the 500th anniversary, our nation numbered as many people as the England of that time. But we had to keep fighting for our freedom, mostly in defense of the Western countries. This stopped the continuity of our development; we had to rise again by our own force. Now is the first instant in history that Hungary is enjoying the sympathy of all cultural nations. We are deeply moved by this. A small nation has heartfelt joy that because of its love of liberty the other nations have taken up its cause. We see Providence in this expressed by the solidarity of foreign nations just as it says in our national anthem: "God bless the Hungarian—reach out to him Thy protective hand."

Then our national anthem continues: "When he is fighting against his enemy." But we, even in our extremely severe situation, hope that we have no enemy! For we are not enemies of anyone. We desire to live in friendship with every people and with every country. By a nation such as the Hungarian whose roots reach deeply into the past, various eras can be recognized by the feeling with which it fills its place among other nations. From the changes and from the differences one can read the signs of its development. But it is a general characteristic of our age that development of every nation is progressing in one direction. The old-fashioned nationalism must be revalued everywhere. A national feeling should never again be a source of fighting between countries, but the pledge of justice and of peaceful cooperation. Let the feeling of nationality flourish in the whole world in the field of common culture. Thus the progress of one country will carry along the other country between nations which according to the laws of nature are more and more reliant on each other. We Hungarians want to live and act as the standard bearers of the family peace of European nations. A peace not artificially proclaimed, but a peace which means true friendship between the nations. And even looking toward more distant parts, we, the little nation, desire to live in friendship and in mutual respect with the great American United States and with the mighty Russian Empire alike. In good neighborly relationship with Prague, Bucharest, Warsaw, and Belgrade. In this regard I must mention that for the brotherly understanding in our present suffering every Hungarian has embraced to his heart Austria.

And now, our entire position is decided by the fact that the Russian empire of 200 million intends to down the military force standing within our frontiers. Radio announcements say that this military force is growing. We are neutral, we give the Russian empire no cause for bloodshed. But has the idea not occurred to the leader of the Russian empire that we will respect the Russian people far more if it does not oppress us. It is only an enemy people which is attacked by another country. We have not attacked Russia and sincerely hope that the withdrawal of Russian military force from our country will soon occur.

Our internal situation is also made critical by the fact that production has stopped in the whole country as a result of what we have said above. We are facing famine. It was a nation worn down to the bone that has fought for its liberty. And so work must be resumed and the possibility for production must be achieved everywhere in the interest of the whole nation. This is essential for the continuation of the nation's life. Having achieved this we cannot lose from sight the following: let everyone in the whole country know that this fight was not a revolution but a fight for freedom.

In 1945, after a lost—and for us, pointless—war, a regime was forced upon us which is now being branded with the red-hot iron of contempt, condemnation, and renegation by its heirs. The regime was swept away by the entire Hungarian people. The heirs should not ask for proof of this. This has been a freedom fight which was unparalleled in the world, with the young generation at the head of the nation. The fight for freedom was fought because the nation wanted to decide freely on how it should live. It wants to be free to decide about the management of its state and the use of its labor. The people themselves will not permit this fact to be distorted to the advantage of some unauthorized powers or hidden motives. We need new elections—without abuses—at which every party can nominate. The election should take place under international control. I am and remain independent of any party and—because of my office—also above it. In my authority I warn every Hungarian, after these beautiful days of unity, not to give way to party struggle and disagreement. This country is now in need of many things, but it needs as few parties and party leaders as possible. Today, politics themselves are a matter of secondary importance. The nation's existence and everyday bread are our worries. The successors of the fallen regime have made retrospective revelations which show that an account has to be made in every field. Through independent and impartial law courts. Private revenge has to be avoided and eliminated. Those who have participated in the fallen regime carry their own responsibility for their activities, omissions, defaults or wrong measures. I do not want to make a single denouncing statement because this would retard the start of work and the course of production in the country. If things proceed decently, according to promises made, this will not be my task. However, I also have to stress the practical framework of things to be done since we live in a constitutional state, in a society without classes, and develop our democratic achievements. We are for private ownership rightly and justly limited by social interests and we want to be a country and nation of a strictly cultural-national spirit. This is what the entire Hungarian people want.

As the Head of the Hungarian Roman Catholic Church I declare, just as the conference of bishops has stated in a joint letter in 1945, that we do not oppose the direction of former progress and that we further desire a healthy development in every field. The Hungarian people will find it natural that we have to care for our institutions which have a great value and a great past. I further mention briefly for the information of the 6.5 million Catholics in the country that in Church life we shall remove every trace of the violence and the characteristics of the fallen regime. This is a natural consequence growing out of our ancestral faith and moral teachings and of laws which are as old as the Church.

I deliberately do not discuss other details in my address to the nation; what I have said is clear and sufficient. As a conclusion, however, one question has to be asked: what do the successors of the fallen regime think? If their predecessors whom they condemn so much would have had a religious-moral basis would they have committed all the things which resulted in their fall? We justly expect the immediate granting of freedom of Christian religious instruction and the restoration of the institutions and societies of the Catholic Church—among other things, her press. From this moment on we shall watch whether the promises and deeds are identical, and the things which can be carried out today. We who are watchful and who want the best for the whole people trust in Providence, and not in vain.

83. Excerpts from the Cardinal's Sermon on the Golden Jubilee, July 12, 1965

When the Church celebrates the golden jubilee of a priest, it does not honor the man himself, or even his office, but rather the priesthood and the sacrament of Holy Orders. . . . Today's jubilee is being celebrated under unusual circumstances. There is no speaker to offer an address, and the primate himself can enter neither the church where he first celebrated Mass nor the cathedral of Esztergom. In the year 1386, the king, monarch of a major power, participated in the ceremonies for the golden jubilee of Primate Simor. The golden jubilee of Primate Csernoch in 1924 was attended by the regent, the Parliament, and the members of the Academy of Science. Renowned Bishop Prohászka was the speaker that day. He told the following story: "Long ago, two Slovak boys were traveling to Esztergom. Today, one of those boys is giving this address; the other is the cardinal and primate of Hungary. He and I are living proof that there is no discrimination against minority groups in Hungary."

The secular leaders of Hungary today have been executed or deported, or have fled. They are not here with their primate, nor is the flock of the faithful. But the primate knows that his fate on this day reflects the fate of his whole nation.

84. Ruling on Appointments to Posts in the Church, August 29, 1957

Article 1. All appointments made to Roman Catholic ecclesiastical positions which, according to canon law, fall under the jurisdiction of the Roman Pontiff, must be confirmed by the presidium of the Hungarian People's Republic. No person shall assume the duties of his office without being first so authorized by the presidium. The same rule applies to transfers and dismissals from Church office.

Article 2. No appointment, transfer, or dismissal shall be considered valid without prior confirmation by the minister of education. This ruling applies to the following positions:

a) All posts normally assigned by the bishop of the diocese, such as seats in the cathedral chapter, the position of vicar general, the directorship of chanceries, deaneries, and the position of pastor in cities and district centers.

b) All positions of rector, dean, principal and professor at all theological academies, seminaries, as well as principals of high schools belonging to the Church.

Article 3. This stipulated that the required confirmation be obtained separately in each case through agreement between the government and the Church until procedures for filling Church positions were finalized by contract between the Hungarian state and the Churches.

Article 4. This made the law retroactive to October 1, 1956.

☿ 85. *Mindszenty's Letter to the Pope (extract), June 24, 1971*

In order for me to dispel this allegation [that I am the "greatest obstacle to a normal relationship between Church and state"] and throw a clearer light on the truthful facts and put an end to the burdens and annoyances of generous hospitality that has been excessively prolonged, I wish to assure Your Holiness that I do not hesitate now, as I have always done in the past, to subordinate my own destiny to the interests of the Church. In this spirit, and after conscientiously weighing my duties as archbishop—but also in order to bear witness to my unselfish love for the Church—I have arrived at the decision to leave the American embassy. I would wish to spend the remaining portion of my life on Hungarian soil, in the midst of my beloved people, no matter what the circumstances that await me. But if the passions that have been nurtured against me, or grave considerations from the Church's point of view, should make this impossible, I shall take the heaviest cross in my life upon me: I am prepared to leave my country and make the atonement of exile for the Church and my nation. In humility I lay this sacrifice at Your Holiness' feet. I am convinced that even the greatest personal sacrifice shrinks to insignificance when the cause of God and the Church is at stake.

Index